C0-AWE-872

WITHDRAWN
A COLLEGE LIBRARY

The Genial Showman

Charles F. Browne.
"Artemus Ward".

THE

GENIAL SHOWMAN

Being
the Reminiscences
of the Life of
Artemus Ward

———— ⟨★⟩ ————

By Edward P. Hingston

———— ⟨★⟩ ————

WITH
AN INTRODUCTION BY
WALTER MUIR WHITEHILL

1971

IMPRINT SOCIETY ★ BARRE, MASSACHUSETTS

CARL A. RUDISILL LIBRARY
LENOIR-RHYNE COLLEGE

Frontispiece
Bust of Artemus Ward by Geflowski

PS
1143
.H5
1971
Sept 1999

© 1971 by The Imprint Society, Inc.
All rights reserved
Library of Congress Catalog Card Number 73-142578
Standard Book Number 87636-014-2
Printed in the United States of America

CARL A. RUDISILL LIBRARY
LENOIR-RHYNE COLLEGE

Contents

List of Illustrations

Introduction

THE BEST WAY to achieve a useful session at a meeting of a learned society is for the chairman to choose a few friends whose literacy, brevity, and sense of humor are equal to their knowledge, tell them the subject, place, date, and time, and let nature take its course. I followed this formula in December 1964 when asked to organize a session devoted to the history of museums at the Washington meeting of the American Historical Association. Clifford K. Shipton, Director of the American Antiquarian Society, Louis Leonard Tucker, then Director of the Cincinnati Historical Society, and Wilcomb E. Washburn of the Smithsonian Institution kept the audience awake and said so many useful things that the University Press of Virginia published in 1967 an expanded version of this discussion under the title, *A Cabinet of Curiosities, Five Episodes in the Evolution of American Museums.*

At this meeting Leonard Tucker began his account of the Western Museum in Cincinnati, 1820–1867, with this quotation from an English visitor: "A 'Museum' in the American sense of the word means a place of amusement, wherein there shall be a theatre, some wax figures, a giant and a dwarf or two, a jumble of pictures, and a few live snakes. In order that there may be some excuse for the use of the word, there is in most instances a collection of stuffed birds, a few preserved animals, and a stock of oddly assorted and very dubitable curiosities; but the mainstay of the 'Museum' is the 'live art', that is, the theatrical performance, the precocious mannikins, or the intellectual dogs and monkeys." This definition so beguiled me that I promptly found my way to its source, Edward Peron Hingston's *The Genial Showman, being Reminiscences of the Life of Artemus Ward and Pictures of a Showman's Career in the Western World,* published in London in 1870 by John Camden Hotten in two volumes and later in the year by Harper and Brothers in New York. The Harper reprint, which was all I could find in the Boston Athenæum, was not prepossessing; it was a grubby affair, with small type set in double columns. But I found myself reading and rereading it, not only for the attractive picture that it presented of its subject but for the remarkable details of American life in the sixties that were tossed in. Somewhere years earlier I had encountered Artemus Ward's description of Harvard College—"This celebrated institootion of learnin' is pleasantly situated in the Bar-room of Parker's, in School street, and has poopils from all over the country"— but that was about all I knew of him, save that he was not to be confused with the Massachusetts Revolutionary general, Artemas Ward (1727–1800). The *Dictionary of American Biography* had settled that matter by a cross reference, indicating that the humorist was, in fact, Charles Farrar Browne (1834–1867), a native of Waterford, Maine, an itinerant printer who wandered from Norway, Maine, and Lancaster, New Hampshire, to Boston, Cincinnati, and Toledo before making a name for himself in the columns of the Cleveland *Plain Dealer* in the late fifties. As the editors of the *DAB* chose their contributors with perception, the sketch of C. F. Browne proved to be by Stephen Leacock, one of the great humorists of our century, who tells thus how his subject acquired the confusing name: "It was at Cleveland that young Browne made his real start in the world. He secured a post on the *Plain Dealer* (at ten dollars a week) which gave him his first opportunity to develop his particular vein of comic humor. Here

The imaginary Artemus Ward, as depicted in "Artemus Ward Visits Brigham Young" in *Vanity Fair*, 10 November 1860

he appears as 'Artemus Ward',—a name selected for fancy's sake from certain old records of land surveyed by a bygone member of his family. In the pages of the *Plain Dealer* he created (beginning Feb. 3, 1858) the quaint fiction of a traveling showman who signs himself 'Artemus Ward', or 'A: Ward' and who is anxious to exhibit wax works, tame bears, and a kangaroo, and is apparently approaching nearer and nearer to the city. The wax works are said to include 'figgers of G. Washington, Gen. Taylor, John Bunyan, Capt. Kidd and Dr. Webster in the act of killing Dr. Parkman, besides several miscellanyus moral wax statoots of celebrated pirates & murderers &c ekalled by few and exceld by none.' This whimsical idea led to the publication of a series of Artemus Ward letters and became the basis of Browne's literary work. Henceforth, as his reputation grew, he was known to the world only as Artemus Ward."

By 1860 Browne, firmly and finally transformed into Ward, was in New York on the staff of the newly founded *Vanity Fair*, which aspired to be an American *Punch*. Two years later, in 1862, when some of his sketches were collected into a volume entitled *Artemus Ward: His Book*, forty thousand copies were sold outright. Abraham Lincoln was one of Artemus's devoted readers. At the Cabinet meeting called on 22 September 1862 to consider the final form of the Emancipation Proclamation, the President opened by reading two chapters of this book, to the no small annoyance of Secretary Stanton. Just as Stanton was considering rising and leaving, Lincoln threw the book down, heaved a sigh, and said: "Gentlemen, why don't you laugh? With the fearful strain that is upon me night and day, if I did not laugh I should die, and you need this medicine as much as I." The draft of the proclamation was then read, after which Stanton approached Lincoln, extended his hand, and said: "Mr. President, if reading chapters of Artemus Ward is a prelude to such a deed as this, the book should be filed among the archives of the nation and the author should be canonized."

Having created the fictional character of a showman called Artemus Ward, Browne decided to try becoming one himself, to the extent of appearing on the lecture platform. He strung together random material from his writings under the title "The Babes in the Wood", which he first delivered at New London, Connecticut, on 26 November 1861, and subsequently repeated in many New England towns, including Boston. After this preliminary reconnaissance in New England, he offered his lecture for the first time in New York City on 23 December 1861 at Clinton Hall in Astor Place. The *New York Times* on the following day observed: "Naturally and justly, those who are acquainted with 'Artemus Ward, Showman,' through his writings only, pictured him, in fancy, as a burly, middle-aged person in somewhat seedy apparel, and with an address more or less suggestive of the 'side-show' type of character. On the contrary, Mr. Browne is a tall, slim, and gentlemanly-looking young man, rather careful in his dress than otherwise, and gifted with an imperturbable expression of face, which adds very materially to the effect of the droll philosophies that are propounded by him. . . . By the gift of nature, Mr. Browne is a comedian. His delivery is provokingly deliberate, and there is a subdued humor visible in every expression of his face."

His title was a characteristic paradox, for having announced it, he said nothing about either babes or woods for an hour and twenty minutes, when he finally remarked: "I now come to my subject — 'The Babes in the Wood.'" After looking at his watch with affected surprise, and assuming an air of perplexity which induced roars of laughter from his audience, he gravely concluded: "But I find that I have exceeded my time, and will therefore merely remark that so far as I know they were very good babes — they were as good as ordinary babes. I really have not time to go into their history. You will find it all in the story-books. They died in the woods, listening to the woodpecker tapping the hollow beech-tree. It was a sad fate for them, and I pity them. So, I hope, do you. Good night!" The *Times* thought the performance a "decided success". Encouraged by this reception, Ward took to lecturing widely. In this new career he was as popular as he had been with his pen. When he "spoke a piece", as the handbills announced that he would, more depended upon his personal charm and his unrehearsed acting than upon the words themselves. As Stephen Leacock perceptively says: "The humor of Artemus Ward on the platform depended in large part on his peculiar personality, on his whimsical assumptions of distress and ignorance, on his sudden flashes of apparent interest, fading rapidly again into despair, not to be reproduced in mere words. In his writings the comic effect is connected on the surface with the use of queer spelling, verbal quips, and puns, long passed out of use and distasteful to the reader of today. Had this been all, Artemus Ward would long since have been forgotten. But beneath

The real Artemus Ward lecturing, as depicted
in *Vanity Fair*, 24 May 1862

the comic superficiality of his written work, as behind the 'mask of
melancholy' of the comic lecture, there was always the fuller, deeper
meaning of the true humorist, based on reality, on the contrasts, the
incongruities, and the shortcomings of life itself."

There was, alas, a truer basis than his audiences realized for the
"mask of melancholy", for physically he was far from robust. Nevertheless, as his fame spread, he lectured in California, Nevada, Salt
Lake City, and Denver, and throughout the eastern states and in
Canada, with a schedule of travel that would have exhausted stronger

The imaginary Artemus Ward
introducing himself on arrival in
London to Mr. Punch, as depicted
by J. H. Howard in *Artemus
Ward in London*

men. From his stay in Utah he developed a new lecture, "Artemus
Ward Among the Mormons", illustrated by a painted panorama,
which opened in New York on 17 October 1864. After two seasons in
New York, with intervening tours on the road, he sailed for England
in June 1866; there his success was as remarkable as in the United
States.

A few weeks after arriving in London, Artemus was elected to the
Savage Club, where he passed many convivial evenings. He became a
welcome contributor to *Punch*. For seven weeks, beginning on 13
November 1866, he filled the Egyptian Hall in Piccadilly with his
lecture on the Mormons and accompanying panorama. The Reverend
Moncure D. Conway recalled of these London performances: "The
refined, delicate, intellectual countenance, the sweet, grave mouth,
from which one might have expected philosophical lectures, retained
their seriousness while listeners were convulsed with laughter. There
was something magical about it. Every sentence was a surprise. He
played on his audience as Liszt did on a piano. . . . His tricks have been
attempted in many theaters, but Artemus Ward was inimitable. And

all the time the man was dying." By 24 January 1867 he was too far gone in consumption to carry on. The performances were suspended; though the lecturer went to Jersey in search of a more equable climate, no benefits resulted and he returned to Southampton, where he died on 6 March 1867, a few weeks short of his thirty-third birthday. His funeral at Kensal Green on the 9th was conducted by Conway; his cronies from the Savage Club were among the pallbearers, while the unhumorous Charles Francis Adams, the American Minister, was one of the numerous mourners. Few men ever went so far so fast. Ward's achievement is the more remarkable when one considers that he was self-educated in newspaper offices, where he began to work at thirteen when his father died.

The real Artemus Ward among London Savages; frontispiece by William Brunton to *The Savage Club Papers* (London, 1867), with Ward's profile near the center of the right margin

Detail of panorama shown in London to illustrate
"Artemus Ward among the Mormons"

Artemus Ward had a genius for absorbing whatever scene he reached. When he was in Boston, he could write of the Common: "It is here, as ushil; and the low cuss who called it a Wacant Lot, and wanted to know why they didn't ornament it with sum Bildins', is a onhappy Outcast in Naponsit." But his books are, nevertheless, heavy sledding for most readers today. It is fortunate, therefore, that for a small part of his life he attracted the devoted Boswell whose biography of him is here reprinted for the first time in a century.

They met by sheer happenstance in Cincinnati in 1861 while Artemus Ward was traveling in the summer to relieve the boredom of working steadily in New York for *Vanity Fair*. Dr. Edward Peron Hingston was an Englishman, apparently engaged in some form of theatrical promotion. How he got to the United States, or when, is not clear, nor is the nature of his doctorate. The *Dictionary of National Biography* knows him not, but the pages of his *The Genial Showman* testify to his sympathetic character. He was obviously fond of Artemus Ward; he seems to have had powers of polite address. He observed keenly, took the United States as he found it, and wrote well. Moreover, he liked to eat and drink, and was not averse to any gastronomic novelties of the country.

During the summer of 1861 Dr. Hingston was on his way to Louisville, St. Louis, and "the Northwestern-States of America" as the advance agent of an unspecified coming "entertainment". During an interminable journey on a jerkwater railroad in Ohio, he fell into conversation with a chatty fellow-passenger, who not only proved to be a friend of Artemus Ward's, but promised to introduce Hingston and Ward to each other in Cincinnati. The introduction was achieved in the lobby of the Burnett House. Very little time elapsed before Hingston and Ward visited the bar of that hotel to "hoist" to the Prince of Wales; Hingston explaining to his British readers that "'to hoist' or, to give the pronunciation more closely, 'to hyst' is, in American parlance, to indulge in a drink." From this promising beginning they made a tour of the shows, concluding the evening at the "Infernal Regions", the theatrical waxworks to which the Western Museum had in its later years degenerated.

The next day being Sunday, Hingston, returning from a walk through the German quarter of Cincinnati, chanced to meet Artemus Ward in Race Street. Finding themselves opposite the First Congregational Church, they went in and heard a strongly political sermon by the Reverend Moncure D. Conway, then its minister, on the text

"Issachar is a strong ass couching down between two burdens." The argument that America, burdened by slavery and "an imbecile administration", should throw both off and allow itself to be ridden by General Fremont, "was not in accordance with the views of poor Artemus", who was a strong Lincoln man. "Little did he think that in a very few years to come that same preacher would use him for a text, and that the same Mr. Conway would be the orator selected to speak the funeral oration in the cold chapel near the temporary grave of the humorist on the day of his burial in the cemetery at Kensal Green in England."

Unsympathetic as the divine service had proved to be, the Sunday morning encounter resulted in Hingston joining Artemus and a few friends for a journey down the Ohio River to Louisville the next day in the United States mail packet *Major Anderson*. The friends ascended to the hurricane deck to enjoy the view. The sight of the Catawba vineyards caused them to drink a morning Catawba cocktail to the health of the owner of those grape vines, the Cincinnati lawyer and horticulturist Nicholas Longworth. Hingston's delight in this drink suggests that he had been in the United States long enough to become a connoisseur of Boston bars, for in retrospect he wrote: "Who but he who has travelled in America during the hot months of the year knows any thing of the glories of a 'Catawba cocktail', made as it is at the bar of the Tremont House, the Revere, or the Parker House in Boston? Flavor, fragrance, and beauty are all united in that delicious draught. Who but an educationally qualified American 'bar-tender' knows how to compound the appetizing, odoriferous, amethyst-colored nectar? Who else but he would understand the precise number of drops of bitter to add to the Catawba, the right mode of using the ice, how to float the freshly-gathered strawberry on the surface, and how properly to 'frost' the rim of the glass with pulverized sugar, so that sweetness should precede amaritude, and perfume be blended with brilliancy? On two other continents besides that of America have I tasted American drinks made by *quasi*-American barmen; but their compounds, compared with those mixed by the true American artist on his own soil, were as different in effect as Verdi's music played by Mr. Costa's band, and Verdi's music on a barrel-organ, with a tamed monkey turning the handle." Clearly Hingston was a perceptive, tasteful, and right-thinking man.

A rainy, windy evening on the river was passed telling stories around the cabin stove, but by midnight the party was comfortably established in the Galt House in Louisville. The next day Hingston got busy with his bill-posters, license, newspaper advertisements, and distribution of free tickets for the forthcoming "entertainment", whatever it was. Ward watched all this with interest; after an evening stroll he said to Hingston on the hotel stairs: "I understand that you are used to management of shows. Suppose one day you manage me?" Hingston asked in what character he was likely to have the opportunity, "and how he intended to constitute himself 'a show'." He replied, with mock gravity: "A moral lecturer. There's nothing else to be made of me but that. And you must take me to England and Australia." They parted that night in Louisville and did not meet again for nearly a year and a half. "Then, when we met, I listened to Artemus as he lectured to an audience of nearly two thousand people; and while the laughter and applause resounded on every side, there came to my memory the night of our parting in Louisville." During their separation, Artemus had moved from writing to "speaking his pieces".

Their second association started in Philadelphia in 1863, when Artemus was giving his lecture "Sixty Minutes in Africa" — the continent that produces "the red rose, the white rose, and the neg-roes." After the lecture, Artemus took Hingston to his room at the Continental Hotel for some Bourbon before going on, in the company of stars from Carncross and Dixey's Minstrel Company, to a fashionable ball "given by the dark-colored population of Philadelphia" to which "no white people were admitted unless they were well known to the committee."

So when Artemus received a telegram from San Francisco later in the year asking him to appear there, he consulted Dr. Hingston, who knew something about California. In consequence of this conversation Hingston agreed to become agent and manager for this western trip, going ahead to prepare the ground. Hingston sailed for Panama on 3 October 1863 in the steamship *North Star*, and crossed the isthmus to embark in the *Golden Age*, which reached San Francisco on the 26th. Artemus Ward followed ten days later by the steamships *Ariel* and *St. Louis*. By the time of his arrival, Hingston had made effective preparations. When "The Babes in the Wood" were "trotted out" at Platt's Hall on 13 November 1863, more than sixteen hundred people paid one dollar in gold for admission, while almost as many were turned away for lack of room.

After three performances in San Francisco, Artemus gave shows in San José and Santa Clara before moving on to Sacramento. Even though winter was at hand, Artemus hankered to return east overland in order to see something of the Mormons in Salt Lake City. So they determined after invading several California mining towns to push east into Nevada, despite the snow in the Sierra. Hingston went ahead to make advance arrangements, although they met frequently to check schedules and concert plans. They were together, for example, in Virginia City, Nevada, in December 1863, where they came to know Mark Twain, then an editor of *The Territorial Enterprise*. Christmas was spent there, and New Year's Day 1864 in the one-year-old town of Austin, Nevada, whose International Hotel stowed away its guests in wooden bunks in dormitories with earth floors. Artemus's lectures in a newly plastered store in Austin and in an earth-floored bar-room in Big Creek were received with joy. On 5 January they left for Salt Lake City in a Concord coach, changing to an open sleigh to cross Diamond Mountain.

Artemus was apprehensive about his reception in Salt Lake City because of the imaginary "A Visit to Brigham Young" that had been published in *Artemus Ward: His Book* in 1862. He had included such flights of fancy as: "In a privit conversashun with Brigham I learnt the follerin fax: It takes him six weeks to kiss his wives. He don't do it only onct a yere & sez it is wuss nor cleanin house. He don't pretend to know his children, there is so many of um, tho they all know him. He sez about every child he meats call him Par, & he takes it for grantid it is so." He had concluded the piece: "I girdid up my Lions & fled the Seen. I packt up my duds & left Salk Lake, which is a 2nd Soddum & Germorrer, inhabitid by as theavin & onprincipled a set of retchis as ever drew Breth in eny spot on the Globe." Artemus was made no more comfortable to learn from Elder Stenhouse, Brigham Young's confidential friend, that his book was in Young's library, and to be told: "He has all the books that have been written about him. You ought not to have made ridicule of our Church." Artemus offered apologies and hope for pardon, which the Elder promised to transmit to the Head of the Church. In due course Artemus was summoned to the presence of Brigham Young, who was "peculiarly affable, gracious, and conversational", and who gave his consent to a lecture in the Salt Lake City theatre. He did not want to let the theatre, but might share the receipts or perhaps give the use of it without charge.

Unfortunately Artemus was suddenly laid low with an attack of typhoid fever, which very nearly carried him off. Poor Hingston was worrying about how to get his corpse to the Missouri River, when he took a turn for the better. As Artemus convalesced, Young sent him dried fruit and wine, while the Mormon ladies brought eggs, dried peaches, jellies, jams, and sweetmeats. Somebody found a dozen cans of oysters brought from Baltimore, which turned the tide. " 'Get out the bills for the lecture,' said Artemus, after the first meal of stewed oysters; 'see Mr. Clawson, and arrange for the date. The show is safe enough, now we've got an oyster basis'." Before long Artemus attended The Apos-

Unflattering representation of the imaginary Artemus Ward repelling the advances of Mormon ladies that illustrated "Artemus Ward Visits Brigham Young" in *Vanity Fair*, 10 November 1860

tles' Ball, at which Brigham Young introduced him to the company generally from a platform, and more specifically to a dozen of his wives.

On Monday evening, 8 February 1864, Artemus presented "The Babes in the Wood" at the theatre. Dr. Hingston notes: "There was a large audience, but the price of admission was low, and many of the chief saints were admitted free. The receipts amounted to no more than four hundred and ninety dollars." It is a wonder they reached that, considering the receipts in kind that were accepted. Chapter XIII of *Artemus Ward, his Travels* listed them thus:

> 20 bushels of wheat.
> 5   "   "   corn.
> 4   "   "   potatoes.
> 2   "   "   oats.
> 4   "   "   salt.
> 2 hams.
> 1 live pig (Dr. Hingston chained him in the box-office).
> 1 wolf-skin.
> 5 pounds honey in the comb.
> 16 strings of sausages—2 pounds to the string.
> 1 cat-skin.
> 1 churn (two families went in on this; it is an ingenious churn, and fetches butter in five minutes by rapid grinding).
> 1 set children's undergarments, embroidered.
> 1 firkin of butter.
> 1 keg of applesauce.
> One man undertook to pass a dog (a cross between a Scotch terrier and a Welsh rabbit) at the box-office, and another presented a German-silver coffin-plate, but the Doctor very justly repulsed them both.

Soon after the Salt Lake City lecture, Artemus and Hingston left by coach for Denver, thence through Nebraska and Kansas to St. Joseph, Missouri, from which point the railway eased the rest of the journey east. Hingston then went about arranging a rapid lecture-tour through Illinois and Ohio en route to New York. Dr. Hingston stayed with Ward during the autumn 1864 presentation in New York of "Artemus Ward Among the Mormons", but was called to Europe before the lecture went on tour through the northern states. So they next met at Euston Station when Artemus arrived in London in June 1866. Ap-

The Genial Showman surveys his show, stored for winter quarters
at Baldinsville, in Indiana; illustration from *The Genial Showman*
in which the real Artemus peers in the door at his imaginary namesake

parently they were often in each other's company during Artemus's last
months in England. At his funeral Dr. Hingston occupied the first carriage with Artemus's physician and valet, while Mrs. Hingston (otherwise unknown to me) appeared among the mourners. Artemus's will
gave one hundred pounds each to Dr. Hingston's sons, James and John
Cincinnatus Hingston, and made the doctor and Thomas W. Robertson
co-administrators of his estate in England.

Although they had spent less than two years in constant association,
Hingston gathered everything that he could about the other thirty
years of Ward's life. In 1865 he edited for John Camden Hotten the
English edition of *Artemus Ward (His Travels) Among the Mormons*,
with an introduction, describing himself on the title page as "the companion and agent of Artemus Ward whilst 'on the rampage' ". To the
1868 volume of *The Savage Club Papers* he contributed an essay, "Artemus Ward Among the Shoshones", which is a lively account of a
prank played by acquaintances in Austin, Nevada. In 1869 Hingston
and Thomas W. Robertson jointly edited for London and New York

publication *Artemus Ward's Lecture* (*As delivered at the Egyptian Hall, London*), to which Hingston contributed a prefatory note on Artemus Ward as a lecturer. In 1870 he edited a new English edition of *Artemus Ward in London*, a collection of contributions to *Punch* and other papers, first printed in 1867, as well as publishing *The Genial Showman*. As he did not include there the account of the Shoshone prank from *The Savage Club Papers*, I have added it as an appendix to this edition.

The most complete and meticulous account of the humorist is, of course, Don C. Seitz's *Artemus Ward* (*Charles Farrar Browne*) *A Biography and Bibliography*, published by Harper and Brothers in 1919, but Hingston's *The Genial Showman* of 1870 remains a valuable and readable contemporary source. Quite beyond its primary purpose, it is a marvelous narrative of western travel in the days before the completion of the trans-continental railroad, as well as an engaging record of details of daily life in many parts of the United States. How else would one know about the literate German cigar-seller, S. M. Ehrlich, in Virginia City, Nevada, who spent his time in the winter of 1863–1864 reading Virgil or German poetry, and who earned the Artemus Ward desig-

Our noble savages on parade in Broadway; illustration from
The Genial Showman in which Bowery Irishmen parade as Artemus Ward Indians;
the real Artemus looks on, accompanied by E. P. Hingston

nation of the "classical cuss" by bringing a farewell present of cigars, with a visiting card on which he had written "Nostra amicitia sempiterna sit." I am glad that the Imprint Society has returned *The Genial Showman* to print after the lapse of a hundred years.

WALTER MUIR WHITEHILL

The Genial Showman

Overture

SOMEWHERE in the Western States of the American Union a newspaper editor was challenged to define explicitly the politics of his journal. He replied: "Up and down the Democratic plank our principles are straight as a ramrod, but we've got some ideas which creep out underneath at the sides. They creep and creep till they get their grip of the whole creation."

The divergent tendencies of that Western editor were, I am afraid, like to those which have influenced me in writing this book. My intention was to write the story of one who was the most genial of showmen. Yielding to the impulse of the moment, I have written of many other people and of many other things.

"Write all that you happen to know of the life of Artemus Ward," advised a friend.

I promised to do so.

"Relate all your adventures among the showmen of America," said another friend. "America has never been pictured from a showman's point of view in any book of transatlantic travel. You have seen the greater part of the North American continent, and must surely have some quaint stories to tell and some odd incidents to describe."

I replied: "Yes."

"Use up those note-books of yours," suggested poor Artemus Ward, on one of the last days of his life, when dying at Southampton; "we fell in with many good things during our wanderings. That note-book was a nuisance on the road, but you should turn it to account now."

My answer was: "I will, by-and-bye."

Hence the volume now presented to the public. It is not a biography, nor does it form a book of travel, nor a collection of anecdotes, nor a treatise on the art of being a showman. It is simply an endeavor to narrate succinctly and amusingly the principal incidents of the public career of Artemus Ward, and the adventures which befell us together; to describe the people we met and the scenes we looked upon; to rescue from forgetfulness a few passing jokes, and to tell over again some of the odd stories heard by-the-way.

Should any critic across the Atlantic object that the stories are not

[3]

all new ones, and that some of them have been told before, my reply is, that they were told to me. If previously related to Brother Jonathan, the Puritan Fathers, or Christopher Columbus, I can not help it, and am far too generously disposed to grudge any one of those gentlemen the pleasure of having listened to a good thing before me.

One word about my non-adherence to the rules of literary composition. I am quite well aware that I have written some chapters in the past tense and others in the present. Wherever I have done so I have written advisedly and with intention. I have changed the key to suit the character of the music. My good intent must be the apology for my transgression.

Note-books and itineraries carefully kept have furnished me with materials. Wherever I have quoted a saying or a speech, I have done so from memoranda made shortly after its utterance. Whether from out of my garden of sweets I have culled the prettiest flowers, I am not quite certain. But the bouquet-paper — thanks to the publisher — may help to sell the nosegay.

In the belief that these pages will furnish some new matter to the reading public, and that the scenes and places described in them are not already too familiar, I venture, as a showman, to open my literary show.

E. P. H.

London, 1870.

∘ 1 ∘

An Introduction to the Showman

ANNO DOMINI 1861. Tuesday, 1 P.M., I was at Versailles; three hours previously I had passed through London; in a few hours more I expected to arrive at Delhi.

"We travel very slowly on this railroad," I ventured to remark to the gentleman seated next to me in the carriage.

"It's a kind-a one-horse one," replied my neighbor. "Travelling on it is about as cheerful as a Quaker meeting-house by moonlight. But Cincinnati will wait for us. It won't move farther down the Ohio because we don't get thar sooner, that's sure."

"Perhaps, gentlemen, you are not aware that this is Artemus Ward's Railroad?" observed a jovial-looking passenger behind me, who had overheard our conversation.

"I haven't the pleasure of being acquainted with Mr. Ward," responded the traveller on my left. "But the Ohio and Mississippi line, which jines on to us presently, was managed by General George B. McClellan; and when he looked after it, it war handled elegantly."

My curiosity was excited. In the course of extensive travel through the United States I had often met with the name of "Artemus Ward" attached to articles of a peculiarly quaint and comic character, copied and re-copied in the newspapers of the North and South. The singularity of humor displayed in these articles, the originality of the style, and the eccentric spelling which the writer used, had caused me, in common, I presume, with many thousands of others, to wish for information relative to the author. Besides, the humorist appeared before the world in the character of a showman, owning some "wax figgers," or "moral wax statoots," as he described them, a "larfable little cuss" of a kangaroo, and a "zewological animal like a snaik under perfeck subjecshun." Any one connected with the "show" fraternity was at that time one whom I very much wished to know.

I use the word "show" in its American acceptation, as comprising every class of entertainment, from opera and the poetic drama downward. Artistes and performers, whether singers, actors, or exhibitors, were ladies and gentlemen with whom I desired to become acquainted. Hence I turned round to my fellow-traveller behind me in the railway carriage, or "car," as they term it in the States, and prosecuted inquiry.

"May I ask you what 'Artemus Ward' you mean?—not 'Artemus Ward' the Showman, whose name I so frequently see in the newspapers?"

"Why, certainly," answered my informant, using the *mais oui* form of affirmation so common in the States. "You are aware that we are travelling through Indiana? Baldinsville must be somewhere about here."

"Then has Mr. Artemus Ward any thing to do with the railroad?" I inquired.

"Not that I am aware of," replied my communicative acquaintance. "But you have seen the paragraph in the papers, in which he describes his visit as the editor of the "Baldinsville Bugle" to the superintendent of the line, to ask him for a free pass. The superintendent told him that the road could not pass him even as an editor. 'Can't it?' said Artemus. 'No, sir, it can't,' said the official. Artemus looked him full in the eyes, and gave it him hot. 'I know it can't,' said he; 'it goes so tarnation slow it can't pass any thing.' This must be the line, and it's just what Browne would say."

"Who is Browne?" was my next question.

"Oh, Browne is Artemus Ward. I know him very well."

"And is he a showman? I know most of the showmen in the West, but I have not met him among them."

"You may meet him this evening; he will be in Cincinnati on business," replied my informant, evading a direct answer to my question.

"Is he an old man—as one would infer from some passages in his writings—or is he merely assuming a character, in writing about Baldinsville, when he states that he has been in the show business twenty-two years and six months?"

There was a pause. My fellow-traveller took a cake of tobacco out of his waistcoat pocket, bit off a piece, and, with a twinkle in his eyes, said,

"Just you hold on; wait till you see him. I have some business with him at the Burnett House in Cincinnati to-night. I will introduce you to him if you like. I guess you'll find he knows more about shows than most of us do. He's smart. He keeps his eyes pretty well skinned, I can tell you. There's nothing of the woodchuck about him. Do you use tobacco?"

I declined with thanks the proffer of the cheering weed. The gentleman who "used" it, seeming unwilling to favor me with any more information at that time on the subject of the eccentric showman, threw himself back in his seat, extended his arms along the mahogany framework of the cushion, and hummed a few bars of one of the then popular martial melodies.

The train jogged on in the direction of Lawrenceburg. I believe that I avail myself of the right verb to describe its motion. Trains in Indiana are not apt to glide, nor to skim the surface of the rails with unfelt celerity. In the West, the "sleepers," to which the rails are bolted, deserve some other name than the technical one accorded to them by the railway engineer. They rest on beds so roughly made as to suggest any other idea than that of sleeping. Very little care is devoted to the preparation of the substratum; and the log which bears the rail has in many instances been cut from a tree that grew but a few yards from the spot. In half the time which in England would be considered requisite for the survey and preparation of plans for a new railway, a railway of equal length is thought of, surveyed, constructed, and the "cars" are running on it in the States west of the Alleghanies. Never mind if there are no towns along the route, they will spring up by-and-by. Never mind if the carriages do get smashed-up now and then, there is wood enough left in the States to build tens of thousands more. Never mind if you are jolted while travelling; if you are bumped, hurtled, bruised, made to feel vindictive, and to wish the engineer of the line to be in the carriage with you, that you might have a chance of throwing him out of the window; all will be forgotten when you arrive at the end of your journey. In the years to come, that line of rail, now running through forests, swamps, new-made clearings, and untilled prairie, will have cities, villages, gardens, and corn-fields on each side—will have lost all its picturesque wildness, all its uncouth crudities, all its youthful eccentricities, and will have developed into as solid, smoothly-conducted and well-behaved a railway as any in the States of that wondrous America, wherein rapidity of growth is as great a marvel as fertility of enterprise.

Arriving at Lawrenceburg, the train waited a few minutes, and then, turning off in a north-easterly direction, proceeded along the bank of the Ohio River. At length it arrived at a swamp, over which, and over the Miami River, an affluent of the Ohio, the rails were laid on a bridge of new timber, and of very suspicious fragility of construction. I remarked to the gentleman who sat on my left that the bridge did not seem strong enough for a place so dangerous, and asked him why it was so newly built, and not of greater strength.

"It's a good bridge enough for where it is," was his reply. "It gets washed away every year."

I was not quite sure whether washing-away time had arrived, and felt more comfortable when the Miami River was crossed, and the bridge in the rear of the train. Shortly afterwards the conductor apprised me that we had come to Delhi, which he pronounced as "Del-eye," with a strong accent on the last syllable. I looked out to ascertain what there was about the place to remind me of the ancient capital of the Great Mogul. Neither palace nor temple was visible; but in front of a whisky-shop a number of old playing-cards were strewn about the road, and I wished to go and turn them over to see if the picture of the East Indian monarch was on the back of them, as I had seen it so often in my own country. It struck me that I might thus trace the derivation of the Delhi of the Occident. But I gave up the thought when I remembered that I had left Switzerland behind me in Indiana, that Athens is in Ohio, that Glasgow and Paris are in Kentucky, and that Rome and Troy are in the State of New York.

The railway terminus, or "dépôt" as it is termed in America, was more than a mile from the city. Omnibuses were in attendance to convey the passengers to Cincinnati. Before taking the one which suited me best, I reminded my fellow-traveller of his promise to introduce me to Mr. Artemus Ward that evening, and I pledged myself to meet him at the Burnett House at the hour he appointed.

Hotels in the United States have been made the theme of copious description by nearly every one who has written a book on American travel; but among the various classes of travellers who resort to them, few experience so much of their comforts and discomforts, or know them so well, as the itinerant showman in the course of his nomadic, unsettled career. By him they are looked upon as among the chief objects of interest in every city which he visits. If he be a true type of the genuine American showman, he will be well informed on the several points of excellence of each of these establishments; he will be personally known to the proprietor of each; he will be on familiar terms with the hotel clerks, and will be fully cognizant of which is the best house to stop at, in order to advertise his entertainment and to dispose of tickets for his show. Prominent among the best hotels of the United

States, from a showman's point of view, let me rank the Burnett House in Cincinnati, of which Messrs. Johnson, Saunders, and Co. were proprietors. Whether they still conduct it after the lapse of seven years, I am not aware; but, at the time of which I write, they illustrated that which in America is thought to be one of the greatest proofs of human excellence—they understood hotel management. When a man falls short of perfection, it is a common mode of pronouncing judgment upon him to say that he is "a very clever fellow, but he can't keep a hotel."

Were a tourist to wander into Cincinnati for the first time, and not be informed to the contrary, his first glimpse of the Burnett House might lead him to suppose it to be the City Hall, the State-house, or the Government offices for the entire West. Its columned portico is approached by a broad and steep flight of stone steps; there are terraces with stone balustrades in front of its windows, and there is a great dome surmounting its central portion, giving to it in the distance the appearance of a small edition of the Capitol at Washington. Its internal arrangements are like those of most Western hotels—the large entrance-hall, the counter with the hotel clerks behind it, and the register-book on the top of it; the leaves of which register-book are being constantly thumbed and turned over by gentlemen who ease their troubled minds by finding comfort in lolling against the counter and studying the list of names. There are advertisements of railways around the walls of the entrance-hall, and, in cold weather, a stove in the centre. Nursing the stove in winter, and lolling on the seats in summer, are the occupations of the gentlemen visitors, some of whom are boarders and others "loafers," who have no better way of employing their time. There is no porter in livery to open the door, nor any policeman on the steps to call cabs and to terrify intrusive little boys. The entrance-hall is a lounge for all who choose to avail themselves of it, an exchange for those who wish to meet on business, and an information-office for those who seek intelligence, or are desirous of learning the latest news. It is a place of continuous bustle, of stirring life and considerable noise; a place resonant with the ring of bells, and reeking with the reek of tobacco.

At the hour appointed I strolled into the Burnett House and looked around among the various groups for my acquaintance of the railway carriage. Presently I perceived him, seated beside a light-haired gentleman of youthful appearance, with whom he was engaged in conversation. Recognizing me, he beckoned me to make my way towards him, and, after first asking me for my name, with which he had not been previously furnished, introduced me to the gentleman with whom he had been conversing. The introduction was without ceremony, and in that easy off-hand manner in which one person is made acquainted with another in the United States.

"Charles," said he, addressing his companion, "I met this gentleman in the cars to-day. He has read some of your writings, and wants to see the great showman of Baldinsville—Artemus Ward. So I told him to come and look at you."

I was bewildered.

I expected to see an elderly man with a shrewd face and "busy wrinkles round his eyes," like those of Tennyson's miller; a man of cunning look and rough exterior, who had mingled much with the world, and who, by travel and long experience of the rough-and-tumble life of a showman, had qualified himself to be the Mentor to so inexperienced a Telemachus as myself. No trace of my ideal presented itself in the gentleman to whom I was introduced. He was apparently not more than twenty-five years old, slender in build, frank, open, and pleasant in demeanor, with ruddy cheeks, bright eyes, and a voice soft, gentle, and musical. Instead of an old showman, I saw a young man, who, judging from his appearance, might have just left college. Instead of the sort of person usually found travelling with a wax-work exhibition, I met a gentleman who might have passed for a youthful member of one of the learned professions. Feeling some doubts about my having been introduced to the right man, and half-suspecting that I was being made the victim of a hoax, I asked hesitatingly if the gentleman were really Mr. Artemus Ward.

"This is my friend Mr. Charles Browne, who pleases to call himself Artemus Ward," replied my introducer. "I'll vouch for him, but not for his show. As for his kangaroo, I don't go any thing on him."

Very little time elapsed before we were on terms of chatty acquaintance. Presently Artemus Ward interrupted the conversation to inquire whether or not I was an Englishman. I replied that I was, when he again offered to shake hands, and said, half in earnest and half in jest,

"I like Englishmen; this is the hotel your Prince of Wales stopped at when he came through here last summer. By-the-by, how is the Prince? Give my compliments to him when you see him. Suppose we go down and hoist to him."

"To hoist," or, to give the pronunciation more closely, "to hyst," is, in American parlance, to indulge in a drink. The bar of the Burnett House is down stairs. Thither we adjourned, and after duly toasting the health of His Royal Highness in some very excellent Bourbon, the genial "showman," addressing me, said,

"My friend and I are going round to see the shows in Cincinnati to-night, and we mean to visit the Infernal Regions. Will you join us?"

"Willingly," I replied; "but pray what are the Infernal Regions?"

"Don't be frightened. Come and see."

Thus it was that I first met Artemus Ward.

*   *   *

It was our destiny that we should become intimate in after years. As we shook hands together for the first time, I felt that we were to know one another better, and that our first meeting was not to be our last.

Among the humorists who rose to eminence during the American War, Artemus Ward was the raciest. Among the satirists of the period, he was the gentlest and the most genial. I write of him as one of whom I saw much, and with whom I travelled far. We planned together many enterprises, travelled as showmen with the same "show," and participated in many odd adventures. Born in that part of New England where Nature wears her sternest and her roughest aspect, Artemus Ward lived to become known as one of the most mirthful and most tender-hearted of her children.

In quiet Elm Vale Cemetery, at Waterford, in his native state of Maine, near the cottage in which he was born, and beneath the shadow of Mount Vernon, the mountain which he climbed in his boyhood — between the grave of his father, who lived not long enough to know of his son's fame, and the grave of Cyrus, the brother whom he loved — Artemus Ward is buried.

In writing the story of Artemus Ward's career, and in relating what I saw of show-life in America while associated with that career, I purpose to give to the public all that I know of Artemus Ward, in the order in which my knowledge of him was gained, from the day of my first meeting with him in Cincinnati to that later and more mournful day when, with dim eyes, I watched the steamer "Deutschland" glide slowly down Southampton Water, bearing among its freight a coffin removed from Kensal-green Cemetery and consigned to a grave beyond the Atlantic.

∘2∘

Enjoying "The Honeymoon" and Visiting "The Infernal Regions"

YOU Britishers can't show an Opera-house like that in your country. Every brick is made of whisky, and all the mortar's pork."

So said Mr. H——, of the "Cincinnati Inquirer," when he first escorted me over Pike's Opera-house in Cincinnati; by which extraordinary metaphor I afterwards understood Mr. H—— to mean that the edifice referred to owed its origin to the successful trade in whisky carried on by the proprietor, Mr. Samuel Naphthali Pike, and that the flourishing state of the pork-exportation business in Cincinnati generally caused money to be plentiful, and the Opera-house to be patronized. Incongruous as the mixture of whisky, pork, and opera may at first appear to be, the idea of incongruity is dispelled when the facts are ascertained that the greater part of the wealth of the inhabitants of Cincinnati has resulted from trading in pork and dealing in whisky; and that with the accumulation of wealth have arisen a desire for amusement, and an inclination to cultivate the fine arts and the drama. At the period of which I write, Cincinnati was singular in its possession of an Opera-house. In the Eastern cities there were establishments much larger in dimensions, devoted chiefly to operatic representations, but, in deference to the puritanical ideas of the citizens, they were called "Academies of Music," not "Opera-houses." In so styling them, there was a distinction without a difference which rendered them more acceptable to the popular taste. Except Maguire's Opera-house at San Francisco, I believe that Mr. Pike's in Cincinnati had no rival by name in the United States.

A very noble building was Pike's Opera-house, and one of which the chief city of Ohio had every reason to be proud. It stood on Fourth Street, presenting a most imposing elevation, and being decidedly the greatest ornament of the town. On the basement story was an extensive bookselling establishment, the pit portion of the auditorium being considerably above the level of the street, the visitors having to ascend a flight of marble steps. Internally the decorations were worthy of any theatre in America or Europe; the seating accommodation was superior to that of our London houses, and an air of sumptuous grandeur in all the appointments caused a stranger, on first entering, to feel no little surprise, especially if his previous ideas of "out West" had led him to anticipate a lack of the refinements of civilization. Still more surprised was he likely to be on learning that no Duke of Bedford, nor Earl Dudley, nor body of shareholders, nor government *subvention* had been required for the erection of a structure so magnificent, but that Mr. Pike had at first traded in whisky, and then distilled whisky, in the course of which processes he had extracted numberless dollars, and obtained a fine spirit of enterprise.

Mr. Pike is a gentleman of musical taste and an excellent flautist. The operatic muse objected to come over the Alleghanies to visit Porkopolis, as Cincinnati is sometimes called, there being no fitting house for her reception. Mr. Pike resolved to build one. He expended a fair fortune in doing so; and let it not be said that Art is without patrons in the West, when one lover of it reared on the banks of the Ohio a temple so worthy of the art he loves. In the course of his tour through the United States, the Prince of Wales accepted an invitation to a ball in the Cincinnati Opera-house, and I believe that Mrs. Pike was honored by being his partner in the first quadrille. The house exists no longer. Fire, that formidable foe of Opera-houses, was no less unkind to Mr. Pike in America than it had previously been to Mr. Gye, or has been, still later, to Mr. Mapleson in London. Playing the old *rôle* of the phœnix, Pike's Opera-house has risen out of its ashes; but finding that it could be a phœnix, it determined to use its wings, and, flying eastward,* has taken up its place of rest in the city of New York, whither Mr. Pike has gone also, and where, with another distillery in full operation, I understand that he cultivates music on a basis of whisky, even as before now literature has been cultivated on a little oatmeal.

I have been thus lengthy in my reference to Pike's Opera-house for two reasons; one of which is that seven years ago it was the grandest place of the kind anywhere in the West, and the second reason being that it was the first theatre to which I went with Artemus Ward.

A dramatic company had possession of the Opera-house, and the play of the evening was Tobin's comedy of *The Honeymoon*. Artemus Ward,

*This building has since become the property of the well-known banker, Mr. Fisk.

two of his friends, and myself, were courteously shown to seats in the dress-circle, with that politeness which is always shown in the United States to the "dead-head," as he is called, or the person who is passed into the theatre without being called upon to pay for admission. The play was very badly acted. The Duke Aranza of the evening was a little worse than usual. Artemus Ward masked his face with his hands, watched the action of the piece with ill-concealed laughter, and when the drop-curtain fell, said, turning to me,

"I am going over to your country some day, and shall want you to introduce me to Mr. Tobin."

Unused as I then was to the pleasantries of my new acquaintance, I felt puzzled, and innocently asked,

"Do you mean John Tobin who wrote *The Honeymoon?*"

"I do. He's a good and great man. I want to thank him."

"John Tobin has been dead these fifty years," I replied. "Is it possible that you are not aware of this being a very old comedy."

Artemus Ward preserved his gravity. Grasping me warmly by the hand, he continued, in a well-affected voice of emotion. "I am sorry, indeed I am sorry. I wanted to see Mr. Tobin very much. Mr. Tobin has done me a great deal of good in his time; Mr. Tobin has been very kind to me. Whenever I have wanted to see any bad acting, I have always found it when *The Honeymoon* has been on the bills; whenever I've had to report an amateur performance, or to take a young lady to the play, I have been sure to see *The Honeymoon*. Much honeymoon is on my brain. It oppresses my heart, and I have hoped one day to be able to go to England just to call on Mr. Tobin to say how grateful I am, and—*to kick him!*"

After that, my first lesson, I learned to be more guarded in my readiness to supply information to Artemus Ward. Subsequent experience taught me that he was very fond of enjoying a harmless laugh at the expense of his friends, and that his manner of joking among them frequently took the form of his joke with me in reference to the old dramatist, whose well-worn comedy is the last resource of many a travelling company in difficulties, and the *bête noir* of many a used-up playgoer.

From Pike's Opera-house we adjourned to Wood's Theatre, in Vine Street, where, not finding some friends whom he expected to see, and not caring to witness the performance, Artemus Ward proposed that our stay should be very brief, and that we should proceed at once on our previously-agreed-upon visit to the *Infernal Regions*.

Partially following the plan adopted in Philadelphia, Cincinnati has a similar arrangement and nomenclature of streets. The streets running parallel with the Ohio River are named in their numerical order, and the streets crossing them at right angles mostly after the names of trees. Third Street is the street of business offices, and Fourth Street the main avenue of the town. In St. Louis and some other western cities, Fourth Street is similarly honored. In Philadelphia, Chestnut Street is the principal of the streets running down to the river, but in Cincinnati, Walnut Street takes chief rank amongst the cross thoroughfares. There are three or four places of amusement in Vine Street, while the National Theatre and the building containing the "Infernal Regions" are both in Sycamore Street, between the streets which are distinguished by the numerals three and four.

Artemus Ward, his friends, and myself, stopped for a few minutes at Mr. John Bates's National Theatre, just to call upon Mr. John Bates, whom we found seated in a grocery store under the front of his playhouse, where he sold bottled whisky and brown sugar, soap, sauces, rum, and raisins, together with other excellent articles common to a Western grocery shop. Unlike Mr. Pike, who had gone from whisky up to opera, Mr. Bates had commenced with theatricals, and was coming down from the drama to the whisky trade. We wished him prosperity, and passed on. Our place of destination was only a few doors lower down; and a very dingy, unattractive place it appeared to be, so far as I could form an opinion from its external characteristics. There were a few dirty bills posted about the entrance; there were the ruins of a hand-organ sending forth doleful sounds inside; there was a dingy light burning in the passage, and there appeared to be a most plentiful supply of dirt and dust in the interior, judging from the samples furnished at the very entrance. The title of "Infernal Regions" had led me to anticipate a strange place, and my first impressions of the exterior were in thorough conformity with that which I had expected. Artemus Ward playing the part of Virgil and I that of Dante, we boldly entered the *Inferno* of the city of Cincinnati.

A hasty glance around the first apartment which we penetrated, and a study of one of the bills therein displayed, were enough to inform me that we were at *The Museum*, and that the manager's name was Mr. W. Allen.

A "Museum" in the United States means something very different from that which we understand by the same word in Europe. There was

Mr. Barnum's Museum in New York, and there is Mr. Kimball's Museum in Boston; but neither of them had nor has any very close resemblance to the national treasure-house of the Louvre, the establishment at South Kensington, or that in great Russell Street, Bloomsbury. A "Museum" in the American sense of the word means a place of amusement, wherein there shall be a theatre, some wax figures, a giant and a dwarf or two, a jumble of pictures, and a few live snakes. In order that there may be some excuse for the use of the word, there is, in most instances a collection of stuffed birds, a few preserved animals, and a stock of oddly assorted and very dubitable curiosities; but the mainstay of the "Museum" is the "live art," that is, the theatrical performance, the precocious mannikins, or the intellectual dogs and monkeys.

Years ago there used to be in Holborn, near the top of Drury Lane, an exhibition, to which the charge for admission was two-pence or a penny. Any one who remembers the place will be able to form an idea of the exterior of the "Infernal Regions" in Cincinnati; but nothing we ever had in London could equal the entertainment provided for the visitor to the Ohio show-shop. In the lower part of the place were broken models and stuffed pigs, rusty swords and guns said to have been picked up on the battle-ground of Tippecanoe, Indian spears, leather hunting-dresses, and oddly-shaped stones. There was a thunderbolt which "had been seen to fall in Kentucky," and some fragments of ancient temples from the ruins of Sodom and Gomorrah(!). All were foul with dust and begrimed with the soot of lamps. An odor of mustiness seemed to emanate from every object, and something suggested the idea of ugly spiders being concealed in every cranny and crevice. In the apartment above, matters were in a little better condition. The stuffed birds still retained some of the original coloring of their plumage, and the hide of the "Horrid Alligator of the Amazon" had been fingered by visitors until its scales had become more polished than they ever had been in the slime of its native river. In a back room was a small and interesting collection of coins and medals; ranged against a wall were a number of glass cases filled with curiosities preserved in spirits. Prominent among these were two bottles, one containing a human head, and the other a human hand. The head was that of a murderer, whose name, if I remember rightly, was "Heaver" or "Hever," and the hand was the actual right hand with which he had murdered his victim. Our guide hurried us away from the inspection of these unpleasant objects, to go with him and see the wax-work portion of the exhibition.

There is no really good wax-work collection in the United States. Were the executors of Madame Tussaud to send over the Baker Street one just as it is, and arrange to show it a month or two in one city, and then a month or two in another, they would rapidly make a fortune. Wax-works in the American cities are about on a par with those which used to be exhibited at English fairs twenty years ago. Those in the Cincinnati Museum I presume to have been originally displayed at Knot Mill Fair, Manchester, or on Glasgow Green. At any rate, the wicker-work bodies and limbs may have seen service there at one time; while the wax faces may really be of transatlantic manufacture, from the *atelier* of some Italian-American citizen.

"I wish we could only get the cases open," said Artemus Ward, looking at them wistfully. "We'd take off General Washington's head, and put it on the shoulders of Queen Victoria."

Whether Artemus Ward had attempted to play any practical jokes at the wax-works during one of his previous visits I know not, but the attendant, after watching us closely for some time, came up and entered into conversation. He had evidently seen our guide before.

"All the same, gentlemen—all the same. We are scass of any thing new. General Fremont is the last; but thar's a mistake in the figger. He's not such a whaler of a man as that; but we had nothing else to spare."

"Whose body have you used for him?" asked Artemus.

"It's the Emperor of Russia's. We'd done with him, and the varmints had got into his clothes."

"And how's the Queen of Sheba? Has she had any snakes in her lately?" continued our guide.

The attendant laughed and shook his head. "Wall no, I guess not," he replied. "She's allus givin' us trouble, but she's had no snakes."

Our curiosity was roused relative to the eccentricities of the Queen of Sheba—a dirty wax figure, dressed in very tawdry robes of colored muslin, and adorned with a large quantity of cheap Connecticut or Massachusetts jewels. One of our party asked the man for further information. He was told that some time back the museum contained, among other attractions, some live snakes from South America. One of these snakes became missing. It was sought for in every corner of the building, but without a discovery being made of its place of concealment. In the wax-work part of the exhibition the Queen of Sheba was represented as bending on the left knee, offering gifts of diamond rings and gold snuff-boxes to King Solomon. The attendants were annoyed at finding the gifts, on more occasions than one, not in her majesty's hand, but fallen on the floor. They picked them up and replaced them, but in no way could they account for their falling. At length, watching the figure, they noticed the body to shake first, and then the arm, the offerings to King Solomon again falling on the floor.

"We were a bit skeart," said the attendant, "for she was awful nervous. I saw her shake all over as if she had the chills and fevers. That was after she dropped the royal presents. When we'd got the people out we undressed her, and thar in her stomach, and half way up her arm, we found that cussed snake."

Many a time afterwards, in rambles through the Eastern States of the Union, in crossing the plains on our journey to Salt Lake City, and during his residence in London, I asked Artemus Ward if his idea of the wax-figure exhibition in his earlier papers had not been suggested to him by one of his previous visits to the Cincinnati Museum. He never gave me a direct answer to the question, but I strongly suspect that it was there where we heard of the disasters to the Queen of Sheba that he received the first thought of "The miscellanyus moral wax statoots of celebrated piruts and murderers, ekalled by few and exceld by none." The story of the Queen of Sheba may also have given him the notion of adding a collection of snakes to his imaginary show.

The hour had arrived for the exhibition of the Infernal Regions to commence, and the visitors began to make their way towards a narrow door leading to an equally narrow and very steep staircase. Thither our party of four proceeded. What sort of an exhibition we were going to see I knew not, but the approach to the place in which we were about to witness it was any thing but inviting. Nor was the way of approach suggestive; up steep stairs to the infernal regions did not strike me as being the correct sort of thing. There was a discrepancy between it and the "*facilis descensus Averni*" of one's school-day reading, though I might have remembered that Dante, "in mezzo del cammin," climbed a steep hill, meeting a panther, a lion, and a she-wolf on the way, before he had the good-fortune to fall in with Virgil, and accept his escort to the world of punishment. Up the narrow, dirty, and rickety staircase we struggled with a dozen or so of other visitors, who were equally as anxious to enjoy the horrors awaiting them above. Arrived at the top of the stairs, our party found themselves to be in a small gloomy sort of room, or gallery very insufficiently lighted. There were a few rows of seats, and accommodation altogether for about thirty or forty people, if tightly packed. The front of the gallery was furnished with a series of bars, extending from the floor to the ceiling; and, looking between these prison-like bars, our first view of the Infernal Regions was obtained.

Somewhere on the continent of Europe there is a church which contains two transparencies; one intended to represent Paradise, and the other Pandemonium. On the afternoon of my visit to that church years ago, a good priest had twenty or thirty children around him, to whom he lectured on the joys of heaven, and the tortures in waiting for the sinful. When he described the future life of the good, he caused the lights to burn brightly behind the picture of Paradise; and when he talked to his young hearers of what would be their fate if they followed a life of wickedness, he had the lights turned up behind the transparency of Pandemonium. By means of hidden machinery, flames were made to dart up and down, while figures of sinners in agony, apparently, writhed in the imitation fire. Had that good priest visited the city of Cincinnati, and gone to the exhibition of the "Infernal Regions," he would possibly have wished to barter for it his Pandemonium, and been willing to throw the Paradise into the bargain; for, looking through the bars, we peered down into a large, dusky, black "chamber of horrors," in which there was just light enough reflected from the dim gas-jets in the gallery to enable us to make out the obscure outlines of many weird and hideous figures. The floor of this chamber was some feet below that of the gallery in which we were stationed.

As the eye became accustomed to the gloom, we could discern that the figures on the other side of the bars were intended to represent demons, fiends, serpents, dragons, skeletons, hobgoblins, and animals of forms more fearfully fantastic than any which Mr. Hawkins has figured as inhabiting a hypercarbonized earth in pre-Adamite times. The face of each figure was turned towards us, and the mouth of each dragon or serpent was wide open. Nearer to the bars than any of the other figures was something not quite an elephant nor a hippopotamus, though its body resembled that of one of those animals; its face was more like that of a lion, while its tail was one of those wondrous structures one might fancy in a dream after a supper of raw pork—one which no comparative anatomist would have the hardihood to classify among the tails of things living, or that have lived. There was another monster, with something like the body of a bull and the head of a satyr. The artist probably intended it for the Minotaur of ancient Crete. Oddest of all the figures was that of the Genius of Evil himself, with the orthodox tail and hoof, but with horns of unnecessary length, and eyes of disproportionate magnitude. In his right hand he carried a pitchfork, while with his left hand he supported his tail, so as to expose to view its barbed extremity.

The little group of visitors in the gallery seemed to be composed of two classes, the perfect strangers, and the knowing ones who had been to the exhibition before. Exclamations of terror from the strangers bore evidence to its being their first visit, while the *habitués* disclosed their acquaintance with the place by pointing out the various objects to those who were with them:

"Thar's Old Nick; you'll see him presently; he's awful good."

"That's the Old Sarpint; wait a bit, he'll skear you."

"I reckon you'll like the Raging Lion; he's like all fury—he is."

Suddenly, and without any warning, the lights in the gallery were turned down; two or three of the visitors yelled with fear, the knowing ones howled to terrify the timid a little more, and the performance commenced.

There was the clang of a gong, followed by a mingled sound of roars and groans. The chamber became more illumined, and it was easily to be seen that the various figures were in motion, the serpents began to crawl, each of them thrusting out a large tongue; the skeleton commenced to glide along a railway laid down upon the floor; and, as it approached the bars of the gallery, to raise the right arm and shake the spear held in its hand. The winged demons flapped their goblin wings, radiant with tinsel and vampire-like in form; the gentleman in black made his way towards the bars with noiseless step, thrust his pitchfork towards the audience, twisted the barb of his tail up to the height of his head, and shook a claw-like hand in the faces of three of the more youthful visitors who had taken front places close against the bars, and who did not seem to be in the least afraid.

"Now for the Ragin' Lion! his dander's risin'!" exclaimed one of the youthful party, as the strange hybrid monster nearest to us began to move its eyes, lash its tail, and turn its head. Then came a loud roar, and a series of shrieks and yells. With these were presently combined the din of some gongs, the discord of what sounded like two or three violoncellos, each out of tune, the shaking of chains, an imitation of an Indian war-whoop, and the roll of a muffled drum. Amidst all the hullaballoo the far end of the hobgoblin's home became strongly illumined, and the regions of fire disclosed to view by means of a bright red transparency with moving flames.

The audience were now supposed to be terrified to the requisite extent, and the time for instruction and edification had arrived. The figure with the horns and the tail, after once more brandishing his pitchfork, commenced addressing the audience, speaking with a very husky tone, but with a deep moral purpose. He announced himself as "Lucifer," and proceeded to inform his visitors that unless they behaved themselves properly he should have to claim them at some future time.

"I shall hev to hev you," said he, an assurance which the three youths in the front replied to by endeavoring to jerk some peanuts through the eye-holes of the mask, a proceeding which the Spirit of Evil resented by endeavoring to strike them with his pitchfork. The Raging Lion, perceiving how things were going, moved ponderously to the assistance of his fellow-fiend. Instantly the shower of peanuts became fierce and furious.

"It's young haythen yez are, ivery one of ye," groaned the Raging Lion, using an unmistakable brogue. "Ye don't riverince the divil yourself, and ye won't allow the ladies and gintlemen to. Ah, get out wid ye!"

A handful of peanuts well aimed passed in between the jaws of the monster and into the mouth of the speaker inside, causing him to cough violently. While the youths were laughing at the effect produced, one of them incautiously placed his arm too far within the bars. It was immediately seized by a hand thrust forth from the mouth of the Raging Lion, and while so held the youth was well cuffed by the gentleman with the tail and horns. Amidst the uproar which ensued, the lights were extinguished in the lower chamber and turned up in the gallery.

The show was over; the audience rushed to the staircase. Artemus Ward stepped towards the Raging Lion, spoke a few words to it, and threw a silver coin into its mouth. From its interior came forth a voice of gratitude—"Thanks, yer honor. It's the likes of ye should come ivery night to the raygions."

No joyous child ever felt more intense delight in the glories of a pantomime than did Artemus Ward in witnessing this grotesque exhibition. When we had passed out of the building and were strolling up

Sycamore Street, I remarked to him that I thought he liked the actors at the Infernal Regions much better than those at Pike's Opera.

"They feel more at home in their parts," was his reply. "It's the best show in Cincinnati."

Visiting the same museum at a later period, I was told that its early history is blended with that of Hiram Powers, the sculptor of the famous statue of "The Greek Slave." My information must be taken *quantum valeat*, but I was assured that while resident in Cincinnati during his younger days, Hiram Powers designed and modelled the hobgoblins and demons in the exhibition of the Infernal Regions.

❧ 3 ❧

The Ohio River · A Showman Afloat

YOUR Sunday in Cincinnati depends for the amount of enjoyment on which side you take it. Taken on the side nearest the river, it is grave; taken on the side farthest from the Ohio, it is gay. Taken one way, it is English or American, taken the other way, it is Continental. Travellers usually prefer a little of both. Running through the middle of the city is the White Water Canal, familiarly designated as "the Rhine;" and "over the Rhine" is the German quarter, or half of the city, with a population exceeding 60,000.

On Sunday evening American Cincinnati is as demure and well-behaved as London or Boston, while Teutonic Cincinnati enjoys Sunday in true German fashion. There may by this time be some alteration in the municipal arrangements, but at the period of my last visit the laws which applied to the city proper did not affect what some people would think to be the city improper, or "over the Rhine." All places of amusement were closed on Sunday evening in Cincinnati of the Americans who spoke English, but among the citizens who spoke German the theatre was open, regardless of the day being Sunday; and the voice of song, together with the clink of lager-bier glasses, could be heard in the "Sanger Halle," the "Arbeiter Halle," and in the hall of the "Turners."

The canal which separates the nationalities is a poor parody on the Rhine. There are no castles on it, but there are some very fine pig-killing establishments; nor is there any Echo of the Lorelei, but in its stead the grunt of innumerable swine, continually grunting their "*Morituri te salutamus*" to the Caesar of the pork-butchers.

Sunday followed the evening of the visit to the Museum. Early in the day I strolled through the German part of the city. Returning down Race Street, I met Artemus Ward. Opposite the place where we met was a chapel, and, at the suggestion of a third party, we went across to it. The preacher was Mr. Moncure D. Conway. His text on that occasion was, "Issachar is a strong ass couching down between two burdens." The sermon was wholly a political one. If I remember rightly, Mr. Conway found in Issachar a comparison for America. He pictured slavery as one of the burdens, and an imbecile administration the other. Unless I am mistaken, the moral of Mr. Conway's discourse was, that the "strong ass" should throw off both burdens, and allow itself to be ridden by General Fremont. The tendency of the sermon was not in accordance with the views of poor Artemus. He left the chapel in a somewhat excited manner. Little did he think that in a very few years to come that same preacher would use him for a text, and that the same Mr. Conway would be the orator selected to speak the funeral oration in the cold chapel near the temporary grave of the humorist on the day of his burial in the cemetery at Kensal Green in England.

It is not within my power to remember on what errand Artemus Ward chanced to be in Cincinnati at the time of which I write; I think that it was upon newspaper business, for he was not then the popular lecturer which he subsequently became. Possibly he was on a visit, for there was at least one family in that city with whom he was well acquainted, and with one member of which, at a subsequent period, his future life was likely to have had a more intimate connection. That his engagement, whatever it was, was not one which restricted his move-ments, was evidenced by his accepting a proposal made by two or three friends to go down the river to Louisville on the next day, or the day following. Having to visit Louisville on business, I arranged to avail myself of the same steamer.

Cincinnati is in the State of Ohio, on one side of the river, and Cov-ington and Newport are in Kentucky, on the opposite side. Seven years ago the Ohio flowed between slavery and freedom. The "Cincinnati

Belle," or the "Newport Belle," was in waiting to ferry you from one to the other. Now you cross by means of a bridge, and the black man can come and go as he pleases. On the morning that Artemus Ward and I went on board the "Major Anderson," United States mail-packet, bound for Louisville, the "Stars and Stripes" were waving from the buildings on both sides of the stream, soldiers in blue uniforms were sauntering on the levée, and the slavery question was in about as muddy a condition as the waters of the river on which we floated.

To a stranger fresh from Europe, an American river steamer is a curiosity: the shape of the boat, the accommodation met with on board, the whole economy of the management, are unlike any thing to which the Englishman is accustomed on the Thames or the Mersey. The "Major Anderson" was not one of the most magnificent boats of her class, but she was a very fair specimen of the vessels on the Ohio. At the clerk's office on board I paid two dollars and a half for my fare to Louisville, in return for which the clerk handed me the key of my cabin, with a long stick attached to it, to prevent its being lost. In the cabin was the following "notice to passengers." I quote it because there are some points about it which render it worthy of imitation:

"NOTICE TO PASSENGERS."

"Life-preservers will be found hanging in the rooms, or under the head of each bed; they are adjusted similar to putting on a jacket or a waistcoat, fastening the straps across the breast. The life-boat, etc., will be found on the hurricane-deck. The doors and blinds can be lifted off the hinges, and make good life-preservers; also the cotton mattresses."

The saloon of the steamer was long, the view from stem to stern being almost uninterrupted; the decorations were white and gold. At the stern end there was a piano, and comfortable seats for the lady passengers; while at the forward extremity of the saloon were the clerk's office, a bar for the accommodation of the thirsty, and a stove with seats around it for those who wished to chat and to smoke. My new friends and I ascended to the hurricane-deck, where we could watch the busy scene at the levée before starting. There were steamboats for Maysville, Portsmouth, Ironton, Ashland, Pittsburg, Marietta, and Gallipolis.

When the steamer glided off, we first passed a suburb of factories, and then between ranges of hills cultivated as vineyards to their very summits. The banks of the Ohio, and those of its tributary, the "Singing Sciota," are famous for the growth of the grape. Chief among the wines of the locality is the celebrated "Catawba," of which Longfellow sings:

> "Very good in its way
> Is the Verzenay
> Or the Sillery soft and creamy;
> But Catawba wine
> Has a taste more divine,
> More dulcet, delicious, and dreamy."

"Sparkling Catawba" has a muscatel flavor, with a dash of bitter intermixed. Who but he who has travelled in America during the hot months of the year knows any thing of the glories of a "Catawba cocktail," made as it is at the bar of the Tremont House, the Revere, or Parker House, in Boston? Flavor, fragrance, and beauty are all united in that delicious draught. Who but an educationally qualified American "bar-tender" knows how to compound the appetizing, odoriferous, amethyst-colored nectar? Who else but he would understand the precise number of drops of bitter to add to the Catawba, the right mode of using the ice, how to float the freshly-gathered strawberry on the surface, and how properly to "frost" the rim of the glass with pulverized sugar, so that sweetness should precede amaritude, and perfume be blended with brilliancy? On two other continents besides that of America have I tasted American drinks made by *quasi*-American barmen; but their compounds, compared with those mixed by the true American artist on his own soil, were as different in effect as Verdi's music played by Mr. Costa's band, and Verdi's music on a barrel-organ, with a tamed monkey turning the handle.

We "took our cocktail" on board the "Major Anderson," and drank in Catawba our morning draught to the health of Mr. Nicholas Longworth, who is, or was, the Perrier, Jouet, Moet, Chandon, and Veuve Clicquot of Cincinnati, all comprised in one individual.

One o'clock was the dinner-hour. A stimulus for the appetite was taken by most of the passengers before sitting down to the early meal. Over the bar was a portrait of Major Anderson, of Fort Sumter fame. Inclosed between glass was a small piece of bunting cut from the flag

which had waved over the fort; and flanking it on each side were portraits of General Lyon and General Franz Siegel. Below this was a
print of that celebrated character, "The Arkansas Traveller," representing him as sitting fiddling in front of a wretched cottage, wearing an
opossum-skin cap with the tail hanging down behind. Just inside the
cottage door was Mrs. Arkansas Traveller smoking a pipe, while a traveller on horseback was vainly endeavoring to extract from the fiddler
plain directions for finding the road to Napoleon, or to some other place
in that cheerful State of Arkansas, where the roads are as eccentric as
the people, and the paths as devious as the ways of the inhabitants.

The pictures in front of the bar were typical of the passengers who
were taking their morning drinks and chatting on the events of the day.
Out of a group of three, two of them were Arkansas men and the third
a Missourian. The straight hair and the sallow complexion, the lean
body and the long arms, were those of the semi-civilized class of men who
act as buffers to the engine of civilization where it comes in contact with
the dead wall behind which the Indian skulks and the wilderness extends.

Side by side with these gentlemen of the backwoods and the prairie
were a group of military personages in blue uniforms, going down to join
the Federal army in Kentucky. One of them was a loud-speaking captain, who criticised in unmeasured terms of reprobation the conduct of
his superior officer. After fully expressing his mind on that subject, he
devoted his energies to abusing General Scott, who had just left for
England.

"Any how you can fix it, he's a slow old fool," was the complimentary
remark of this newly-fledged captain, referring to the famous old general. "His policy was always to have his men chawed up—chawed up
for nothin'. It's jest what he did at Lundy's Lane years ago. Now, if you
call chawin' up fightin', I ain't that way of thinkin'."

The opinions of the outspoken little captain were not very favorably
received by two roughly-bearded men, who were each addressed as
"doctor," and who in their turn addressed the bar-keeper as "doctor"
also, when they requested him to mix them another cocktail.

In the midst of his denunciations, the captain was interrupted by an
impudent Jewish-looking youth, whose age could not be more than
sixteen, but whose expressive face seemed to notify that he had already
laid in the whole stock of villainy required for the next twenty years of
his life.

"Jine me in a game of seven-up, Cap?" The captain declined the invitation, and the youthful gamester applied to the two doctors. They also declining, he solicited Artemus Ward and myself. Again disappointed, he addressed himself to the Missourian. The offer was at once accepted, and, as the youth sat down to play, the handle of a bowie-knife peeped out from under his jacket.

Artemus Ward and his friends were quietly watching the sharp play of the Missourian and the youth, when a gentleman of very pleasing address stepped up, and addressing Artemus as "Charley," politely asked him to take "a scintillation," an invitation which was afterwards as politely extended to our little party. The phrase was a new one to me, but in the course of the day I discovered that it was the favorite euphemism of the affable gentleman for a small quantity of whisky. Not that he drank at all himself. A cigarette seemed to be his own chief enjoyment, but he was ever ready to offer "a scintillation" to any one to whom he was introduced. In the course of a brief conversation I ascertained that he was agent for a show, and that he was going down to Louisville to survey the capabilities of that city as a field for money-making.

"Are you still in the Crimea, and does my friend Lord Raglan hold on to his gallant steed as well as usual?" inquired Artemus Ward, in an affected tone of solicitude.

The question startled me, for the date of the year was 1861, and I had been among the spectators a few years previously when the funeral procession of Lord Raglan passed through Bristol.

"The Crimea came to an end in Canada; Lord Raglan is Major Anderson now," was the enigmatical reply. "Still the same old horse, though. Goes over the field of battle at night just the same. The professor understands his business. It's a big show — a very big show. Gentlemen, won't you take a scintillation?"

Accustomed as I was to shows of various kinds, I felt puzzled about this particular one. Artemus Ward noticed my perplexity, was amused at my inability to understand the conversation, and requested the "Colonel," as he called the agent, to explain to me the merits of his particular show.

We adjourned to the hurricane-deck for the second time before dinner; and as the steamer glided down the Ohio, with Indiana on our right and Kentucky on our left, the "Colonel" described his show. Being a

man of some education, he spoke without any very marked peculiarity
of accent, and, being aware that two at least of our party were acquainted with show-life, he conversed without reticence.

"Ours is a *Theatre of Arts*," said he. "There is Thiodon's, and there is
ours. Thiodon is in the Canadas now, with the Holy Sepulchre and the
Shipwreck. His is a very good show, but ours can knock spots out of it.
It wants life. Ours is bright, and nothing but animation. Our machinery
is perfect, and we always light up well. Light's the thing. Gas, if you
can get it. If not, spend your dollars on camphine, and don't be afraid.
Audiences like lights high and music loud. We had nothing but the musical glasses first; now we have a self-acting organ with cymbals in it.
The boys like the cymbals. Here's our programme—Panorama of
Europe to begin with. Panorama not too large, but A No. 1. Illumina-
tion of St. Peter's at Rome to finish off Part I. Then a little minstrelsy;
not too much. Then the Grand Pictorial and Mechanical Animated and
Moving Representation of the Taking of Fort Sumter. That used to be
the War in the Crimea and the Siege of Sebastopol. The Crimea got
played out, and we turned it into Fort Sumter and Charleston Harbor.
Ours are all cut figures. The Russians did not want much painting to
turn them into Secessionists, and we had only to paint out the red-coats
of the British and color them in blue to make the Federals. Sebastopol
stood a little too high on the rocks for the city of Charleston, but we
have painted the rocks down. We turned Balaclava into Castle Pinck-
ney, and we had room enough in the Black Sea to slip in a very nice
Fort Sumter. The same holes which did for us to puff the smoke
through, in bombarding the Malakoff, do for us in firing at Sumter, and
Sumter had to have a few holes made for it. All fits in, and costs no
trouble. We put the licks in. We did it ourselves. There was a night
scene in the Crimea with a horse to move, and Lord Raglan to go out
on it, to look at the dead on the field of battle. Horses are all alike in
pictures. Lord Raglan makes a good Major Anderson; but, as no one
was killed at Fort Sumter, all we can do is to suppose the Major to be
surveying the ruins from James's Island before going on board the
steamer for New York. Our exhibition is particularly well suited for
schools. Moral, instructive, and cheap—that's what schools want. In
making my arrangements ahead, I call upon the schools and contract
with them. Five cents each in New England. No getting any more
there; ten or fifteen cents anywhere else."

As nearly as I can remember, I have quoted the very words in which the "Colonel" described his show. The last time that I endeavored to remember and to quote them was when the Mr. Thiodon referred to volunteered his services, and came from the Crystal Palace to assist poor Artemus in fitting up the panorama of the Mormons at the Egyptian Hall.

The sound of a gong announced the arrival of dinner-time on board the "Major Anderson." To any one who has never travelled except in England, the ceremony of taking dinner on board an American river steamer is peculiar. When we descended to the saloon from the hurricane-deck we found the majority of the male passengers standing up against the doors of the state-rooms, or holding on to chairs, waiting for the customary signals. The table extended down the saloon, the stern end of it being assigned to the ladies, and the fore-part to the single gentlemen. A small bell was rung, and the ladies at once proceeded to take their seats, those who had cavaliers being escorted by them in the usual manner. Until all the ladies were seated, the gentlemen at the lower table remained standing. Then a gong sounded—not a bell—and plump went all the gentlemen at once into their chairs with a rush. Piled up in huge dishes on the table were the several kinds of meat provided, already carved and cut into slices. Americans are proverbial for eating rapidly, and on river steamers in the West they eat more rapidly than they do anywhere else. In twenty minutes from the time of commencement the ceremony of dining was completed. Supper, as it was called, took place at six o'clock. It was conducted in like manner, but with even more rapidity. After supper the company broke up into small parties; the ladies occupying the after-part of the saloon, to play the piano, read, and flirt, the majority of the male passengers selecting tables nearer the bar to indulge in one or other of those never-failing sources of solace to the Western traveller—the games of euchre, poker, and seven-up.

Artemus Ward was not a card-player. Indeed I very much doubt if he knew at any time during his life how to play the simplest game. His friends proposed that we should amuse ourselves with euchre. Artemus turned away from them with a look of pity, and sought the society of the ladies. Among the fairer portion of the passengers was a very retiring, quiet young lady, who wore spectacles, and who appeared to have the manners, air, and bearing of one whose occupation in life was to impart her knowledge to others in some college or seminary; that, at least, was the guess which Artemus and I had made about her. We had noticed her during the afternoon busily engaged in reading About's story of "Le Roi des Montagnes." As soon as supper was over she resumed her reading, cutting the leaves of the book with a pocket paper-knife as she read on. By what means my friend contrived an introduction I am not aware; but I found him in conversation with her when I went to request his company to smoke a cigar with me and the two military doctors.

"Excuse me," said Artemus. "This lady was asking me if I read French. It is a serious question, and I was reflecting whether I do."

The lady seemed to be a little surprised, and explained to me that she had simply asked if my friend knew the French language, as she wished to recommend to him the story she herself had been reading during the afternoon.

"It is a story about brigands in Greece," said she; "and it is so charmingly picturesque that I can almost fancy myself to be in that classic land. As I read, the blue skies of Greece seem to be over my head, and the Ægean Sea to be sparkling in the glorious sunlight!"

Then followed a question from Artemus, which I quote as literally as I can remember it:

"Pardon me, madame, but do you think that glorious sunlight in Greece is constitutional—that is to say, if early be the dream of youth—whenever they are so—and you know, I presume, that George Washington, when young, never told a lie—that is, Greece—in the blue skies, I mean. You understand me, of course?"

Instead of understanding, the lady appeared to be utterly bewildered. At first she seemed to doubt whether she had heard distinctly. Then the expression of her face indicated that she had a suspicion of her not having paid sufficient attention, so as to enable her to comprehend the interrogatory.

"Do I understand you to say that George Washington went to Greece in his youth?" she asked. "I scarcely think that I perfectly understood you."

Artemus Ward maintained his gravity, and proceeded to explain.

"I was about to remark," said he, "that, so far as Greece is concerned, he was more so."

"More so of what?" asked the lady, still more perplexed.

"More so with regard to it viewed morally. Because the Ægean is a sea—a blue sea, which might, if not under those circumstances—in parallel instances—very truthfully though; but before breakfast—always before the morning meal. You agree with me, I hope?" And Artemus smiled and bowed politely.

The lady closed her book, laid it on the table, and, raising her spectacles, so as to enable her to see better, regarded Artemus with amazement. The ladies and gentlemen around who had overheard the conversation looked at the speaker with equal astonishment. Artemus shook his head mournfully, and in a deploring tone of voice observed:

"Blue Greeks—blue Ægean brigands, dead before their breakfast!"

"Mercy me!" cried the lady. "The poor fellow is out of his mind. Has he no friends with him? He is much to be pitied."

"It is nothing, madam," replied one of our party; "nothing, I assure you. He usually wanders in this way when he has snakes in his boots."

"Snakes in his boots! And has he got them now?" cried the lady, rising quickly, and recoiling from the man whom she had just been regarding with tender pity.

"He has, madam. He's apt to see them now and then, but—"

An outcry of terror from the sympathetic lady led to a scene of confusion, in the midst of which the gentlemen passengers made their way to the forepart of the saloon, while some of the ladies took refuge in their state-rooms.

At that time I was not better informed than the lady I have referred to as to the meaning of the phrase "Snakes in his boots." On inquiry I found it to be the Western idiom for *delirium tremens,* and it was explained to me as a curious physiological fact that the hard drinkers of the South and South-western States are apt to imagine that their boots are full of snakes when they themselves are suffering from the mental hallucination produced by excessive intemperance.

The incoherency of speech and strange behavior of my fellow-passenger had not, of course, resulted from any such cause, but was merely a humorous freak on his part; a specimen of a peculiar description of fun in which he was very fond of indulging at a subsequent period of his career. At the time of which I am writing he was a stranger to me. Being unaccustomed to any such style of joking, I was as much bewildered with his rambling remarks on the Greek brigands as appeared to be the lady to whom he addressed them.

In later years, during summer months spent at his home at Maine, in company with his friend Mr. Setchell, it was a great source of amusement for him to seek out some of the stolid, half-witted townsfolk and befool them in the same manner. Mr. Setchell and he would maintain a long conversation together in which there would be no coherency, nor relevancy of subject between any two sentences. If by so conversing the agricultural mind could be thoroughly confused, and the country bumpkin be made to express his opinion that the two conversationalists were a pair of crazy idiots, the end of the joke was gained, and, being gained, was thoroughly enjoyed.

Before we arrived at Louisville, the lady, who had evinced so much enthusiasm about Greece and so much astonishment at the conversation of Artemus Ward, was duly informed of the perfect sanity of the gentleman with whom she had been talking. I had reason to think that she fully accorded her forgiveness for having been made a participant in the jest, for I noticed her conversing very pleasantly with my friend, and not manifesting the least uneasiness about the proximity of the boots which had been said to be filled with unpleasant reptiles.

The agent for the *Theatre of Arts*, the captain, the two doctors, and myself, sought seats around the stove, beguiling the time with anecdote and jest. We did not expect to arrive at Louisville till about midnight. So inclement had the evening become that none of us seemed anxious to leave the warm and comfortable saloon of the steamer to encounter darkness, rain, and wind, by promenading on the hurricane-deck. Each of us volunteered to tell a story. The stormy evening suggested the topic of most of the tales, and by far the best one was told by one of the passengers who had hitherto amused himself by playing poker — its excellence consisting in the gravity with which it was related, and in its being illustrative of a quality of humor more keenly appreciated by Americans than by Europeans.

"I used to reside at Apalachicola, in Florida," said the teller of the tale. "While I was located there I kept a little yacht of my own, which I had built for me at Portsmouth, in New Hampshire. She was a sweet beauty of a craft, and I used to go out in her considerable; sometimes taking a trip to Cedar Keys, and sometimes rounding Cape St. Blas, and going to St. Andrews. Down there, in the Gulf of Mexico, we got awful storms. When it thunders the heavens are as mad as all wrath, and when it lightens the electric fluid is something wonderful to see.

The little puff of wind and rain we have to-night don't bear talking about in comparison. Early in the fall, the weather being confoundedly hot and sultry, I took a trip in my yacht round to St. Joseph, and I was on my homeward voyage when there came a dead calm. I had only two men with me to sail the yacht, and as the wind fell and the sky darkened away to the sou'-west they began to get scared, wishing themselves safely round the cape. I knew we were to have a thunder-storm, and I reckoned upon our having it pretty smart. When it came it was a caution. Such thunder, such lightning, and such electricity of the heavens I had never seen before. I saw a great thunder-bolt, all one blaze of fire, go plump into the water like a cannon-ball, and presently, as I was standing looking on, the lightning struck my yacht and almost blinded me. I felt as if I had a flutter-wheel in my head, and I could feel the electric fluid running all through me like streams of hot water. My men helped me down into the cabin, and there I sat for some time, feeling the lightning trickle, trickle, trickle through my bones. When I got better and could stand up I found my feet quite burdensome to me, and my boots swelling out with something which felt like warm oil. I got my men to pull them boots off for me, and I reckon there was close on to a quart of electric fluid in each boot!"

"How did you know it was electric fluid?" asked the bar-keeper, who had been listening to the veracious story-teller.

"Know it? Wall, I reckon there wasn't much trouble in knowing it. We poured it into the sea, and it lighted up the Gulf of Mexico for miles around."

While we were laughing at the manner in which the narrator of the story confirmed the truth of his assertion, the bell rang to warn us that we were in sight of Louisville.

❦ 4 ❦

Louisville · Among Panoramas and Minstrels

KENTUCKY had experienced very little of the excitement caused by the war of the Great Rebellion at the time when Artemus Ward and I chanced to visit Louisville; but regiment after regiment was daily passing through the city *en route* for the southern part of the State. Buckner was at Bowling Green, and Zollicoffer at Cumberland Gap. Soldiers from Indiana, Ohio, and Minnesota, most of them tall, gawky, and half-drilled recruits, were assembled in groups upon the levée; and General Buell had just superseded Sherman in command of the district.

The hotel to which we went was the Galt House, the place at which to obtain the best accommodation in the city. The charge for board and lodging was two dollars and a half a day. Having to do with an entertainment about to visit Louisville, I put in my claim to the privilege of being treated with that amount of leniency with regard to charge, always accorded to showmen in the United States. Hamlet's instructions to see that "the players are well bestowed," is invariably attended to by the hotel clerks across the Atlantic. I stated who I was, registered my name in the book, and was politely asked to "take a drink." Having come through the wind and rain, I accepted the invitation. Late as it was in the evening, and though Louisville was then under martial law, the bar-room of the Galt House was thronged with customers. More than half of them were soldiers attired in the blue uniform of the Federal army. Most of them were young men, and none of them, I presume, had seen any thing of the stern realities of actual warfare. To them fighting seemed to be a matter of no more importance than a game of base-ball would be to an American, or a cricket-match to an Englishman. They were soldiers fresh from home; their gilt adornments bedazzled them, and where they might have seen thistles they saw but roses; their swords had been buckled to their sides by fair hands, which they had pressed only a few days previously; and the parting words of parents, brothers, and sisters still sounded in their ears like the echoes of soul-inspiriting music. That there could be any thing in store for them but victory, any thing in waiting for them but promotion, laurels, another night at the Galt House on their way home, and a speedy return to the loved ones they had left, scarcely seemed to oppress the minds of any one of them. The South was to be crushed at once, and they had only to go and crush it. The "Star-spangled Banner" was to be sung in every city of "Secessia," from the Cumberland River to the Florida Reefs, and they were to go and sing it.

The young soldiers were mostly recruits from the North-western States — fine stalwart men, who had been accustomed to the use of the axe in the backwoods, and who felt no more doubt about clearing away their enemies on the fields of Alabama or Tennessee than they had of their ability to hew down the forests of Michigan or Minnesota.

They were all colonels, captains, or lieutenants — those young men in front of the bar. Nor was it derogatory to their ideas of military etiquette to loll about, smoke their cigars and drink their whisky together in a bar open to all comers. Unacquainted as I then was with the military customs of the Western World, the free-and-easy manners of these youthful officers was matter for surprise and study.

I was surveying the scene with great interest, when there entered the bar-room a gentleman whose coming seemed to be regarded by the soldiers with unusual satisfaction. He wore a common black coat, such as we wear in England for morning dress, and a pair of black trowsers. On his head was a cocked hat, with feathers in it, having on one side a gilt shield ornamented with the stars and stripes. He was stout in build, and, from his ruddiness of color and other characteristics, might have been mistaken for an Englishman.

"Glad to see you, Gen'ral. Take a drink with us; some very good Bourbon. Hurrah for the old flag!"

The General acknowledged the compliments paid him, and "took a drink." On inquiry, I found that he was General Buell, the new commander of the district. That he should accept a glass of whisky from his young subordinates appeared to be regarded as in no way improper.

Fighting was near at hand, but festivity was the order of the night. To add to the amusements, there came into the bar-room a negro, answering in description to that "tall, broad-shouldered, impudent black fellow" whom Addison, in the last volume of the "Spectator," causes to describe the "Widow-club." He carried with him a thick stick, and, without being at all intoxicated, offered to allow any one present, on payment of the small sum of ten cents, to strike him on the head with the stick as hard as they might please.

I was told that he made money for himself and his master also by going round the city and submitting to be struck on the head by any one who would pay first and strike afterwards. That the cranium of the negro is thicker and harder than that of other men is, I believe, an admitted fact; but no Irishman at Donnybrook Fair ever enjoyed the touch of a shillalah on the top of his head so much as this Louisville negro, who seemed to enter into the sport of being battered.

No one in the bar-room being willing to strike him, he tried a few hard blows on himself, making no feint in the wielding of the weapon; then with a smiling expression, as though he had done himself much good, he made a collection among the audience and spent a part of it in whisky. Since that exhibition I have fully comprehended the difficulty of educating the negro.

To prepare the way for an entertainment about to take place in Louisville was, as I have stated, the purport of my visit. Artemus Ward was then more of a "showman" in theory than in practice; and when in the morning I prepared to go out to arrange with the music-sellers, call upon the editors, give orders to the bill-posters, and confer with the city officials, he met me, and we started on the expedition together.

The first place to visit was the hall in which the entertainment was to be given. It was called the Masonic Temple. The accommodation was for about a thousand people, and the rent seventy-five dollars a week, including the gas. Like most of the halls of the United States, it contained a stage and proscenium; but the latter was of the most extraordinary description, resembling an organ front of Gothic design, painted very vilely blue. Coming out from the hall, we noticed a number of heavy boxes, and inquired what they were.

"Panoramas!" answered Mr. Matthews, the hall-keeper, or "janitor," as they call such an official in America. "There's 'The Holy Land,' 'The Sights of Paris,' and 'Bunyan's Pilgrim's Progress,' and 'The Drunkard's Career.' They are all there for rent. Panoramas generally get stuck here, and the owners go dead broke. You can have 'The Holy Land' very cheap if you want to buy it; but the gentleman who owns 'Bunyan's Pilgrim's Progress' has gone down to Cumberland to trade whisky to the army. He'll be back with some chips."

"And of course he will redeem his panorama?" I suggested, knowing that by "chips" Mr. Matthews intended to imply money. Mr. Matthews thought he would, adding, thoughtfully, "He has a fancy for the picture, and always cried to the school-children when he lectured on it. His liking to it, I reckon, comes from the face of Christian being painted, all the way through, a portrait of himself. That's awful stuff of whisky he's taken down to the army—sudden poison, I should think; but I hope he'll sell it and clear out his panorama."

"A lesson for me to have a panorama," remarked Artemus Ward as we passed out of the hall. Three years after that he had one painted for him in the city of New York.

Opposite the Masonic Temple lived Mr. Richard Moore, the bill-poster. In the order of business it was requisite to call upon him next. We found him in a small shop, where he retailed butter, eggs, and poultry. As I entered he was engaged selling squirrels to a lady; not living ones, but squirrels skinned ready for cooking. There was a chestful of them in the shop. "Them squarrels is cheap at a dollar for six," said he, addressing the lady. So I thought, reflecting on the sensation Mr. Moore could cause in Leadenhall-market by taking over a cargo of them.

I introduced myself, and requested to know how many bills of different sizes he could put up for me, how soon he would do them, and what contract he would make with regard to charge. His answers were satisfactory on all the three points of my inquiry, but he hesitated as I was about to leave, and in an anxious manner said:

"Did I understand your show to be a panorama?" I replied that it was not, and fully explained its characteristics. Mr. Moore's face brightened, as he replied: "Them bills shall be out at onst, gentlemen. I can see my money. But there's no use my leaving my butter business to go fooling after panoramas. Circus-work is what I like; but we can't expect many more circuses through here, now we've gone to fightin'. War is against circuses; thar's the evil of it."

Leaving Mr. Moore to his reflections on the wickedness of war in general, we proceeded on our way. The hall having been arranged for, and the bill-poster duly secured, the next thing requiring attention was to see the mayor and obtain the license; for, in the United States, every travelling entertainment has to take out a separate license in each town it may visit.

In going to see the mayor, it is as well to put a few free admission tickets into your pocket, that you may make his worship a present of some of them, and also extend a similar invitation to the aldermen. In many towns, especially where the aldermen have large families, these free admissions, or "dead-heads," as they are called, will obviate the payment of any money for the license. Under any circumstances I believe that it is good policy to "dead-head" the mayor, the aldermen, and the city clerk.

The newspapers of course have their prescriptive right to be "dead-headed." Then it is not bad policy to "dead-head" the chief clerk at the telegraph-office, that he, in return, may "dead-head" any telegram you may have to send; and there is wisdom in "dead-heading" the postmaster; for the postmaster has boxes in which he places the letters of the townsfolk. In those boxes he can place the programme of your concert or the circular of your lecture. He can aid you: he has a small family, and he talks through the little window to the ladies and gentlemen who come to fetch their letters. He may chance to talk about *you*, therefore "dead-head" him.

Relative to the subject of obtaining a license for an entertainment, I remember being in Lancaster, Pennsylvania. My business was to arrange for some amusements to take place in Fulton Hall. I sought out the bill-poster and accompanied him round the town, to see where there were any fitting places for the display of bills. He pointed out many, and urged the necessity of my giving him the bills at once. I told him that they were at the railway station, and that he should have them after I had obtained the license. He assured me that the license was "all right," and that I need not trouble about it. I instanced to him the fact that, at a neighboring town, the giver of a concert had been heavily fined some few weeks previously for allowing his concert to take place without having first applied for the license. The bill-poster smiled, and assured me that I had nothing to fear in Lancaster. He went with me to the station. The bills were duly handed over to him, to be used for placarding the town.

"Now," said I, "be good enough to show me the way to the mayor."

"I am the mayor!" was his reply. Another illustration of Lord Houghton's often quoted line, that

"A man's best things are nearest him."

There were two newspapers in Louisville — the "Louisville Journal" and the "Louisville Democrat." The "Journal" was edited by the celebrated Mr. George D. Prentice, an editor whose humorous paragraphs, pithy remarks, and trenchant sarcasms long ago won for him high renown in the literature of American journalism, and who was a celebrity worth travelling into Kentucky to see. Unfortunately he was not to be seen at the period of my visit. Business, therefore, had to be transacted with Colonel Wallace, the "local editor," an obliging, courteous, and shrewd member of the press, who listened attentively to the request I had to make, readily comprehended the character of the entertainment, and undertook to herald it into public notice in a manner befitting the "Louisville Journal." I offered to pay for the insertion of a "puff preliminary," but the offer was promptly declined. The Colonel had no objection to come out, stroll, and have a chat; and, accompanied by him, we went to the Medical College, where prisoners were then confined for political offenses. On the way we met an acquaintance who was in a great hurry. "I'm off to Paris," said he; "it's no use hanging about here. I was going to California. But quinine is better than gold now. If I can only ship over a cargo of quinine, and send it to where I want it to go, I'm a made man." We left him hurrying off to Paris, and the Colonel explained to us that quinine "down South" was in great request, and likely to be still more scarce. He had some Memphis and Nashville papers in his pocket. Taking them out, he pointed to the number of advertisements relative to the drug which our street-acquaintance was going over to Paris to import.

Later in the day I called at the "Democrat" office, and offered five dollars for a puff which I wished to be inserted. Messrs. Hughes and Harney not only accepted it, but volunteered to treat me with whisky in return for my fair dealing. As a rule, out West, I always found the Democratic editors to be better patrons of whisky than the Republican ones. There is a vein of whisky running through Western Democracy, as characteristic of the genial Democrat as the "blue blood" is of the Vere de Veres of aristocracy.

We dined at the Galt House, partaking of a very excellent dinner, and meeting many officers of the Union army who afterwards won distinction on the field of battle. Judging from the conversation, the ladies were more warlike in their disposition than the men; but those nearest me at the table were more strongly in favor of the Secessionists than of the Federalists. As an indication of their political feeling they wore the colors of the South in ribbons around the neck, just as they flaunted them in the streets by means of dyed feathers stuck in their little jaunty hats. For personal beauty the ladies of Louisville are deserving of especial notice. The Kentucky belle has a freshness of color and a roundness of form not so general among her fair sisters in other States of the Union. These characteristics are the result, I believe, of much out-door exercise. To be able to ride, and even to shoot, are not unusual accomplishments of a Kentuckian fair one. A young lady of the same age in Massachusetts would prefer to be able to read Virgil, and to stand an examination in physiological anatomy.

Louisville is not a city of any great architectural pretensions, nor has it the business life and "go" in it which characterize most of the large cities of the West. It is built on the Ohio, and is frequently designated "the Falls City," on account of the falls of the river being about two miles down the stream. I strolled to the levee to look at the steamboats, ranged in a row, the greater number of which were said to be taken up by the Government for the conveyance of troops. There were the "Argonaut" and the "Shenango" for Pittsburg, the "Trio" and the "W. W. Crawford" for Henderson, the "Dove" for the Kentucky River, and the "Sir William Wallace" for I know not where; but the name of the great Scotchman who gained the victory at Cambuskenneth and lost the field at Falkirk, painted on a steamboat floating on the muddy waters of the Ohio, seemed to be a little out of place. To a Scotchman's mind it might possibly have been some slight compensation for the murder which the first Edward wrought. Doubtless the boat was owned by an Americanized Scotchman.

Nationalities were plenteously represented in Louisville. Names of Scotch and Irish extraction figured over the whisky-shops, and Jew clothiers were numerous in the long row of buildings which looked down upon the levee. And a wild, dirty, bleak, windy, unattractive place that levee is — a steep bank sloping down to the edge of the river, with winding paths traced out on it for the carts to load and unload the steamers. On the opposite bank of the stream, looking as forlorn and as melancholy as it is possible for a town to look, is Jeffersonville, in Indiana. All the towns in Indiana are dreary, but Jeffersonville, I think, would be likely to win the prize in a contest for the honor of dreariness. It belongs to that State in which Artemus Ward describes his celebrated town of Baldinsville — a State wherein every place has more or less of a bald, graceless, raw-boned, and unadorned appearance — where, in every town, the streets are purposely made wide that the sun may have every chance of warming you in the broiling summer, and the wind lose no opportunity for sweeping along in one huge ferocious blast during the cold days of winter. Yet Jeffersonville is a town of some importance. It contains the railway station, where you take the train for Indianapolis, and the Penitentiary, in which many of the wild spirits of Indiana enjoy the sweets of repose and chew the cud of reflection.

A stroll along the chilly banks of the Ohio late in the afternoon was a good stimulant for a visit to the cosy little Louisville theatre in the evening. The lessee of the theatre was Mrs. Mary Lorton, and the manager Captain Fuller. There was a touch of the brigand in the captain's appearance, something which called to my mind Fra Diavolo, Schinderhannes, Zamiel, the late O. Smith, and the deep-voiced heroes of the Surrey theatre. He wore a large cloak and a broad-brimmed felt hat; and as my friends and I approached him, his arms were folded under his ample cloak, as if in the act of clutching a dagger. His reception of us was most courteous. Beneath the guise of a brigand we found the manners of an Alfred Jingle, with the hospitality of a Mr. Wardle, and the warm-heartedness of a Mr. Pickwick. The interior of the house was a little dingy, but very comfortably arranged. A "star" was in possession of the stage, and that star was Mr. Neafie, a tragedian well known to American play-goers. Had he not been playing the character of "Metamora" we might have staid longer to witness the performance; but the play of *Metamora* itself is one of those wondrous dramas so well characterized by a Western critic—"One in which the unities are admirably observed: the dullness which commences with the first act never flagging for a moment until the curtain falls."

Far more interesting than the tragedy to Artemus Ward was a chat in the theatre with a friend of the famous Mr. Rice, who introduced "Jim Crow" to the English public at the Adelphi Theatre in 1836, and who had but recently died in New York. The "burnt-cork profession," as that of negro minstrelsy is frequently termed in the United States, was one towards the members of which Artemus Ward had a special attachment. Their peculiar mode of life and singularities of habit rendered them favorite subjects of study to one who delighted in absurd, grotesque, and out-of-the-way developments of character. Rice and "Jim Crow" were therefore more enjoyable topics than "Metamora" and his Indian friends. We adjourned to where we could talk without disturbing others, and there it was that I found myself to be a pilgrim at the shrine of the birthplace of "Jim Crow."

"Yes, sir-ree," said our informant, "it was in this city of Louisville, in 1829, that Daddy Rice first jumped Jim Crow. Whar's all your minstrels spring from but here? Whar's all the beautiful melodies of every ministrel band going take their start from but from old Kentucky? I helped to black Daddy Rice's face the first night he sang; and if thar had been no Daddy Rice whar would have been your Bryants, and your Christys, and your Moores, and your Eph Horns, and your Morrises, and your Pells? Whar — why, just nowhar. Yes, sir-ree! that's whar."

"I thought that Nicholls was the first man to sing Jim Crow?" remarked Artemus, inquiringly.

"As a clown, he was. Yes, sir-ree. Thar you are right. It was in Purdy Brown's Circus, too. But he blacked his face after Daddy Rice did his, and then he sang 'Clar de Kitchen.' I can hear Daddy Rice at it now:

'First on de heel tap, den on de toe,
    Every time I wheel about I jump Jim Crow.'

Thar was singing. Thar was something to listen to. Whar is it nowadays? Thar's more on the stage to show off the art of the thing, but the art is nowhar. You can't see it. That's what's the matter. Yes, sir-ree!"

"We have some very good black artists now," responded Artemus Ward. "Good, noble, whole-souled lovers of their art, who love it — for the dollars and the whisky."

"Thar you are right again," chimed in our informant. "It's whisky in their souls that half of them have got. But Daddy Rice warn't upon that lay. He made Jim Crow as great a piece of acting in his way as Forrest makes any thing in Shakspeare. Yes, sir-ree."

I had seen enough of that curious race of performers, the black minstrels, in America and in other parts of the world, to wish to know a little more about their origin and history. Fortunately a gentleman happened to be present who appeared to be better informed on the subject than any one else. Waiting till the eulogist of Daddy Rice had departed, he favored us with a few facts, of which I made notes at the time. It may interest some of my readers to know that the first white man who publicly sang a song with his face blackened was a personage known as Pot-pie Herbert. His song was entitled "The Battle of Plattsburg," and was sung by him on the stage of the theatre at Albany, in the State of New York, shortly after the little victory gained by the Americans over the British on Lake Champlain. So successful was Pot-pie Herbert with this song that he was engaged to sing it at the Park Theatre, New York, then the fashionable theatre of that city. His career would have been more brilliant had it not been for his having the fatal habit, to use an expression of poor Ward's, of "concealing too much whisky about his person." Long afterwards, Mr. Keller, a low comedian, blackened his face and sang "The Coal Black Rose;" while a Mr. Barney Burns, with similar facial adornment, treated his audiences to the enlivening melody of "Sich a Gittin' Up Stairs." But not until 1842 did a company of "Nigger Minstrels" appear in combination before the public.

For the information of any one who feels an interest in the history of amusements, and who has wondered at the origin of the idea of a group of men singing songs in the character of negroes at a popular hall in London, or less artistic performers of the same class executing grotesque vagaries on the sands at Ramsgate, it may not be out of place to mention that the original troupe started as a quartette party. They made their first appearance at the Chatham Street Theatre, in New York, calling themselves "The Virginia Minstrels." Their names were Richard Ward Pelham, Daniel Decatur Emmett, William Whittock, and Francis Marion Brower. The first song they sung was the still popular melody of "The Boatman's Dance."

When Macaulay's New Zealander shall disinter a fossil banjo from among the ruins of Piccadilly, these facts may have interest for the editor of "Notes and Queries" in the world's metropolis of the Feejee Islands.

The discussion on the origin of negro minstrelsy being brought to a close, Artemus Ward and I strolled through the streets of Louisville at night. Our conversation related chiefly to the various forms of amusements, and the eccentricities of those who make it their business to amuse. Many were the odd stories about minstrels and circus-men told me by my companion in the course of our desultory ramble.

During his engagements as reporter and editor of the "Toledo Commercial" and the "Cleveland Plain-dealer," Artemus Ward had met with most of the travelling showmen of celebrity, and become intimately acquainted with their history. He knew their good points, their shortcomings, their peculiarities of character, and their eccentricities.

The social life of the showman had been to him a special subject for study. He knew the showman at home as well as abroad — knew him in his show and in his chamber, knew him in his unconventionalities of thought and understood him in his views of society, as well as in the under-current of feeling resulting from early experiences. Droll anecdotes and shrewd remarks followed one another rapidly, until we found ourselves at the hotel, parting company on the stairs. Then, after a few moments of silence and reflection, my friend said:

"I understand that you are used to the management of shows. Suppose one day you manage me?"

I replied that the proposal was one which I felt very well disposed to consider favorably, but expressed a wish to know in what character I was likely to have the opportunity of managing him, and how he intended to constitute himself "a show." He replied, with mock gravity:

"A moral lecturer. There's nothing else to be made of me but that. And you must take me to England and Australia."

We bade each other "good-night!" and parted laughingly. The next morning I left by the train for St. Louis. Thence I started on a journey of many months' duration through the North-western States of America. Artemus Ward and I did not meet again till nearly a year and a half had passed away. Then, when we met, I listened to Artemus as he lectured to an audience of nearly two thousand people; and, while the laughter and applause resounded on every side, there came to my memory the night of our parting in Louisville. The "moral lecturer" was before me. Were we ever to go to England and Australia together?

The question was left for Time to answer. In a very few years came the full reply. We were destined to be associated in California among the gold-miners, and in Salt Lake among the Mormons. We were to travel the United States, and be friends in London; but never to visit Australia, nor, after leaving American ground, were we to meet upon it again any more.

In this chapter and those which precede it the reader has been made acquainted with the circumstances that led to my first personal knowledge of Artemus Ward. By the help of notebooks I have endeavored to recount faithfully the incidents of our first meeting, and to depict the scenes among which we met. Before I proceed with the narrative of our acquaintance, and previous to detailing any further reminiscences of show-life in the Western World, it may be proper, perhaps, that I should devote a few pages to the early history of him the story of whose life I have undertaken to tell. Let me premise that the few facts I have to relate about the youth of "the Showman" are mainly gathered from his statements to me during the period of our intimacy. Relative to his own affairs he was always reticent, and, when interrogated about his early career, seemed to regard the subject as a farce worthy only of being treated with laughter, or, rather, as a transient jest, which had served its purpose, and merited nothing more than to be laid aside, unthought of and never to be recalled.

❧ 5 ❧

Maine · The Home of the Humorist

CHARLES FARRAR BROWNE, whose *nom de plume* was "Artemus Ward," was born at the upper village of Waterford, Oxford County, Maine, on the twenty-sixth of April, 1834. His father, Mr. Levi Browne, was a land surveyor and rural justice of the peace. His mother, Caroline E. Browne, still lives, and is a hale active lady of advanced years, who has survived the loss of husband and children, and whose physical strength still enables her to take long journeys in the summer weather, when she leaves her secluded home in Maine and travels to see the busy world as represented in the pleasant city of Portland, or in the thronged and noisy streets of charming old Boston.

The family of the Brownes dates back to the days of the Puritans, and has been long resident in the State of Maine. There appears to be an uncertainty in the family as to the correct orthography of the patronymic. In signing his proper name, Charles Browne used a final "e." I have before me letters received from him in America, and the visiting-card which he used in London. The name in each instance is spelt "Browne." But I also have letters written by his mother in which the final "e" is omitted from the signature. Noticing this variation of spelling, I once took occasion to question Artemus Ward on the subject. His reply was to the effect that he believed the final vowel was always used by his ancestors, but that his father at one period of his life omitted it in his signature, and that some of his relations retained it, while others dispensed with it as being superfluous. I was anxious to know if he possessed any information relative to the English county whence the family originated in pre-Puritanic times. He replied jocosely:

"I should think we came from Jerusalem, for my father's name was Levi, and we had a Nathan and a Moses in the family. But my poor brother's name was Cyrus, so perhaps that makes us Persians."

Maine is the Scotland of the United States; it is the

"Land of the mountain and the flood,"

the land of pine-forest and the moose-deer—of the lonely lake and the narrow glen—of the cloud-kissing hill and the torrent leaping in madness from crag to crag. It is the most northern as well as the most eastern of the States of the American Union. The uncleared lands of Canada, and the secluded glories of the lower St. Lawrence limit it on the north-west; the forest solitudes of New Brunswick and the fierce waves of the Atlantic are its boundaries on the east; while on the south-west the snow-capped White Mountains of New Hampshire guard it like grim sentinels, jealous of its wealth of scenic grandeur; for in Maine there are lakes fifty miles in extent, and mountains five thousand feet high. Historic associations are all that Maine requires to render it as much the favorite resort of the tourist in search of the picturesque as it is now the chosen ground of the hardy hunter and the adventurous sportsman. Its climate is cold, bleak, and invigorating—a climate where the summer is brief but glorious, and the winter lengthy but thoroughly enjoyable—a blue sky overhead, hard, shining, sparkling snow covering the ground, the wind making music among the pines, and the sleigh-bells tinkling as the sleighs glide swiftly over the frosty plain. "Caledonia, stern and wild," may be, as Scott expresses it, "meet nurse" for a poet; but the wild magnificence of rock-bound, icy, dark-forested Maine would hardly seem to be the fitting cradle for a humorist who evinced very little appreciation of the beautiful or grand in natural scenery, but cared infinitely more to notice, to study, and to enjoy the comic side of conventional city life.

A traveller arriving at Quebec, after having made a tour through the Canadas and being about to visit the United States, would be most likely to avail himself of the facilities offered by the Grand Trunk line.

He would take the train at the terminus on the St. Lawrence, opposite Quebec, travel through the forest wilds of Canada down to Richmond, and on through Sherbrooke, till, crossing the boundary-line of the States, he would enter Vermont, and come to a stop at the romantic station of Island Ponds. Arriving there late, he would most probably stay a few hours and sleep at the hotel specially intended for his halting-place. Rising very early in the morning, and waiting for the engine to get up steam, he would have time to notice the solitary beauty of the locality, the gloomy grandeur of the woods around, and the placid brightness of the miniature lakes, whence the station obtains its name of Island Ponds. The clearness of the morning, the sharpness of the air, and the grateful fragrance of the pine forest, would most likely tempt him to indulge in some breakfast before taking the train for Portland. He would do well to let that breakfast be substantial, and never mind being told that Paris is near, and that he can breakfast there. It is just possible that the name of the place might suggest ideas of luxurious cafés, looking out upon gay boulevards—of breakfasts with the most tempting of viands and the most unexceptionable wines. Would the traveller know the difference between Paris and Paris? He has only to wait. After being whirled through the forests, and hurried through the mountain gorges, over streams roaring amidst the rocks, and "foaming brown with doubled speed," as they rush through their channels of gray granite; he would catch a distant glimpse of the Androscoggin River to his left, and see peaks of the White Mountains glittering far off to his right. If he became very hungry, he might glance at the back of the little card-check the conductor had given him, count how many miles there were yet to be travelled before arriving at the refreshment station, and having entered the State of Maine, would suddenly come to a halt, be told that he had arrived at South Paris, and that he might refresh to his heart's content. Probably he would find—as the writer did, when very hungry—that some squash tarts—"pies" they call them in the States—some cold pork and beans, and some wretchedly poor coffee, would comprise the whole *menu* of the railway restaurant at South Paris. But if more fortunate, able to obtain a good repast, and disinclined to travel on to Portland by that train; and if, being an admirer of the writings of Artemus Ward, he felt inclined to pay a visit to the birthplace of Charles Farrar Browne, he might make inquiry, and learn that the village of Waterford was only a few miles off, amidst some charming scenery, wherein the rougher aspects of nature are commingled with the rustic characteristics of a "Down-eastern" agricultural district.

Oxford County, in which the upper and lower village of Waterford is situated, forms a part of the south-west angle of the State of Maine. More to the north the industrial pursuits of the inhabitants of the State are chiefly directed to the lumber trade—that is, to felling the fir-trees, floating them down the rivers, and converting them into timber. But in Oxford County agriculture can be made a more remunerative source of profit, while the excellent pasturage opens up another avenue for the hardy inhabitants to derive wealth from the soil. There is an extensive culture of Indian corn and potatoes, and the trade in wool is very considerable. The country is well watered by the Androscoggin River and two smaller streams, the Margallaway and the Saco. It contains also some small lakes, yielding plenteous sport to the angler. Paris is the chief town of the county; but the nearest city of any size is the very beautiful one of Augusta, about forty miles distant, the capital of the State of Maine, and the seat of learning for that part of the country. Portland, the chief commercial city of the State, is many miles away to the south-east. It is one of the most handsome cities in the Union, and makes a pleasing impression on the European tourist who chances to see it in summer; so beautiful is its position on the shores of a lovely bay; so shady are its streets, with their stately rows of trees; and so clean, bright, and well-constructed are its buildings.

The people of Maine are a hard-working, strong, and adventurous race, the ladies being especially notable for their beauty of form and freshness of color. As the State in which the celebrated Liquor Law originated, and the home of Neal Dow, the traveller is prepared to meet with a very temperate community. In passing through Portland he will see a notice over one of the doors of the old Town Hall, if it be still standing, that strong liquor can be obtained there on production of a medical certificate; but do not let him run away with the notion that it can not be obtained anywhere else, nor without medical permission. The hotels have each a bar down stairs in the cellar, and there are quiet whisky shops all over the city. But there is none of the open, and even obtrusive, allurements of the bar-room noticeable in cities farther south. The men of Maine are men of clear head, sinewy frame, large bone, and iron muscle—men who formed the sturdiest among the pioneers of

California, and the hardiest of soldiers in the great American war. Poor Artemus Ward, with his thin, spare form and delicate organization, was by no means a representative man with regard to the physical qualifications of his countrymen.

If the reader will turn to one of the humorous papers of Artemus Ward, entitled "Affairs Round the Village Green," he will meet with a description of the birthplace of the author, as pleasantly joked about by himself. The "village green" is his own native village of Waterford. "The village from which I write to you is small," to quote from the paper to which reference has just been made." It does not contain over forty houses all told; but they are milk-white, with the greenest of blinds, and for the most part are shaded with beautiful elms and willows. To the right of us is a mountain; to the left a lake. The village nestles between. Of course it does. I never read a novel in my life in which the villages didn't nestle. Villages invariably nestle. It is a kind of way they have." To this village, in the hot days of the American summer, Artemus Ward was always glad to retire, that he might rest during warm weather in the home of his youth. A humble home, but a very comfortable, cosy little farm. A homestead which he loved with the fondness of one who was intense in his affections. At the death of his father that little home was not secured to the family. To secure it for his mother was the ambition of his youth; and one of the first uses he made of the money derived from his writings and his lectures was to see his mother safely housed for life in what he used to refer to endearingly as "the old homestead." To escape from the enervating influences of New York or any of the large cities, and to retreat to that "old homestead" down in Maine, was his panacea for all the ills that might overtake him, for there he found the recruiting-ground where health came back to him in the air he had breathed in his boyhood, and where, loitering through the long summer days, he would become reinvigorated and ready for his winter campaign.

He who has been imprisoned in the streets of London for ten or twelve months, and then has the opportunity of rushing off to the Highlands or becoming a Cook's excursionist to Switzerland, can appreciate the luxury of a month in Maine, after spending three parts of the summer in noisy New York, monumental Baltimore, or prim Philadelphia.

How much the poor humorist appreciated the delights of that rural home "away down in Maine"—how proudly he remembered that it was his home, and how keenly he enjoyed the pleasure of returning to it when opportunity offered — may be estimated from the opening paragraph of the paper from which I have already quoted. Artemus is exultant when he writes:

"It isn't every one who has a village green to write about. I have one, although I have not seen much of it for some years past. I am back again, now. In the language of the duke who went about with a motto, 'I am here!' and I fancy I am about as happy a peasant of the vale as ever garnished a melodrama, although I have not as yet danced on my village-green, as the melodramatic peasant usually does on his * * * Why stay in New York when I had a village green? I gave it up, the same as I would an intricate conundrum — and, in short, I am here. Do I miss the glare and crash of the imperial thoroughfare? the milk-man, the fiery, untamed omnibus horses, the soda-water fountains, Central Park, and those things? Yes, I do, and can go on missing them for quite a spell, and enjoy it."

And most thorough was that enjoyment, especially when he could induce some old friend or companion of his boyhood to accompany him to his Eastern home and spend a few days or weeks with him among its simple-minded inhabitants.

"The villagers are kindly people," he writes; and then sarcastically adds, "they are rather incoherent on the subject of the war, but not more so, perhaps, than are people elsewhere. One citizen who used to sustain a good character subscribed for the 'Weekly New York Herald' a few months since, and went to studying the military maps in that well-known journal for the fireside. I need not inform you that his intellect now totters, and he has mortgaged his farm."

To stroll around among these "kindly people;" to chat with the villagers, storekeepers, and mechanics; to converse with the farmers about the produce of their farms, and to discuss with the owners of horse-stock the value of horses; to joke with the more astute of his old school-fellows, and to test the crass density of intellect among the country clowns by propounding to them political and social conundrums, to guess which they were simply incapable, were the favorite modes of dissipating the dullness of rural life which Artemus Ward adopted. He wrote very little during these summer recesses. Most of his humorous papers were written in the great cities and under the stimulus of literary society. When at home among the hills of Maine, he preferred the company of jovial companions, and was especially fond of that of Mr. Setchell.

To the possession of great talents as a low comedian, Mr. Setchell added the qualifications of one whose flow of animal spirits was almost inexhaustible, and whose jocose vein of humor was in admirable harmony with that of his friend. Artemus Ward and Mr. Setchell would ramble out together on a summer evening, fall into the company of any visitors to the village who were not well aware of their manner of seeking amusement, and commence a conversation on some singular topic, which they would carry on in a seemingly irrational manner, after the style of the chat about the brigands with the lady on the Louisville steamer, as related in a previous chapter. To mystify and thoroughly muddle the intellect of Bœotia was the point of the joke, and to be looked upon as a pair of lunatics just escaped from the State Lunatic Asylum, was fully to succeed in their waggery. But poor Setchell said many good things in his time, and was original in his facetiousness. He was the very man for a host who could appreciate humor to select for his guest, especially as the guest had that constant vivacity which frequently accompanies redundancy of health, while the host was occasionally moody through the presence of physical weakness. It was the misfortune of Artemus Ward to lose by death most of his youthful jovial companions. Among that number was Mr. Setchell. He sailed from San Francisco in a ship bound for Australia. I believe that neither he nor the ship was ever heard of again.

From that which I have stated relative to the "village green," the reader must not suppose Artemus Ward to have spent the whole of his time when at home in the country in making merry with the villagers and jesting with the playful spirits whom he might invite to visit him. Though he wrote but little, he read much in a desultory manner, and was careful to keep himself well informed on the political condition of his country, as well as very fairly acquainted with the current light literature of the day. He took great interest in the education of the young, was especially fond of the society of children, and delighted in making happy the juvenile portion of the community of "the village green." With the fair sex he was always a favorite; "I like little girls— I like big girls too," as he used to remark in one of his lectures. But to question children, to ascertain their little wants, study their quaint fancies, and sport with them in the moments of his leisure, was as much a characteristic habit of his earlier years as it was of the last days of his life, when he bequeathed his library to the best boy in his native village.

Waterford, like every other place large or small in America, has its "store," at which articles of the most heterogeneous description may always be found on sale.

"The store—I must not forget the store," writes Artemus. "It is an object of great interest to me. In it may constantly be found calico, and nails, and fish, and tobacco in kegs, and snuff in bladders. It is a venerable establishment. As long ago as 1814 it was an institution. The country troops, on their way to the defense of Portland, then menaced by British ships-of-war, were drawn up in front of this very store and treated at the town's expense." Referring to the customers who frequent the store, the writer continues: "I usually encounter there on sunny afternoons an old Revolutionary soldier. You may possibly have read about 'Another Revolutionary Soldier gone;' but this is one who hasn't gone, and moreover one who doesn't manifest the slightest intention of going. He distinctly remembers Washington, of course. They all do. But what I wish to call special attention to is the fact that this Revolutionary soldier is one hundred years old, that his eyes are so good that he can read fine print without spectacles—he never used them, by-the-way—and his mind is perfectly clear. He is a little shaky in one of his legs; but otherwise he is as active as most men of forty-five, and his general health is excellent. He uses no tobacco; but for the last twenty years he has drunk one glass of liquor every day—no more, no less. He says he must have his 'tod.' But because a man can drink a glass of liquor a day and live to be a hundred years old, my young readers must not infer that by drinking two glasses of liquor a day a man can live to be two hundred."

However, the Revolutionary soldier is an apt illustration of the healthfulness of the district, while the daily habit in which he indulges exemplifies one of the uses of "a store" even in the antibibulous State of Maine.

Endeared as it was by youthful recollections, the old "store" was not the only place near home which Artemus Ward loved to visit. Nowhere in his writings does he more pleasantly betray the gentle spirit and kindly nature which underlay all his rollicking frivolity and all his sarcastic matter-of-fact, than where he describes a house in the neighborhood of "the village green" which he was in the habit of going to occasionally. Thus he pictures it, and thus he permits the reader to know more of his feelings and his inner self than he at all times cared to display:

"Sometimes I go a visiting to a farm-house, on which occasions the parlor is opened. The windows have been close shut ever since the last visitor was there, and there is a dingy smell that I struggle as calmly as possible with, until I am led to the banquet of steaming hot biscuit and custard-pie. If they would only let me sit in the dear old-fashioned kitchen or on the doorstone — if they knew how dismally the new black furniture looked — but never mind. I am not a reformer. No, I should rather think not. Gloomy enough this living on a farm, you perhaps say; in which case you are wrong. I can't exactly say that I pant to be an agriculturist; but I do know that in the main it is an independent, calmly happy sort of life. I can see how the prosperous farmer can go joyously afield with the rise of the sun, and how his heart may swell with pride over bounteous harvests and sleek oxen. And it must be rather jolly for him on winter evenings to sit before the bright kitchen fire, and watch his rosy boys and girls as they study at the charades in the weekly paper, and gradually find out why my first is something that grows in a garden and why my second is a fish."

Chatting with me one day relative to the people among whom his boyhood had been spent, Artemus thus characterized them:

"They are very rough, but they are a lot of good old souls. They don't understand me. Some of them — bless their kind hearts! — think I ought to be sent to the State prison for having changed my name. Most of them pity me for a poor idiot. Some of them want to make me good. They would give up all their time in trying to make me so, and be self-forgetful enough to let themselves run to the bad. They'd howl for the old flag, and never buy a bit of new bunting to mend it with when it got to tatters."

The father of Charles Farrar Browne died while his sons were very young. He was a shrewd man, with much geniality of disposition and some amount of humor. Though in comfortable circumstances, he was not in a position to acquire much wealth, and could leave no fortune to his children. Charles was educated at the high-school, where he learned the rudiments of knowledge. He was taught English grammar, arithmetic, recitation, the facts of American history, and the elements of physiology. He smiled when he informed me of the tuition he had received in this last branch of learning. According to his own account and the testimony of those whom I have interrogated on the subject, he was an apt pupil, without any power of application — one who was reputed to be able to learn well if he would but apply himself, but who very much disliked the trammels with which study too often vainly tries to hold the student. A hatred of routine and a lack of method were characteristics of the man, as they had been of the boy; and no one more than himself, in later years, deplored this.

I called upon him one day in London, just after he had had an interview with Mr. Mark Lemon. He appeared to be more than usually grave, and on asking him the reason for his apparent depression, he replied:

"Mr. Lemon tells me that I want discipline. I know I want discipline; I always did want it, and I always shall." Then, in a serio-comic mood, he added: "Can you get me a stock of discipline, old fellow? You have more of it over here than we have in the States. I should like some." Referring to the extent of his early learning, he told one of his friends that when he left school he had "about enough education for a signboard." And when he gave instructions for the drawing up of his will, he directed that his page George should be sent to a printing-office first, and afterwards to college, remarking at the time, "In the printing-office he will find the value of education, and want to learn when he gets the chance. I lost the chance before I felt the want."

While at school, declamation was that part of the curriculum of duties which the boy Charles Browne liked the best. In the education of American youth elocution is made more a matter of study than it usually is in England. Every school-girl is taught to recite Tennyson's "May Queen," and there are few youths who have not declaimed to their brother scholars some of the glowing periods of Daniel Webster, or selections from the stately versification of William Cullen Bryant. I am told that Charles Browne preferred Shakspeare to either Webster or Bryant, and that *Richard the Third* was a play which appealed the most forcibly to his youthful fancy.

Waterford and its neighborhood were visited occasionally by travelling shows. In the summer one or two circus companies were pretty certain to wander that way; and a circus was something better even than Shakspeare. Artemus Ward in his maturer years seemed to regard a circus as being a greater source of amusement than a theatre. He knew all the circus clowns in America, had all their jokes by heart, and was frequently sought after by them to provide them with a few new jests. When a boy, he constructed a circus in his father's barn. A school-fellow acted as ring-master, while Artemus would play the part of clown, dressing himself up for the occasion with colored pocket-handkerchiefs. He made sundry attempts at private theatricals. According to his own confession, he never acquitted himself very successfully in any of the principal characters of the drama. He told me that he once tried to play Romeo, but forgot the words, and had to ask Juliet, in front of the audience, to hand him the book from her bosom, that he might read that which he had to say to her. His brother Cyrus gave me a much more favorable account of the histrionic ability of Artemus, and ventured an opinion that he would have made a good comedian.

Cyrus Browne died a few years before his younger brother, Charles. I last saw him in Portland, looking very worn and haggard. He was then anxious for information relative to the British North American provinces, and meditated a trip through them with his brother, but scarcely seemed to have health enough for so long a journey. Cyrus was a man of considerable talent; more reserved and more methodical than Charles. I believe that he was connected with newspaper literature during the greater part of his life, and that he was at one period on the editorial staff of the "New Bedford Standard," at New Bedford, in Massachusetts.

Family circumstances induced the parents of Charles Browne to take him from school when quite a boy, before he had the opportunity of proceeding to the higher branches of study. The occupation selected for him was that of a printer. He was sent to learn the rudiments of the craft at a small newspaper office in the little town of Skowhegan, some miles to the north of his native village. To the last days of his career he had a bitter remembrance of his first experiences in a printing-office. He was accustomed to set up a howl of derision whenever the name of Skowhegan was mentioned. He seemed to be gratifying a long-cherished revenge on the little place by holding it up to ridicule, and alluding to any thing rough, uncouth, and unpleasant as worthy of Skowhegan.

Artemus asked a friend once, in my presence, whether his acquaintance with the American press was very extensive. The person interrogated replied that he knew most of the American newspapers. Whereupon Artemus inquired if the "Skowhegan Clarion" was among the number? On being replied to that it was not, he looked pityingly at the party with whom he was in conversation, and said, "I am sorry for you if you don't read the "Skowhegan Clarion." It is your duty to read it. There is no paper like it in the States—nor anywhere else!"

Before he was sixteen years of age Charles Browne left his home, bade farewell to the "Skowhegan Clarion," and quitted his native State of Maine to seek his fortune in the metropolis of New England. He was not "Artemus Ward" then, had no influential friends to tender him a helping hand, nor any well-filled purse to console him for the loss of old companions; but he had ambition, a light heart, and excellent spirits; in addition to all of which, he was in a land where the willing hand can always find work to do, and where youth is thought to be of some value —a land where a man can get his chance before his hair is gray, his strength gone, and the freshness of his intellect has faded forever.

○ ⑥ ○

Cleveland · How Mr. Charles Browne Became "Artemus Ward"

MRS. PARTINGTON" is an old lady who once enjoyed extensive celebrity in the United States, and who still lives in the memory of her friends as one who contributed largely to their mirth, and helped to make happy many of their hours of ease. She is a most eccentric old character, apt to raise many ridiculous objections, say many absurd things, and commit herself in various egregiously inconsistent actions. She is the national Mrs. Malaprop. Her utterances are always provocative of laughter, while her opinions and deeds are a never-failing source of amusement. She owes her birth to Mr. B. P. Shillaber, of Chelsea, near Boston, who, when I travelled in America with Artemus Ward, was one of the editors of the Boston "Saturday Evening Gazette."

A small and mildly-comic journal, entitled "The Carpet-Bag," was the organ of "Mrs. Partington's" communications with the public. Mr. Shillaber—one of the most genial, warm-hearted, sincere, and thoroughly estimable of men—was the editor of "The Carpet-Bag," and the author of the sayings and doings of the celebrated old lady. Charles

Browne, fresh from Maine, a mere youth, with all the crudities of the country about him, and of a singularly lean and lank appearance, offered himself as a compositor in the office of "The Carpet-Bag," and readily found employment. Among the contributors to the paper were Mr. Charles G. Halpine, who, under the *sobriquet* of "Miles O'Reilly," achieved much reputation as a humorist; and Mr. John G. Saxe, one of the most accomplished authors of American light literature, as well as one of the most eloquent and fascinating lecturers in the United States. Day by day, as the youthful compositor from Maine set up the articles of these talented writers, he studied and enjoyed their humor, until at length the idea crept into his mind that possibly he could write a funny article, if not as well as they could, at least well enough for it to have a change of getting into "The Carpet-Bag." Then why not try? "He listened to that 'still small voice' in the heart"—to quote the words of the elder Disraeli—"which cries with Correggio and with Montesquieu, '*Ed io anche son pittore!*' " So listening, he tried, wrote an article, disguised his handwriting, put his contribution into the editor's box, and enjoyed the triumph of having it given out to him to set up at case, without the editor knowing that the compositor to whom he gave it was the youth by whom it had been written!

"I went to the theatre that evening—had a good time of it, and thought that I was the greatest man in Boston," added Artemus Ward, after telling me this anecdote of his first success. His eyes glistened while he spoke, and the animation of his manner betrayed that he lived his triumph over again in remembering the joy with which it was won. His narration of it reminded me of the preface to "Pickwick," in which Mr. Charles Dickens recounts how he dropped his first essay "with fear and trembling into a dark letter-box in a dark office, up a dark court in Fleet Street," and how, when it appeared in print, he "walked down to Westminster Hall and turned into it for half an hour, because my eyes were so dimmed with joy and pride that they could not bear the street, and were not fit to be seen there."

A statement has appeared in some of the American papers, to the effect that "Mrs. Partington" was the model which Charles Browne used for the creation of that peculiar display of humor which characterizes the writings of "Artemus Ward;" but I have the authority of the author's own statement to me for recording that the humorous writings of Seba Smith were his models, so far as humor thoroughly *sui generis* can be said to have had any model whatever. It is true, as one transatlantic writer has suggested, that the satirical vein in which Mr. Saxe writes of the commonplaces of society, and the sarcasm with which Mr. Halpine treats political topics, may have influenced the mind of the young humorist from Maine, and contributed to form the characteristics of his style; but John Phœnix was an author of whom Artemus Ward was accustomed to speak in terms of admiring familiarity, more than of either of the above-named contributors to the comic literature of America.

While resident in Boston, Charles Browne availed himself of every chance of visiting the theatre. He studied the plays, and courted the society of the actors and actresses. There were few of what are by courtesy termed legitimate plays with which he did not become acquainted while a mere youth. Boston soon seemed to be too circumscribed a place in which to remain any longer. Naturally nomadic in disposition, he left the great city to go and see the greater world outside. Plays of a grander character, and actors and actresses of far more importance, were awaiting him there. Like a German artisan, Charles Browne wished to learn his craft while travelling from city to city, and while studying the habits of many men. According to his own confession, the early career of Mr. Bayard Taylor as a travelling journeyman printer had stimulated him to imitation, and the vocation of a compositor offered him peculiar facilities for earning his bread, in whatever town he might be led by circumstances or by caprice. He wandered through the State of Massachusetts, made two or three halts in the State of New York, and, after a year or two had passed away, came to a stopping-place at a little town called Tiffin, situated in Seneca County, Ohio. He once told me that at that time he could seldom keep five dollars in his pocket; and, if I am rightly informed, he walked into the town of Tiffin with much less than that amount, and with a change of clothes rolled up in a bundle and carried on his back.

The wandering life led by Artemus Ward in his earliest years has been instanced by some of his less kindly critics as proof of an aimless, purposeless character. On the contrary, it was in full accordance with his youngest ambition, and with the well-considered design of his boyhood. He wished to see the world; he desired to be a traveller and emulate Bayard Taylor. With a "composing-stick" to use as a workman, and the ability to pick up his "ems" a little faster than some of his fellow-craftsmen, he thought that he could accomplish his design. "I didn't

know but what I might get as far as China, and set up a newspaper one
day in the tea-chest tongue," was his remark, when upon one occasion
he alluded to this period of his career.

In the town of Tiffin, Artemus Ward undertook the double duties of
reporter and compositor. His salary amounted to four dollars per week,
and much of the chief work of the Tiffin newspaper was intrusted to him.
Though the remuneration was slight, the life he led was a joyous one.
His cleverness and frank good-humor won him many friends, while the
chances he had of saying a good word for those who deserved it caused
him never to be without a dollar. In a newspaper sketch of his life written by Mr. Townsend, the writer says: "People in Tiffin remember him
still, in the luxury of new apparel, purchased by a notice of our enterprising townsman, the dry-goods merchant, and making free with strangers in the town of which he was the crowning hospitality. Every travelling show that happened in the place found in him a patron, and he was
most generally behind the scenes, happy as a king in the friendship of
clown and acrobat, who recognized in him the traditional good-fellow
and incipient genius."

Tiffin could not hold its new hero of the press forever. Fortune beckoned him to take a trip to Toledo, and to Toledo he went. Not to Toledo
of the Spaniard and the Moor; not that glorious old Toledo where the
Jew stored his learning and the Saracen found his steel, but a very different Toledo indeed — a young Toledo, situated at the western end of
Lake Erie, with Dundee not far off, and Vienna close at hand. "The
Toledo Commercial" was the name of the journal which wooed Artemus
Ward from his temporary home in Tiffin, and, to become engaged on it
at a slight increase of the salary he had been receiving, he migrated
with high hopes and a light heart. It was a wild harum-scarum sort of
town to migrate to — that Toledo of the West. I retain a lively recollection of two days spent in it during winter; and when I wish to go
somewhere to spend two cold days in winter another time I think that
I shall not select Toledo. It has left upon my mind a picture of a town
half built, a picture of wooden sidewalks and roads knee-deep in mud—
of canals and rough-mannered boatmen — of one hotel over the arch of
the railway station, with din enough beneath to prevent any one from
sleeping; and of another hotel much larger, and dismally grand, away
out in the fields, to which I tried to get home in the dark, along a plank
footpath, and narrowly escaped suffocation in a pool of watery mud.

But, for all that, the town is a very busy one, the inhabitants are go-ahead people, and as they are aware that the Spanish namesake of their town was famous for its swords, they also have started a "Toledo Blade;" only it happens to be a newspaper with that title instead of being an article of cutlery. Happy Toledo, where they have no use for their "Blades" except for the exercise of their pens!

While engaged on "The Toledo Commercial," Artemus Ward acquired his first reputation as a writer of sarcastic paragraphs. He commenced as a compositor and rose to be a reporter. The reporter of the other paper and he waged continual war. Western editors are by no means sparing in their abuse of one another, and frequently mistake unwarrantable vituperation for galling satire. Toledo required excitement, and the new "local editor" was permitted to be as vivacious as he pleased. Permission was given him to cut and slash. What fairer chance could a very young author desirous of making a name possibly want? But Artemus did his work with talent as well as energy. He could be humorous as well as caustic; he could be witty as well as ferocious. Therein he had the advantage of his opponent on the antagonistic journal. His column of the paper soon became the one which every body read. The articles in it were purely of local interest, and not worth reprinting; but they served their purpose admirably at the time. The skill of the writer attracted attention, his fame travelled along the shore of Lake Erie; and in the summer of 1858, when Charles Browne had attained his twenty-fourth year, he received an invitation from Mr. J.W. Gray, of Cleveland, to change his place of abode to that city, and become local reporter of "The Cleveland Plaindealer" at a salary of—twelve dollars per week!

In all the great State of Ohio there is not a more pleasant city than Cleveland. In winter it partakes of the general cheerlessness of the new cities of the West; but in summer its broad streets, most of them ornamental, shaded with green trees, and kept cool by the fresh breezes off Lake Erie, render it a delightful place of residence. There is one street called Euclid Street—though what the old geometrician of Alexandria had to do with it I am at a loss to imagine—which for its beauty, its leafy trees, its well-built villas, its stately aspect, and its cleanly condition, would be worthy of Paris, in the neighborhood of the *Bois*, or of Berlin, in the vicinity of the Brandenburg Gate. In a stroll along this beautiful street, on a moonlight evening, some five years ago, Artemus

Ward detailed to me many of his early experiences in the fair city of Cleveland; how he journeyed to it from Toledo; how he toiled as a reporter on the "Plaindealer;" how he wrote himself into celebrity; became "Artemus Ward, the Showman;" and, having gained a name throughout the United States, was at length invited to leave the seclusion of Lake Erie, and became an editor in the great metropolis of New York.

Cleveland is a goodly city to look upon, if you look at it in the right direction. "Every medal has its reverse," says the old Italian proverb; so has every city. There are few cities, among some hundreds with which I am acquainted, that have not their work-day and their holiday side. Cleveland is a most agreeable town in the neighborhood of Euclid Street or of the public square, but it is a very noisy place round about Pittsburg and Kinsman Streets on market mornings; and a very dirty, smoky one where the Cuyahoga River, down in a deep valley, flows past manufactories with tall chimneys, and work-shops grimy with the soot of forges and the smoke of furnaces. The office of the "Cleveland Plaindealer" is at the corner of two streets. The approach to it along the main street is pleasant enough, for that is broad, open, and airy, but the corner on which the newspaper office stands is one where the traveller in search of the beautiful would not be likely to linger long. Why the light of the press should be given forth from narrow courts, dingy back streets, pestiferous alleys, and uncomfortable corners, is a problem requiring solution. But an awkward building, hard to find, and unpleasant to visit, is in too many instances the one chosen for the home of the daily or weekly journal, and the abode of gloom in which the slave of the pen shall write brilliant leading articles or sparkling paragraphs, using the pyrotechny of his art to light up the darkness of his studio.

The office to which Mr. Charles Browne was consigned was no exception to the general rule. Whatever of the bright, the cheerful, and the sunny was destined to emanate from the pen of the young journalist had to be "evolved from his inner consciousness," for there was nothing suggestive of any of these qualities in the dreary room wherein he was expected to write his articles. Nor had he an apartment allotted to himself alone: a desk among desks, a corner among the corners of a many-cornered small room, was all that was allowed him. There he was supposed to write out his reports and jot down his humorous fancies, amidst the interruptions of an editor's room in the West, open as it is to pretty nearly all comers, from the politician boiling over with some exciting political news, to the agent of the showman anxious to expatiate on the merits of a coming show, or the enterprising tradesman, willing to pay his fair price for a laudatory notice of his new stock of goods. In such an office there is pretty sure to be near at hand a whisky-bottle, with some Bourbon or Monongahela whisky in it; the chairs are usually very much "whittled;" and there are marks made by the heels of boots on the desks and on the tables. In some offices pencils take the place of pens, and the annoying sound of your fellow-workman's goose-quill is thereby obviated; but Artemus Ward had much faith in the stimulus of moist ink. His little desk, still preserved in the office at Cleveland, is thoroughly well ink-stained, while his arm-chair bears in its cut and carved defacement copious evidence that when the penknife had nibbed the quill it was carelessly used as a convenient tool for "whittling."

The politics of the "Cleveland Plaindealer" have always been what in the political technology of the United States is entitled Democratic. In England we use the word "Conservative" to express something nearly allied to the same idea. As it was the first, so I believe the "Plaindealer" is now the only thoroughly Democratic daily paper in the north of the great State of Ohio. The politics of Artemus Ward were never very clearly defined by him, and I doubt if he ever had any clear political creed. In America politics are a trade. The tricks of the politicians were too evident to the glance of the genial humorist for him to attach much value to the trade or the tradesmen; he laughed at the comicalities of the trade, satirized the rottenness of the business, and ridiculed the pretensions of the traders. For all that, his connection with a leading Democratic journal influenced his views, gave a bias to his thoughts, and a color to his writings. Not but that by nature he was a Conservative. I remember his going into raptures over his discovery of that paragraph in one of our Ex-Premier's novels, where Mr. Disraeli defiantly asks the question: "Progress to what? — progress to Paradise or to Pandemonium?"

Artemus had very little faith in popular cries, and some doubts about the "vox populi" being the "vox Dei." His skepticism in this respect is frequently apparent in the sayings of his imaginary old showman. It crops out in many sly hints and caustic jests.

While engaged on the paper in Cleveland, his associates were mostly men who belonged to the Democratic party, and among them were some of the most talented. Mr. Joseph W. Gray, the proprietor and editor of the "Plaindealer," was a man of brilliant wit and great ability. His contributions to the literature of the day were copied all over the Union; and he was the confidential friend and adviser of the celebrated Stephen A. Douglas, who contested the election for the Presidential chair with Abraham Lincoln. Mr. John B. Bouton, a New York journalist of eminence, was another of Artemus Ward's associates during his reporting days. There was not a clever man in Cleveland — or indeed in Ohio, no matter what his political sentiments or his peculiar tendencies — with whom the young Western humorist did not become acquainted before he threw his pen down for the last time on the little desk in the editorial room of the "Plaindealer." Later in life it was said of him that he knew more gentlemen of the Press in America than did any other man.

To chronicle the local changes in the town, attend public meetings, report the proceedings of the municipal magnates, notice concerts and criticise the performances at the theatre — Ellsler's "Academy of Music," I believe, it was called at the time — were among the duties which first devolved upon Artemus Ward. They were duties which led him largely into society, and caused him to mix with various classes of people, especially with that class of which he was most fond — actors, actresses, showmen, and public entertainers generally. With this latter class he was "hail-fellow, well met!" in the free-and-easy manner of the Far West; but in the midst of hilarity his eye was still watchful and his powers of observation ever on the alert. His reports were characterized by the happy manner in which they reflected the spirit of the meeting; his criticisms were piquant, witty, and sometimes good-humoredly severe; his notices were brimful of mirth; and whenever he could lighten up a paragraph with a pleasant jest, he unfailingly availed himself of the chance.

Engaged as he was in other duties, he found time to sketch a series of caricatures of the local politicians. The "Western Reserve," as that part of the country was then familiarly designated, had many politicians who had talked themselves into notoriety, among whom were the names of Giddings, Tilden, D. K. Cartter, and Wade. All these gentlemen were fair game for the young humorist to shoot at. He shot like a skillful marksman. His shots told, and his skill gained him ready renown. Besides, it was fun of a sort which suited the journal on which he wrote, and was something more amusing than the dull duties of a "local editor." What Artemus thought of those duties may be gathered from a short paragraph which appeared from his pen in the columns of the "Plaindealer." It is here transcribed:

"*Editing.*—Before you go for an editor, young man, pause and take a big think! Do not rush into the editorial harness rashly. Look around and see if there is not an omnibus to drive, some soil somewhere to be tilled, a clerkship on some meat-cart to be filled, any thing that is reputable and healthy, rather than going for an editor, which is hard business at best. We are not a horse, and consequently have never been called upon to furnish the motive power for a threshing-machine; but we fancy that the life of the editor, who is forced to write, write, write, whether he feels right or not, is much like that of the steed in question. If the yeas and neighs could be obtained, we believe the intelligent horse would decide that the threshing-machine is preferable to the sanctum editorial."

Secure in his seat as "local editor," with his reputation well established for drollery and humorous fancy, the mirthful journalist conceived the felicitous idea of impersonating a character, and embodying the experience he had gained of the life of showmen in general, in the conception of a quaint old hypothetical showman of his own creation, who should at once take rank in the literary world as an author, relating incidents in a showman's manner, and describing places visited from a showman's point of view.

Happy as the idea really was, the full conception of the character and its surroundings evinced the most marked felicity of inventive genius. The shrewdness of a Barnum was to be united with the stupidity of an uneducated itinerant exhibitor, who had gained his experience by roughing it in the West among the towns and villages on the outer edge of the circle of civilization, and in a state of society where the more refined forms of amusement are comparatively unknown. The old showman was to have the smartness of a Yankee, combined with the slowness of one whose time had been chiefly spent among the backwoods; he was to blend humorous stupidity with unscrupulous mendacity, to have very little of the reverential about him, a modicum of the philosophic, and a large amount of the broadly comic. His home was to be in Indiana, that being a State of the Union abounding in quaint specimens of uncultured and eccentric people; and he was to be the possessor of a show consisting of "Three moral Bares, a Kangaroo (a amoozing little rascal, 'twould make you larf yerself to death to see the little cuss jump up and squeal), wax figgers of G. Washington, Genl. Taylor, John Bunyan, Captain Kidd, and Dr. Webster, besides several miscellanyous moral wax statoots of celebrated piruts and murderers."

The idea of the showman being conceived, and the character of the show being settled, a name was required for the supposititious new author who was to give forth his experiences to the world. Hitherto literature had numbered Charles Browne amidst the rank and file of its army — henceforth it was to enter upon its roll-call the name of "ARTEMUS WARD."

There is, I believe, a mistake made by some people who suppose that a real veritable entity of a showman once existed whose name was "Artemus Ward," and that he and Mr. Charles Browne were once acquainted. I think I may safely assert that there never was an individual of the name among the showman fraternity. On more than one occasion I have heard Artemus Ward interrogated relative to how he came to choose that *sobriquet* for his imaginary character. His explanation was that he scarcely knew why he selected it in preference to any other, that he was in want of a name for his old showman and remembered "Artemus Ward" as being that of one of the generals who fought in the army of the first American Revolution. The name had impressed itself upon his memory, being, as he considered, a very droll one, and, for the lack of a better, he called it into service. When he signed it to the first letter he wrote as a Showman to the "Cleveland Plaindealer," he little thought of the celebrity to which it would attain, and that in a few years the coffin-plate of the writer would bear the inscription, following the record of his own proper name — "Known to the world as 'Artemus Ward.'"

In the orthography of the name the humorist took occasion to deviate slightly from the accepted method of spelling "Artemus." He substituted "u" for "a" in the last syllable. The old major-general who commanded the troops of New England before Washington was a general, figures in history as "Artem*a*s Ward." The records of Massachusetts also include the names of Artemas Ward of Roxbury, who filled the singular position in society of being a contractor for the feeding and fattening of pigs, and of Judge Artemas Ward, who was for many years Judge of the Court of Probate in that State. But it was the

Revolutionary general from whom the humorous old showman of "Baldinsville, in Injianny," received his prenomen and his family name. Originally the property of a warrior, they became a *nom de guerre*.

The letters of "Artemus Ward" in the "Cleveland Plaindealer" were not the result of any preconcerted and well-matured plan of writing a series of amusing articles. The first one was written on the spur of the moment, merely to supply "copy" for the paper when the writer had nothing better with which to fill up a column. It now forms the first of the papers in the volume entitled "Artemus Ward, His Book." Being the first of the series, and descriptive of the imaginary eccentric old showman, as well as of his heterogeneous and oddly-assorted show, I transcribe it to these pages as an important and interesting record of its author.

"To the Editor of the 'Plain Dealer.'

"Sir—I'm moving along—slowly along—down tords your place. I want you should write me a letter, sayin' how's the show-bizniss in your place. My show at present consists of three moral Bares, a Kangaroo (a amoozin little Raskal—'twould make you larf to deth to see the little cuss jump up and squeal), wax figgers of G. Washington, Gen. Taylor, John Bunyan, Dr. Kidd, and Dr. Webster in the act of killin' Dr. Parkman, besides several miscellanyus moral wax stattoots of celebrated piruts and murderers, etc., ekalled by few, and exceld by none. Now, Mr. Editor, scratch off a few lines sayin' how is the show-bizniss down to your place. I shall have my hand-bills dun at your offiss. Depend upon it. I want you should git my hand-bills up in flamin' style. Also git up a tremenjus excitement in yr paper 'bowt my onparaleld show. We must fetch the public somehow. We must work on their feelins—come the moral on 'em strong. If it's a temperance community, tell 'em I sined the pledge fifteen minits arter ise born. But on the contrary, if your people take their tods, say that Mister Ward is as genial a feller as we ever met—full of conwiviality, and the life and sole of the soshul Bored. Take, don't you? If you say any thing 'bout my show, say my snaix is as harmless as the new-born babe. What a interesting study it is too see a zonological animal, like a snaik, under perfeck subjection. My Kangaroo is the most larfable little cuss I ever saw—all for 15 cents. I am anxyus to skewer your inflooence. I repeet in regard to them hand-bills, that I shall git 'em struck off up to your printin'-offiss. My perlitical sentiments agree with yourn exackly. I know they do, becauz I never saw a man whoos didn't.

"Respectfully yours,
A. Ward.

"P.S.—You scratch my back and Ile scratch your back."

The originality of this letter, its quaint fancies, its odd spelling, its satire and its humor, caused it to be copied and recopied in hundreds of newspapers throughout the United States. The owner of the "onparaleld show" was thought by most people to be a reality instead of a pleasant fiction. More letters from him were anxiously desired, and the public throughout America became the friends of "The Genial Showman."

❧ **7** ❧

New York
The Verdict in the Cellar

DOWN at Pfaff's the verdict was given. And down at Pfaff's they were accustomed to conduct trials with rapidity, return verdicts with emphasis, and pass judgment with honeyed kindness or with savage severity.

The verdict in this case was favorable down at Pfaff's.

Literature and the drama were the two classes of crime adjudicated on at Pfaff's. Young authors, new books, the last dramatic importation from England, the *débutante* at the opera, the novice who had appeared at Niblo's or at the Winter Garden—these were the criminals to be tried and sentenced, acquitted or condemned.

Down at Pfaff's the verdict was, that "A Visit to Brigham Young," by Artemus Ward, in the number of "Vanity Fair" just issued, was by far the funniest article contributed to that journal during the second period of its career. It was the first article from the pen of the new author published in "Vanity Fair," and the journal in which it was printed was the leading comic paper of the city of New York. The verdict it received down at Pfaff's was heartily indorsed by the public in the streets above—for Pfaff's was under the street.

It was in the number of "Vanity Fair" bearing date November 10, 1860, that the contribution above alluded to appeared. The jury down in Pfaff's cellar knew very well that Artemus Ward at that time had never visited the Mormon territory, and that his account of the interview with Brigham Young was simply pleasant fiction.

They knew every thing down at Pfaff's. That which they did not know they assumed they did, which, being about the same as knowing it, the grammatical construction of this paragraph holds good. Many of them being young men, and all of them critics, the gentlemen who assembled at Pfaff's were encyclopædic in their information, and never suspected the correctness of their opinions.

Pfaff's cellar in Broadway was a singular place. At the date of which I am writing it ranked as the head-quarters of Bohemia in New York. It was situated near to the well-known Winter Garden Theatre, the destinies of which were then controlled, I believe, by Mr. Dion Boucicault. In the great cities of the United States it is a common thing for the places of refreshment to be situated in an under-ground apartment in one of the principal thoroughfares, a flight of steps giving direct access from the street. In New York many of these cellars are at prominent corners, and have very well painted signs, and extremely large lamps to attract the attention of passers-by. Some cellars are famous for the quality of the whisky sold, some for the excellence of the lager-beer, and many of them for the first-class oyster suppers which they furnish.

It was one of these cellars which lured Mr. Thackeray to its fascinating depths. The author of "The Newcomes" chanced to be wandering up Broadway, when he perceived a sign on which was written, "Oysters cooked here in thirty-six different ways." Impelled by curiosity as well as a good appetite, he descended the steps and astonished the waiters by asking for oysters "cooked in thirty-six different ways." As a rule, such requests are seldom made in a New York oyster cellar.

So little is apparent from the street, that a stranger merely peeping down would fail to form an adequate idea of the luxurious style in which many of these cellars are furnished. Nearly all of them have a bar with a marble top to it for the sale of drinks, and a counter, similarly fitted up, on which oysters are placed in carefully stacked piles, with a huge lump of glittering ice crowning the summit of each pile.

The cellar is likely to have one or two, if not more, cabinets or private rooms for parties wishing to sup quietly; and there are sure to be about a dozen boxes or alcoves, each furnished with its little table, its well-stuffed seats, and its crimson curtains, to exclude the occupants from the view of other customers. The wood-work in most instances is of mahogany or walnut, while the floor is very often of white and black marble arranged in diamond-shaped pieces.

Varied is the reputation of these cellars for the class of refreshment furnished, but still more varied is the character of the frequenters of each. One will be the resort of gentlemen of the theatrical profession, another will be the favorite haunt of the young men about town, a third will be the meeting-place of the sporting fraternity, and a fourth will be especially patronized by those interesting songsters who make visual semi-tones of their features before proceeding to sing, so that the black face between the two halves of the white shirt-collar reminds one of the key-board of a piano-forte. But some of the cellars of New York are frequented by the very scum of its strange cosmopolitan community, and have arrangements for beguiling their visitors with singing and dancing of the most inferior description. Until recently these underground dens were the nearest approach to the type of the London Music Hall; but enterprising Americans have lately taken across from England not only the models of the Alhambra and the Canterbury, but many of the performers, who have appeared at both those places, and have fitted up a transatlantic Alhambra of their own, side by side with the grand and fashionable house devoted to Italian Opera. Americans are very apt to think that they are ahead of the Old World in every particular; yet they have allowed us to have many years' start with the Music Halls, and they have only just come up to us in a Hansom cab.

To return to Pfaff's cellar. It was not like others in the same city. Descending to it from Broadway, the visitor found himself in a large apartment under the shop above. On one side was a long counter well supplied with tempting articles of refreshment, and in front of the counter were rows of tables and chairs for the guests. The place had a celebrity, well merited then, and possibly still enjoyed, for its German wines and its foreign dishes. Furthermore, every thing was sold at a reasonable price, and he who went there, if his purse happened to be light, could breakfast, dine, or sup without fear of having too large a bill to pay. But the one great attraction of the place was an arched cellar under the pavement of the street. Round against the walls of this cellar were barrels, and in the middle space a large table and a requisite number of seats. The arch was dimly lighted, had a weird, dull, and gloomy appearance, and was nothing more than a capacious vault, undecorated and somewhat unsavory. Yet here Bohemia at one time loved to congregate. Down in this vault the King of Bohemian New York held his court.

That court of Bohemia has been in mourning many times since I was first presented at it down in Pfaff's cellar. Very few of the brilliant young men who figured at it then are living now. Among them was Edward Wilkins, the dramatic critic of the "New York Herald," a talented and kind-hearted man, long since dead. Associated with him were Fitz-James O'Brien, the graceful poet; George Arnold, the thoughtful and sprightly essayist, poet, and humorist; Frank Wood, Henry Neil, and Artemus Ward. All have deserted forever that memorable Bohemian court. None of them will ever descend those steps again to salute Mr. Pfaff, and be merry round the table in the cellar of that bland and portly Teuton.

There were good Bohemians and there were bad Bohemians among the patrons of Pfaff's. Some there were who played at Bohemia, and supposed that to loiter at Pfaff's during unseasonable hours, drink foaming beer or good Rhine wine, play cards, carry unread books about under the arm, and lead a listless, heedless, aimless life, made them naturalized subjects of the Bohemian kingdom; and that they came into the possession of genius as a natural consequence. Others there were who were to the manner born, and who had the true type of legitimate natives of that eccentric realm. Some of these latter have risen to eminence, and cast off all allegiance to the Bohemia of their youthful love, though they once held high office at its court, and were enrolled in its Legion of Honor.

Among the frequenters of Pfaff's cellar was one whose imagination was brilliant and whose poetry was good, but who had a strong antipathy to having a lodging of his own. He had the address of a gentleman, but no address as a citizen. His friends were many. They would invite him to come and stay with them. He would borrow their latch-key and retain it when once lent to him. His pocket was full of latchkeys; and, as his fancy prompted him, so he would select where he would sleep, letting himself into the house at any hour of the night or morning. A servant going into a room to open the shutters or draw up a blind would find an unexpected guest asleep on the sofa. If he had been a frequent visitor to the house, he would be known to the domestics, but on more occasions than one he was mistaken for a burglar.

There was another *habitué* of the cellar who had played the part of a Bohemian in Paris, and who, because he had lived in Paris, considered himself to be the chief authority on all matters affecting civilization and the arts. As an author he had the faculty of writing an essay that would read like sprightly music, but be utterly devoid of ideas. As a critic he would be stingingly sarcastic or nauseously laudatory, according to the terms on which he was with the artist criticised. Being a great poker-player, he would invite those who were open to criticism to take a hand of cards with him. If they were desirous of praise, they would do so; and, as they lost their money on the Monday, console themselves by anticipating the eulogium which would fall to their share in the paper of the following Saturday. A gay and festive patron of the cellar was the gentleman to whom I refer. Though neither young nor an Adonis, he knew more pretty actresses than almost any other man in New York.

Like the company at "The Owl's Roost" in Mr. Robertson's comedy of "Society," the people down at Pfaff's were gentlemen. One of them belonged to an aristocratic Irish family; another once owned ancestral halls in England. One there was who had been brought up to the Church at Oxford or Cambridge, and who had all the dignity, suavity, and learning to qualify him for being a bishop, but who much preferred writing plays, engineering shows, and being an old Bohemian. There was another who had figured among the gayest of the gay world of London, who could paint a picture, write a drama, make very good poetry, display much critical ability, and rival the Admirable Crichton in general proficiency; but who, amiable and estimable as he was, could do much for others and little for himself. And there was yet another who would wear a sombrero hat and carry a thick stick. In his personal appearance he presented the Henry the Eighth type, and his face was always ruddy. In his talents he was versatile. When he had nothing better to do, he would write plays—he could do his three acts at one sitting. At other times he would indite a religious essay or furnish comic copy. Then, to vary his occupation, he would get up a "Gift-distribution enterprise" of gold watches, or turn "literary agent" to a circus, or go down South to exhibit a hippopotamic pig, or a phenomenon of a

horse with sky-blue hair and feathers on its mane. Like the rest, he let
the cares of life sit lightly on his shoulders; and, like the rest, was more
disposed to do a good turn than a bad one to those with whom he
chanced to come in contact.

These were the gentlemen who pronounced a favorable verdict on
Artemus Ward's first paper in "Vanity Fair." They voted for his coming to New York, and to New York he came.

The first letter in the "Cleveland Plaindealer," purporting to emanate from an old showman on his travels, gained immediate popularity.
Its author quickly followed it up with a second one. In using cacog-
raphy, or eccentric spelling, he had recourse to a legitimate source of
humor, not of his own invention, but admirably in harmony with the
character he had chosen to personate. There was no reason why he
should not employ the same means for raising a laugh on the other side
of the Atlantic, which Thomas Hood had already used so successfully
on this side. Bad spelling was to be combined with "Down-Eastern"
dialect. Of this latter Artemus Ward was perfect master: his place of
birth and the people with whom he associated in early youth had rendered him thoroughly familiar with the quaint and oft-times ludicrous
idiomatic expressions of the uneducated provincial native of New
England. Though the average American does speak very good English,
he is not quite a sinless Lindley Murray, as Mr. Reverdy Johnson would
have had us believe. When, for instance, after you have told a young
lady all that you know on the subject relative to which she requires
information, she exclaims energetically, "Du tell!" a stranger to the
land is apt to be puzzled as to which he should regret—her perverted
English, or her greed for further knowledge.

Three letters with the signature of "Artemus Ward" affixed to them
sufficed to insure the popularity of the writer. They were copied in the
"exchanges" of hundreds of papers throughout the United States, the
postal system of that country permitting the editorial craft to exchange
their newspapers with one another free of postage. The author of the
oddly-spelt, quaintly-conceived, and intensely comic letters was sought
for by the proprietors of journals in cities remote from Cleveland. Applications were made to him from Boston to return to the city wherein
his earliest contribution to literature had been printed. California sent
him an invitation to make merry the shores of the Pacific; and New
Orleans was quite willing that the old showman should pay her a visit

to scatter a few jokes around the Gulf of Mexico. But to be asked by New York to be one among her citizens, and rank among her staff of editors, was that which best accorded with the ambition of the youthful humorist. There he would have a fulcrum on which, with the already tested lever of his fun, he could raise a laugh throughout America.

Like leaving a cheerful home to go to a large public school, was that change from the small Western city to the great metropolis. Mr. N. G. Hoyt, one of Artemus Ward's fellow-reporters, writes of him:

"In Cleveland, Browne was the cynosure of all the wits of the town. By them he was throned a monarch of mirth, and at his feet were spread the rarest tributes of their excessive adulation. He quitted Cleveland and came to New York with letters to distinguished authors which he never presented. He won his own way here, as he had won it in the West." And, referring to his social characteristics at this period of his career, Mr. Hoyt says: "To him every thing wore a comical aspect. He saw fun in every thing. His lips were always smiling. It was impossible for him to frown. Genial to all, every thing that came within his quick, penetrating, observant eye, wore its grotesque shape. * * * He never assumed to be any thing more than he was; and he was as much at home in one place as in another, if the people were only human and natural. He utterly scorned all and every attempt at cant and hypocrisy, and was as keenly alive to his own demerits and deficiencies as the most acute of his critics."

Such was the character of the man to whom New York held out the hand of fellowship. The hand that clasped it was one which never shook hands but with sincerity.

Comic journalism in New York has not been a great success. Whether the talent requisite to uphold a comic paper has failed to exist in sufficient quantity; whether the tastes of the people are antagonistic to the successful career of a periodical conducted on the principles of "Punch," "Fun," or "Judy," whether sufficient enterprise has never been manifested, or whether the right sort of paper has never been started, I will not pretend to decide; but the fact is undeniable that many attempts have been made, and many failures resulted; and that, in cases where temporary success has been achieved, it has scarcely owed any thing to the originality of the contributions. Perhaps the most praiseworthy of any of these attempts was the journal to which was given the name of "Vanity Fair." The paper was well started, had a talented staff of writers, and an open field for development. Unfortunately it flickered with unsteady light through periods of radiancy and shade, to go out altogether before its brilliancy had become fully known and recognized.

There were two periods of existence in the career of "Vanity Fair." In its second period the editorial management was intrusted to Mr. Charles G. Leland, whose humorous poem in German-English, entitled "Hans Breitmann's Barty," has recently become so popular in this country, as well as in America. While Mr. Leland was editing "Vanity Fair," Artemus Ward sent to him from Cleveland the article detailing the interview of the old showman with Brigham Young, the head of the Mormon Church. And down at Pfaff's that article was accounted quite sufficient to warrant the verdict that Artemus Ward was superior in humor to Major Jack Downing, and that he ought to take up his abode in New York city without delay.

I have already stated that when Artemus Ward wrote the article he had never visited the Mormon region. When he did go there he remembered with fear and trembling that which two or three years previously he had written in fun. Had Brigham Young seen it? He had; the book was in his library.

Let the reader turn to the article itself, and he will find that Artemus Ward asserts that he called upon Brigham Young, who asked him: "Do you bleeve in Solomon, Saint Paul, the immaculateness of the Mormin Church, and the Latterday Revelations?" Replying favorably to which, he was invited by the prophet to see his family, and was introduced to all his wives. The result of the interview and of his visit to Salt Lake being that, to quote the words of the article: "I packed up my duds and left Salt Lake, which is a 2d Soddum and Germorrer, inhabited by as theavin' and onprincipled a set of retchis as ever drew Breth in eny spot on the Globe." This declaration of opinion, though very prejudicial to the writer when he really did visit Salt Lake, was excellently well fitted to the times when it was written, for the Mormons had attracted the attention of Congress, and an outcry been raised against them which threatened their total extinction. The contribution to "Vanity Fair," therefore, owed as much of its success to its being felicitously opportune as to its being inimitably humorous.

In a very few weeks after becoming a contributor to the funny paper of New York, Artemus Ward received a letter from its proprietors offering him the position of assistant editor. In a communication written and sent to me by Mr. Charles Dawson Shanley, one of Charles Browne's earnest New York friends, and also one of his literary executors, Mr. Shanley states that—"Late in the summer of 1861 Mr. Leland retired from the management of the paper, and 'Artemus' became sole editor of it, a position which he held only for a brief period." But during that "brief period" many of his best contributions to the literature of his country were given to the public. And whatever there was of any merit in the columns of "Vanity Fair" from the time he assumed the editorial duties, emanated from his own pen. There were elements of dissolution in the journal which no antiseptic power or restorative energy on the part of the new editor was adequate to combat successfully. Artemus Ward succeeded in galvanizing it into a vigorous imitation of life, but its days were already numbered, and, having struggled into its seventh volume, it ceased to exist.

"They say that I can write comic copy," remarked Artemus Ward to a friend. "Comic copy was what they wanted for 'Vanity Fair.' I wrote some, and I killed it. The poor paper got to be a conundrum, and so gave itself up."

There were reasons, however, why the Showman of Baldinsville should have succeeded as an exhibitor of his own curiosities when he started his show in "Vanity Fair," and reasons equally as cogent why he should not be successful in managing the entire ground of which he himself occupied but a portion. The duties of an editor require qualifications beyond the talent sufficient to constitute a good contributor. Above all, they demand application and an attention to routine. Now routine was simply hateful to Artemus Ward. He was far too *journalier*, in the sense which the French attach to that word as an adjective, to be an exemplary illustration of it as a noun.

To be no more than twenty-eight years old, and to be the editor of the chief comic paper in the metropolis of the United States, was an achievement affording cause for self-congratulation. Yet the position rendered Artemus none the less amiable and none the less modest in New York than when he had been a mere reporter in Cleveland. The world hailed him as a young man of great ability, but he always distrusted that ability himself, and manifested no jealousy of the literary talent possessed by any of his associates.

His articles in "Vanity Fair" gained him a very large circle of acquaintances. From among them he selected a few friends. With him friendships once formed were destined to be lasting; and being durable, they were ardent, thorough, and sincere.

During his literary career in New York city, Artemus Ward occupied lodgings in Varick Street, the house being the first on the right hand entering from Canal Street, and between Canal Street and St. John's Park. His place of abode was known to very few of his companions. They met him at breakfast or dinner at a restaurant, and late in the evening they would find him down in Pfaff's cellar with the wit and the talent of the great city there congregated, and its representatives busily intent on discussing the topics of the day over Rhine wine or Bourbon whisky, with the elucidatory assistance of a short pipe or a fragrant cigar.

The contributions of Artemus Ward to "Vanity Fair" were collected, collated, and arranged for publication by himself in the volume issued by the publishing house of Messrs. G. W. Carleton & Co., of Broadway. I presume that every article which its author thought worthy of republication was reprinted.

Mr. Shanley writes to me: "My impression is that, with the exception of a very few paragraphs, jokes, and such-like, Artemus gave no unsigned contributions to 'Vanity Fair.'" To ferret out and republish paragraphs which he himself thought most fitting to let pass out of memory would hardly be respectful to the dead or interesting to the public.

Sitting up in bed at Southampton on one of the days of his last illness, Artemus Ward attempted to write a brief autobiography. Using for the purpose a black-lead pencil, he succeeded in writing a single paragraph, and then threw away the pencil in despair, finding himself too much exhausted to proceed. I have preserved the half-sheet of note-paper. The lines written upon it are the last that the gentle humorist wrote. As they contain one characteristic little jest, they are here given to the public:

"Some twelve years ago I occupied the position (or the position occupied me) of city editor of a journal in Cleveland, Ohio. This journal—'The Plaindealer'—was issued afternoons, and I was kept very busy indeed from eight o'clock in the morning till half past three in the afternoon in collecting the police reports and other items that might be of local interest."

I have hitherto endeavored to trace the career of Artemus Ward as an author from his earliest article in the Boston "Carpet-Bag" to his becoming editor of a paper in New York. It is now time to regard him in the next character he assumed — that of a public lecturer. Tired of the pen, he resolved on trying the platform. Instead of merely writing as a showman, he determined to be one, and boldly to face that public which hitherto he had addressed from the dark recesses of a printing-office. Down at Pfaff's he was assured that he would succeed. In Cleveland, where he had previously entertained the idea, some of his friends had discouraged him. At Pfaff's it was voted to be a matter of certainty that he would make a hit as a comic lecturer; and — as I have stated before — they were always right down at Pfaff's.

❦ 8 ❦

The United States • Lectures and the Lecturing System

AMERICA is a lecture-hall on a very extensive scale. The rostrum extends in a straight line from Boston, through New York and Philadelphia, to Washington. There are raised seats on the first tier in the Alleghanies, and gallery accommodation on the top of the Rocky Mountains.

There may be some truth in the hyperbole of the morning drum-beat of the British army unceasingly encircling the globe; but yet more true it is that the voice of the lecturer is never silent in the United States. The subtle strains of wisdom which have their birth in Boston; the pleasant orations delivered in New York; and the dreary diatribes dealt forth in Washington, resound at earliest morning along the shores of the Atlantic, and are echoed and re-echoed at latest night in the cities beside the Pacific.

The lecturer is indigenous to American soil. No Darwin is required to explain the origin of his species, for his *fons et origo* are in the very nature of things. Every American believes himself to be the repository of extensive information; within him is the pent-up source of knowledge; his amiable spirit of benevolence prompts him to let it flow forth for the enlightenment of his benighted fellow-citizens, and the outer world of darkness generally.

Two sins not alluded to in the Decalogue are thought to be transcendent trangressions in America; if committed, I believe that they are regarded as amounting to actual crimes. One is to grow old; the other is not to know.

"I don't know," is an English phrase; as much so as that thoroughly English idiom for expressing helplessness—"It can't be done." Across the Atlantic they are phrases seldom or never heard. Any thing can be done there; and a school-boy who, interrogated, should chance to reply that he "didn't know," would blush, not at his own ignorance, but that he had used the expression.

Educated as he is to know a little of the rule of three and human anatomy—of Latin, hydrostatics, botany, navigation, and political economy—it is no wonder that the American school-boy, peppered with science, and salted with history, should be a sciolist, with a strong inclination to teach. The "Pierian spring" being tasted only, the usual result follows. But better that it should, and better far that some results open to criticism should flow from the system of national education, than that there should be no system at all to produce such results. The universal knowledge of the superficially educated American is infinitely preferable to the profundity of ignorance which we too often meet with in England. Besides, that which an American knows, or thinks he knows, he is always ready to impart willingly and politely. He is not churlish enough to wrap himself up in the robes of his own knowledge, and refuse to lend a corner of his ample garment to keep warm the knees of a shivering fellow-traveller. In the States it is every man's duty to be informed, and you have only to ask for information to have it supplied to you in profusion. The clerk at the hotel, the conductor in the railroad "car," and the policeman on the street, are only too happy to oblige, if you will but ask them in a civil manner for that which you want to know. But speak to them as though you were addressing an equal: though they know that they are servants of the public, they will not submit to any domineering from you as a supercilious master.

The heterogeneous elements which enter into the education of a young American citizen, and the varied acquirements he is supposed to possess, are national characteristics, which have been amusingly burlesqued by the Boston humorist, Mr. B. P. Shillaber, who makes his celebrated "Mrs. Partington" say—"For my part, I can't deceive what on airth eddication is coming to. When I was young, if a girl only understood the rules of distraction, provision, multiplying, replenishing, and the common denunciator, and knew all about rivers and their obituaries, the convents and dormitories, the provinces and the umpires, they had eddication enough. But now they have to study bottomy, algebery, and have to demonstrate supposition about the sycophants of circuses, tangents, and Diogenese of parallelogromy, to say nothing about the oxhides, corostics, and the abstruse triangles."

A young lady educated as "Mrs. Partington" describes would possibly become as muddled in her mind as a young man chanced to be whom I once met at Birkenhead. Desirous of educating himself, he had purchased two volumes of an excellent work, entitled "The Popular Educator," in which the Arts and Sciences are made easy of comprehension in a series of condensed elementary treatises. I asked him what order he observed in his study of the various subjects. He replied that, wishing to educate himself thoroughly, he had resolved to begin from the beginning, and, to do so, had taken the alphabetical index of contents for his guide. He had commenced with "Acoustics," and gone on to "Anatomy," "Architecture," and "Astronomy." Thus he meant to go through with his studies gradually, and finish off with "Zoology."

That there are reasons why a man should not know too much is illustrated in an anecdote told by the well-known Mr. J. H. Hackett, in the "New York Leader." He tells it of a certain Mr. John Robinson, who offered himself as candidate for the office of Sheriff somewhere in Tennessee. Two farmers met one another on horseback, and the one asked the other whom he was going to vote for.

"John Robinson," was the reply.

"Vote for him!" rejoined the other; "why he's so ignorant he can't spell his given name, 'John;' and, what's worse, he is so stupid, I would bet you ten dollars you couldn't larn him to spell it between now and to-morrow noon."

The bet was made, a place of meeting arranged for its decision, and the farmers parted. He who had made the bet rode off to the house of John Robinson, told him of the conversation and the bet, and ascertained that the poor fellow really could not spell his own name. The farmer proposed to teach him, and to divide the winnings. Robinson assented, and persuaded his tutor to stay all night.

"Next morning at breakfast"—to tell the anecdote in the words of Mr. Hackett—"on John's being asked to spell the name, he did so readily enough; but his friend wasn't satisfied, and said, 'John, there may be some crooked ketch, after all, in such politics. There's time enough between now and noon, if you have a mind, to larn the whole alphabet. I'll larn you from first to last—that is, from A to Izzard—the latter being the common mode in America of naming the letter 'Z.' John agreed to be so high larnt; and before noon could say every letter from A to Izzard. Off they started at noon for the place appointed, where four or five of the neighbors had got together on purpose to hear John Robinson, and to judge whether he was able to spell his given name. Five men were appointed as judges, the bet recited, and John asked if he was ready to spell his name. John said, 'Try me.' And the judges said, 'Well, spell John.' So John began with 'J.' All the judges looked at him and at one another, and then nodded and said, 'Right—next letter.' 'O,' said John. They all looked at one another, as if there was some doubt about the letter, and said, 'Right; now next letter.' Said John, 'That's H.' John's friend, seeing the judges, by halting in giving a judgment after each letter, had somewhat bothered him, cautioned him to keep cool till after the judges had done fooling, and had agreed and said 'Right.' Now for the next letter, when his friend assured 'John, we are all right now, but the *last* letter—don't forget.' John hesitated, and thinking he meant the last letter of the alphabet, which he had just taken the trouble to learn, bellowed out, 'Izzard, by thunder!' and—lost the bet."

Mr. Hackett draws the moral from his anecdote that people are apt to know too much, and to suffer in consequence. Without indorsing to the full that deduction, I honestly believe that if the good people across the water had fewer individuals in their midst who feel themselves effervescing with information, and under such high pressure that they must impart it without delay, there would be a less number of lectures, and many a patient audience would escape being bored. As it is, every thing is lectured upon, from the destinies of humanity down to the proper method of making a pumpkin-pie. The poor President, no matter which, affords the most fertile theme. He is lectured upon before he is elected, lectured to all the time that he is in office, and made to serve as a frightful example to point a lecturer's moral, or adorn a lecturer's tale, after his term of office is concluded.

Lectures certainly count among the list of "shows" in the Western World. All the arts of the showman are employed in aid of their popularity; and the chief showman, Mr. P. T. Barnum, having abandoned the exhibition-room for the rostrum, goes forth to enlighten the multitude for the small fee of one hundred dollars per night and his expenses.

I am not thoroughly acquainted with Mr. Barnum's views concerning the art of lecturing. But his idea of a lecture-room was certainly somewhat original. Within his renowned museum on Broadway the largest apartment was designated "The Lecture-room." Performances were given in it every evening, and almost every afternoon. In reality it was the theatre of the establishment, and was devoted to the representation of stage-plays. To have called it a theatre would not have suited Mr. Barnum's purpose. His patrons being composed of sober-minded young men from the country, and innocent young maidens from the city, it was necessary that every thing should be exceedingly proper to please the tastes of youth in search of amusement and ladies desirous of edification. The theatre was therefore described on the bills as *The Moral Lecture-room*. The propriety indicated by the title being illustrated by playing sensation dramas, and charging twenty-five cents additional to the lower seats. Between the acts of a drama it was customary to exhibit a giant, a dwarf, or any malformed being suitable for the purposes of a moral show.

The old style of conducting public lectures in the United States is very like that of this country, but the system of later date is in accordance with the go-ahead character of the times, and is markedly different. There are venerable institutions on the other side of the Atlantic, which have their analogues in similar institutions on this side. For instance, in Boston, looking up a court off Washington Street, may be noticed a large gloomy door-way, with a baker's shop on one side of it. Bostonians know the building in the rear as the Lowell Institute. They who desire some information can obtain tickets gratis at certain seasons of the year, and at the Lowell Institute attend a series of lectures on Geology or Comparative Anatomy, delivered by the learned, eloquent, and estimable Professor Agassiz, or a course on the History of the United States, by one of its most erudite historians. The place, the audience, the lectures, and the general arrangement, remind one of Gresham College in London. Like that, the Lowell Institute was endowed by a wealthy founder, and lectures have to be delivered in it at fixed periods of the year. Then there is the Smithsonian Institution at Washington, the gift of an Englishman to the people of the United States, and unfortunately partially destroyed by fire a few years ago. Lectures on scientific and historic matters are given there after the model of those delivered on Friday evenings in Albemarle Street, at the Royal Institution. In New York there is the Cooper Institute, endowed like the Lowell one in Boston. There is no Polytechnic, with a Professor Pepper presiding over it, in the States at present; but there are Lyceums, Athenæums, and Literary Societies without end. Then, every town has its hall for lectures, concerts, and entertainments. Not dingy little rooms, with broken and dirty seats, built over a market-place, or down a back street, but large, elegant, and well-situated buildings, many of them exceedingly capacious, and fitted up with a stage and scenery for the use of any travelling dramatic company. In the cities of the West the popular hall is usually on the first or second floor, the basement of the building being occupied by stores. The smallest town will have its hall, while in most there are two or three, each being the result of private enterprise, and not the property of the city corporation.

Churches and chapels are frequently used for lecture halls in the Western cities. Even in Brooklyn, the sister city of New York, the celebrated Rev. Henry Ward Beecher allows his very large church to be hired for political and amusing lectures. I remember visiting it one evening to hear the well-known Mr. George Francis Train lecture on his travels. He spoke from the pulpit, wearing a blue coat with brass buttons, and was as voluble in his narrative of what he had done, seen, and suffered, as he was violent in his denunciations of England. Though perched up in a pulpit, he joked without restraint; telling funny stories and outrivalling a dozen Baron Munchausens in details of adventure, to the infinite delight of the crowded and hilarious congregation, who applauded, laughed, and cheered the veracious lecturer most uproariously. Mr. Train is a quotable specimen of the American gentleman of universal information, to whom I have referred in a previous paragraph. On the evening of his lecture in Brooklyn, he adverted to the condition of the army of China, and, having been astonishingly statistical all the evening, one of his audience took occasion to interrupt him to inquire what was its numerical strength. Mr. Train replied without a moment's hesitation, giving the number to a unit. Whereupon his interrogator requested to know the number of guns.

So many thousand, so many hundred *"and five; but two of them are cracked,"* replied Mr. Train, with charming accuracy. Could the whole of the Ordnance Department together have answered as rapidly and as precisely with regard to the guns of the army of Great Britain?

It is not to be wondered at that the clergyman who preaches at the most popular church in Brooklyn—Plymouth Church, as it is called—should sanction its being occasionally let out for amusing lectures. The church altogether is conducted on the paying principle, and the seats in it are annually put up at public auction to the highest bidders. As a lecturer, the Rev. Henry Ward Beecher is most eloquent, fascinating, and humorous, abounding in apt illustration and felicitous anecdote. He lets himself out to lecture at so much per night, and, being highly attractive, receives quite as large an honorarium as Mr. Barnum.

Political lecturers of high renown, like the Hon. Horace Greeley, Mr. Wendell Phillips, or Henry Ward Beecher; literary lecturers of celebrity, like Mr. George Curtis, Mr. Emerson, Dr. Holmes, Mr. E. P. Whipple, and Mr. Saxe; together with a few of the more prominent of the professedly humorous lecturers, always command their one hundred dollars per night. Mr. Beecher, I believe, has now raised his fee to two hundred dollars. Lecturers so well known are in constant request throughout the lecture season, and in the Western cities receive higher pay than they can obtain in most of the Eastern ones.

Every thing in America is managed by agency. The Lyceums, which are very much the same in character as our Mechanics' Institutes or Athenæums, are supplied with lecturers by means of committees and agents. The Lyceums of various cities extending over a large tract of country band together, form an organization, correspond with one another, and appoint a central committee, with a manager or agent, whose business it is to look up the most attractive lecturers and arrange with them for a tour, so arranging that the talented gentleman engaged shall not waste time, nor be subjected to unnecessary travel, but go on from the place at which he lectured on Monday night to the town at which he has to display his eloquence on Tuesday. The lecturer experiences very little trouble except that inseparable from travel. All his arrangements are made by the society's agent. When he arrives at where he is to lecture, there is sure to be a committee-man waiting to receive him, and when he has finished his lecture and received his fee, he will be either escorted to his hotel by some of the chief members of the Lyceum, or invited to sup and sleep at a private home, where he will be regarded as a lion, and treated more as a member of the family than as a stranger.

Samaritans, however, are not always found among lecture committees, or, if Samaritans in their intentions, they do not carry out those intentions agreeably. Some six years ago I accompanied a popular lecturer to a lecture in the large school-room of a church not far from the city of New York. The time of year was mid-winter, the night was bitter cold, snow was on the ground, frozen into sharp little spiculæ of ice, the stars were steel-like in their frosty splendor, and the wind seemed to be disposed to stab wherever it could strike. My friend the lecturer hoped to find some warm refreshment when he arrived at the schoolroom. There was water only. When the lecture was over, we were invited by the gentleman who paid the fee to go across to his house, be introduced to his family, and partake of something to eat and drink. Visions of a large fire and a hot supper were before us as we hastened shiveringly across the road. Our host ushered us into a library where there was no fire, and invited us to admire the splendid binding of the volumes in his very elegant book-cases, while he left us to order the repast. Freezingly we waited. When the good things did arrive, accompanied by the family, we found our appointed supper to consist of a plate of apples and a jug of cold cider! The gentleman was a vegetarian and a philosopher.

Within the last few years a successful attempt has been made in New York to organize a central agency on a large scale for the supply of lecturers all over the United States. It is entitled "The American Literary Bureau," and has its office in Nassau Street, in the neighborhood where all the newspapers are published. In one of its prospectuses the following business-like statement is made:

"In enlarging the field of operations, it is proposed to introduce the principle of co-operation, as calculated to be of essential service to Lyceums. By that system the hundreds of lecture-committees in the Eastern, Central, and Southern States will be enabled to obtain the best talent at the lowest rates; they will also secure a higher average of lectures. Other benefits will follow upon the plan, and Lyceums can not further their own interests better than by putting themselves into immediate correspondence with the Bureau, when all necessary explanations will be made in full. Lecturers will readily perceive that their interests will not less be subserved by our system, and we invite all who have not already registered their names on our books to do so at once. Address to American Literary Bureau, P.O. Box 6701."

Since issuing the prospectus from which I have quoted, the Bureau has extended its operations, and, under the superintendence of its energetic manager, Mr. James K. Medbery, has pushed its operations to the farthest West, and enrolled among its members a most efficient army of lecturers. Nor has it restricted its energies to enlisting American lecturers only, but has been enterprising enough to secure talent from Europe. In a circular recently issued, it advertises that it has upon its books the Rev. Prof. W. C. Richards, A.M. "Terms, 50 dollars and expenses (with modifications). Subject: 'Thomas Hood, the Humorist and Humanist.' " The Bureau is also in possession of "Z. R. Sandford, Esq. Terms, 50 dollars (with modifications); reading and recitation of his original poems, 'Fringes.' — The Rev. Robert Laird Collier, of Chicago. Terms, 100 dollars. Subject: 'The Personality of a Poet.' — J. O. Miller, the eloquent Orange County Farmer, a highly reputed humorist. Terms, 50 dollars (with modifications). Subjects: 'Model Husband,' 'Model Wife.' " Then it announces a gentleman whose "modifications" are stated in the advertisement thus: "George M. Beard, M.D. Terms, 75 dollars to 30 dollars. Subjects: 'Our Crimes against Health;' 'Stimulants and Narcotics.' " But it is not stated whether the eloquent doctor charges 75 dollars for the "Crimes" and 30 dollars for the "Stimulants," or *vice versa*.

Not content with the purely American element, the Bureau notifies that it has on its books Mr. Henry Nichols, of London, Mr. William Parsons, of Ireland, and Mr. Justin McCarthy, "the editor of the London 'Morning Star,' " who is prepared to lecture on "The Progress of Democratic Ideas in England," "The British Parliament," "Goethe, Schiller, and Moliere."

Nothing can be done in the United States, any more so than elsewhere, without the society of the ladies. The "American Literary Bureau," therefore, informs the world that it has at its disposal Miss Julia Crouch, of Mystic, Connecticut, and that the topic of her lecture is "Wisdom and Folly." No price is named for her services, nor any statement made or not whether she permits "modifications;" but as she is comparatively new in the market, and has not attained that position which warrants her being quoted in the price-list of lecture-stock, the following extracts from newspapers are appended to the advertisement:

> "Miss Crouch makes a very graceful appearance before an audience, with elegant form, full medium height, very fair complexion, keen, sparkling black eyes, and as sweet a voice as we ever heard on any platform."—*Norwich Bulletin*.

"She bows gracefully and modestly to her audience,
and proceeds in a most unexceptionable manner, with
eloquence of movement as well as eloquence of utterance."—*New London Democrat.*

"She speaks with an agreeable, clear, silvery voice."
—*Mystic Pioneer.*

"We regard her as a successful platform speaker.
She has received calls as a lyceum lecturer that will be
flattering to her talents."—*Hartford Post.*

Nothing like the "Bureau" exists, I believe, in this country. Yet why
it should not, and why the lecturer is not better known and better paid
among us than he is, it might be difficult satisfactorily to explain. Perhaps we have not come up to the time; perhaps we have passed beyond
it. Let a thorough system of national education be introduced, and the
thirst for knowledge would then, perhaps, cause the itinerant higher-
class lecturer to be as popular and as well rewarded in the towns of
Lancashire and Yorkshire, and the villages of Somerset and Devon, as
he now is on the banks of the Mississippi or on the shores of the great
American Lakes.

In devoting so much space to the Lyceum lecture system in the
United States, I have been actuated by two motives: first, to render its
peculiarities perfectly understood by the reader, as distinct from that
style of lecturing which approximates more closely to the calling of the
showman; and, secondly, because it was with Lyceum committees that
Artemus Ward had to make some of his earliest arrangements as a
lecturer.

He who engages himself to the "Bureau," or who lets himself out to
Lyceums, has to manage his business in a manner different from that
in which he conducts it if, to use an expressive American phrase, he
lectures "on his own hook." Then, unsupported by committees, and
unassisted by the working members of a literary society, he has to fight
his own way and rely upon his popularity, his business talent, the
efficiency of his agent, and the excellence of his bills and posters.

The timid man, he who is indisposed to exertion, and he who dreads
any thing which resembles showmanship, will remain passive and thoroughly respectable in the hands of the committees. He who has more
daring, more energy, and who cares only to make money, no matter

what people may have to say about his showman's artifice, will "go it on his own hook." Perhaps, if the purse of the latter be not too heavily laden, or his speculative spirit be not sufficiently bold, he will dispose of himself to a capitalist for a certain time, either for a stipulated sum, or on equitable sharing terms. As a rule, in the States the lecturers who are simply lecturers fit into the machinery of the Lyceums, while those who approach in character to entertainers trust to their own powers of management, or share with some one whom they consider to be capable to manage them. Artemus Ward tried in turns each of these three systems.

A lecturer or entertainer who makes up his mind to be his own showman in America must have no compunctions of conscience about puffing himself to the world. There must be no hiding his light under a bushel, nor any disinclination to work. An agent, to go ahead and make his arrangements, is absolutely indispensable. To get a good one is a matter of difficulty, for the best are always engaged by those who know their value.

Here in England the nature and office of an agent to a showman is by no means thoroughly understood. There is the same lack of enterprise in the management of a show with us that we develop in many other respects. In the United States the agent or business manager has, or should have, unlimited power to do as he pleases conceded to him by his principal. He should be of gentlemanly manner, that he may herald his attraction fittingly; he should be a man of tact, that he may make his moves properly; he should be a man of education, so that when he is asked in a Western office to sit down and write the notice which he desires, he should acquit himself skillfully, and in accordance with the politics of the paper; he should understand human nature, so that in dealing with people he should accomplish his aims with ease, never bore and never disgust. Above all, he should be used to the business, know the country in which he is travelling, have a constant fund of good-humor, and a zealous determination to make his lecturer or his show successful, no matter what difficulties he has to overcome, nor what impediments may present themselves. If he knows all the railway conductors, so much the better for his trips along the rails; if he is acquainted with all the newspaper editors and reporters, so much the more easy for him to get hold of the long end of his great lever, the press; and if he is known at all the hotels, and friendly with all the hotel clerks, so much superior will be his boarding and his lodging, and so much the more will he be reckoned up as a specimen of that valuable class of people who are said to "know their way about."

There are a few minor accomplishments which it is just as well that he should possess. For instance, he should be able to take a hand at poker, be a good judge of a cigar and know where to buy the best, have a fair knowledge of how to handle a cue, and able to drive a buggy. It is also advisable that he should have no politics, and be always enthusiastically of the same opinion as the company among whom he happens to be thrown. That which he privately thinks, and his ideas on things generally, acquired during his roving career, he can lay aside in the storehouse of his brain until his agency is over.

Having secured his agent, the show-lecturer will be careful about the manner and matter of his bills and posters. If at all fitted for his vocation, he will understand the value of pictures on his bills. The advantage of pictorial placards is much better understood in America than it is here. We are beginning to comprehend it in the lithographs, plain and colored, which our theatrical artists and showmen cause to be displayed in shop windows. When Mr. Sothern came over from the States, he brought with him, and did not forget to use, the pictorial style of advertising. He was adventurous enough even to astonish the Parisians with it in the year of the great Paris Exhibition. Mr. Boucicault, arch-priest as he is in the Showman's Temple, has always appreciated the value of a sensation-scene pictorially rendered on his show-bills; while Mr. Toole, in his ideas of the picturesque in announcements, would almost induce a stranger to believe that he had learned his business on the other side of the Atlantic, whither he has never been.

Artists of considerable talent, and business firms with great resources at their command, undertake the production of pictorial bills in America. There are some offices — as, for example, Clarry and Reilley's in New York, and the "Cincinnati Inquirer" in Cincinnati — that have presses of immense size for pictorial printing. Where in England we should have to use four sheets of paper to print a large wood-cut, at the offices I have named they use but one. Our "double-crowns" and "double-demies" sufficed for America in the days of her youth. When she had grown up to be old enough to have territories, the paper-makers provided her with a "mammoth" sheet; and when she grew to be the owner of California and had gold-mines of her own, they made her a sheet of paper larger still, and called it a "mastodon." I am told that, now the Pacific railway is completed, the paper-makers are coming out with a "megatherium."

The pictorial printing establishment in New York, to which I have just referred, is a marvellous place for the supply of illustrated mural art. In a vast repository of racks are stored up engraved wood-cuts of every possible variety of show. If you are a giant or a dwarf, and wish to make a show of yourself, you have only to pay a visit to Spruce Street, and you will be able to take your choice of an engraved block of any kind of dwarf or giant you desire to represent yourself to be. There you are drawn and engraved. In the process of printing it is very easy to give you nationality. Wishing to exhibit yourself as a martial giant, the printers will print you in blue if you desire to be an American, in red if you wish to be British, or in a prismatic mixture if you intend to be Asiatic in your origin. Perhaps, instead of being a giant or a dwarf yourself, you are simply a showman and a lecturer. You have a "living skeleton," an "erudite pig," or a "woolly fish," which you are anxious to exhibit and to lecture upon. In Spruce Street the printers will show you in an instant wood-cuts of living skeletons of every degree of thickness, erudite pigs of every breed of swine, and woolly fishes with or without dorsal and ventral fins, just as you please. They keep on hand professors of conjuring, well cut out in flowing robes for the trick of "The bowls of water," and in evening dress to illustrate simple tricks with hats and coins. They have wood-blocks of horses illustrative of every "trick-act" a circus horse was yet known to perform; while for the purposes of menageries they possess cuts of all the larger animals, including the hippopotamus taking its bath, and a monster elephant fanning itself with a lady's fan.

Mr. Barnum set the example, and all showmen in the States follow it, to have a lecture explanatory of whatever curiosity they may please to exhibit. A lecturer or two, able to describe an object of interest, and tell a few good stories about it, was always found to be of advantage in the Old Museum of New York. Perhaps a few peripatetic lecturers exercising their vocation at certain times, or on certain days, would help to throw a little life into the British Museum in London, rendering the collection more interesting to visitors, and more useful to the public at large. "What! make a show of it?" exclaims some good old horror-stricken conservative. Yes, decidedly. It is a show. Nine-tenths of its visitors go to see it as a show. Among its trustees there should be at least one good showman.

Some of Mr. Barnum's exhibitions with lectures were characteristic of the showman and his show. When he could arrange for the curiosity to lecture on itself, and be, in a reflected sense, theory and example, he seldom omitted to seize the chance. Had he a "Lightning Calculator," he would cause that "Lightning Calculator" first to lecture on himself, and then illustrate his electric powers of arithmetic. Had he a "double-voiced" singer, the vocalist with the dual gift had first to lecture on his peculiar endowment, and then proceed to illustrate it. One of Mr. Barnum's happy thoughts in this way was to catch a female spy and cause her to relate her adventures. Her name was Miss Cushman—a good and great name in the States. She had played the part of a spy in one division of the Union Army, and coming to New York, offered herself as a curiosity. Engaged by Mr. Barnum, she appeared on his stage in the "moral lecture-room." After giving a brief lecture on the nature and office of the military spy in general, she narrated her own adventures in particular. Her preliminary matter was delivered while she wore very pretty and fashionable attire. Then she exhibited herself in military disguise, and changed her dress to illustrate her exploits. People just then were very bellicose in their way of thought, and the lecture by a female spy harmonizing well with the times, the show became popular.

In Boston, Mr. Barnum had an exhibition of another sort, in which he employed the services of an adventurous lady. The Bostonians had been anxious to see a live whale. Mr. Barnum had one captured expressly for them. It was a white one, and not so large as to be unmanageable. An extensive glass tank was built up for it in the exhibition-room—the tank being filled with sea-water pumped up from Boston harbor. The whale made a pretty sight from the gallery around the hall, whence the visitor could look down upon the tank and see the creature take its circular swim by way of exercise. An interesting lecture on the whale was easily concocted, but every school-girl knew as much about whales as the lecturer did. Hence something more was desirable to give interest. It required genius to find that something.

Mr. Barnum found it. Attach a car to the whale, harness the whale to the car. Dress up a pretty woman as a nymph or sea-goddess, and do circus business inside the tank. That was the idea which struck the mind of the whale's owner, and the idea which he fully carried out.

Unfortunately, the whale became disgusted with being subjected to so much degradation, and ingloriously died, committing suicide by eating some broken glass.

The show lecturer and the Lyceum lecturer are usually gentlemen of very different temperament. He who adheres strictly to the orthodox proprieties of the rostrum, and who exalts the didactic as being far above the entertaining, is, as a matter of course, less jovial and more saturnine than the lecturer who is not afraid of being heralded with a picture poster, whose aim is solely to make money, and who thoroughly believes in the world's thirst for knowledge being subordinate to its hunger for enjoyment.

Before he adopted the profession of a lecturer himself, Artemus Ward amusingly caricatured a species of the didactic order of lecturers not uncommonly met with on the Western Continent. The burlesque is so apt as to merit quotation:

"Poplar lecturs as thay air kalled, in my pinion air poplar humbugs. Individooals, who git hard up embark in the lecturin' bizniss. Thay cram thairselves with hi-soundin' frazis, frizzle up thair hare, git trusted for a soot of black close, and cum out to lectur at 50 dollers a pop. Thay haint overstockt with branes, but thay have brass enuff to make suffishunt kettles to bile all the soap that will be required by the ensooin sixteen ginerashuns. Peple flock to heer um in krowds. The men go becawz it's poplar, and the wimin folks go to see what other wimin folks have on. When it's over the lecturer goze and regales hisself with oysters and sich; while the people say, 'What a charming lectur that air was,' etsettery, etsettery, when nine out of ten of um don't have no moore idee of what the lecturer sed than my kangaroo has of the sevunth speer of hevun."

❧ 9 ❧

New York • "Babes in the Wood" at Clinton Hall

CLINTON HALL, New York, has been the test-ground for many an ambitious young lecturer. Some of the most talented and best qualified lecturers of America have spoken therein. Some of the very worst have spoken there also. It is not a very grand place, nor is it a remarkably cheerful one.

It was in Clinton Hall, on the 23d of December, 1861, that Artemus Ward, having already made his position in New York as an author, endeavored to ascertain his popularity as a lecturer.

The hall stands upon memorable ground. It occupies a portion of the site of the old Astor Place Opera-house, the scene of the fatal riot on the occasion of Mr. Macready, the tragedian, performing there some years ago. On the ruins of the Opera-house has arisen a large building, which includes within its walls Clinton Hall and the Mercantile Library. The neighborhood is the very focus of information. Close by is the magnificent Astor Library—the great public library of reference; not far distant is the Mission House, whence America disperses religious knowledge over the world; and very near at hand is the Cooper Institute, an admirable establishment, wherein, through the benevolence of its charitable founder, the working-classes have excellent facilities afforded them for self-education.

Singular people have presented themselves before the public at the Cooper Institute and in Clinton Hall.

It was in the lecture-room of the Cooper Institute that the Davenport Brothers astonished and perplexed New York with their ingeniously-contrived mechanical Cabinet; and, in 1860, the walls of New York were placarded with posters announcing that Miss Adah Isaacs Menken would lecture on "The Age of Irrepressibles" in Clinton Hall.

Poor Artemus Ward used to shiver when reference was made to his own appearance at Clinton Hall. How he came to lecture there may be briefly told.

While writing for the newspaper in Cleveland, the hard-worked young reporter was called upon in the course of his duties to visit the different exhibitions which chanced to come into the town, and to attend the performances of the various nigger-bands, circuses, and itinerant entertainers. He noticed the peculiarity of humor which seemed most to please the public, made notes of the characteristics of the several entertainers, and was observant of what an audience requires in order to be amused, and what it is in an entertainment that is superfluous or simply wearisome. He readily perceived how much vitality there is in a good old jest, and how a venerable joke, if properly retailed by "Mr. Merryman" in the ring, or by "Bones" upon the minstrel platform, still retains its power of raising a hearty laugh. And more than this, he listened to some of his own humorous fancies, that had done duty in the newspaper for which they were originally written and in fifty other papers into which they had been copied, served up again by the clown or the wandering jester, and received with acclamation by hilarious crowds. Having thus heard, seen, and noticed, he went home and reflected.

To make jests for the printer brought but poor pay. Besides, the printer required the jest of to-day to be different from the one of yesterday, and he would want a new one altogether on the morrow.

The *viva voce* diffuser of jokes received good pay. A limited stock-in-trade sufficed, and the brain work was comparatively slight. That which passed current as a good thing in the town visited yesterday could be re-uttered in the town stopped at to-day, and could be used for the delectation of the multitude every day for the next year to come.

Of such nature were the reflections which stimulated Artemus Ward to be a lecturer. He desired to accumulate money not only that he might see the world and better his own position, but also that he might secure to his mother the old homestead in Maine, and aid those whom he most loved. Newspaper work was not likely to produce him affluence, nor even sufficient means to carry out his most moderate ambition. But to start in life as a comic lecturer, and achieve success in the new calling, was to effect that which in a land like America offered every prospect of eventually realizing a competency.

Poor Artemus was acquainted with many of his literary brethren who possessed great talent but made little money. He was also familiar with showmen innumerable whose intellectual gifts were few, but who could load their caravans with golden dollars and paper the inside of their shows with bank-notes. His experiences as an amateur did not inspire him with a wish to adopt the stage as a profession, any more than did his lack of musical ability prompt him to become a concert-giver. As a comic lecturer he thought that he might succeed; and he thought so with increased belief, the more that he was assured by many of his friends that the idea was a happy one, and one which he should lose no time in carrying out.

But all the friends of the ambitious young reporter were not equally as encouraging. There were sure to be some among those immediately around him who were disposed to act the part of the wet blanket, ready to quench the fire of energy, and say, "Don't do it, you will certainly fail." What man of enterprise has ever lacked that order of friends? America does not produce them as plentifully as do some older countries, but they are indigenous to every soil; and too frequently, where they think they act the serviceable part of the break to the train, are only the log of wood placed across the rails to throw the locomotive off the track.

In some prefatory notes prefixed to the little volume in which Artemus Ward's "Lecture on the Mormons" has been printed, I have briefly detailed a conversation I had with the lecturer himself in Cleveland relative to his first attempt at composing a humorous lecture. The idea of becoming a public entertainer had taken possession of his mind, and the nature of the entertainment he should give had been made matter of study. From time to time he had jotted down on slips of paper things that he had heard, and quaint fancies as they had suggested themselves, with the intent of working up the whole into an entertainment. One day he chanced to go out and leave his slips of paper on his desk. Mr. Gray, the proprietor of the paper, happened to notice them, and, perceiving their peculiarity, inquired for what they were intended, and in what way they were to be used in the columns of the "Plaindealer." The gentlemen in the office could not inform him. Artemus himself was therefore appealed to for information.

"Those slips are notes for my comic lecture," was his reply.

His comic lecture!

That the "city editor" should turn lecturer seemed beyond the belief of his interrogator, who, when assured that the assertion had been made in all gravity, and that the intention was seriously entertained, burst into laughter.

"They laughed at me, and called me a fool," said Artemus, relating the circumstance to me some years after, in the course of an evening ramble through the town in which it had occurred four or five years previously.

When a man believes that he sees his way clearly before him, and has even a moderate amount of self-reliance in his character, laughter is not very likely to stop him from journeying on the road which he has chosen and take another path, however much it may cause him to halt and be a little more anxious to read the finger-post correctly. Artemus allowed those who laughed at him to remain behind in Cleveland, while he, with the idea of the comic lecture germinating in his brain, went on to New York.

Stimulating in the extreme to the mind of the emulative man who has not met with many great rebuffs from Fortune is the air of a great city. To him who has ventured much, and been defeated often, it is air that is full of noxious vapor—an atmosphere with the density of carbonic acid and a pressure which no barometer can measure; but to the sanguine and the fortunate, to him who has friends to cheer, hope to inspirit, and unchecked courage to sustain him, the air which plays around multitudinous chimney-pots, and vibrates incessantly with the hum of labor, the roar of the Bourse, and the clash of contending citizens, is invigorating, bracing, and full of food to ambition and to energy. To the wearied and the disappointed it is an air which withers like the blast of the Sirocco. To him who feels assured that with exertion he can win his way, it is air which seems to be meat, drink, and life itself, like the breezes I have felt blow round me on the hill-tops of Australia and on the grand mountains of Oregon.

"Going out gunning in the country is all very well, and makes a man feel good," remarked to me one of the editors of a Milwaukee paper, who was fond of using long words. "But I like to get back into the city among people; that's what *refocillates* me most."

In the great city of New York, Artemus Ward found himself surrounded by those who were more disposed to stimulate than to discourage. Down at Pfaff's cellar the young Bohemians, who were positive in their knowledge, and the old Bohemians, who were oracular in their wisdom, alike told him that he had only to turn comic lecturer in order to make a fortune. As to the matter of the lecture, and the order of its arrangement, there was considerable difference of opinion. Some offered to suggest the subjects to be treated on; while others, kinder still, obligingly tendered to write the whole lecture. But Artemus had his own opinions.

Among various schemes which had suggested themselves to him was that of a string of jests combined with a stream of satire, the whole being as unconnected, and one jest having as little relation to another, as the articles in any number of a comic periodical. He could not distort his countenance for the impersonation of character, like Dr. Valentine had done, or as Winchell or Alfred Burnett did. He had not the pulpit *prestige* of Mr. Beecher, nor the Maine Liquor Law back-ground of Mr. Gough. He had no panorama, nor any thing to exhibit but himself; therefore, to become a humorous lecturer, with simply humor, fun, and satire blended together to form the basis of his entertainment, appeared to him to be that for which he was most fitting, and that which would best suit the public. The lecture was put together with great care and with studied incoherency in some of its details. A burlesque upon a lecture, rather than a lecture in the accepted meaning of the term, was precisely that which it amounted to. Then came the great difficulty— what should be its title?

"I first thought of calling it 'My Seven Grandmothers,' " said he, in reply to my inquiry of how it was he came to choose the title at length determined upon.

There was nothing whatever in the lecture about "Seven Grandmothers;" but the title seemed a droll one. The young lecturer had studied the showman's art long enough to know how much there is in a name. At the suggestion of a friend, and not able to think of any thing better at the time, he ultimately concluded to entitle his lecture "The Babes in the Wood;" and with the borrowed name of the well-known story which has charmed so many children, and formed the ground-work of so many pantomimes, the lecture was introduced to the public.

Prominently brilliant among the group of bright young men who at that time occasionally illumined the gloom of the vault under the street down at Pfaff's was Mr. Frank Wood. He was one of the contributors to "Vanity Fair," and one who to considerable literary talent added the qualifications of a most fascinating manner and a sympathetic, amiable disposition. Artemus Ward and Frank Wood became great friends. Artemus required a nurse for his "Babes in the Wood," in the form of an agent, who should pioneer the way and attend to the business affairs.

Frank Wood offered himself in that capacity, and strongly urged his friend to let him start off and engage Clinton Hall for the experimental attempt at lecturing. To this Artemus would not agree. He wished to try the country first. Outlying the neighborhood of New York are numerous small towns, each having its lecture-hall, its literary institute, and its share of lecture-loving people. The "Babes" were as yet in their cradle, and the idea of Artemus was, that during their infancy, and while gaining strength to step out of the perambulator and walk alone, it would be much better to train them in country air than to exercise them in the streets of the metropolis. Mr. Frank Wood consented to the arrangement, and the "Babes" were taken for their first airing to the small town of Norwich, near New London, in the adjacent State of Connecticut.

Nervous in temperament, and manifesting anxiety in all that he did, Artemus Ward made his *début* as a lecturer under strong excitement. I have been told by one who heard him that his audience, though they laughed immoderately, thronged around him, when the lecture was over, to sympathize with him, believing that the purposely odd and disjointed character of the lecturer was the result of intense nervousness on the part of the lecturer, and that in his confusion of thought he had forgotten to tell them any thing about the Babes. He had never intended to. Therein lay the gist of the great joke which constituted the so-called lecture.

Having made a trip through the rural districts, and taken a hasty run out West, the lecturer returned to New York, and adopted Mr. Frank Wood's advice to try his fortune at Clinton Hall.

New York is not a city wherein the inhabitants are much given to attending lectures. Boston and Philadelphia are far more disposed to yield their patronage to him who mounts the rostrum. In New York the people prefer the theatre, circus, or museum, to the hall in which there is nothing to see, nor any thing but the voice of a lecturer to hear. They love excitement, and find no great pleasure in sitting still to be talked to for an hour together, unless the speaker is a man of very great renown, or has some remarkable eccentricity combined with his powers of eloquence. Such being the character of the people of New York, neither Artemus Ward nor his agent had any good reason to anticipate great financial results from the experiment they were about to make. Something better than did result they certainly expected.

The lecture was well advertised, and the poster on the walls was quaint and striking. The latter contained very few words, but they were displayed in large roughly-formed white letters on a black ground, and underneath them a printed slip informed the passer-by where the event was to take place and the time of opening the doors. Throughout his lecturing career, down to the last week of his delivering a lecture in London, Artemus Ward used that same form of poster. The following is a copy on a very reduced scale:

ARTEMUS WARD

WILL

SPEAK A PIECE.

Every boy and girl who looked at the bill knew that the notification conveyed by it was to the effect that a recitation was to be delivered, or an oration made. Just as in England we use the phrase "Christmas-piece" to express something intended to be read or recited at Christmas, so to "Speak a Piece" means, in the phraseology of New England, to deliver orally something in prose or poetry, either as a lesson or by way of amusement. It is a favorite mode of expression with children, and for that reason seemed to harmonize admirably with the idea of the "Babes in the Wood." Wherever it was seen posted on the walls, in the various towns of the United States, it invariably succeeded in attracting attention, eliciting a smile, and in causing the reader to be aware that the lecture to which it referred was intended to be quaintly humorous.

The night of the twenty-third of December came about, and the doors of Clinton Hall, when opened, had to be half-closed again immediately, for snow and rain were descending together in a mixed shower, and a fierce wind drove the sleet into the entry and numbed the fingers of the money-taker, who sat waiting for the crowd which resolutely refused to come. The poor "Babes," though young in their career, already experienced the melancholy fate assigned to them in the ballad. "Frank Wood was one babe and I was the other," said Artemus, referring to that night of disappointment:

> "These pretty babes, with hand in hand,
>   Went wandering up and down,
> But never more could see the man
>   Approaching from the town."

There were a few faithful friends, and a few dauntless and curiosity-led members of the public, who, regardless of the pitiless inclemency of the night, ventured to make their way through the storm. The lecture was given, and thoroughly enjoyed by the scanty audience. When the lecturer and his agent came to make up the accounts the next day, the pecuniary loss amounted to a little more than thirty dollars. It was the first and the last lecture which Artemus Ward gave in Clinton Hall. But the snowstorm alone was to blame.

New York can do well in the way of snowstorms occasionally. And the pride which a patriotic American can manifest in the snowy capabilities of his country is well illustrated by the story of the "Down-Eastern" youth who was shown in England a picture of a snowy landscape painted by a Royal Academician. "I guess that's not much like our snow," said he. "Our snow is whiter and thicker, and colder-looking, and a deal more snowy than that."

"But do not you consider the snow excellently painted?" observed the exhibitor of the picture.

"Painted!" replied the American with disgust. "Do you call that painted? I hev a brother who is an artist tu home, and he painted a snow-picture so natural, sir, that my sister-in-law left her little baby a sleeping in the cradle close by it, and when she got back to the room, the child was frozen to death. Our snow's too cold to bear painting. No sir, nohow."

◦ 10 ◦

Washington and Philadelphia · An Embalmer's Workshop · Sixty Minutes of Africa in the City of Brotherly Love

"THE *Beautiful Art of Embalming the Dead taught in Six Lessons.*"— That among other strange announcements attracted my attention as I hurried into Washington on business one day during the war. The ghastly oddity of the notice struck me forcibly; but Washington was full of horrors just then, and there were other public intimations quite as startling. My engagements took me to Willard's Hotel, where the military element was so strongly represented, that the house I had previously known as the most fashionable hotel in the city had become more like a barracks than a hotel. Soldiers were thronging round the door-way; officers in blue uniform, and wearing cocked hats, were parading themselves in the passages; and the clank of military heels resounded through the various rooms on the basement-floor. Troops were departing down the Potomac by steamer, to be landed at Aquia Creek, and detachment after detachment was being sent across the Long Bridge to see service on the fields of Virginia. Washington was a scene of confusion, excitement, dissipation, and uproar. Never at any time the most delightful of cities, it was just then one of the most annoying and most to be avoided.

The hotel-clerk at Willard's knew me. When I asked him to be accommodated with a bed, he apologized for not being able to offer me any thing better, and told me that there was only one to spare, but that it was in a room where there were seventeen others. I went to look at it. There was a soldier in a state of mad intoxication on the bed next to the one that I could have. I declined the offer, and made up my mind to seek rest elsewhere. Passing out of the hotel, I was roughly pushed against a gentleman who was just entering. As our faces met I recognized an old acquaintance, whom I had last seen in New York, and who was then practising the profession of a dentist. Before he took to dentistry he had been a showman, and had managed very successfully a theatrical company.

"What are you doing in Washington?" I asked, after the first few words of recognition had been spoken. "Have you come down to set the edge of the soldiers' teeth before going to battle, that they may have no trouble in biting cartridges?"

"No; I have given up dentist work for a time," was his reply. "I am an embalmer."

"And have you an establishment in Washington?"

"Yes; come and see me. My place is on the Avenue. Here is my card."

He gave it me, and I read "*Dr. Charles Brown, Embalmer of the Dead. Office, Pennsylvania Avenue, Washington, D. C.*" I had my lodgings for the night to look after before doing any thing else. So, taking the card, I promised to call and see the doctor on the following day.

Next morning, having transacted the business which had taken me to Washington, I strolled up Pennsylvania Avenue in search of the embalming establishment. I found it to be on the right side of the road going up towards the Capitol. The purpose to which it was devoted was advertised by means of a sign painted in very large letters. Some men were taking in the body of a dead soldier as I arrived.

Dr. Brown being within, I readily obtained admission. There was a large apartment on the level of the street, the windows of which were so obscured as to balk the curious gaze of the world without. At one time the apartment had apparently been used for a store-room. But at the period of my visit it was turned into a workshop, where the artists of death were busily employed. Placed on tressels in various parts of the room were the bodies of eleven soldiers, some already embalmed, and others waiting for the doctor to commence or complete the process. Business was brisk with the doctor, and Virginia was yielding him a plentiful harvest.

In the United States it is a common and a loving desire to wish to preserve the body of a dead relative or friend, that it may be inspected months or years after death. Americans resemble the old Egyptians rather than the ancient Romans, in preferring the mummy to the cinerulent urn. Even at home in their great cities, when death comes among them, it is customary to call in the services of the embalmer. In the cemeteries of Greenwood and of Mount Auburn there are many silent inhabitants resting on stone shelves, their faces still visible, and

CARL A. RUDISILL LIBRARY
LENOIR-RHYNE COLLEGE

wearing something like the look of life, though the bunches of flowers placed upon their breasts have long since faded into little heaps of brown vegetable matter. During the war, brave sons fell in battle, and heroic husbands left the soft delights of home to uphold their flag on the contested field, and there met their death: fond mothers and heart-broken wives wished to see the faces of those they had loved and lost—wished the dead body to be sent to them a thousand miles away—wished to show their children once again the features of him who had once made home so happy. To them the embalmer stepped kindly in, as the last friend whom Death had left them to appeal to, as one was more kindly than the grave-digger and more consolatory at the moment than even the priest. Hence the reason of the strange signs in the city of Washington.

The doctor was appropriately dressed for his business. His assistants were around him. He had just completed the injection of a body recently brought to him to be preserved, and was contemplating his work with satisfaction.

"This is very different to being a showman, and far more unpleasant," I remarked. "How came you to take up with so strange an occupation?"

"It is my patent," he replied. "The process is the new French one. I went to Paris. Got it there. Have patented it for the States. I have another establishment in the West, and I grant licenses for the use of the invention. See," said he, showing me a figure which appeared to be life-like, the face having been carefully painted, and glass eyes having replaced those which death had made dim forever; "see! here is a sample of my process. The flesh is almost as hard as stone. Listen!"

He tapped the neck of the embalmed body very lightly with the handle of a paint-brush. The flesh was firm and resonant.

"Your establishment is very well situated on the Avenue," I observed; "but it is rather noisy. What is that noise overhead?"

"Oh, they have a German dancing-room up over me, and they are giving a few lessons. The noise you hear at the side and underneath comes from the printing-offices, where they are rolling off the evening paper."

Thus was death wedged in between life, in the Washington of half a dozen years ago. Neither Dr. Brown nor his assistants seemed to be struck with the horribly grotesque situation of their place of work. They

CARL A. RUDISILL LIBRARY
LENOIR RHYNE COLLEGE

worked as artists, and regarded the result of their work with similar satisfaction to that with which a painter surveys his finished picture or a sculptor examines his completed statue. If the doctor remembered his Horace, *Debemur morti nos nostraque* must have been a quotation which now and then occurred to his mind.

Having seen all that the doctor had to show me, I said to him:

"The Browns seem to me to be a very singular race. They follow eccentric pursuits. There is Artemus Ward, who represents himself to have been a showman like you. I undertand that his proper name is also Browne. Is he any relative?"

"None whatever," replied the doctor. "He is a very clever fellow, though. As I passed through Philadelphia yesterday, I noticed that he is to lecture there this evening. If you are going to New York, you should stop on your way and hear him."

The opportunity was one for which I had waited. Since I had last seen Artemus Ward in Louisville, about eighteen months previously, I had read and heard of the great reputation he had acquired as a humorous lecturer; but though I much wished to listen to him, no chance had offered itself for my so doing. In Dr. Brown's establishment I found a gentleman who also wished to gratify a similar curiosity. We arranged to go to Philadelphia together.

The train was delayed on its way from Baltimore. When we arrived at the Musical Fund Hall in Locust Street, where the lecture was to be given, we found the hall to be already crowded. Every seat was occupied, and there was that description of standing-room left which has been defined as no place for standing. Thanks to the courtesy of Mr. Beckett, the keeper of the hall, we were politely conducted into a recess on one side of the platform, where through an opening we could hear very well, and have a full view of the faces of the audience, together with a side view of the face of the lecturer.

Artemus Ward had just stepped out on the platform—a tall, thin, gentlemanly-looking young man, with light-colored flowing hair. He wore a black coat, such as in this country we wear in the morning, but which in the States passes as dress; his waistcoat was a white one, and in his hand he carried a roll of white paper, which he twitched nervously in the course of his lecture. The subject of the lecture, according to the bills, was "Sixty Minutes in Africa;" but the matter of the discourse, as I afterwards ascertained, was pretty much the same as that of the "Babes in the Wood," only that in Philadelphia, the abolition of slavery being a favorite topic, any thing about Africa was likely to be acceptable. Besides, the "Babes" had already visited Philadelphia, and Artemus was careful not to take them twice to the same place, unless specially desired.

In the book to which I have already referred, "The Lecture on the Mormons," I have detailed the characteristics of Artemus Ward's style of lecturing, and given a sample of the matter of which it was composed. Any one of his lectures, previous to the delivery of the Mormon one, was simply a heterogeneous collection of jests, interspersed with dry, witty, telling observations on the fashions and follies of mankind, and pleasantly wrapped-up sarcasms on the social and political topics of the day. The humor of the lecture was more in the man than in his matter — his manner of saying a funny thing was infinitely more funny than the thing itself. Yet his lecture was a grand display of mental fireworks, coruscation succeeding coruscation, and rocket-flight following rocket-flight, without giving his audience time to think or to count the number of pieces. While people listened they laughed. When all was over they wondered what it had been which they had listened to. When the next morning came about, they remembered several of the good things and laughed at them again.

The lecture that evening at the Musical Fund Hall was illustrated by a map of Africa, suspended at the back of the platform. Except in the way of burlesque the map was useless. The lecturer commenced by telling his audience that his subject was Africa, and alluding to some of the natural productions of that country. When he told them that it produced "the red rose, the white rose, and the neg-roes," they yelled with laughter. When he informed them that in the middle of the continent there was what was called "a howling wilderness," but that for his part he had never heard it howl nor met with any one who had, the audience shouted approbation; and when he told them that he believed the African to be his brother, but was not so fond of him as to believe him to be his sister, wife, and grandmother as well, the political feelings of the good Philadelphians were roused, and while the Democrats laughed uproariously, the Republicans enjoyed the joke with a dubious smile. All that the lecturer said was spoken by him as though it fell from his lips without premeditation; but from the position in the hall which I chanced to occupy, I could notice that his eyes were keenly fixed upon his audience, and that he carefully watched the manner in which every sentence was received. Never once did he allow his countenance to relax from its continuous grave expression. Instead of joining in the laughter he had elicited, he seemed to wonder whence it had arisen, and to be slightly annoyed that he could not speak without being laughed at. Some of his audience entered into the spirit of the affair, and were boisterously merry. Others attempted to be critical, but occasionally manifested their vexation at not being able to grasp any thing which they could criticise; and some there were who simply regarded the speaker as a lunatic, and seemed ashamed that they had caught themselves laughing at him like the rest.

There were nearly two thousand people in the hall, the heat was oppressive, and the merriest of the audience began to feel that ceaseless laughter was very hard work. Artemus Ward perceived that he had spoken long enough; and having just told a funny story, the scene of which was in Massachusetts, suddenly changed his tone of voice and said:

"Africa is my subject. You wish me to tell you something about Africa. Africa is on the map. It is on all the maps of Africa that I have ever seen. You may buy a good map of Africa for a dollar. If you study it well, you will know more about Africa than I do. It is a comprehensive subject — too vast, I assure you, for me to enter upon to-night. You would not wish me to — I feel that — I feel it deeply, I am very sensitive. If you go home and go to bed — it will be better for you than to go with me to Africa!"

Thus abruptly, and without any further peroration, the lecture was brought to a conclusion. When it was over I sought an interview with the lecturer in his dressing-room, and reminded him of our last meeting, far away in Kentucky. Recognition was immediate and reception cordial.

"Come home with me to my room at the Continental," said Artemus.

I accepted the invitation and went, two or three of the lecturer's friends accompanying us. We had not been long in conversation when half a dozen young men entered the room and saluted the host familiarly.

"Glad to see you, boys! Sit down — take some Bourbon," said Artemus. "I hope you have had as good a house this evening as I have had."

"Pretty good," was the reply. "But we didn't have many clergymen. You must have had the best of us in the best seats, as the people in the gallery said, when the hankey-pankey fellow threw all the bon-bons out of the hat to upper-tendom in the dress circle, and flung them the wrapping-paper."

Our little party in the small room on the fourth or fifth floor of the Continental Hotel soon became convivial. In a very few minutes I ascertained that the last arrivals were the principal members of Carncross and Dixey's Minstrel Company—a negro minstrel organization as famous in Philadelphia as that of the Bryants was in New York, or that of Morris, Pell, and Trowbridge in Boston.

The gentlemen of the minstrel company were well known to Artemus Ward. Their entertainment had often afforded him amusement, while his jokes had largely assisted them in amusing the public. One of the number had been present at the Musical Fund Hall that evening, to take notes of any thing new in the lecture admitting of being dovetailed into the minstrel entertainment.

Anxious to meet Artemus, the minstrels had left their own establishment in haste. One of them, in his hurry, had failed to wash from his face all traces of the burnt-cork coloring he had worn during the concert. His friends noticed the omission, and some little banter passed. As the professional gentleman wiped away the black marks, he remarked to his host:

"I am as bad as Mr. B—— was when being thanked by Queen Victoria."

Any thing about Queen Victoria being very interesting on the other side of the Atlantic, the gentleman was asked to explain.

"I was once in the company of the H—— Theatre," said he. "Mr. B—— was the manager. The play was 'The Wicked Wife.' Queen Victoria was present. The manager had to see her Majesty out of the box; and his stage-manager advised him to hurry up with his washing, lose no time, and be ready to bow her Majesty to her carriage. Mr. B—— is a little hard of hearing. He made haste, and was rubbing his eyes dry when he met the Queen coming out of her box. 'Ah! Mr. B——,' said her Majesty, 'I see that this beautiful piece has made you cry, as it has me. I have been to see it four times.' The manager did not catch the words. 'Your Majesty,' said he—'what did you please to remark?' 'I said that it is a very beautiful piece, and do not wonder that it made you cry.'

'Yes, your Majesty,' replied Mr. B——, 'I washed in a hurry, and haven't got the soap out of my eyes.' "

The story was well received. It was one which I had not previously heard, and made a note of accordingly.

The gentlemen appeared to be inclined to personality in their jests, and one of them accusing the other of a want of veracity in his statements, the accused retorted on the accuser by saying:

"You bring to my mind the fellow who went stumping the country down South. He made a speech, and he told more lies in the course of it than there are bricks in Philadelphia. Presently he paused and said, 'Now, gentlemen, what do you think?' 'Think!' said one of his audience—'Well, I reckon that if you and I were to stump this part of Alabama together, we would tell more lies than any other two men in the State, sir; and I'd not say a word myself during the whole time, sir."

Thus pleasantly did the visitors of the evening beguile the time. There were some very talented artistes among the members of Carncross and Dixey's band. Philadelphia has always of late years maintained a good band of minstrels, some of them being no less enterprising than humorous. Perhaps one of the best performances ever given by minstrels in the Quaker City, was that wherein they burlesqued a famous exploit of which the hero was the well-known comedian, Mr. John Brougham.

Before narrating what Mr. Brougham did, or telling how the minstrels burlesqued it, let me explain the meaning of the word "Gag'—a most expressive word in the lips of the showman. Used as a noun, "a gag" is something added to another thing to give it factitious and extrinsic interest; and used as a verb, "to gag" a show, is to devise or invent some method of raising excitement which shall either be for the purpose of starting the show well on its way, or for drawing attention to it anew if its interest is diminishing. The good gag is the showman's happy thought. To the professor of the art of showing, the theory and practice of "gagging" are matters of serious study. Practised skillfully, so as to whet the appetite of the public without cloying it, success is the result. In the hands of a bungler there results disgust in the mind of the public.

Mr. John Brougham had for some time been playing in a favorite piece at New York. His popularity was very great. He had played the same piece at Philadelphia, where also his popularity was assured. Philadelphia and New York are nearly as far apart as London and Birmingham. Could not Mr. John Brougham's celebrity be greatly increased, and considerable money made by his playing the same piece in both the cities on the same night? That was the "gag" which struck the mind of Mr. Brougham, or of his speculative and clever friend, Mr. Jarrett. When an American conceives a happy idea, he carries it into execution immediately, if possible. So the two performances were settled upon, advertised, "worked up," and accomplished. The play was acted in New York to a crowded house. A ferryboat was waiting to convey actors, actresses, and as many of the New York audience as chose to accompany them, across the river to Jersey City. There an express train, with many cars attached, received its histrionic cargo of passengers, and at once started at full speed through the State of New Jersey to Philadelphia. And at Philadelphia the same play was again played that had already been performed that evening in New York, the same artists performing, and among the spectators being many who, not being content with having seen the performance in one city, had rushed a hundred miles to see it repeated in another.

Always on the look-out for novelty, so good a "gag" was not to be lost sight of by the Philadelphian minstrels. Forthwith a poster was issued to the effect that Mr. John Brougham's feat would be entirely eclipsed by the gentlemen of the "burnt-cork opera." There are two halls at opposite extremities of Philadelphia. The minstrels pledged themselves to give the same performance at both on one and the same evening, and to make the journey from one to the other, as well as convey as many of the audience as were willing to accompany them — *in wheelbarrows!*

A plenteous supply of wheelbarrows was obtained, and the enterprise successfully conducted. Philadelphia, usually one of the most demure, respectable, and properly conducted of cities, never swerved more from its pleasant routine of dullness than when it turned out some thousands of order-loving citizens to yell "Bravo!" to a troupe of artistes, dressed in black, their faces being black also, but their shirt collars large and white, their musical instruments in their hands, and they themselves whirled through the town at full speed in a score or two of wheelbarrows. The gag answered its purpose. One of the wheelbarrows was required to take the proceeds to the bank.

Artemus Ward, and Carncross and Dixey's Minstrels, seated in the little room at the Continental Hotel, soon became engaged in a warm discussion relative to the respective professional merits of the sons of Mr. E. P. Christy, the once famous minstrel of New York. And now, as I write, gentlemen in London are contending as to who has the right to the title of Christy Minstrels in this country. None of the sons of him who bore the name are, I believe, alive at the present time. Not more suggestive of melancholy reflection to Hamlet is the tossing up out of the grave the skull of poor Yorick, than was it to see in a law court of the United States the last ghastly jest in which the originator of the Christies figured. In a fit of mental aberration Mr. E. P. Christy threw himself out of the window of his house. He was not killed by the fall, but lived for many weeks, and while so living made a will. After his death, the amount of property he left being large, that will was contested. It was argued that the injury he had sustained by the fall from the window had been of a nature to render it impossible that he should afterwards be of sound mind. In his lifetime he had often handled dexterously the "bones" with which mock Ethiopians are apt to "discourse most eloquent music." After his death two of his own bones — the *atlas* and *axis* of the cervical vertebrae, were tossed across the table from lawyer to lawyer, in the course of the discussion in open court as to whether or not the injuries they evidenced were not sufficient to prove that the nervous system of the poor minstrel must have been so affected as to have rendered him incapable of performing any legal act or deed.

"I had a new joke in my lecture to-night," said Artemus, addressing his Philadelphian friends. "If George Christy had known I was going to have it, he would have travelled a hundred miles to borrow it for his own. As it is, I have no doubt that he will have it telegraphed to him to-morrow. But come, gentlemen, I hear there is a nigger-ball on to-night. Shall we go?"

The suggestion was received with satisfaction. One of the company was in possession of a sufficient number of tickets of admission, and we started for a distant part of the city where the ball was to take place. I think that the name of the building was Mahogany Hall, but in this I may be mistaken.

Whether in freedom or in slavery, the negro race are proverbially fond of gayety, and especially delight in dancing. The ball to which we went was given by the dark-colored population of Philadelphia, and no white people were admitted unless they were well known to the committee. About a hundred negroes and nearly that number of negresses were present when we arrived. The colored gentlemen were dressed in evening costume, and seemed for the most part to be waiters from the various hotels. Their partners were arrayed in finery of the most glaring description. Some of the ladies were attired in white muslin, with bright blue ribbons of most unnecessary length. One lady of very large proportions, and of remarkably broad features, wore a ruby-colored dress with flounces to it of a gamboge tint; and there was one who had attired herself in bloomer-costume, her coat or outer dress being of lilac color, with a gilt leathern cincture round her waist, and her pantalettes of a pale-green hue, terminating in white frills. Every lady had a bouquet of enormous size; and both ladies and gentlemen bore evidence, in the beads of moisture on the face, to the spirit with which they were entering into the enjoyment of the evening.

For a band, the ball committee had provided six instruments—two violins, one double-bass, a flageolet, a flute, and a triangle. Perched on an elevation at the end of the room was the master of the ceremonies calling out the figures of the dance.

"Ladies' Chain—Hurry up, ladies! Set and turn partners—Gen'elmen, what are you 'bout, mind de figgers. Fus' couple 'vance! Now retire—'vance again. Now de gen'elmen returns. Lebe lady on de left of de op'site gen'elman. De ladies cross to op'site sides. Hurry up—hurry up! Change de corners. Gen'elmen pass 'tween de ladies. Now de ladies cross. De gen'elmen go back to dare places—Fus'rate, bery fus'rate! Now fus' copple set and turn—Good! Now den, all of ye, de last figger!"

The embalming office of Dr. Brown in the morning—the negro ball in the evening! In the life of the showman, light and shade are often so contrasted!

◦ 11 ◦

Across the Continent · A Strange Telegram · The Babes Transformed into Ghosts

THERE came a message by telegraph three thousand five hundred miles or thereabouts across the American Continent. On its way that message had passed through the mining camps of California, darted over the summit of the Sierra Nevada, traversed the region of the silver miners, and passed into a little wooden house on one side of Main Street, Salt Lake City, where it paused for a few minutes to take fresh electric breath, and then to start out anew from the city of the Mormons to hasten onward to the city of New York.

When the telegraph clerk received it at his lonely little office in Salt Lake City, he wondered at its meaning. Months afterwards he told me that he did. His business was to send it onward.

Onward it went, flying over the heights of the Rocky Mountains and swooping down upon the boundless plains of Colorado and Nebraska. Indians attired in furs and feathers, the face painted, the hand grasping a spear, looked up at the wires as the message hastened on; prairie dogs, each standing on his own little mound of earth, yelped as the message flew by; and the backwoodsman, resting on his axe in the newly-felled clearing, amused himself by thinking what those wires, of which the wind of the wilderness was making an Æolian harp, could possibly be transmitting from one side of America to the other.

When the message arrived at New York it read thus:

> "*Thomas Maguire, Opera-house, San Francisco,
> California,
> to
> Artemus Ward, New York City.*
> What will you take for forty nights in California?"

The verb "to take" has various significations. Hence the message required to be carefully studied. After giving to it the gravest consideration, Artemus Ward returned the following answer:

> *"Artemus Ward, New York City,*
> *to*
> *Thomas Maguire, Opera-house, San Francisco,*
> *California,*
> BRANDY AND WATER."

Puzzled as the telegraph clerk in Salt Lake City was with the message from San Francisco, he was still more so with the reply from New York. Had the Indians on the plains been able to read the message as it flew by them, they would have been disposed to wonder what sort of a person it was who offered to take "fire-water" for forty nights in California. But the most puzzled man of all was Mr. Maguire when the answer was brought to him, as he stood sunning himself in front of his Opera-house. The sort of reply he expected was "Ten thousand dollars." Then he was perhaps prepared to offer five thousand, and afterwards to "split the difference;" but "brandy and water" astounded him. He was not quite sure but that it was a sporting phrase unknown to him, and signifying a certain sum of money; just as the word "monkey" may mean five hundred pounds, and the word "pony" twenty-five pounds among the sporting fraternity of England. So Mr. Maguire took the message round to his friends and asked their interpretation of the mystery. Their reply was that it was one of Ward's "goaks," and that he undoubtedly did not desire to visit California.

Mr. Maguire's friends were not quite right in their guess; neither were they quite wrong. The telegraphic answer was certainly a joke, but Artemus Ward was anxious to see the shores of the Pacific. Why he returned so absurd a reply to the message was simply that he did not wish to engage his services to Mr. Maguire, nor any body else, but to take a trip to California on his own account and make money for himself.

Out of Mr. Maguire's perplexity some good came. The manager of the Opera-house exhibited the strange message to his friends; they told the gentlemen of the press, who soon constructed it into a paragraph for the newspapers. Once in the papers, the inquiry and the reply found their way over the continent. And when Artemus Ward did visit California, he discovered that his telegraphic answer to Mr. Maguire had resulted in one of the very best advertisements he could possibly have devised. The joke was precisely of that description which appealed to the fancy of the gold-diggers, and to the mirthful spirits of California, Oregon, and Nevada. Artemus Ward was voted to be a genial show-man.

The receipt of the telegram from San Francisco was fully sufficient, even if invitations previously received had not been amply indicative, to assure Artemus Ward that his fame had travelled beyond the Rocky Mountains, and that he had good reason to entertain the idea of taking a trip to the gold regions of the Pacific. The "Babes in the Wood" had become a little exhausted by travelling in the Atlantic States. They required sea-air. A sail down to the Isthmus of Panama, a skip across the Isthmus, and two weeks of pleasant steaming up the Pacific, were probably all that was needed for their health. After having consulted many friends on the subject, Artemus sent a message to me, asking me to meet him at the Revere House in Broadway, New York.

"What do you think of my going to California?" he asked, when, responding to his message, I found him waiting my arrival.

My opinion was to the effect that he could not pay a visit to any country likely to yield him more profit, if he went to it as a lecturer and did not stay too long. I had known the Golden State of the Union at a time when its mines were easily worked, when large nuggets of gold were frequently found, when the mining camps were prosperous, and when miners spent their money with careless prodigality. Being well aware that affairs had changed, and, that although San Francisco had increased largely in wealth and population, the interior of the country was not in equally as flourishing condition, I advised a brief visit, a rapid march through the State, lecturing at one town to-night and at another to-morrow evening, and a speedy return to New York with the dollars resulting from the enterprise.

Artemus listened to that which I had to say, and then desired to know if I would join him in the trip, to act as agent and manager. He made various proposals, and to one of them I readily assented. Thus much being arranged, it became a question whether we should return by the same route that we intended to take in going out, or whether we should come home across the plains, and drop in among the Mormons at Salt Lake City.

To this latter proposal there was one great objection. We were going to California in the autumn—"the fall" as Americans term that season of the year. By the time we had visited the various mining towns the winter season would have arrived. To cross the American desert in winter, and to traverse the Rocky Mountains amidst snow and ice, were by no means agreeable prospects. I suggested another plan, but Artemus was strong in his desire to see Brigham Young.

"There was a man in the next street to me who committed suicide a week ago because he could not get on with two wives," said Artemus. "I want to see how a man can get along who has fifty."

I remarked, in reply, that my curiosity was more excited relative to the fifty ladies who lived under the dominion of one lord. Finally, an arrangement was concluded that Artemus Ward and I should come back from California by way of Salt Lake, if we found the route to be open, practicable, and comparatively free from danger, at the termination of our visit to the towns of the Pacific coast; but that if circumstances were not favorable to our making the acquaintance of the Mormons, we should run up to British Columbia, return to California, take the steamer again to Panama, and pay a flying visit to the West Indies. To me the greater part of the ground to be gone over was already known; but to my intended companion it possessed the charm of novelty, and offered plenteous scope for him to meet with much humorous incident, as well as to see many strange characters.

Some forethought was devoted to the preparations for the journey, in order that the trip might be productive of pecuniary success. Artemus Ward's publisher, Mr. G. W. Carleton, of Broadway, undertook to publish a book, the materials for which were to be collected during our stay among the Mormons. It was settled that I should go to California by the mail steamer preceding that in which the lecturer himself was to make the voyage. I was to take with me the requisite posters by the aid of which, among other means also to be used, the coming of Artemus Ward to the Land of Gold was to be made publicly known, and the miners were to be informed that he would "Speak a Piece" to them on his arrival. When Mr. Booth, the printer, had printed the bills and I was seeing them duly packed, Artemus observed:

"I hope you have kept a couple of bills out loose?"

I told him that I had reserved a dozen to take with me in my travelling-valise, and intended to have one posted at Aspinwall, another at Panama, and one or two in the Mexican towns of Acapulco and Mazatlan, if the steamer chanced to put in at both.

"That's all very well," said Artemus; "but I want you to have two loose in your pocket, with a hammer and some nails."

"To use where?" I asked.

He answered me gravely:

"When the steamer gets to San Francisco it will have to pass through the Golden Gate.* Now I have never seen that gate myself; but as you go through I want you to stop the steamer, and just nail up one of my bills on each side of the gate."

Besides posters, I was provided with some lithograph portraits of the lecturer, and a hundred copies of "Artemus Ward, His Book." The volumes were nicely bound in cloth, and were intended to be used as presentation copies to editors, civic functionaries, and clergymen. There was a thorough understanding between Artemus and myself that the lecturing expedition was to be regarded in the light of a scheme for making money, and that no feeling of delicacy relative to attracting the attention of the public by means of extensive advertising was to be allowed to stand in the way of doing any thing that might conduce to popularity and profit. That which would not do in steady-going old Boston might answer very well in lively and excitable San Francisco.

I notified Artemus, in pleasantry, that if I found other means to fail in getting up rapid excitement about him in the Californian metropolis, I should organize a torch-light procession on the night of his arrival.

"Do it before I arrive," said he; "and have a great wax-figure of me in a chariot, with my 'Babes' on each side of me."

He was a genial showman, and thoroughly understood his profession.

In the course of the few weeks that elapsed between the time that our preliminaries were settled and that the steamer on which I was going was to sail, there was an opportunity for Artemus Ward to lecture again in New York. The suggestion was made to him, I believe, by his friend Mr. De Walden, who offered to engage the lecturer as a speculation. Poor Artemus remembered his previous experience at Clinton Hall, and felt some reluctance; but the great inducement was, that it would cause his name to be brought again before the public in the New York papers, and that the popularity so gained would be capital on which to trade in California. Mr. De Walden proposed that the lecture should

---

*The name of the entrance to the harbor of San Francisco.

be given in Niblo's Saloon,* a very handsome room adjoining the large theatre known as Niblo's Garden. To this proposal Artemus Ward agreed.

Where the lecture should be given having been arranged, the title of it became a matter of discussion. As for the matter, there was no difficulty. The well-tried jokes which, as "orient pearls at random strung," had done duty in "The Babes in the Wood," and in "Sixty Minutes in Africa," were all ready to be made available, but the lecture required to have a new and catching title.

Just at that period "Pepper's Ghost," as the famous ghost illusion was familiarly termed, had attained to great notoriety in England, and had been imported to America. Two or three speculative comedians had taken a trip across the Atlantic, seen how the "Ghost" was worked in London, and brought it over to the United States. In a very short time itinerant "stars" were travelling in every direction, carrying with them huge sheets of plate-glass instead of extensive wardrobes. Wallack's Theatre was the first to produce the "Ghost" in New York city. The Boston Theatre very quickly followed: "Macbeth," "Hamlet," "Richard the Third," and half a dozen new plays were made the vehicles for exhibiting the reflective powers of plate-glass; and the "Ghost" became the dominant sensation. What better title could Artemus select for his lecture? Not that he knew any thing about the mechanism of the ghostly illusion, nor that he intended to make it the subject of his discourse. The public who came to hear him, if they knew any thing at all of Artemus Ward, came with the intention to laugh—not to be instructed in optics. The few who were not familiar with the style of the lecturer enjoyed the burlesque, and passed the joke on to their friends.

Here is the way in which the entertainment was announced. It will be perceived that it is entitled an "Entirely New Comic Oration," and that the orator is styled "The Eminent Young American Humorist." I have reason to believe that Mr. De Walden was guilty of these deviations from Artemus Ward's usual manner of making his announcements. A "comic oration" was thought to suggest something more attractive than would have been implied by advertising a humorous lecture.

---

*Since then, I believe, the saloon has been converted into the dining-room of the Metropolitan Hotel.

NIBLO'S SALOON,

568 BROADWAY.

———

WEDNESDAY EVENING,

September 30, 1863.

———

THE EMINENT YOUNG AMERICAN HUMORIST,

ARTEMUS WARD,

(CHARLES F. BROWNE,)

IN HIS ENTIRELY NEW COMIC ORATION,

THE GHOSTS.

———

Admission Fifty Cents.

The "comic oration" was successful. Niblo's Saloon was crowded, and the orator had a fair start for California. I had arranged to land there a fortnight before him; and during the interval that was to elapse between the sailing of the steamer on which my passage was taken and that which was to take him, he determined to go down to Maine and bid a temporary farewell to his relatives.

In the slang of the stage, for "the ghost" to "walk" simply means that when salary-day arrives there is money in the treasury. It is a sorry day for the actor—and such days have been known even in the largest theatres of London—when "no ghost walks!" As Artemus Ward placed in my hands the morning papers of New York with the report in them of the "Oration" on "The Ghosts," he smilingly observed:

"Take them with you, and have the notices copied. We shall want the ghost to walk in California!"

And the ghost did walk there with the steps of a strong and lusty spirit.

๐ 12 ๐

The Atlantic Ocean
Showmen on the Sea

OFF to California! The third day of October, 1863, is bright, breezy, and sunny. The "North Star" is a large and sea-worthy steamer. Captain Jones is a cheery, ruddy-faced, good-tempered-looking captain, and his officers seem to be the right men to manage the business of the vessel on her voyage from New York to Aspinwall.

It wants a few minutes to noon. The "North Star" is alongside of Pier No. 3, North River, and at twelve o'clock she is to sail. Her decks are crowded with passengers starting for the land of gold. The rickety, battered, dirty, wooden pier is equally as crowded, and the policeman who stands at the gate can not keep back the thronging multitude who are pressing in to bid "good-bye" to departing friends. Twelve o'clock has arrived, and as the bell of the City Hall clock announces the arrival of noon the paddle-wheels of the steamer begin to revolve.

Handkerchiefs are waved, huzzas are given, hats are flourished, hands are kissed to those who throw kisses back in return. There is one poor lady who has come to bid farewell to him she loves, and who, as the steamer moves off, sinks fainting among the cheering, weeping crowd. The Stars and Stripes are flying above us—the "us" comprising more than a thousand tightly-packed passengers. To the stern of our steamer is the Hudson River. We are heading for New York Bay. New York itself is on the left, Jersey City on the right, and Staten Island, green and shady, in front.

Two other steamers start almost at the same minute. The one ahead is the "Illinois," also laden with passengers for California, but belonging to the "M. O. Roberts Line;" while the "North Star" is owned by Commodore Vanderbilt, and carries the United States mails. The steamer closely following ours is the "Bavaria," bound for Hamburg.

In little more than an hour we are steaming through "The Narrows." Brooklyn—the "City of Churches"—has just been passed and is off our port quarter. Staten Island is to starboard. Away ahead is

Coney Island, with its wilderness of sand, the resort of happy New Yorkers on Sunday. To the left of it, but near to us, is Bath, where, in a snug villa just among the trees, lives Mr. Barney Williams, the actor; and there is the Bath Hotel, at one of the windows of which Carlotta Patti is probably watching our steamer slide by. Almost hidden by trees, but close to the shore on the Brooklyn side, is a small hostelry known as the Beach House, kept by a buxom English landlady named Mrs. Dobbinson, and down to it I know that kindly friends have come with telescopes to take a parting glance as the "North Star" steams rapidly onward.

Three o'clock and our steamer has made Sandy Hook. We stop to part from our pilot, and to send off with him two detectives who have come with us down the bay to make search for a murderer. On Sandy Hook we may observe that a fort is being built; and, if we noticed carefully as we steamed through the Narrows, between Fort Richmond on the one side and Fort Hamilton on the other, we might have wondered whether the stoutest ship of an enemy could by any possibility steam up the bay unscathed, to inflict injury on the city of New York.

Sandy Hook is passed. The highlands of Navesink are in sight; and as the "Bavaria" steams off to the east towards the Old World, the "North Star" ploughs her way down the Atlantic, to take us to the first station on the road towards the world which is new.

Pleasant it is to feel the ocean breezes disporting around us—to see the green waves rolling, mounting, leaping, and prancing on every side—to watch the white spray playing merrily in our path, and the shadows of the scudding clouds reflected in the sunlit waters. After all, there is something jolly in the life of a "show-artist"—to use a phrase invented by a friend. There is jollity in the company amidst which he is thrown, jollity in the variable life with which he becomes acquainted, and exquisite jollity in the feelings with which he welcomes the change from the theatre or the hall, with its atmosphere of gas-smoke and the breathings of a multitude, to the enjoyment of unobstructed sunlight, and of the uncontaminated air wafted over the stimulating and health-giving ocean.

We have made 177 miles in our first day's run. The weather is pleasant. People around are chatty, and much gratuitous information is offered. For instance, the captain is pointed out as being a remarkable man. We are told that he commanded the "Ariel" when she was seized by Captain Semmes of the "Alabama," and that he bonded her for over two hundred thousand dollars, "payable three months after the recognition of the Southern Confederacy." We are told that his pay on board the "North Star" is two hundred and fifty dollars per month and a percentage on the freight. Then we are told that the management of the Vanderbilt line of steamers is so close and niggardly that our doctor has to act as purser also; that he is mail agent, freight agent, and express agent into the bargain, and that his pay is only fifty dollars per month. We learn that we have one thousand three hundred souls on board, of which number six hundred are in the steerage; and we are informed that, in consequence of the "North Star" being so crowded, there will have to be a first and second table for each class of passengers, as well as extra tables for the children, so that from the first meal at six in the morning the stewards and waiters will be employed at furnishing meals till seven o'clock in the evening. But the stewards are gentlemen of color, and are well accustomed to the work. At sea they have to bestir themselves. When on shore they seek for enjoyment with avidity, and appreciate fully the luxury of idleness—appreciate it with that active rather than passive sense of appreciation which indolence communicates to the mind of the African.

Reeling up to us comes a poor muddled fellow who has just been to the "bar" behind the wheel-house, where he has visited again and again for the last few hours. In his weak, whisky-addled brain there is a strange mixture of patriotism and love of the sea. He was inebriated when he came on board, and as we steamed out of New York he commenced singing a song, the only words distinguishable in which were:

"Spread wide the sails,
And blow the gales;
The old flag's floating o'er us!"

He has been desiring the sails to spread, and bidding the gales to blow, all through the night. By midnight he had become a little confused, and commanded the gales to spread and the sails to blow. This morning he had a fresh relay of whisky for his breakfast; since then he has had a reinforcement of whisky for his luncheon, and now the song has become more incomprehensible. The latest version of it is:

"Spwide ol'gales,
Blowth-sails;
Flag's a-fightin' o'er us!"

And he is desirous of fighting some one himself. Floundering along, he comes plump against the man who is hauling up the ashes from the engine-room. In a moment the bucket of ashes is emptied over the singer's head, and "the old flag" is grievously dusty.

Our second day at sea is a little more orderly than our first. But Mr. Daly is doing a good business in his bar behind the wheel-house. He charges ten cents a drink for beer and fifteen cents for spirits. His drinks are bad, but his customers many.

We left New York on Saturday at noon. It is now five o'clock on Tuesday morning, and we are passing stormy Cape Hatteras, off which so many a brave ship has gone down. The sea is true to Cape Hatteras, and will not let the "North Star" pass without causing it to behave in a most unsteady manner for a fixed star with so good a reputation for keeping its place.

Yesterday the weather was chilly. To-day we feel pleasantly warm, yet the sun is not shining any more brightly. Whence the agreeable change? Please to notice the blue tint of the water in our wake, and the sea-weed tossing on the crests of the waves around us. We are passing across the Gulf Stream. The warm balmy air owes its warmth to that bright blue water which has laved sunnier shores than even those of the Carolinas. We shall leave the Gulf Stream in the afternoon, and again see the green waves and feel the bracing breezes of the Atlantic. Along paths of sapphire and on a road of emerald we are hastening to the Land of Gold.

"No lights allowed on deck in the evening." Why an order so arbitrary? "The ship is to be kept perfectly dark." Why the precaution? Simply because we are sailing under the Stars and Stripes, and may fall in with privateers. Captain Jones has a lively remembrance of his having once fallen a prey to Captain Raphael Semmes; and as the "Ariel" was not a tricksy spirit enough to keep out of the way of danger, our careful commander prudently consults our safety by not allowing the "North Star" to shine. We shall be convoyed by-and-by, but the time is not yet. Meanwhile we sneak along in the dark, and take our chance of being run down by any vessel that may happen to meet us in the gloom.

Latitude 28° 35' N., by noon on Wednesday. The indicator informs us that our paddle-wheels have made 65,000 revolutions since we left New York. "They have to do about 180,000," replies the engineer, to an inquiry from a passenger relative to how many turns of the paddlewheel are averaged between New York and Aspinwall—a distance of about 1980 miles.

Magnificent weather! Sunset. A golden glow over cloudless sky and waveless, sparkling ocean. Away in the direction of Florida a few clouds are discernible, but of the fleeciest texture, while the heaven in which they float is radiant with tints of gleaming amber, royal purple, and a green that has all the delicate beauty of the beryl. We seem to breathe sunlight with every breath of air.

On an evening so delightful every passenger is on deck. Let us notice a few of them, and we shall see that we are not the only showman on board.

There, in a rocking-chair, sits a lady who has been reading George Eliot's "Romola" all day. Her fingers are blazing with diamond rings, and the little brooch with which her shawl is fastened is worth at least a thousand dollars. Very lady-like in her manner, very pleasant to converse with, she can maintain a conversation in three different languages, and can quote poetry to you by the volume. You would hardly think her to be the wife of a professional gambler, and a woman who has helped to ruin a score of men. But we, who happened to know her, know that she is that which we say. By chance, also, we know that she is not going on with us to California, but will leave us at Panama on her way to Valparaiso, whither she is travelling to look at some property recently won by her husband at the gambling-table. Reading "Romola" as she is, you would give her credit for being better mated and better minded. The story of Savonarola and those diamond-ringed fingers hardly accord. Yet they are both parts of a show. She wears the diamonds to attract some; she reads that she may be able to attract others. We who have travelled know.

There is another lady, who has gleaming white teeth, which she will persist in causing you to see. She is conversing with the owner of one of the wealthiest estates in California. Many years ago she appeared as an actress at the Adelphi Theatre, in London. Now she is a Spiritualist, and is going out to San Francisco to lecture on Spiritualism. A rapping-table constitutes her show.

Beyond her is a clergyman whose talent is well known, and whose eloquence has rendered him remarkable. He belongs to the sect of the Universalists, and preaches sermons wherein he quotes largely from the profane writers. Shakspeare in the pulpit is his show.

Just beside the clergyman is a lithe, active, beady-eyed little man, who has smoked cigars from the time we left New York till now, and will continue to smoke them from here to South America, whither he is going to purchase some horses of a peculiar breed. When we met him years ago he owned a circus. Now he is the proprietor of a "race-track," and of some very good trotting ponies. The horse constitutes his show.

Here is a real showman in the person of a friend from Philadelphia, who is travelling to San Francisco to take a theatre and produce his own plays. He has brought a boxful with him. None of the Philadelphian managers will play them. Hence he is going to California to hire theatres and play them himself.

Here also is another genuine "show artist." He plays the violoncello. Last evening he became confidential. And, in the course of conversation, stated that his violoncello is on board, contained in a box made from the wood of a tree which overshadowed his birth-place. He is voyaging to California to try change of air, his lungs being weak. "If I die," says he, "I intend to be buried in that violoncello-case. It is made large enough. Two partitions take out, and so make it a comfortable coffin."

Poor violoncellist! He has never been to England, and does not know of the eccentricity of an English provincial manager whose habits were parsimonious, who rambled much from town to town, and whose wife was in a very ailing condition. Rambling as he did, he had to take a theatrical wardrobe with him. The wardrobe required a packing-case, and the wife would one day require a coffin. The manager chanced to be at a theatre where wood had been left behind by a previous lessee, and where he had to engage a stage carpenter. For motives of economy he had a strong coffin made to pack his wife's stage dresses in. When the poor wife died the coffin was ready.

There are many others on board the "North Star" this bright evening who are showmen or show-women, in the fullest sense of the word. There is a Californian legislator who is going to bring in a new Bill this coming session at Sacramento. He is a capital "wire-puller," and will work his Bill with the use of the same arts to gain popularity which the showman employs for his show. Beside him is a fashionable milliner from New York, who is travelling to San Francisco with patterns with which she will open an exhibition that will bedazzle many a fair Californian, and cause the loss of some scores of dollars to many a stout son of the Pacific. Showfolk every one, *Messieurs et Mesdames*, disguise it how you may. On this great stage of twenty-four thousand miles in circumference, with its "sinks" and "traps," its shifting scenes and illusory "gauzes," its complex machinery, moved by influences from above or mechanism beneath, the play goes bravely on; and are not "all the men and women merely players?"

Thursday evening now, and we are off Turk's Island. At midnight we descry out at sea two red lights with a white one over them. Our captain knows those lights. He has been waiting and watching for them. They are on the "San Jago de Cuba," the steamer destined to keep us company and protect us as we steam along between Cuba and San Domingo. So up go our lights also. He who wishes to light a cigar on the deck may fearlessly use his matchbox. We have our big brother to fight for us. Who's afraid now?

All day on Friday the convoy steamer continues to play around us. She is very small, has eight guns and a pivot one at her stern. The "walking-beam" of her engine is fully exposed to view. If Captain Raphael Semmes should chance to put in an appearance and fire one well-directed shot at that walking beam, would our big brother be able to fight for us then? The question *will* suggest itself.

Thanks, however, to the company of the "San Jago de Cuba," we can have lights on the deck to-night. We are within the tropics and are too warm to do any thing during the day but loll lazily in shady places. So in the evening we desire amusement. A concert is proposed and given. One of the officers can play a guitar, and many of the ladies can sing.

Here is the programme of our concert—"John Brown's Body," "Columbia the Gem of the Ocean," "My Country, 'tis of Thee," "Rally Round the Flag, Boys," "Kingdom comin'," "Annie of the Vale," "Do they Think of me at Home?" and "The Star-Spangled Banner." The very names of our songs are indicative of time, place, and circumstances. American is shooting down American in that fair land to the north of the waters on which we steam and sing.

Saturday finds us in the Caribbean Sea. On Sunday at noon we are 328 miles from Aspinwall. After prayers, up with the baggage to the weighing-machine, that every passenger may know how much he has to pay extra for that which belongs to him before it is transferred to the Panama Railway. Monday night, and we enter Navy Bay. We sight the lighthouse at two in the morning, and cruise about till sunrise. The planet Venus has already risen. Not the same modestly bright Venus we have seen in the North, but a Venus of dazzling brilliancy, seemingly twice as large, and shining with twenty-fold splendor.

This is Colon and this is Aspinwall. The English will call it Colon. The American persists in terming it Aspinwall. Whichever name you please, ladies and gentlemen, but oblige the Captain by stepping on shore.

◦ 13 ◦

The Isthmus of Panama · Showmen in the Tropics

WE are at Aspinwall, standing on a coral reef in the Island of Manzanilla, and in the Republic of New Granada. Weary travellers who are not partial to the sea are glad to arrive at Aspinwall. Timid passengers who have a fear of fever are glad to hasten away from it as rapidly as they can. All that there is to be seen can be seen in an hour. There have been expeditious travellers who landed early in the morning and were buried by midnight.

Some such experience fell to the fate of the poor Frenchman who came here across the Isthmus, bringing with him a pet monkey. The Frenchman was a naval officer. He arrived at Aspinwall early in the morning. While he was at breakfast, his monkey made its escape. He had brought it with him from South America, and was unwilling to lose it. The monkey fled to the outskirts of the town, and its master went in pursuit. The monkey was captured in the forest which forms the background to Aspinwall. Wearied with the pursuit of the animal, and probably feeling suddenly ill, the poor Frenchman rested himself on a fallen tree, securing his captive by chaining him to the loop of one of his boots. Neither man nor monkey returned to Aspinwall that evening; but next morning the monkey made its appearance in the town dragging its master's boot after it, and with the gold band off its master's cap paraded around its neck. Search was made and the Frenchman discovered. Fever had seized him. He had died on the borders of the tropical forest.

The monkey, to free itself, had either played the part of a boot-jack, or the dying man had kicked off the boot in his last struggles with the fever-fiend.

Very grand is the appearance of that tropical forest as we view it from our place of landing. Before us is a long row of white houses built of wood, and each having a capacious verandah. Some of them are hotels, some shops, and some offices. In the distance, away behind the row of white houses, is the dense, luxuriant, richly-green swamp-forest. Still farther away in the distance is a range of mountains, misty and indistinct among the vapors which rise from the wilderness of vegetation at their base. These mountains we shall have to cross on the little railway on which we shall presently travel. In crossing them we shall traverse the narrowest portion of the backbone of the Western World. Southward it constitutes the Andes; while northward, where it becomes the Rocky Mountains, the great ribs of granite and of prophyry attached to it stretch out and form the giant sides of the North American continent.

We bid "good-bye" to Captain Jones and to the "North Star." The wharf we tread on is part of a coral reef stretching nearly a thousand feet into the bay. Ten days ago we saw cocoa-nuts for sale in the shops of New York. This morning we may see them hanging from the cocoa-nut palms. Please to notice that the wharf has a metallic roof, and that through the boarded floor the cocoa-trees shoot up and flourish, claiming their full right to the soil whereon their parent trees flourished, when Columbus in the course of his third voyage walked with the step of a conqueror where we are now hustling one another.

Queer-looking hotels are these in the row of wooden houses. One of them is named the Howard House, another the United States, and a third the St. Charles. Their touters are very anxious that we should take breakfast, and as every body else who has come by the steamer from New York seems desirous to try the novelty of breakfast on dry land, we had better imitate the example. The charge for breakfast is one dollar. We ask for a little fresh milk with our coffee. "Berry sorry, massa," replies the black attendant; "no milk. Cows don't gib any milk in Aspinwall." Then, on inquiry, we learn that we are not indebted to the Republic of New Granada for our butter; but that we have in a considerate manner brought it on with us in the steamer from the States. We offer payment in greenbacks. At once we discover that we are in the land of President Señor Mosquera, and not in that of Mr. Abraham Lincoln. "Forty per cent. discount here on greenbacks, sir. This dollar bill is worth only sixty cents." With the evergreen forest in the rear of their little town the Aspinwallians do not value greenbacks as we do.

Breakfast being over, let us take a stroll. Here is a notice posted up that "The train at ten o'clock is for steerage passengers only." Ladies and gentlemen who have voyaged first or second class on board the steamer may stay in Aspinwall till eleven o'clock. The railway runs along the open street in front of the hotels and shops. We may notice, too, that there is an Isthmus Telegraph, and that the posts which support the wires are built up of concrete, and look like stone. Wooden posts would quickly rot in this climate. Here are the ruins of half a dozen burnt houses. The fire which consumed them very nearly had a chance of consuming the whole town. Opposite the burnt houses is a steamer stranded, with her back broken. She is the "Avon," belonging to the Royal West Indian Mail Steam Packet Company, and was driven on shore in a hurricane. The locomotive getting up steam in the middle of the road is the "Obispo." She is preparing to take the steerage passengers to the Pacific.

An odd population is this we notice in the streets of Aspinwall. It has more streets than one, as you may perceive. Here we meet with Americans from the United States; a little farther on is a group of Spaniards; beyond them are some Jews; and sprinkled over the whole place are Jamaica negroes with very wide brims to their straw hats, and Jamaica negresses with very yellow handkerchiefs bound round their brows of jet.

Turn off round here to the right and we are in the native market-place, the "Mingillo" as it is called. The negroes we see here are not from the West Indies, but are the descendants of the slaves who were once owned by the Spanish rulers of the country. Here, too, are a few aboriginal Indians from San Blas, men whose ancestors the *Conquistadore* never conquered. They are in full-dress, having a piece of colored cloth tied round their loins. To men such as they are—to their forefathers, who, like them, had straight black hair and high cheek-bones, Columbus talked when he was as great a stranger on these shores as we are to-day.

We stop a little merry-faced, large-eyed, graceful negro girl who has a school-book in her hand. She goes to school, as she admits. We ask her a few questions, and finally promise her a silver quarter-dollar if she will tell us who King David was.

"Guess you s'pose I don't know who Kin' Dabid war?" she laughingly replies.

"Then say who he was, and you shall have the quarter."

"Guess you want to know 'bout de ole Kin' Dabid?"

"Yes; the old King David."

"Why de ole Kin' Dabid, massa, war de kin' who come from England to fight Gen'ral Washington in New York—S'pose I don't know?"

We give her the quarter-dollar and pass on; buying on our way five oranges for ten cents, or a "real," as they call it here, some bananas, and two bottles of claret, sold at a stall in the open street, paying for them *un peso, cuarto reales*, or one dollar and a half.

Aspinwall bears all the characteristics of a temporary town. Its birth was yesterday. It is alive to-day. To-morrow, perhaps, it will have no existence. While it is alive it does its best to take rank among the towns of the world. Our fellow-passengers are peeping into the freight dépôt of the railway. Let us take a peep also. Those huge piles of pork, beef, bread, cheese, and flour are collections from various parts of the United States, and are destined to feed the inhabitants of towns on the coast of the Pacific. Those strongly-made boxes contain gold ore from California, silver ore from Nevada, and Mexican dollars from the cities of Mexico. Heaped up to the very roof of the building we may notice bundles of sarsaparilla bark from Nicaragua, bales of quinia bark from New Granada itself, and bags of coffee and cacao from Costa Rica and Ecuador. In the corner to our right we see some tons of pearl-oyster-shells from the pearl fisheries of Panama, and here to the left are thousands of hides from all sorts of places between California and Patagonia. Here, too, is cochineal from Guatemala, indigo from San Salvador, and guano from lonely isles of the Pacific. As a commercial "show" this little town of Aspinwall acquits itself very well. Here are riches enough for any town of moderate ambition. Then why is it that there is no roof to the stone church over yonder, and why—oh, why—are those filthy, stagnant lagoons allowed to remain in the middle of the town to generate miasma and render the place more unhealthy than it would be simply from its geographical position? Has President Señor Mosquera no Board of Health, or is it thought that the turkey-buzzards, which roam at large up and down the streets picking up the offal, are sufficient Sanitary Commissioners?

Perhaps, however, there is another reason why Aspinwall does not take more care of itself, and that is a consciousness of its own fate. When the railway is completed across the American continent from New York to San Francisco, very few indeed will be the travellers to California by way of Aspinwall; and, when the canal is cut across the Isthmus of Darien, will Aspinwall be at the Atlantic end of it, or will she be left to mourn the days departed, while another town, the streets of which are not yet made, shall collect the tolls of vessels passing from the eastern to the western side of the world?*

Poor Aspinwall! The undeniable fact is that you owe your existence, after all, to what billiard-players designate as a "fluke" or a "scratch." If the adventurous Scots, who sailed for Darien in 1698, had succeeded in their enterprise, and if William III. had protected with his fleet the town of New Edinburgh, there would probably have been no Aspinwall. You are but a development of the little railway to Panama; and should the trains on that little railway cease to run, you would not be wanted in the world, nor would you make for after ages even a respectable ruin.

There is the signal! Eleven o'clock has arrived. Our engine, the "Gorgona," has her steam up. The train is ready. We take our seats. A Jamaica negro stoker shovels more coals into the furnace; Jamaica negro brakesmen attend to the machinery of the train; and Jamaica negro signal-men, having already cleared the road, notify us that we have a clear start. Our train glides slowly along the open street, past the hotels where the black chamber-maids are lolling over the verandah, past the Jew slop-shops and the Yankee stores, past the stalls in the street at which are being vended fresh oranges with their rinds still green, and bottles of claret bottled in every variety of bottle. To our right are the waters of Navy Bay. Behind us far away are the sunlit waves of the Caribbean Sea; and in front of us, to be plunged into immediately, and rushed through with what speed the "Gorgona" can command, are all the richly-green and luxuriant glories of the primeval tropical forest. We are on one of the most wondrous little railways in the world.

*Since I crossed the Isthmus last, the Legislature of the State of New York have granted a charter of incorporation to the Darien Canal Company. According to a letter from Dr. Cullen, in the "Athenæum" of March 6th, 1869, "The line selected by the promoters (Messrs. Cooper, Vanderbilt, and others) is that from Caledonia harbor to the Gulf of San Miguel, so long advocated by me." Dr. Cullen states in the same letter that the Republic of Colombia has conceded the lands, and that the engineers of the company will at once commence operations.

"That's so," observes an American friend on the other side of the car. "No two ways about its being wondrous enough. A railroad not fifty miles long that charges you twenty-five dollars to see both ends of it is a pretty steep kind of a rail."*

"But bear in mind, gentlemen, how much this railway cost to make," observes another passenger. "Not only in money, gentlemen, but in lives. I have heard say that almost as many workmen died in making it as there are sleepers under the rails. Irish workmen were tried, but they died off quickly. New Orleans niggers were tried, but they couldn't stand the pressure. Coolies were brought over, and they can stand considerable, but even they caved in. The West Indian nigger was found to be the fellow to battle the climate best. We have to thank them and Colonel George M. Totten, the engineer, for this road to Panama."

We remark that it is a very good road, and that the engine seems to glide smoothly over the rails. Whereupon our communicative friend continues:

"Yes, gentlemen, all the sleepers on this road are made of lignum-vitæ. No wood but that will resist the boring worms. Lignum-vitæ, gentlemen, means wood of life, but you may count every sleeper as being the monument to a dead man. Even these telegraph-posts would rot in no time if they were made of wood. They look like stone, but they are all cast out of cement."

We thank our informant for his explanations, and look out at the open window to notice the wondrous scenery around us; the wealth of vegetation, the gorgeous tints of waving leaves and trailing stems, the evergreen palms with their bunches of ripe fruit, bright in color as though each bunch were a cluster of rubies; the mangrove bushes with their pendent boughs drooping down and taking root in the ground; the cedro-trees towering up and thrusting out their strong branches, branch interlacing with branch, and one grasping the other as with the arm of a giant; palms whose pinnate leaves are nearly twenty feet in length—palms from under whose crowns hang down tassels of gold—palms around whose trunks entwine clasping flowers of every conceivable hue and every exquisite tint. Nature seems to riot in prodigality of verdure. Here, where summer dwells forever, where ceaseless sunshine steeps the whole scene with light and color and glory, where the very air

*Twenty-five dollars, or about five pounds English money, was the railway fare across the Isthmus by the steamer train.

seems as full of life as it is of perfume, it is difficult to believe that miasma can have sway, or that to live here continuously through the long
summer days could be unlike abiding in Paradise. One would think it to
be the very luxury of living.

Listen! we seem to hear the trees growing and the flowers opening,
just as we really do hear the palm nuts drop and the ripe bananas fall.
The scarlet-breasted bird with the huge beak uttering that strange cry
is the toucan; the cooing sound which comes to our ear from the recesses
of the forest is the call of the turtledove; that singular whistle is the
voice of the pretty black and golden turpiale; and that harsh scream
proceeds from the throat of the green and crimson parrot. The tropical
forest, with all its richness of coloring, is rendered still more variegated
with the plumage of bright birds and the gleaming wings of gaudily-
colored butterflies.

In less than half a mile from Aspinwall we left the Island of Manzanilla, and are now travelling over the main-land. We have passed Mount
Hope, on which is the cemetery of those who perished in making the
road on which we travel. The river just crossed was the Mindee. We
notice tall bamboos flourishing along its banks: and, if we stopped to
seek for them, we might find any number of alligators in its waters.
Sometimes they crawl out and bask upon the rails on which we journey.
If the "cowcatcher" in front of the engine fail to throw them off, a
crushed alligator by the roadside will tell the story of the locomotive of
modern civilization having penetrated to the haunts of creatures
whose form is typical of the living things which inhabited an earlier
earth.

Seven miles from Aspinwall and we pass Gatun Station, with its
large two-story timber building wherein reside the superintendent of
this part of the line and his workmen. Those fifty or sixty huts built of
cane and thatched with palm leaves constitute the native town of Gatun. To our right is the Chagres River. In its waters we may notice a
number of dusky natives bathing; some of them are men, and some
young women. American ladies—and there are some in the cars—
please do not look out of the windows as we pass by; the New Grana-
dians have not your ideas of decency. There are young girls standing on
the river bank gazing at our train rushing past. Do they endeavor to
conceal themselves? Not they. Yet the only dress they wear is that rich
brown tint with which Nature herself has clothed them, and the sun of

the tropics dyed their dusky skins. There are older women with naked "pickanninies" riding straddle-legged on their hips, and there are children playing on the river's edge, as amphibious in their childhood as are the alligators of which they have no fear.

The "Gorgona" is steaming away briskly. We cross the Rio Gatun by an iron truss girder bridge ninety-seven feet in span, and plunge into a forest so dense that the trees seem matted together, each being inextricably bound to its neighbor with living cordage. Vines seem to rise everywhere from the ground—to rain down, as it were, from the very heights of the forest—to droop, to trail, to climb, to twine, to hang in rich festoons and wreathe into arabesque networks of intricate beauty, marrying tree to tree, wedding the mangrove to the palm, and the bread-fruit-tree to the banana; and clothing all with a rich embroidery of green and gold, in interminable profusion extending deep and far through all the sleepy lotus land.

We pass Lion Hill Station, and our conductor or guard points to some beautiful white flowers growing in the swamps by the roadside. We ask him the name, and he replies:

"That, gentlemen, is the *Flor de Espiritu Santo*, or the Holy Ghost flower."*

We wonder at the name, and make inquiries. A lady chances to have one of the flowers, and we examine it. Here is the origin of its Spanish designation readily discernible within the flower itself. In the tulip-shaped cup of the flower is what appears to be an exquisitely modelled image of a snow-white dove, its head bent forward on its breast, its little bill tipped with a ruby tint, its wings folded gracefully, and its plumage of matchless purity. The plant is an orchid, and the flower gives forth a delightful odor which perfumes the railway-carriage, causing our passengers to praise its fragrance as much as they do the extreme beauty of its marvellous formation.

Merrily we rattle over the rails. This station is called "Ahorca Lagarto," which we know to mean something about hanging a lizard; but what lizard was hanged, or where the lizard is hanging, or why any lizard should be hanged at all, is more than any one of our merry company can explain. Here we are at "Stephens's Tree," a wondrous sample of tropical luxuriance. It is a cedro-tree, at least one hundred feet high. Vines trail up its trunk in clustering beauty, and drape themselves in

*So called by the Spaniards. It is known to botanists as the *Peristera elata*.

curtains, garlands, and wreaths of pendent verdure over the roofs of our carriages. Close to the roots of the great tree grow some sensitive plants, which, sentient to the vibration caused by the engine, curl their leaves as we glide past. A little farther, and we pass the cottage where Stephens, the explorer of Central America, once lived. A few miles more, and we are at Frijoli Station, where the natural wonders of the region we are traversing most abound. The flowers on our left are passion-flowers, the birds flying round are orioles or hanging-birds. Hereabout are boa-constrictors and tarantulas, monkeys, opossums, ant-eaters, iguanas, cougars, and tiger-cats. The proprietor of a menagerie might stock his exhibition here in the course of a few days; and if desirous to experiment, might have himself bitten by centipedes, scorpions, musquitoes, sand-flies, and chiggers all within the time that might elapse between his breakfast and his dinner.

Again the Chagres River. The bridge by which we are whisked over it is of wrought iron, six hundred and twenty-five feet long. Our conversation in the railway-carriage turns on the subject of alligators. We have at least sixty travellers in the carriage, and among them is a lady who is anxious to know if the natives catch the alligators, and, if so, by what process they are caught. A gentleman seated in front of us volunteers some information on the subject.

"They are generally caught, madam, by tickling them," says he.

"How very extraordinary!" exclaims the lady. "Pray explain how the nasty creatures are captured. It must be a singular operation."

"Very singular indeed, madam," replies the gentleman, closing one of his eyes as he speaks. "Them alligators are queerly-made critturs, and they have queer fancies. If you look at one of them you will see that he has hard spines upon his tail. Examine them spines, and you will see the last one at the end of the tail to be the largest, to be very sharp and strong, and curved back towards the head of the critter like a hook. Now alligators, madam, are very sleepy things—always a going to sleep in the mud. The brown-skinned gentlemen who live hereabouts go out to catch them with a cane and a long pole. When they see one alseep, they tickle the point of his tail very gently with the cane so as not to wake him. The alligator feels it, and turns his tail away from the tickle. Then they tickle it a little more, and it turns it further away, curving it sorter round, as you see. They go on tickling, and the critter goes on bending round his tail till he gets it right opposite his mouth.

Then they give it a hard tickle. The critter wakes, opens its mouth, snaps at its own tail, gets the point of it between its jaws, and the hooked spine driven clean into its palate. It has just made itself into a ring, you see, and can't help its tail out again. The natives have tickled it enough. All they've got to do is to put the long pole through the ring the critter has made itself into, hoist the two ends of the pole on their shoulders, take the critter home, and kill it quietly. It's a scientific sort of way of catching them, madam, but it's very satisfactory."

We accept the explanation *cum grano*. The lady looks a little skeptical. While some of the passengers are laughing, the train stops at Matachin. Travelling is apt to engender thirst. A native of New Granada has here established a refreshment-station. Let us dismount and regale ourselves with English beer, French claret, "dulces," oranges, monkey-apples, guava, or wild mangos. Here is a buffet in the tropics, and here are fruits not easily to be found elsewhere. Gentlemen, what will you take for refreshment?

◦ 14 ◦

Panama • *The Laocoon at Santa-Fé de Bogota*

WHEN the valiant Spaniard of old time stood on the mountain-top from which he obtained a view of both the great oceans of the globe, and when he reflected that, since the beginning of this world, he was the first white man who had beheld those two oceans at almost a single glance, his sensations must have been joyous and his appreciation of his own fierce spirit of adventure most intense.

It was something for that plucky Spaniard to stand

"Silent upon a peak in Darien,"

where fellow white man had never stood before, something to look back at the waves of the old Atlantic which washed the shores of his home, and something to catch the first glimpse of the waters of that new Pacific, flowing westward he knew not where.

Not quite so picturesque must have been the position of Vasco Nunez de Balboa, when perceiving the Pacific rolling beneath him, and believing himself to be the discoverer of the new ocean, he rushed down to its shores, ran up to his neck in the water, and, striking the waves with his sword, claimed them as being the property of Spanish majesty, and the exclusive water-privilege of the Spanish crown.

We will not do as Nunez de Balboa did; but, as we are approaching the highest point of the railway—"the Summit," as it is called—we are as anxious as Nunez was to catch a peep at the Pacific. The "Gorgona" is puffing and snorting. Empire Station has been passed. When we arrive at Culebra, or "the Snake," we shall be higher up in Central America than at any other point of the present journey.

Very grand is the scenery around us. Tall forests and lofty mountains. Our road winds round the side of a great cliff of basalt, with columnar crystals projecting from the rock—each crystal being from ten to twelve feet in length, and three or four feet in circumference. Here is a structure like to that of the caves of Staffa, or the Giants' Causeway, on the height of an extension of the Andes. A few miles more and we are at Paraiso, or "Paradise" Station. Still a few more, and, having passed the Rio Grande, the city of Panama opens to our view. Beyond it, glowing brightly in the sheen of the tropical sun, are the placid waters of the Pacific.

Are we in America? There is nothing about the appearance of Panama which reminds us of any city in the United States, nor even of poor little Aspinwall at the other end of the rail. The towns and cities we have seen lately have all been new, but Panama takes its lustre from the touch of time. Its great buildings, never wholly completed, were built in the days of early Spanish rule. The towers of the cathedral, the red-tiled roofs of the houses, the crumbling walls and turrets of the ancient fortifications, the high volcanic mountains rising up behind the city, and the peaceful waters of the great ocean, studded with islands and alive with canoes floating over it and pelicans flying above it, make a picture which would cause a landscape painter to feel happy with himself and all the world. This little shed, covered with corrugated iron, is the terminus of the railway. We have a few hours to spare for a stroll into Panama itself, and if we use our time well we can see as much of a Spanish city of the past as we shall care to look at now in the days of its decay and unwholesome sanitary condition.

"Be careful, gentlemen," advises a railway official on the platform.

"You may go into the town; but the small-pox is about, and they are dying at the rate of twenty a day."

We have been a little too far to be frightened easily, and, thanking the official of the *Ferro Carril*, proceed on our way. There is one of us at least who has been in Panama before.

A guard of honor is drawn up on the platform. We pass the soldiers respectfully. They are part of the army of the Republic of New Granada, and are clothed in blue jackets and white trowsers. Their faces are those of negroes, and their fixed bayonets are not over bright. We appreciate their services, and walk on.

Though the sunshine is warm enough, the coloring of all objects in Panama is warmer still. The tints of walls and roofs, houses and churches, are all red and brown. As a relief to the general warmth, the spires of the cathedral are of a cool gray. We enter the town by taking the course of the dilapidated walls alongside the bay; find the streets to be very narrow, and the houses to be in most part built of adobe or sun-dried brick.

There is just time to run out to the ruins of the Church of St. Felipe, which have reminded some travellers of the Baths of Caracalla. The nave has become a natural hot-house of tropical plants, and the wild vines hang in curtains, fringes, and lace-work from the arches down to the floor. We wish we had that old church nearer home that we might ramble to it often.

Here is the Hotel Europe, and here is the Aspinwall Hotel. We seek the latter to ask for a cool drink. Before us there is a splendid old wall for the display of a poster, and we think that we should like to see a poster pasted thereon. In our pocket is one of Artemus Ward's bills. With a little trouble we find a man who will put it up; and in the course of ten minutes "*Artemus Ward will speak a piece,*" is an announcement on the walls of Panama. The natives stare at it in wonder. The American residents look, laugh, and make inquiries. We know that Artemus Ward will not "speak a piece" in the ruinous, effete, and almost lifeless city; but it will amuse him when he comes along by the steamer train in two weeks hence, should he chance to find the bill still upon the wall, and his name known in the ancient capital of the Isthmus.

When the poster has been fastened up, we return to the hotel. One of our fellow-passengers, who wears a slouch hat, and has diamond rings on his fingers and a diamond cluster for a breast-pin, quietly asks:

"Are you connected with that show?"

We reply in the affirmative.

"Circus, I guess?"

"No, not a circus."

"Magic-lantern or tableaux vivants?"

"Neither."

"Maybe it's a parlor entertainment?"

We answer that we are not inclined to regard it as an entertainment of that class.

"Then it's no use in these parts," rejoins our acquaintance. "I have done my show all over these towns, and they are picayune, every one of them."

We ask what his show is, and are informed that it consists of athletic performances and illustrations of ancient statues; that our performer's name is Professor Riley—but he is not acquainted with the well-known Professor Risley, though, from the similarity of the name, we half suspect that he wishes to be occasionally mistaken for him; and, that having been across to the West Indies, he is now going on a professional trip to revisit some of the South American towns. He strolls with us back to the terminus, and while we wait for the boat to convey us to the steamer "Golden Age," Professor Riley relates a few of his experiences.

We remark to the Professor that if all the towns hereabouts are like Panama they must be very dreary, and we ask him what sort of a place the capital of New Granada is, and whether a show would be likely to prosper in Santa-Fé de Bogota.

"Bogota!" he shrieks in derision. "Don't make a pitch there with any thing. Nary Bogota. They had me there once. That's where I nearly got murdered for doing the *Lakune*."

Not understanding what the Professor means, we ask him what a *Lakune* is. He answers thus to our inquiry:

"The Lakune is the old man with his two sons a fightin' the sarpints. It's one of the ancient classic statoos."

A suspicion steals over us that our informant refers to the Laocoon; and, as the boat is not yet in sight, we desire to know what the Laocoon could possibly have to do with causing a man to be nearly murdered in Bogota. So we light up a cigar while the Professor proceeds with his story.

"My entertainment is the most elegant one they've had in these parts. It's a little one-horse perhaps, but it would not pay if it warn't. There's myself, my son, his wife, and her brother. My son's wife can play half a dozen instruments, and can make a whole band out of a piano and a guitar. She used to do a little dancing, but she broke her leg falling off a mule goin' over the mountains in Chili, so she's nothing on the dancing now. Her brother is as good as I used to be on the horizontal bar, and can take a flying leap with any man in the profession. My son and I give the best parlor entertainment out. There ain't a man goin' can beat me at balancing, and my youngster is as strong in the muscle as a bunch of Herculeses. When we do the statoos, there's neither of us ever wink an eye or stir a hair. Firm as a rock, sir; solid as a bit of iron. Feel that, sir—feel it. That's the stuff for statoos."

The professor holds up one of his legs and invites us to feel the muscles of his calf. With the intention of showing that no impression can be made upon the muscular development of that part of his body, he punches his calf with the knuckles of his closed hand, and applies similar treatment to other parts. We ask him for a programme of his performances and receive his reply.

"In three parts, sir. With our talent we can give variety. The parlor entertainment and the tumbling come last, the statoos first, and in between my son plays the concertina, and his brother-in-law does the licking the red-hot iron business. There's nothing can stand against so much talent. You've heard of Madame Anna Bishop, I guess? Well, she and her concert party came to Quito on the same night I was playing there. Quito is a good city for a pitch, but not for two shows at the same time. Madame Anna Bishop gave her concert, and we gave our entertainment. We beat her, sir—beat her hollow. She sang songs in about ten languages, and had a strong concert party; but bless you! in these South American places people like to see more than to hear. So we did a parade in the daytime, and in the evening my daughter-in-law's brother juggled some cannon-balls red-hot. Talent did it, sir. Quito turned up trumps that night."

We remind the Professor that he has not yet told us the story of Laocoon. He laughs, and plays with the diamond rings on his coarse fingers while he narrates his story.

"Well, that was at Bogota. It's a roughish kind of a place, is Bogota. It's not quite a dead place, and it hasn't got much life in it. The farmers at some of the ranches round about are pretty rich, but the people haven't the money like they have in the cities further south. I guess it was a mistake to build Bogota for a capital up in the mountains. Capitals ought to be down by the sea. Then they get fresh air and grow. That's what's made New York, and New Orleans, and Valparaiso."

We interrupt the Professor by remarking to him that the sea has not made much out of Panama. We point to its crumbling walls, and then across the railway station to where glimmers the Pacific—

> "Thick set with agate and the azure sheen
> Of Turkis blue and emerald green."

Whereupon the Professor screws his diamond rings around his fingers and remarks:

"This here ought to be a city, and I guess it will be when Uncle Sam gets hold of it. But Bogota will never amount to much. The whole country round about would only make a big rancheria for Uncle Sam to let out in ranches. I gave them a good show in Bogota, and the Lakune is just one of the best things we do. We've got a property sarpint we carry with us. It's very long, elegantly painted, and has a head to it that would deceive a sarpint itself. It's made out of brass. I had it cast for the purpose. When my son and his brother-in-law and I get that sarpint twisted round us, and I am made up for the statoo, and hold the sarpint's head up high in my right hand, and press it so as to make its forked tongue go in and out, it's a show, sir, that can't be beaten. It's the Lakune to the life, just as natural as ever it was seen by any one."

"But was it so appreciated in Santa-Fé de Bogota?" we ask.

"That's what I'm coming to. We'd got the right pitch in Bogota. Our fixin's were all complete. It was one of their *fête* days, and I'd booked the alcalde and all the ayuntamiento to come and see our show. The house was good—very good for Bogota. The statoos came first —they were all classic and good. New lamps, too, to light them up. We gave them Hector and Andromash, and Ajax defying the thunder and lightning, Herculeses labors, Apollo playing on his little harp, the Greek fellow throwing the ball in the bowling-alley, Virginus sticking his daughter—attitude one, two, and three, and then we came to the Lakune. Every thing had gone off right enough up to then. The statoos had all been done smart—right up to the handle, and the Lakune was to finish the first part of our entertainment. Now how was I to know about a priest having been killed by a boa-constructor?"

We are surprised at the sudden manner in which the Professor asks a singular question, and mildly suggest to him that we are in a state of fog about the priest and the "boa-constructor," not exactly comprehending their relation to the story of the Laocoon.

"There's where it was," he continued, rolling up a new cigarette as he speaks. "There's where it was. What did I know about the priest and his big sarpint? Why didn't the alcalde send to me and let me know? Why didn't he tell me? I told him the Lackune was part of our show. It was his business to have said 'Don't do it!' How was I to know his brother had been killed by a boa-constructor?"

"And was that the difficulty?" we ask.

"Of course it was," continues the Professor. "They've got biggish-sized sarpints in this country. They call them boa-constructors—that is, the people don't, but the travellers do. I don't think they are. But *quien sabe?* [who knows?] as they say hereabouts. The priest had been a good old man, and was one of the alcalde's brothers. He had gone out in the country to see a poor fellow who was dying, and he chanced to fall in the way of a big sarpint. Seems he was found dead, with the sarpint twisted round him. Now the moment our curtain drew aside and showed us doing the Lakune, the idiots thought we were burlesquing the poor priest. We had made the announcement through the curtain that we were about to show the Lakune and the sarpints, being a copy from the antique; but they didn't know anything about antiques, and were as ignorant of the Lakune as a dead jackass would be. Soon as the curtain opened, and they got sight of us, with me holding up the head of the sarpint and making the spring-tongue work, there was an outcry of '*Cuidado! cuidado! no hay culebra aqui!*' which means in their lingo, 'Look out, we don't want no snakes here!' And there was a rush at us all at once. The alcalde spoke to his men, and two fellows drew their swords upon us. We didn't know whether they wanted to kill us or to take us into custody, so we unwound our big sarpint quickly, and, holding it tight by the tail, swung the brass head around us to keep off the crowd. Some of the Bogota roughs had got their machetas with them, what they use to cut wood with, and they made at us, howling like a pack of Coyote wolves. 'Hold on, Tom, to the traps!' I cried out to my son; 'hold on, and let me sling the sarpint.' And I did sling it—you bet! I slung it round and round and round so fast they couldn't see which way it was a comin', and I guess them who got a knock from the brass head knew what sort of a boa-constructor I'd got."

"And you escaped safely?" we ask.

"Just with a few scratches, and a smash-up of some of my traps. But I tell you what, they don't see Professor Riley in that city again. No, sir! Not if I know it will they ever have another Lakune in Bogota."

◦ 15 ◦

Poker and Euchre on the Pacific

AFLOAT on the Pacific. Our steamer is the "Golden Age," whereof Captain Lapidge is commander. The tender has taken us off to her late in the afternoon. We pace the hurricane-deck, and glance back at the picturesque town we have just left.

Though the "Golden Age" does not sail till midnight, we feel that it is much better to be on board her, and to lounge about her clean and spacious decks, than to saunter in the streets of close, unpleasant-smelling, and unwholesome Panama. Even the principal thoroughfare of the city is so wanting in stir and bustle as to suggest oppressively the idea of death. It has none of the characteristics of the chief streets of other cities of the same great continent, and is no more like the Calle Victoria of Valparaiso, or the Rua Direita of Rio de Janeiro, than it resembles the Broadway of New York, Canal Street, New Orleans, or Montgomery Street, San Francisco. But under the enchantment of distance Panama is fair and fascinating; looking at it as we do now, steeped in sunlight, sleeping at the foot of a mountain, with palm-trees listlessly waving their large green fronds over ruined wall and quaint red-tiled roof, and the ripples of the peaceful ocean of the world breaking gently on the almost noiseless shores.

By the light of an unclouded moon, the brilliancy of which seems unusual, we steam out of the Bay of Panama at midnight, past islands rich with tropical foliage, and rocks covered with valuable deposits of guano. We are told that this is the Island of Taboga, on which are the work-shops of the company owning the English line of South American steamers, and that that is the Island of Taboguilla, the name of which means "little Taboga." That here on one island may be seen the lava of an extinct volcano, and that on another are the graves of the foreign wanderers who have died in Panama, and found on a little island in the Pacific peace at last, and rest from all adventure.

We retire late, but rise early with what one of our companions phrases as "a noble appetite" for breakfast. After breakfast we take a tour of inspection along the hurricane-deck, which, high up as it is above the main deck of the steamer, is sought by all who are not afraid of fresh air, and who are desirous of looking at the magnificent scenery, the Island of Quibo, the promontory of Veraguas, and the distant mountains of Costa Rica. On board the "Golden Age" we meet most of our fellow-voyagers by the "North Star." Some who came with us from New York as far as Panama have deserted our company to find their way to one or other of the South American cities, and some have remained behind in New Granada; but, to make up for the loss, we have acquired others who have come up from the South to join us, and who, like ourselves, are going in search of dollars to the golden land.

Seated on an American rocking-chair, a book on her lap, and her long fingers intertwined, sits the lady who is a lecturer on spiritualism. She will persist in showing those large white teeth, sunning them, as she is doing now, in the sunshine of the tropics, and talking meanwhile to a gentleman who, we are told, is a very rich government contractor. We notice that she has a habit of engaging in conversation with the richest and the oldest of the male passengers, and we presume the habit to be part of her business in connection with her show of rapping-tables, "mediums," and "spirit-circles." We regard those teeth in the light of advertising posters, and if we are mistaken we beg most sincerely to apologize.

Here, pacing slowly up and down the deck in abstracted mood, and talking in a low tone to himself, is our friend from Philadelphia, who is going out to California to start a theatre and produce his own hitherto-rejected plays. We suggest to him that as there appeared to be no theatre open at Panama, he might have made a start there, and might have easily obtained a small company from New Orleans or elsewhere. He smiles, and with a knowing look replies:

"Not for the child from afar."

We appreciate his good sense and join him in his promenade.

Day after day we steam along towards the Gulf of Tehuantepec. Twelve days from New York, and we are off the coffee-tree plantations of Costa Rica. Three days more, and away in the distance we catch a glimpse of Nicaragua. Sunday arrives; and as we happen to have among our passengers the Rev. Mr. Lee, an Episcopal clergyman, he is called upon to conduct religious services on deck under the awning. Then, just as we are about to sit down to dinner on Sunday, the steam-whistle gives forth a discordant screech, the cry of "Fire" is heard, and every one, springing to his feet, hastens for the deck. Strangely enough, the ladies do not scream, nor manifest any serious alarm. When we get up stairs we find that the sailors have already taken up their positions, the hose being rapidly uncoiled from out of the place in which it was stowed, the water-buckets being handed out, the engines stopped, and the steam-pumps going, the officers issuing orders which are instantly obeyed, the boats about to be lowered, ourselves taken in charge and assigned to the care of so many of the ship's company, the steam-whistle still screeching, but no symptom visible of the ship being actually on fire—no smoke, no flame, no burning odor, no crackling of wood in process of combustion. Then do we learn, though we in part suspected it before, that the alarm is a false one, simply intended as a rehearsal to teach every one what to do in case of real calamity, and to see that all the ship's officers thoroughly understand their duty in the event of emergency. Once again during the voyage a similar false alarm is raised, but at night instead of midday. The calm and collected behavior of the lady passengers is fully explained when we learn that they have been previously forewarned and cautioned by the stewardesses, and that many of our female voyagers are old travellers on the Pacific.

Sixteen days from New York and we are off the coast of Mexico. There is no wind, the weather is intensely hot, the ocean is one huge glittering sheet of smooth glass, the sun seems to have acquired an extra supply of heat, and the Mexican mountains look uncomfortably red and fiery. Our latitude is 15° 53′ N., and our ice is a quarter of a dollar a plate, with a decided tendency to become a plateful of water in a very few minutes after we have purchased it. With a plate of ice, a bottle of claret, and a few green oranges still in stock from among those we bought at Panama, existence is made comparatively easy; but how fares it with the poor fellows of whom we catch occasional glimpses down in the engine-room below? Even on deck the weather is too warm for the passengers to take exercise during the day-time. But down among the furnaces the temperature must be almost unendurable; yet there we see the stokers busily at work, opening the door of one furnace after another, shovelling coals into the red-hot iron receptacles, the fire lighting up their faces with a fiendish glow, and the perspiration pouring down their cheeks as if each man were becoming metamorphosed into a fountain. Presently one poor man is brought up and laid on the deck. The heat below has been too much for him, and he has fainted. As he recovers we tender him plates of ice, whisky cocktails, and jugs of claret. Afterwards we learn that he is not used to the stoking business; that he is a "stow-away" who smuggled himself on board at Panama, having no money with which to pay his passage. When discovered, he had been ordered down to the furnaces to assist in feeding the fires. Were he a strong man he might be left to do the duties assigned to him, but he is thin, weak, and bears in his countenance the signs of having suffered mentally and physically at no very remote period. A showman now comes to his aid. The violon-cellist who is travelling his instrument in the case which is to be his coffin, and to whom we have already referred, steps forward and proposes that we open a subscription at once to pay the passage of the "stow-away." Five dollars is the amount which the violoncellist himself contributes. In half an hour the whole fare is collected, counted out to the clerk on board, and a ticket for the voyage handed to the penniless man, that he may not go down again among the furnaces. When your violon-cello-case becomes your coffin, as you wish it one day to be, may you sleep peacefully in it, good and kindly violoncellist!

Strolling round the deck as the day wanes and the atmosphere becomes cooler, we notice that many of our fellow-passengers are busily engaged in card-playing. Nothing seems to relieve the tedium of a long voyage more effectually with those who are accustomed to excitement than a little gambling. Your Californian adventurers are not all of the reading class, and many of them would much prefer the labor of washing a ton of gold-dust to that of reading a single book. Here and there on the steamer we see a man with a book in his hand, but where there is one reader there are twenty card-players. The lady who lectures on spiritualism always has her book on her lap. She has it just now. Not that she is reading it; for while she suns her white teeth in the rich sunlight of the Pacific, she is conversing learnedly with a passenger with whom we have not previously seen her in conversation. The poor man seems to be fascinated by her eloquence, and will inevitably make one more purchaser of a ticket to her lectures in San Francisco.

Here, in almost the same spot on the deck which they have occupied every afternoon since we left Panama, we see a young couple whom we have ascertained to be newly married. The lady is very pretty, the gentleman very like a man who never has done, nor ever intends to do, much hard work. For amusement they have brought with them a small mahogany box of circular form, inside which is a rotating wheel painted in rays of black and red. Around the periphery of the wheels are numerals. The box has a lid to it, and in the lid is a small hole. Through this hole in the lid the lady drops a pea, causes the wheel to rotate, and watches the number at which the pea rests. Then the husband performs a similar operation. They are playing to see which can soonest make the various turns amount to one hundred. When they have completed the sum they will begin again, and when tired to-day will recommence to-morrow. They must have already spun that black-and-red wheel round four or five thousand times, and are likely to spin it four or five thousand more before they arrive at San Francisco. We have our doubts whether they are playing for amusement only, or whether to solve some great problem of their future fortune. Whether, in fact, the man is not an American Protesilaus, revolving "The oracle upon the silent sea," and the lady a Laodamia of the present day bound for California. Not Mercury, but gold, leading Protesilaus back to earth, and Laodamia not likely to be willing to go back to Hades with her husband, but to try the divorce court in San Francisco or Sacramento.

In quiet nooks and secluded corners of the deck are groups of bearded men playing the never-tiring game of "poker." It is an open question whether the paddles or the screw of an American steamer would continue to revolve without some poker-playing on board the vessel. A pack of cards—a "deck" of cards, as they phrase it across the Atlantic —would seem to be as indispensable to a steamer having the stars and stripes for its flag, and sailing on western waters, as the boilers which generate the steam, or the machinery used for propulsion. And of all games played with cards, poker is the one in which your true Western traveller finds his chief solace and his never-failing source of amusement. Tobacco is thought to be good to have; whisky is regarded as a very desirable item, and brandy is by no means objectionable; but to the rough-and-ready passengers on board the steamer, especially those in the steerage, a game of poker is better than all. Poker is preferable to breakfast, is almost a substitute for dinner, and is much superior to supper. Meals have their times and seasons, but poker is thought to be good always. It must have puzzled many an American to think how Robinson Crusoe got along without it. According to a Californian's way of thinking, had Friday and Crusoe been able to play the game, and had they had a little Western training, they would never have tired of the Island of Juan Fernandez.

Your showman of the West is seldom one who can lay his hand upon his heart and solemnly assert that he never once played a game of poker. To profess ignorance of a game so sublime, so important, and so necessary to know, would be to render yourself despised in the eyes of the noble backwoodsman, the Mississippi trader, or the California adventurer. Yet, common as it is in the Western World, poker is a game of which very little is known in England. We may be pardoned, perhaps, for teaching the elements of it in a very few words.

In playing common "draw-poker" five cards are dealt to each player. No trumps are turned up. Each player can then make a bet if he pleases. He looks at his hand. If he have four aces in it he has the strongest hand there can be, and, having a certainty, can not bet. Four cards of any kind constitute a strong hand. Next in value comes a flush. Then a "full," which consists of three of one kind and a pair; then three of a kind—next in excellence two pairs, and then one pair. Each player can, after looking at his hand, discard three cards and take three others from the pack. The dealer then makes his bet, say five dollars. His opponent can accept it or "raise it," saying, "I see your five, and raise it to fifty." If the dealer object to the raising, he simply throws up his cards and loses his five dollars. If he accepts his opponent's challenge and shows a winning hand, he gains fifty dollars. Poker is purely a betting game. There is no memory nor science required, but great daring, combined with coolness and caution. Study your adversary's face, and guess his hand by his features. In other respects poker resembles our English game of *brag*.

There is another game of cards which our fellow-passengers are playing, and some of the lady passengers are joining in it. The name of it is *euchre*. It is not purely a gambling game like poker, in which the player "anteys-up" his quarter or half dollar; but a very lively and very interesting mode of using a pack of cards for amusement, and purely American in its origin. In playing euchre all cards of a lower value than seven are first discarded, a two and a three being used to mark the five points which constitute the game. Five cards are dealt to each player, two at a time first, and then three. Trumps are then turned up. The value of the cards in euchre is not as in other games, for the most valuable card of all is the knave of trumps, which takes the name of the "right bower"; while the next in value is the knave of the suit of the same color, which for the time being assumes the name of the "left bower." The right and left bowers are superior in value to ace, king, and queen. In playing, making three tricks scores a point, making all the five tricks constitutes "a march," and scores double. The game can be played with two, three, or four players. When only three play it is called "cut-throat euchre." In playing, the "elder hand," or first player, after studying his hand and finding that with it he can not, as he thinks, take three tricks, either says "I pass," or raps his knuckles on the table to express that he does so. But if he perceives that he has enough trumps in his hand to warrant him to believe that he can beat his opponent, he says "I order up," when it becomes the duty of his opponent to discard a card, face downward, and supply its place in his hand by the card which had been turned up for trumps. Should the player who "ordered up" fail to make his three tricks, he becomes "euchred," and loses two points to his antagonist. But, supposing that in commencing to play he does not "order up," but says "I pass," then the dealer has his choice of discarding and taking up the trump card, or turning the trump card face downward on the pack. The dealer having done that, his opponent can make the trumps as he pleases. For instance, if the elder hand perceives that he holds in his hand the knave of hearts, the knave of diamonds and the ten of hearts, he unhesitatingly says, "make it hearts," and hearts at once becomes trumps, though spades may have been trumps before. But, having made trumps, he must take care to win three tricks and score one point, else he will be euchred, and his antagonist triumphantly score two instead of one. Should the elder hand decline to make the trumps and "pass" again, it falls to the option of the dealer either to declare new trumps and stand the chance of being euchred, or to throw up his hand for the cards to be dealt again.

We are very well aware that we are not supposed to be writing an American edition of "Hoyle's Games," and we are equally as well aware that poor Artemus Ward knew very little of card-playing, but here are our fellow-passengers playing cards everywhere around us. The phrases made use of in playing poker and euchre are used more than once by Artemus in his writings, and we have never seen in any English work an explanation of either of the games. To the ear of him who has travelled far in the United States, and become familiar with the slang of the less cultivated classes, many phrases will recur, the exact meaning of which can only be understood by him who is acquainted with the games of old sledge, poker, and euchre. "I'll euchre you," "I pass," "That's my best bower," and "Now then, antey-up," are common expressions, all of which owe their origin to American uses of a pack of cards.

A transatlantic humorist whose writings are partially known in England, and who hides himself under the *nom-de-plume* of Josh Billings, expresses his opinions on the game of euchre in the following style. We copy his statements, but not his mode of spelling:

"This ill-bred game is about twenty-seven years old. It was first discovered by the deckhands on a Lake Erie steamboat, and handed down by them to posterity in all its juvenile beauty. It is generally played by four persons, and owes much of its absorbingness to the fact that you can talk and drink, and chew and cheat, while the game is advancing.

"I have seen it played on the Hudson River Railroad, in the smoking-cars, with more immaculate skill than anywhere else. If you play there you will often hold a hand that will astonish you; quite often four queens and a ten-spot, which will inflame you to bet seven or eight dollars that it is a good hand to play poker with; but you will be more astonished when you see the other fellow's hand, which invariably consists of four kings and a one spot. Euchre is a mulatto game, and don't compare to old sledge in majesty any more than the game of pin does to a square church-raffle. I never play euchre. I never would learn how, out of principle. I was originally created close to the Connecticut line in New England, where the game of seven-up, or old sledge, was born, and exists now in all its pristine virginity. I play old sledge to this day in its native fierceness. But I won't play any game, if I know my character, where a Jack will take an ace and a ten spot won't count a game. I won't play no such kind of game, out of respect to old Connecticut, my native State."

With all due respect to Mr. Josh Billings, it is as doubtful whether the game of euchre originated on a Lake Erie steamboat, as that the game of old sledge had its birth-place in Connecticut, but where games did originate is really matter for very curious inquiry. The spelling of the word "euchre" offers an etymological puzzle; and where was the game of *besique* first invented? Five or six years ago it was advertised in a shop-window in Broadway, New York, as a game just imported from France; while in the shop-windows of London it is announced at the present moment as the "new American game." We believe that there is no statue of Columbus in the United States, but there will be one some day. Should Americans wish to put up a statue out West to the memory of the discoverer of poker or of euchre, where will they find the portrait from which to make the model?

❀ 16 ❀

Coffee-Trays and Cigar-cases in Mexico • The Showman at Acapulco

AN hour past midnight. Sixteen days' travel from New York, and we are in Mexico.

No glimpse of the Pacific can be obtained. We are in a land-locked harbor. At anchor in a cosy little bay, round which rise dark mountains, and over which we discern one little patch of sky and a few groups of stars. There is no breeze, no movement in the air. We seem to be at the bottom of a huge pit where the heat is suffocating. Looking over the sides of the vessel we perceive troops of dusky demons, each carrying a torch. Other demons with torches are coming off to us in boats, which glide silently over the black water. More demons seem to be dancing on the shore in the distance. The atmosphere is full of a sickening odor of cocoa-nut oil, the heat is that of a furnace, and the scene is weird enough for any witch-drama or grand hobgoblin spectacle. The red light from the demons' torches falls upon the face of the lady lecturer on spiritualism, and her teeth are no longer white, but have a sanguinolent hue. Can it be she who has called up the dusky forms which hover everywhere around?

The place is Acapulco, and yonder in the darkness is the old Mexican town, founded by the Spaniards in their days of conquest on the Pacific. We shall see it when morning breaks, and we shall have a chance of landing. Meanwhile let us glance at the scene around us.

Watch the demons with the flambeaux! They are coming close to us. Some of them are about to scale the sides of our ship. As they come close to us we perceive that they are not demoniac, but simply natives of the place, very dark in color, wearing scarcely any attire, some having a shirt on and others not, but nearly all of them carrying a piece of lighted sugarcane, which, as it burns, throws a lurid light over surrounding objects. Some of the dark figures are engaged propelling towards us heavy barges on which are stacked up little bags of coal. We want 250 tons, the captain says. We ask if it is Mexican coal, and find that it has been brought from Pennsylvania, and made the voyage round Cape Horn. It has been shovelled into the bags by women. We want fresh water also, and here are more dusky Mexicans approaching us with another barge. When they come up close with us they screw a hose to the side of our vessel, and pump away in the glare of the torch-light. We survey the strange scene with a showman's eye, and think, as we look upon it, that if we could only transfer it to the stage of Drury Lane or Covent Garden, in an appropriate drama by Boucicault, Wilkie Collins, Halliday, or Watts Phillips, we know how many people would pay to the pit every night for the first two months of the run of the piece.

Day breaks about half-past five. We have slept an hour, and awake to find the scene thoroughly transformed. The dark water of the bay has become bright and sparkling, and is beating on a sandy beach. The black hills have become covered with verdure, and the patch of sky over head is blue and cloudless. Rows of cocoa-nut palms are growing close down to the water's edge. Acapulco is peeping out behind a rocky point. There are high hills behind us, one with an old fort on the top, and there are high hills in front of us, on the summit of one of which are the ruins of a battery, lately shattered by a French vessel of war. We go on shore early in a small boat, which has a flat, oblong canvas awning to it supported by upright rods. Fifty cents is the charge for our boat-ride. With a good appetite, we step on shore to breakfast in Mexico.

In Mexico! Shall we see any traces of Gautemozin, Montezuma, or Hernando Cortez? Shall we have a peep at any ruins of a pyramid like to those of Cholula, or any palace like to that of Chapultepec? Nothing of the kind here in Acapulco. Ancient as it is, it wears no aspect of past grandeur. It is Mexico away out on the Pacific. A different sort of thing to the Mexico we have seen in days past on the table-land of the interior. The houses are mostly one story high, and are built of "adobe," or mud shaped into bricks and dried in the sun. To the right on entering the town is the American Hotel—a very sorry affair. The landlady stands at the door and invites us to take a cup of coffee and some cake for twenty-five cents. We decline with thanks; but purchase a pineapple for a *real*, or sixpence, and leisurely eat it as we ramble through the town.

Acapulco is a well-laid-out city. The names of the streets are painted up legibly, and we have no difficulty in finding our way about. We ramble up the *Calle San Diego*, thence into the *Calle San Francisco*, and on through the *Calle del Correo* and the *Calle Nueva*. Presently we find ourselves in a market-place forming an open square, having an old church in the middle of it, and a well in front of the church. Men and women are squatting on the ground selling oranges, beans, pumpkin-seeds, cocoa nibs for making drinkable cocoa, unpurified sugar, candles, fish, and meat. The meat presents a most unpleasant appearance, consisting for the most part of long strips, which seem to have been torn asunder rather than cut, and to have been dried in the sun. There are large lumps of offal for sale, and some legs of pork are being chopped into small pieces on great stones by very uncleanly-looking female butchers. Close at hand, on the towers of the church, are perched large ugly black turkey-buzzards, waiting in their capacity of scavengers for the carrion which will fall to their share.

There are two hotels at either of which we are told that we can procure a good breakfast for the small cost of a dollar, and at both of which English is spoken. We look in first at the Louisiana, and, not liking that, pass on to the El Dorado. Our breakfast consists of stewed chicken, fried eggs, fried bananas, raw tomatoes, and coffee. We are waited on by a woman of unprepossessing appearance, being thin and bony, having very little hair on her head, and wearing a pair of greasy old black trowsers, as if she were a man. We are told that she is the wife of the proprietor. The husband waddles towards us with a billiard-cue

in his hand. He is very stout, very greasy, and very bluff in his demeanor. We ask him if he is an American.

"I scorn the name," is his reply. "I am a Secesher. That's what I am.
I'm for the South, right through me down to the heel. I reckon thar's
not a drop of Yankee blood to be found in my veins—not the smell of
a drop. You see that billiard-table thar. Captain Semmes, who is scaring
the Yanks with his 'Alabama,' used to play billiards on that when he
war in the United States navy, and his ship lay here. Here in his room
war whar he told me he war off to fight for the South. I reckon he'll
chaw up every ship the Yanks have got before long."

Having finished breakfast and lighted a cigar, we proposed to the
landlord that he should take a glass of liquor with us, a proposal which
he bluffly accepts. We wish to try a little *pulque*, as the fresh juice of
the maguay is called, but are informed that it can be obtained in the
interior of the country only. "You can have some *muscal*," says our
landlord. Muscal we knew to be the fermented juice of the same plant,
and having tasted it in times past, respectfully decline to renew our
acquaintance with it. Our host recommends his brandy, and we try that
while we lead him into a conversation relative to the political condition
of this portion of Mexico.

Acapulco is in the province of Guerrera, the present governor of
which is Señor Juan Alvarez, whose name we see attached to certain
decrees posted up here and there in the town. Later in the course of the
morning we chance to see the Señor, and find him to be a stout jolly-
looking man, seeming more like a negro than a Spaniard or a Mexican
—Liberal in his politics, belonging to the Juarez party, and holding the
rank of general in the Liberal army. We also learn that he is a gentleman of considerable intelligence, a pious Catholic, and a great patron
of sport in the way of cock-fighting. We ask our landlord what he thinks
of the General. His reply consists of a long whistle. We then ask him
how he likes the French, and whether, the French having recently
visited Acapulco and shelled it, he thinks it to be likely that they will
come again.

"They'll be here again in a month and stay for good, I hope," is his
reply. "These fellows don't amount to any thing. When the French
came they behaved like gentlemen. They asked for water and cattle.
They whar refused, so they shelled the town. Very proper too. They
did no harm to any house. Our soldiers worked the battery upon the hill

pretty well, but they vamosed from the battery on the shore after the second shell war fired at them. They are no good, I tell you. They fight! It isn't in their constitutions. The captain threw away his sword and fled. Five people whar all that were left in the city. All fled to the hills. French fellows whar gentlemen. Yes, sir-ree! They committed no outrages. Here they came, and here they sailed away again. They paid me for what they had, and I charged them double what I charge you."

In the course of the morning we make the acquaintance of the very courteous American consul, Mr. Eley, and of an American of the name of Rector, who is going a hundred and fifty miles into the interior to fit up a cotton-mill. Presently we drop upon a communicative man from Ohio who has travelled all over Mexico, and who now owns a small store built of adobe, where he is engaged in the manufacture of cigars. He informs us that he pays three dollars per month for his store, and that his board costs him one dollar per day. With ordinary industry he contrives to earn four dollars per day, and appears pleased with his residence in Acapulco. Around him in his store, smoking cigars, are three or four Mexican tradesmen. The political state of affairs becomes the topic of conversation, and the expression of opinion amounts simply to a strong protest against things as they are, and an earnest desire for a complete change. "Let us have Napoleon and General Forey, Maximilian, the French, the United States, England, or even Spain; any would be better than the government we have."

"But you have a liberal ruler," we observe in reply. "On the wall of the Adouana Maritima we noticed a picture this morning of your Mexican arms. An eagle is fighting with a serpent, and has the neck of the serpent in its beak. Then there is the red cap of Liberty emitting rays of sunlight, and the word '*Libertad*' on it as large as possible. What more can you want?"

"Take a walk ten miles into the country and you'll find," is the answer we get. " '*Libertad*' means leave to rob. It means a knife at your throat, and your purse in another fellow's pocket. That's what '*Libertad*' means hereabouts. The sooner we get an end to it the better."

The group of smokers in the cigar-store and the landlord of the hotel are not the only parties to express to us a similar opinion in the course of our ramble. We begin to suspect that General Alvarez is not peculiarly gifted by nature for a ruler, especially when we learn that though Acapulco is the great Mexican seaport on the Pacific, there is no highway leading from it to the interior, no coach road, no coaches, no wagons, no spring-carts, nor any drays. The ingenuity of the inhabitants has expended itself in getting as far as wheelbarrows and pack-mules. There arriving, it has come to a pause. Going on at the same cheerful rate, under the same enlightened government, there may be a railroad in the province of Guerrera in five hundred years hence.

Strolling through the town we notice that the stores or shops have iron bars instead of glass windows; that some of the stores are well stocked, and that the articles on sale chiefly consist of printed calicoes which we will warrant came from Manchester, gaudily-colored pocket handkerchiefs, boots, shoes, combs, soap, and bottles of brandy. There is no attempt at tasteful display of the goods, and no restriction with regard to variety.

A walk up the Alameda, along a pleasant road shaded by large, branching, gnarled trees, brings us to the fort, whither we have come to have a peep at the soldiers of the Republic. Nine of them are guarding the gate—nine brave, noble, stalwart, martial defenders of "*Libertad.*" The tallest is not more than five feet six; all of them look as if fighting would be less congenial to them than cigar-smoking, and they loll on the draw-bridge, each with a modest droop of the head as though they were much disposed to meditate on the vanity of all Mexican affairs. The soldiers of General Alvarez and of "*Libertad*" are clothed in white shirts, and have no trowsers. On the head of each is a black sombrero, and across the chest of each is a black strap, to which is attached the sheath of a bayonet. One of them is armed with a rusty musket. We ask to pass into the fort, but are refused admission, being told that sickness prevails inside. On the wall of the fort we notice a single cannon; while in the bush and scrub outside the walls are four or five more cannon, and as many broken gun-carriages reposing peacefully among the verdure, asserting the cause of "*Libertad*" in graceful tranquillity.

We walk round the fort and turn down into a pretty valley, wherein there are cottages thatched over with palm leaves, cocoa-nut palms shading the roof of each, and little gardens in which oleanders are in full bloom. Presently we find ourselves again in the Calle Nueva, a long straggling street with adobe huts on each side of it. We cross the Calle del Correo, and pass along the Calle San Francisco to the back of the old church. Here we fall in again with our friend from Ohio, and with the landlord of one of the American hotels. We have just seen what the martial element of Acapulco is like. There is an old priest passing into the church, and we are prompted to make inquiries relative to the religious portion of the community.

"Have you a hard-working clergy in this part of the world?" we ask.

"Well," replies our American acquaintance, "they are pretty good at chicken-disputes."

"What kind of argument or exercise is that?" we innocently inquire.

"Why, I reckon it's cock-fightin'. They go in well for cock-fightin'. We've got some fine old priests out in the country parts, who own each of them a hundred or two of the finest cocks for fightin' you ever saw."

As we saunter with our companions across the plaza some bright-eyed Mexican girls advance towards us, and in the most polite manner make us a present of some common steel or iron pins, each with a lump of sealing-wax or piece of glass for a head to it. We wonder what the gift means, but are soon given to understand that the generous-hearted young ladies expect a present of money in return, and that Acapulco etiquette dictates that the amount of money should be twice or thrice the value of the gift we have accepted. Whereupon we bless the generous hearts of all the young damsels who afterwards accost us, and nobly refuse to deprive them of any more wax-headed pins. It may not be etiquette for us to do so, but we have that within us which conquers etiquette.

As we return to the hotel to refresh, after the long ramble through the dusty little town, we suddenly remember that we have not as yet posted up the name of Artemus Ward in Acapulco. We have a couple of bills with us, ready for the purpose, and, producing one of them, request our friend from Ohio to oblige by having it displayed in some prominent part of the town.

"Entertainments are no use here," says the kindly cigar-maker. "A game of monti or a good chicken-battle is all these fellows care about."

"Do you never have any shows stop here?" we inquire, with an eye to business.

"They wouldn't get much if they came," is the reply. "And if your friend does come with his show, don't let him bring any coffee-trays or cigar-cases."

This last piece of cautious advice puzzles us exceedingly. Why Artemus Ward should bring or should not bring a coffee-tray or a cigar-case with him is a question which does not readily suggest an answer. We assure our adviser that we have never once contemplated the importation of any such articles into Acapulco, and request to know why we have received the caution.

"Well, we had a fellow with a show come here some months ago," answers our informant. "He came across the country, and had been travelling in the interior with two mules. He'd got a magic lantern for a show, and had sent on to him here a consignment of little coffee-trays and cigar-cases. The trays and the cases were prettily painted, and looked worth a lot of money. On the cigar-cases was a portrait of Juarez, and on the middle of each coffee-tray was a picture of the Virgin sitting on the Mexican eagle and cactus. He was a smart Yankee, who had seen a good deal of the world, and spoke Spanish better than any of these natives. So he got up a lottery. These people like lotteries. He showed his magic lantern, charged two reals to see it, and gave every one who came a ticket for a chance in his lottery, which was to come off on the last day of his being here. So many of the Juarez cigar-cases and ever so many of the coffee-trays, with the Virgin sitting on the Mexican eagle and cactus, were to be drawn for on the last day of his stopping among us. Nobody wanted coffee-trays or cigar-cases here, but they looked so pretty many thought they'd like to have one. He showed up his magic lantern, and he sold his tickets. He was right smart, and managed the thing well. The lottery was drawn, and the people got their coffee-trays and cigar-cases. The day after the lottery the fellow vamosed this ranch, and went up to Manzanillo in the steamer."

"And why should not another showman come and give away coffee-trays and cigar-cases?" we ask of our friend.

"There was his artfulness. That was what he was smart in. But it won't do for any other *estrangero* to try it here again in a hurry. You see, he had those trays and cases made for selling in the city of Mexico, or Vera Cruz, or Guadalupe, or somewhere where the French were, or where the people were for Miramon or his party. The cigar-cases looked so pretty as to make the fellows who won them carry them about to show to others. In carrying, the paint rubbed off bit by bit, and before many days there weren't the likeness of Juarez among the whole lot of 'em. They'd all turned into Miramon."

"And the coffee-trays with the Virgin sitting on the Mexican eagle and cactus. How about them?"

"Well, they looked pretty too. I reckon the women who got them set a great deal of value by them. They rubbed the picture on them every day to keep it clean and bright. The first few rubs made a mustache come upon the Virgin's face. A few rubs more and her hands, which were clasped together in front of her throat, changed into a pointed beard. The eagle and cactus soon rubbed away altogether. Instead of the Virgin they'd got the Emperor Napoleon, just the same as he sits on his throne at Paris, in France."

"And did not they like him for a picture quite as well?"

"Like him! Well, I reckon not. Nor the pictures of Miramon neither. It was as good as treason to have them. You might look a considerable time for one of them coffee-trays or cigar-cases in Acapulco just now. Don't let your friend try to have them with any more picture lotteries."

We assure our kind adviser that Artemus Ward does not intend attempting any such enterprise, and again make a request that the poster announcing that "Artemus Ward will Speak a Piece" shall be duly posted in the town. We are promised that our wish shall be complied with, and being in Mexico, and at a *fonda* where we can get frijoles and tortillas, we order a lunch, previously to embarking.

"You want some pepper-sauce with those frijoles," suggests an American.

"Why do the Mexicans take so much pepper-sauce?" we ask. "Surely the climate is warm enough outside without the people peppering their interiors."

"It's good for them when they travel," replies a neighbor. "If they go dead on the road, the vultures or the turkey-buzzards won't eat them. They are too well seasoned for any thing to touch, and they keep without burying."

After lunching we proceed to dispose of our second poster by fastening it up on the wall of the *fonda*. The landlord looks at it attentively and says, "What is this Artemus Ward? Is he a United States officer?"

We pause for a moment, and then make answer: "He's a general." For we know that he must have a title to be considered any body, and nothing less than a general will serve our purpose.

"Then if he's coming along by the next steamer," says our host, "we'll get him to express his sentiments. The sooner this place and all the rest of the land belongs to the United States the better. If he's big on the stump, we'll get him to give our people a monition."

About noon we steamed out of Acapulco. When, two weeks later, Artemus Ward arrived in San Francisco, we asked him how he was received in Acapulco, and if he was called upon to give a "monition" to the people.

"Why did you put them up to such nonsense?" he replied. "That old fellow at the hotel saluted me as general, and called upon me to make a speech to a crowd of his friends. I said a few words to humor him, and thought I was doing him a good turn by advising them all to go in and take a drink to support the house. They all did. They took two drinks each. When I was just about going, the hotelkeeper stopped me. He said all his friends had taken their drinks, but none of them had paid. It cost me seven dollars for that 'monition.' Don't make me a 'general' any more."

◦ 17 ◦

Landing the Show in California

ACAPULCO behind us, and again we are on the Pacific. Eighteen days out from New York, and still steaming past the rocky coast of Mexico. A grand and interesting coast along which to steam or sail. We pass Manzanillo, and about nine miles beyond it get a glimpse through a telescope of the wreck of the fine steamer once famous as the "Golden Gate," but which caught fire at sea and was burnt some few months ago. We fully value the precautions against fire observed on board the vessel on which we voyage.

Bright and clear in the air of early morning we discern at a distance of nearly a hundred miles the peak of the great Mexican volcano, far away in the province of Jalisco. The captain points it out to us. "That's Mount Colima," says he. "It's sixteen thousand feet high. That and Popocatapetl, which is seventeen hundred feet higher, are the two biggest hills in Mexico."

The morning being very warm, the white snow on the summit of the volcano of Colima tempts us to wish that, with an alpenstock in hand, we were scaling its steep sides. Albert Smith made the ascent of Mont Blanc—how would the scaling of Colima do for a show?

Twenty days on our voyage. We have crossed the Gulf of California, and at early morning are off Point Falso, Cape St. Lucas, the southern extremity of Lower California. Just after breakfast we pass the steamer "Oregon," from San Francisco, bound to Mazatlan, La Paz, Guaymas, and other places in the Californian Gulf. No land could be more unpromising in appearance than California, as we first see it here at Cape St. Lucas. Huge masses of white slaty-looking rock are piled up heap upon heap, each vast pile of rock having a jagged summit. There is no vegetation whatever; neither tree nor grass. Down by the shore the rock has been washed by the waves into a fine white sand. The shore is white, the land is white, the hills are white. With the fiercely bright sun glaring on all the ghastly whiteness, the scene is intensely suggestive of arid sterility and dreary desolation.

A sperm whale makes its appearance. One of the officers of the vessel informs us that this is a great fishing-ground for whalers, and that many fishermen land on Cape St. Lucas. Forlorn and barren as the place appears to be, there are fertile valleys inland, far away behind the hideous white rocks.

In the evening we pass the Island of Santa Marguerita. We have left the tropics, and are now in the temperate zone. White coats disappear from the decks, and passengers array themselves again in the sombre warm garments they wore when leaving New York.

MONDAY, OCTOBER 26. — Twenty-three days from New York. It is afternoon. We are passing between two islands; Santa Cruz is on our port side, and Santa Rosa on our starboard. We anticipate arriving at San Francisco by midnight to-morrow. Late at night we see the friendly rays of the light-house on Point Concepcion, and, retiring to rest, wake up early the next morning to spend our last day at sea.

A sky of cloudless azure and a sea of merry waves dancing in the streaming sunlight; the atmosphere fully charged with some powerful invigorative force, which produces a sensuous feeling of how good a thing it is to live, and breathe, and be one among the millions of humanity. We feel the air of California to be even more valuable than its gold, and its sky to be more resplendent than the riches of its rocks. Yet in a few days November will be here. We think of the Novembers we have known in England, and we bless the good fortune which has floated us thus far on the North Pacific. We have seen the brightest sky of the Mediterranean, and have experienced the exhilarating influence of the atmosphere of Australia, but never have we felt more than we do to-day that the consciousness of existence is in itself a source of positive delight, and that merely to breathe is luxury in the superlative degree.

"Guess there's considerable ozone about to-day," remarks a friend at our elbow.

We reply that we are not aware whether it is "ozone," or what it is; but that there is something very bracing in the air, causing a sensation nearly akin to that produced by a slight excess of Champagne.

"That's so," rejoins our friend. "It makes a man feel good. They do drink an awful lot of Champagne in 'Frisco. Maybe the gas out of the bottles gets into the air and floats out to sea."

We doubt the correctness of our fellow-traveller's hypothesis, but feel too good-natured and too full of amiability to discuss the question with him. Enough for us to experience, as we glide over the sparkling waters, that which Byron phrases as

"The exulting sense, the pulse's maddening play,
That thrills the wanderer o'er the trackless way."

We feel that we are strong in the nerves, and can endure this sort of "thrill" to an indefinite extent.

We are off that part of the coast of California which is situated in the county of San Luis Obispo, and are approaching the Bay of Monterey. Can it be that the hills hereabouts are coated with gold, and that the mountains which slope down to the sea are covered with layers of golden ore? If not so, why have they that golden glow in the midday sunlight?

We borrow an opera-glass from the lady who lectures on spiritualism, and look at the golden hills. Glance number one reveals to us that the surface has a slight undulatory motion; while glance number two, with the glass better focused, satisfies us that California has sown her wild oats very plenteously, and that they are ripening in rich harvest on her mountain slopes. Being a young State of the Union, she can afford to be thus lavish with her wild oats. Here on the rock-walls which shield her from the sea, there are oats enough to feed all the mustangs of Mexico, or all the steeds of Arabia.

Nine o'clock in the evening, and we see a bright light in the distance. It proceeds from the light-house on the North Head of the entrance to the harbor of San Francisco. The mountains behind it are three thousand feet in height. In majestic grandeur they sentinel the approach to one of the fairest and most flourishing cities in all the Western World.

Half past ten o'clock and we are steaming through the Golden Gate, the "Portal to the Paradise of Plutus," to use the pleonastic alliteration of one of the local newspapers. The gateway is not broad, but very grand. The rocky hills which form the gate-posts on each side are bold in outline, and admirably adapted by nature for the defense of the entrance. We regret, as we steam through, that we can not affix a large-size announcement-bill on each of those posts of the Golden Gate in accordance with Artemus Ward's suggestion. Were it possible to accomplish the feat, we should feel much satisfaction in attaching one large poster to the wall of the light-house on the left, and another to that of the fortress on the right. Both headlands could be converted into very noble bill-posting stations for the information of all who come to California. It is almost wondrous that some enterprising speculator from New England has not made a tender for them. The idea is not a romantic one, but eminently practical.

As yet we can not see the city of San Francisco. It is round a promontory, where the bay curves to the southward. On a solitary rock in the middle of the strait through which we are passing is Fort Alcatraz. Far away in the distance, shadowy in the moonlight, is Monte Diabolo, and here in front of us is the Island of Yerba Buena. A few minutes more and the lights of the great city burst upon us, flashing along the shore and glistening from terrace upon terrace, where reposes beautiful San Francisco on her throne of hills in an amphitheatre of rock, with a footstool of richly-laden wharves and warehouses stored with accumulations of all the treasures of the Pacific.

As we steam up to our anchorage, one of the passengers, who happens to be a very well-informed Californian citizen, obligingly details to us how the bay received its name. He tells us that in the year 1769 a certain friar, Juan Crespi, started from San Diego with instructions to found a mission at Monterey. Travelling up the coast northward, he arrived at the place to which he had been sent, but found that the harbor was not a good one. Friar Crespi mingled ideas of commerce with his zeal for the propagation of the Christian faith, and determined to seek a better place for shipping still farther north than Monterey. Plodding on patiently through what are now known as Santa Cruz, Santa Clara, and San Mateo, the good old priest came to a bay of glorious

size, with a harbor of corresponding excellence. He believed himself to
be the first white man who had seen it, adopted it at once as the site of
his future mission, and named it after the founder of the order to which
he himself belonged—San Francisco.

Still the old mission stands, and the bay that Friar Crespi named just
one hundred years ago has given its own name to that of a city, in the
streets of which are to be seen the latest fashions of Paris—a city certainly not behind any other in the world in its possession of the good
things that tend to make life pleasant, and the act of living a continuous occupation of rose-gathering.

Dear old England of ours! Why do you so often play the part of the
Fat Boy in "Pickwick," and fall asleep so frequently? Had you been
but wide awake, this California in which we now are would have not
belonged to the Spaniard, nor to the American, but to you. The treasure
was in your hands—the prize was at your feet. You did not stoop to
pick it up, nor close your fingers upon it when it was within your grasp.
Your own adventurous mariners ploughed these waters of the northern
Peaceful Ocean, and returned to tell you of the rich possessions at your
command. Still, to the present time, the memory of your loss survives
in the name of a picturesque indentation of the coast not far north of
San Francisco, where the waters of the Pacific shine at noon and surge
at midnight in *Sir Francis Drake's* Bay!

The "Golden Age" has come safely to her moorings off the wharf at
the bottom of Folsom Street, San Francisco. We have all thanked Captain Lapidge for his courteous attentions during a pleasant voyage of
three thousand miles, and are each eagerly desirous of stepping on
shore. Twenty-four days have passed since we left New York, during
which time we have travelled more than five thousand miles, going
down the North American Continent on one side and up it on the other.
The time is near at hand when travellers who wish to pass from New
York to California will no longer come by the route we have taken. The
Pacific railroad will be an accomplished fact; the iron horse will career
across the plains, snort on the summit of the Rocky Mountains, and
neigh in locomotive fashion amidst the snows of the Sierra Nevada.

Where again are you, dear drowsy England? You should have had a
railway already in course of construction, if not already completed,
from one side to the other of that British America which you hold in
separate colonies, from Canada westward through the valleys of the

Saskatchewan to British Columbia, where you have gold mines of your own. The engineering difficulties are not equal to those which the Americans have to encounter in building their iron way, and you have wealth enough at your command to engage all the labor that would be required. The time must come when there will be a highway for the steam-engine straight through from Halifax, Nova Scotia, to New Westminster, on the Fraser River—England's own road to China and Japan. France may gain an engineering glory in marrying the Mediterranean to the Red Sea, but England will have a greater triumph with her engineering army when she has completed two parallel rows of iron bands, extending through her own possessions from the Atlantic to the Pacific.

From Folsom Street wharf we drive to the Occidental Hotel, where we at once find ourselves to be at home. No better hotel do we wish to stop at, in whatever part of the world we wander. We announce our relationship to the showman's fraternity, and are gladly welcomed. Our arrangements are soon made. A nice commodious room is assigned to us, and we are free of the house for the sum of two dollars and a half per day, payable in gold. Greenbacks are not current in California. There is a State law that payments shall be made in coin. As a matter of course, it can not override the Federal enactment, by which greenbacks are made legal currency throughout the Union, but Californians accept greenbacks at a discount to pay taxes with and to trade with their brethren in the East. Among themselves the golden dollar and the beautiful twenty-dollar gold piece are the coins in daily use. They have a mint of their own in which to coin them; and the letter "S" on the face of them attests to their being coined in San Francisco. Money coined at New Orleans has an "O" upon it; while that coined at the great mint in Philadelphia is without any distinctive letter. There are but three mints in the United States.

For the English reader to understand what we get for two dollars and a half per day at the Occidental Hotel, it is necessary to take a cursory peep at the hotel itself. So very different is it in its arrangements from that which an untravelled man might expect to find far away out here on the extreme western edge of civilization.

There are five brothers of the name of Leland who are engaged in hotel business in the United States. They have establishments in New York, at Saratoga, here in San Francisco, and elsewhere. In New York they conduct the great Metropolitan Hotel in Broadway, inside which, like a kernel in a nut, is the theatre known as Niblo's Garden. The Lelands have a special talent for hotel-keeping. It seems to have been born in their blood, and—*vires acquirit eundo*—to develop itself with more force the more hotels they build. The Occidental, San Francisco, is managed, at the time of which we are writing, by Mr. Louis Leland, who is at hand ready to receive his guests just arrived by the steamer. An air of sumptuous splendor and easeful comfort strikes us, immediately we enter the doors, as being characteristics of the house. Newly built, only a portion of the intended edifice completed, and the grand staircase not yet opened, the Occidental is but an incomplete sample of that which it is intended to be. The interior fittings are those of a first-class hotel; the bedrooms are airy, the beds soft and large; the salle-à-manger is a spacious hall, with elaborate embellishments and columns of noble proportions. There are breakfast-rooms and supper-rooms, hot and cold baths for every body, well-carpeted stairs, elegant drawing-rooms for the use of the ladies, pianos of the best manufacture, and lounges and rocking-chairs of the most luxurious construction. The attendance is far better than in most English hotels, with none of that bowing and scraping servility among the waiters which constitutes the most offensive form of attention. Our two dollars and a half per day includes attendance. The waiters do not expect to receive a gratuity for every little act of duty they may chance to perform; but if they know you to belong to a show and likely to give them a free pass, they will shower upon you every civility they can manifest.

Americans have a *cuisine* of their own; not always acceptable to Europeans. The dishes are not such as an Englishman is accustomed to at home, and to some of them he may very possibly object. If he is fastidious about having his joint roasted instead of baked, he is likely to meet with disappointment in the course of his American travel. Should he like his beef underdone, he may feel annoyed at Americans liking theirs well done, and at the cook sending up the meat brown instead of red. To compensate for these little drawbacks, he will find more than a balance of advantage in the copiousness of the *menu* and the numerous luscious dishes peculiar to the Western Continent. There is no roast turkey in Europe comparable with the roast turkey of the United States, and there is no vegetable so delicious as a cob of green corn served up hot on a white napkin with butter, pepper, and salt. Here, at the Occidental Hotel, the bill of fare comprises every thing which the Pacific coast produces, and any number of luxurious dainties imported from Europe. The tables groan with good things—with beef from Contra Costa and potatoes from Bodega, with richly-tinted apples from Oregon and the juiciest of grapes from Sonoma, with strawberries from Oakland and peaches from Marysville. There is breakfast to be had at any hour of the morning, with any dainty or any number of dainties you may please to select to accompany it. The milk rich, the butter magnificent. There is luncheon at midday, the tables covered with tempting dishes and the best of fruits. At dinner the dishes are numerous, and the dessert one to which Apicius might sit down and be happy, or Lucullus himself feel that he had done the right thing in coming to California. When you express a desire for tea, you are furnished with some of the rarest flavor and fragrance; and when you come in late and seek your supper you will find it waiting for you, laid out in the very best style. All these we obtain for two dollars and a half per day.

But there is more to be had for your money yet. Pass down stairs and you will find a large reading-room furnished with newspapers from all parts of the United States, and with magazines of every description. Here, too, you will find the latest numbers of the "Times," "Punch," and the "Illustrated News" that have arrived from England. Do you want to know how they are getting on with the war in Virginia or Kentucky? Here are the latest telegrams posted on the wall, and here are abstracts of the state of the money-market in New York this morning, and of the discussions in Congress yesterday. Here, too, in the same reading-room, is a telegraph office, if you wish to send a message; here are desks for writing, and a library, if you desire to read a book. More still beyond. Pass into this back apartment, and you are in a museum of the mineral products of California. With most commendable care for the comfort of his guests, Mr. Leland has provided a collection of specimens of every variety of gold ore from the different diggings of California, and with properly labelled exemplifications of the various rocks and earths to be found throughout the State. There is more information to be obtained in this room in one hour, relative to the geology of the Pacific coast, than a week of reading would furnish. Then the excellence of the idea—a museum in the hotel! and we get it all for two dollars and a half per day. We know that some people pay three, and some a little more, but we do not.

Fresh from our voyage, and about to part with pleasant acquaintances whom we have become familiar with during our ocean trip, we descend to the bar to partake of a social glass. Were we in England we should order it into our room, but, being in California, we do nothing of the kind. The bar is the right place at which to take it, and to the bar we go. Our host accompanies us; for no one better than he knows how to speed the parting guest, or welcome the coming one.

Ubi mel, etc. The bar is fitted up with great taste, and the good things with which it is stocked are numerous; consequently full a score of the gentlemen passengers by the "Golden Age" have already found their way there. It is a commodious apartment, luxuriously appointed, scrupulously clean, and radiant with white marble, gilt fixtures, and glittering crystal. Nothing to remind one of the garish glare of polished brass, the greasy mahogany, or the unpleasant odor of black beetles, occasionally to be met with in hotel bars of certain English towns.

Behind the counter is one of the most distinguished, if not the chief, of American "bar-tenders." His name is Jerry Thomas—a name as familiar in the Eastern States as it now is out here in California. Bartending, as it is called, is an art in the United States, and Mr. Jerry Thomas is an accomplished artist. In the manufacture of a "cocktail," a "julep," a "smash," or an "eye-opener," none can beat him, though he may have successful rivals. For instance, there is Mr. William Pitcher, of the "Tremont House," Boston, who, because he has obtained proficiency in the making of cocktails, and is accustomed to make them for the students of Harvard, and for other learned imbibers, mingles Greek with his gin, and entitles himself on his card "Professor of Kratisalectronouratation." But Mr. Jerry Thomas is author as well as artist, and has written a work on the art of compounding drinks. He is clever also with his pencil as well as with his pen; and behind his bar are specimens of his skill as a draughtsman. He is a gentleman who is all ablaze with diamonds. There is a very large pin, formed of a cluster of diamonds, in the front of his magnificent shirt, he has diamond studs at his wrists, and gorgeous diamond rings on his fingers—diamonds being "properties" essential to the calling of a bar-tender in the United States. Unless he already possesses them, it is said that no member of the craft can expect to attain to a high-class position. Mr. Jerry Thomas, we are told, can command his hundred dollars, or twenty pounds, weekly, for wages. It must be remembered, however, that he is in California, and that he is engaged as a "star." The interest on the value of his diamonds is worth the money.

In the Boston Theatre there is a large central chandelier. I have heard it said as a joke that bar-tenders and negro minstrels avoid the Boston Theatre on its account. It is heart-breaking to them that they can not have a diamond breast-pin as large or wear the chandelier instead.

We are recognized by an old acquaintance whom we have met before in Nevada City among the mines.

"Come to engineer another show?" he asks.

We reply in the affirmative, and, being requested to state what show, we publish that Artemus Ward is our hero, and that he will be here shortly.

"He'll do, you bet," asserts our interrogator. "He's sound on the goose too—isn't he?"

We know that the question has to do with the political principles of Artemus Ward, and we boldly declare that his soundness is unimpeachable.

"Then we'll drink to his success, and I'll shake hands with him when he comes. Gentlemen, order your drinks. Here's the old toast—'Thus we cross the Yuba!' Success to Artemus Ward."

⚬ 18 ⚬

Waking the Echoes in San Francisco

FOUR or five o'clock in the morning was about the time. The place was the Occidental Hotel, in San Francisco. I had scarcely had three hours' sleep when I was roused by some one shaking my arm and saluting me familiarly, saying,

"How are you, old boy? Just heard you had arrived. Was down at the steamer, but did not see you. Glad to see you back among us. I've brought you up a cocktail. Just had a nice stiff one made on purpose for you."

The speaker was an enthusiastic young Irishman engaged on the "Alta California" newspaper. During a previous visit to San Francisco he had rendered me some literary assistance, and was always ready to tender his aid in furthering the interests of a showman.

"Just got through at the paper," he continued. "Was going home to bed. Heard you were here, and came along at once to be the first to shake hands. You are going to sling us Artemus Ward, are you?"

I replied that I had come to San Francisco as the precursor of that gentleman, and expected him to arrive by the next steamer.

"Well, my boy, we'll put him through. We'll bedazzle him with Californian glory, and show him the ropes as well as give him the rocks. We want a new sensation. Had nothing lately except Menken. Finish your cocktail, and let me go down and get you another. They'll make one for me here at any hour. Artemus Ward coming. Well, that's mighty good! We'll wake the echoes for him, and give him a good time."

I thanked my warm-hearted friend for his expressions of good-will; declined to accept another cocktail at that unseemly hour, and begged to be allowed to go to sleep, having had very little rest the previous night. With reluctance the echo-waker shook hands and departed, consenting to forego "waking the echoes" until later in the day.

After breakfast came the task of opening up the campaign in California. There was much to be done, and done quickly. Artemus would be in San Francisco by the next steamer. Every thing must be prepared for his arrival. One great point had to be ascertained with promptitude, and that was whether Artemus Ward should "speak his piece" at his own risk and venture, or whether a speculator was to be found who would buy him up at a price so good as to render it better to accept a certainty than to take the chances of success or failure without any one but ourselves being interested in the enterprise.

There were good reasons, if a liberal *entrepreneur* could be found, that the business should be left in his hands. Though I knew California very well from previous experiences there; and though how to launch and to steer an entertainment had been my study for some years, San Francisco had altered somewhat since I had last visited it, and a local manager was likely to know better than a comparative stranger the mode of commanding a large audience, and of working the venture successfully. To find such a speculator, the best method of procedure seemed to be to have my arrival in San Francisco announced at once in the evening paper, as well as the object of my coming, and the hotel at which I was residing; then to allow twenty-four hours to pass away, and wait to see what fish would nibble at the bait.

On a slip of paper I noted down the agenda of the day. That which was to be done first coming first in order.

1. To send a telegram across the continent to New York to announce to anxious friends the safe arrival in California.

2. To call at the "San Francisco Evening Bulletin" office, and secure the insertion of a paragraph stating that Artemus Ward is coming, that his *avant-courier* is here, and that headquarters are at the Occidental Hotel.

3. To call at the Opera-house, see Mr. Thomas Maguire, the Manager, who telegraphed to Artemus Ward in New York to ask what "he would take," and ascertain if Mr. Maguire would be willing to make a good offer.

4. To unpack the box in which were the hundred copies of "Artemus Ward, His Book," on the title-page of each of which was written "With the compliments of the Author." Then to take a conveyance, go round the city, present the letters of introduction I had brought with me, as well as call on old influential friends and leave a copy of the book as a present wherever the so leaving it would be productive of good results, or, to use the language of my Hibernian friend, assist in "waking the echoes."

5. To be sure to call first on the Rev. Mr. Starr King, the most popular preacher in San Francisco, and for whom I had a special copy of Artemus's book. Before leaving New York, I had been particularly requested by Artemus Ward to see the celebrated clergyman of San Francisco as soon as possible after my arrival, and solicit his aid in promoting the success of the first lecture. Also, if practicable, to get him to occupy a seat on the platform.

6. To call on the editors of the various papers, present them each with one of the books, so that they might have the material ready at hand from which to make extracts, and enlist their aid in the great cause of Artemus and popularity.

7. To drop in at the chief book-stores and at the "Mercantile Library Association," announce the object of my visit, and ascertain the probable chances of success.

Here was work enough for one day, but the seed had to be sown copiously in order that the harvest might be abundant. To adopt the phraseology of showmen, "You must work your show if you want to make a go of it."

The dispatch of the telegram to New York was the first thing to be done. In a very few minutes the message was delivered to the clerk at the telegraph office in Montgomery Street. Before noon it was re-telegraphed on from Salt Lake City, and before evening it was read on the other side of the continent, in the city of New York, three thousand five hundred miles away.

A call at the "Evening Bulletin" office was the next duty to perform. Had I gone to England on a similar errand, I should have spared myself the trouble of calling at the "Times" office; but San Francisco is not London, although the "Bulletin" is one of the most respectable, well-conducted, and high-principled of newspapers. Travellers are apt to come home and write sensation paragraphs relative to the eccentricities of Western journals; but he would be a very hypercritical traveller indeed who would undertake to represent the "San Francisco Evening Bulletin" as other than a first-class paper, well written, well edited, and invariably accurate in its reports. Unlike some other journals of the Western World, it does not open its columns to paid-for puffery; never indulges in "highfalutin" or bombastic language in its articles, and carefully eschews the insertion of any paragraph which might render its pages unacceptable to the most fastidious family circle. It had for its editor a well-educated English gentleman, who was at one time, I believe, a frequent contributor to the "Edinburgh Review."

As I walked down Montgomery Street towards the "Bulletin" office, I was irresistibly reminded that I was in San Francisco and nowhere else. Overhead was a bright sky without a cloud, around me an atmosphere which seemed to communicate elasticity, nervous tone, and lightness of spirits. Before me were buildings which in their whiteness and airy appearance suggested Paris or one of the cities of the Mediterranean. But not the clear sky, nor the bracing atmosphere, nor the brightness of the buildings, was so corroborative of the fact of my being in San Francisco as were the developments of social life around me. The ladies out walking were dressed as in England they would dress for carriage-riding only, and the gentlemen wore for morning attire black trowsers, black coats, and shirts with fancy fronts. I met Chinese in the costume of the Flowery Land, and in the habiliments of natives of the Western hemisphere. I passed miners fresh from the mines, and emigrants recently arrived from New York. At the corner of one street stood a group of Spanish residents, and on the other side of the way were the brown faces and broad-brimmed *sombreros* of men who had lately journeyed from Arizona, Chihuahua, or Sonora. Then, when I halted before the "Bulletin" office, I found a crowd assembled around it, and, becoming recognized by one of the number, my hand was tightly grasped, and he who welcomed me said:

"I am right glad to see you! Why, where on earth have you come from? Have you got any feet?"

The question puzzled me. I hesitated before answering that I believed I was the owner of two.

"Well, that won't do," continued my acquaintance. "I am glad to see you—I *am!* If you've got no feet, I've got a whole pocket full, and I'll give you some. Good ones too. Gould and Curry are up this morning."

Ignoramus as I was, the meaning of the benevolent Californian was a mystery to me. If Gould and Curry were up I did not care, not knowing the gentlemen; and where they had gone up to was a matter I cared about less; but I own that my curiosity was a little excited concerning the "feet" my friend stated he had in his pocket, and I was anxious to know more about them, as well as what possible benefit they could be to me if he carried out his profession of generosity.

A few words of explanation, and I understood all. Since my previous visit to California the silver mines of Nevada had been discovered and worked. The "Gould and Curry" was the richest of those mines. Mining property in the land of silver was not reckoned up in shares, but in "feet." The area of each mine was measured off, and the owners allotted so many feet each. With their "feet" they went into the share-market, with their "feet" they assembled in Montgomery Street, bought, sold, speculated, won or lost. In London, at that very time, the jest of the streets was to inquire in senseless *badinage*, "How's your poor feet?" While six thousand miles off, in San Francisco, the familiar question everywhere was, "Have you got any feet?" or, "How are feet to-day?"

My errand at the office of the "Bulletin" was soon accomplished. The paragraph with which the first "echo" was to be started was to appear that evening.

Turning up Washington Street towards the Plaza, I found Mr. Maguire, the proprietor of the Opera-house, just in the same spot where I had parted with him a few years previously. He was standing in front of his place of business, smoothing down his beard in the sunlight, precisely as I have seen him engaged morning after morning in time past. It was his habit to transact all his business on the footpath in front of his theatre. There he had settled on the production of new pieces, engaged companies, dispatched agents to Europe, made contracts for building new theatres up the country, purchased mining stock, bought the best horses in California, heard calmly the news of his losses by fire in some distant part of the State, paid over ten thousand dollars at a time, and lectured refractory actresses on their duties while on the stage. Among the representative men of California there is not a more noticeable one in his way than Mr. Thomas Maguire; nor would any history of San Francisco be complete with his name omitted from its pages. Commencing life in a very humble position in New York, he went out to California in its earliest days; speculated in shows, played at faro, fought duels, built theatres, saw them burn one after another in the great fires which from time to time desolated San Francisco; and, nothing daunted, when one theatre had become ashes, fell to work and built up another immediately. Among his last enterprises was to visit London, and, in conjunction with Mr. Richard Risley, bring over the Japanese acrobats and jugglers. He engaged Her Majesty's Theatre for their performances. About a week previous to the date on which they were to appear, he and I stood at the corner of Suffolk Place and saw the grand old Opera-house make red the midnight sky. It almost broke the heart of the plucky Californian manager. "Haven't I had enough of that kind of luck in San Francisco?" said he to me. "What has it followed me here for?"

Mr. Maguire received me in the most friendly manner, there, in front of his theatre in Washington Street of the Californian metropolis. Presently he inquired: "What did your Mr. Ward mean by replying to my telegram in that way, saying when I asked him what he'd take to come out here, that he'd take brandy and water? Well, it was a good joke. It went into all the papers, and it will do him good. Of course he'll come to me. You should let me handle him. How much do you want for him for the whole State?"

My reply was to the effect that Mr. Maguire had better make his own offer. He did so immediately. I declined to accept, and left him to think the matter over. Returning to the hotel, I unpacked my parcel of books, and, taking a dozen or two with me, proceeded to make a series of calls.

The Rev. Starr King, the head of the Unitarian Church in San Francisco, was the first gentleman I selected to visit. There were many reasons for my doing so. In the first place, there was Artemus Ward's expressed wish that I should endeavor to enlist Mr. King in his favor, and secure his attendance on the first night. Then there was the fact of the reverend gentleman's great popularity in California, and the influence he had over all classes of citizens in San Francisco. In addition, to see Mr. King and obtain his advice were desirable points to be gained. He was himself a popular lecturer, and something of a showman. Some years before I had heard him lecture in San Francisco on the life of Socrates to a church so crowded, that although a dollar, I believe, was charged for admission, many persons paid simply for the privilege of standing in the porch and listening as best they could. Then, again, a new and beautiful cavern was discovered up the country. When it was opened to the public, the Rev. Starr King was called upon to play the part of exhibitor, and deliver an oration on its beauties. Whenever a public occasion required the delivery of an eloquent speech, or wherever oratory could be brought in to aid a good work, his assistance was sure to be sought, and he was always as courteously willing as he was unquestionably competent. His place is now filled, I believe, by the Rev. Horatio Stebbins, formerly of Boston, a very thoughtful and excellent preacher, but the grand voice of the truthful, eloquent, and enthusiastic Starr King must still linger in the memory of those who heard it as one the like of which is not soon to be heard again upon the Pacific coast.

A brief and most agreeable conversation, and my object in visiting the reverend gentleman was attained. He expressed how much he had already enjoyed the writings of Artemus Ward, was prepared to give him a warm welcome, would do his best to advertise him among friends, and would unfailingly attend on the first night. So far, so good. He was better than a large poster.

Many more calls were made during the morning, and many presentation-books distributed. Then came a chat with the booksellers, and a little interested advice to them to make a show of some of their copies of Artemus's book in their shop windows. For the adornment of their premises as well as for the satisfaction of public curiosity, I left them each one or two portraits of the coming lecturer. All alike were encouraging enough to express but one opinion; and that was that there would be large audiences and golden dollars in satisfactory plenitude. Let me add that the bookstores of San Francisco are an honor to the city. Their size and the large stock of standard works they each contain bear evidence that brains as well as "feet" are valued in the Land of Gold, and that the *auri sacra fames* is accompanied with a constant thirst for knowledge.

The newspapers had yet to be called upon; a few little courtesies to be exchanged, and the editorial pulse to be properly felt. He who neglects the newspaper in America commits a worse fault than if he sinned against the Constitution of the United States. There is no difficulty in seeing an editor or a newspaper manager. Your visit is not intrusive, provided you have the common sense not to bother. On the contrary, it is regarded as a compliment, and an act of attention worthy of being duly reciprocated. That your visit may be thoroughly acceptable, the rule is to say all you have to say in a few words, afford all the information you can, place as much matter at the disposal of the editor as may be desirable, and take your departure without delay. Sow the seed and wait the result. Of course you have a few "deadhead" or complimentary tickets with you. Take care that you give them to the proper persons.

Among the morning papers the "Alta California" was the chief. I believe that it still retains that position. For commercial news, for stocks, "feet," public companies and auctions, it holds pre-eminent rank, and possesses the means of obtaining very copious information. Being known to Mr. Noah, who was then one of the editors, I had no difficulty in effecting the object of my visit. The coming of Artemus Ward would be heralded in the "Alta California" precisely in the way in which I wished it to be. There would be a short paragraph the following morning, and longer ones in due course.

The next newspaper to be attended to was the "Morning Daily Call," a remarkably spirited and chatty little journal, published at a very cheap rate, having a large circulation, and being full of piquant paragraphs, bits of scandal, sensation "items," and special scraps of news interesting to its numerous lady readers. I placed myself fearlessly in the hands of Mr. Barnes, one of its editors and proprietors, and had no reason afterwards to regret that my confidence had been wrongly intrusted, or that my intention in calling had been misconstrued. In the office of the "Morning Daily Call" I chanced to meet one of the most able and most original of Californian authors—Mr. Bret Harte— whose contributions to the literature of the Pacific will most assuredly be one day collected and published in London. My announcement to him that Artemus Ward was about to visit San Francisco was quite enough to secure his good-will and hearty literary cooperation.

Then I went across to the office of the "Golden Era," a weekly paper, excellently well printed, always full of entertaining matter of literary merit, and having a circulation which ranges over all the western coast of English-speaking North America. I had a letter of introduction to Colonel Lawrence, co-proprietor and editor. The colonel chanced to be at his desk, and received me very graciously. My mission was soon executed. The assuring phrase of "We'll put him through," was enough to satisfy me that the cause of Artemus Ward would be quite safe in his hands. I wished to know how much matter relative to the lecture and the lecturer I could contribute to the next number. The colonel smiled. "You are stopping at the Occidental, are you not?" he asked. I replied that I was. "Then," said he, "I'll drop in there late to-night, and take a drink with you and we'll talk it over."

There chanced to be one or two other gentlemen in the office of the "Golden Era" at the time. One of them paid particular attention to all I had to say about Artemus Ward coming, and then remarked:

"We know a good deal about Mr. Ward, and I've no doubt he'll *corral** some very good audiences. But you should bring along out here some of your great English writers whose books we have all read."

I inquired which of them the gentleman thought would draw the best houses.

"Well, there's Charles Dickens. He goes out with a show of his own now—don't he?"

I explained that Mr. Dickens simply gave readings from his own works.

"Well," rejoined the speculative Californian, "I wouldn't mind going in a few thousand dollars for him to come and read his books out here; but there's your Bulwer. His Last Days of Pompei-i is a smart book— as smart a book as I know. He ought to be brought out too. Now I'll give you an idea. There's a pile of dollars in it—*you bet*. Bring out your Dickens and your Bulwer, and let them read together on the same night. First Dickens a bit out of his books, and then Bulwer a bit out of his. One down and the other come on. Sakes alive! they'd have a good time out here in old California! My columns would be open to both of them,"

Corral, Spanish for an inclosure. *To corral* is a Californian phrase meaning to gather in, or get together.

added Colonel Lawrence. "They could just have as much space as they liked to write themselves up in the 'Golden Era.' "

The "Dispatch," another weekly paper of much importance, and one or two other journals of minor position, remained for me to visit. But the day was over, and further calls had to be postponed. Dinner, and a stroll round to the theatres in the company of the friend who had promised to "wake the echoes," occupied the evening. Late at night, the moon shining brilliantly and the stars in the clear sky of California seeming to be larger than the stars we see above us in England, I rambled along Montgomery Street, and though the night was chill and the walk a very lonely one, made my way up Telegraph Hill, that I might look upon the Golden City of the West by moonlight.

There are a few cottages on the side, and a signal-station on the summit of Telegraph Hill. No one was about. I had brought with me one of Artemus Ward's posters, and material for fastening it up. My fancy was that the first bill announcing our enterprise in California should be posted on the signal-station. There it is that the arrival of vessels is notified, and there, it seemed fitting to me, should be the earliest notification of the coming of Artemus Ward. The poster duly affixed, I wrapped my outer coat around me, for the wind was keen, and sat down to enjoy the prospect.

Beneath me, to the east, lay the commercial portion of San Francisco, built along the shore of its magnificent bay. Lights gleamed from the windows of houses perched up on the three great hills which back the city. I have been told that San Francisco, like Rome, is built on seven hills, but I could never enumerate that number. Lights glimmered down in the bay among the shipping and on the island of Yerba Buena. Lights, too, were dimly discernible across the bay at Contra Costa. Grim and silent in the midst of the placid waters slept Fort Alcatraz on its throne of rock. Westward were the grand portals of the Golden Gate; beyond them the waters of the Pacific. Twenty years ago and the country around me was almost a solitude, except having here and there a Spanish mission. Now there was a great and gay city, filled with rich and energetic inhabitants, a harbor crowded with vessels, and the whole commerce of the western half of a continent centring in this one spot— a commerce that must perforce go on increasing and still increasing, until the "star of empire," taking its way still farther westward and travelling across the Pacific, Yokohama and Canton shall become the centres of the civilized world, the Orient regain its ancient supremacy, the circuit be completed, and the days of the millennium accomplished.

Seated there in solitude on the summit of Telegraph Hill, thoughts chased one another rapidly through the brain, and imagination pictured out the great wastes of Oregon and of Washington Territory away to the north; the coral isles visited in days gone by in the peaceful ocean flowing to the south-west, and the dreary deserts of the great continent to the east which would have to be traversed, if, as projected, my homeward path should be taken that way. But overhead the stars were bright, the moon brilliant, the sky clear. Around all was tranquillity and beauty. To the memory came the grand lines of Tennyson:

> "I hear at times a sentinel
>   Who moves about from place to place,
>   And whispers to the worlds of space
> In the deep night that all is well."

Five minutes afterwards the poetry of the situation was ruthlessly destroyed by a watchman asking me what I was doing at night on Telegraph Hill.

I felt that there was solid prose in the watchman's question, and after chatting with him and bidding him "good-night," descended the hill, sought out the Occidental Hotel, and went to bed, feeling that the "echoes" had been roused enough for one day.

◦ 19 ◦

San Francisco from a Showman's Point of View

TWENTY-FOUR hours to let pass and wait the results of what had been already done. That was the plan I laid out. Meanwhile there was time for a stroll round San Francisco, to notice its changes and improvements, revisit old friends and form a few new acquaintances. A lengthy description of the city would be foreign to the purpose of these pages, but a brief reference to its amusements and its varied developments of show life will perhaps be expected by the reader. The city itself affords material enough for half a dozen volumes, so varied are the scenes to be met with in its streets, so motley is the character of its inhabitants.

Imagine a city built where there was no place to build one. Imagine a bay, a narrow strip of shore alongside that bay, and steep hills rising from it, their summits stony, and their bases almost washed by the waters of the bay. On the strip of shore San Francisco had its origin. The narrowness of the strip soon became an inconvenience. What was to be done? Three things. First, build out on piles into the bay; secondly, build on some of the hills as they stood; and, thirdly, hew out the stone, and remove, by the process of blasting, a portion of the rock of which the hills are formed, and turn hilly paths into level roads. All this has been done. Roads have been made through the rock by engineering skill, and street after street, with rows of warehouses, hotels, and offices, built parallel with the strip of shore skirting the bay, on piles driven into the mud. The city is now as up-hill as have been the lives of most of its inhabitants.

Pretty and picturesque is the up-hill part of San Francisco. Charming villas and delightful little residences, all of them very white in color and some of them most fanciful in design, are perched up one above another on hewn crag and rocky summit. From the windows of some of them can be seen the glimmer of the sunlight on the Pacific through the open Gate of the Golden Land; while from the windows of most of them may by obtained views of the beautiful bay, of majestic Monte Diabolo, of Oakland with its paradise of pretty trees, and of the gay and brilliant city, which has the brightness of Marseilles, the sky of Athens, and the atmosphere of Eastern Australia.

Away in the rear and to the north-west of the pretty up-hill residences, is the Old Presidio; while to the east is the quaint old Mission Dolores; so that in less than an hour you can leave behind you American San Francisco of to-day, and look upon what remains of Spanish dominion in the days gone by.

Descend to the Plaza, or Portsmouth Square, as it used to be called some years ago, and you are in the heart of San Francisco. Wander round the pretty inclosure, and you will meet with exemplars of the nationalities of all lands. You will notice Americans just arrived from

Boston, New York, or New Orleans; Englishmen from British Columbia or from Vancouver's Island; Australians from Sydney or Melbourne; Chinese from various parts of the Celestial Empire; Japanese from Hakodadi or from Jeddo; Mexicans, with their sarapes rolled around them; Spaniards from Cuba or from Spain itself; Peruvians with their heads thrust through their picturesque ponchos; brown-skinned Kanakas from Honolulu; Chilians, with their dark, flashing eyes; Brazilians, with their black, shining hair; Digger Indians from the interior, dressed in their rags and feathers; miners from the mines in their rough costume; Germans, puffy with lager-bier; and Frenchmen, dressed as though they were on the Parisian boulevards. On the Plaza and along Montgomery Street there is a continual midday masquerade.

On the Plaza, too, stands the City Hall, opposite to where the alcalde used to hold his court in former times. The City Hall occupies the site of the Jenny Lind Theatre, burnt many years ago. Music halls, or low-class concert rooms, are as numerous, in proportion, in San Francisco as they are in the large towns of England. On the Plaza is one which has been long established, and to which miners go to get rid of their surplus gold. It is known as Tetlow's "Bella Union." On another side of the Plaza is Gilbert's "Melodeon," with its windows decorated with large sheets of painted linen, on which are figures of nigger minstrels, Irish jig dancers, ladies of the ballet making very angular pirouettes, and infant prodigies doing any thing but what a good child ought to do.

A city so cosmopolitan as San Francisco must have amusements to suit all tastes. Consequently, in Jackson Street there are any number of dance-houses for sailors, Mexicans, Sonorians, and South American rough customers. In one of the suburbs are the ruins of the wooden amphitheatre in which bull-fights once took place, but the Spanish and Mexican portion of the inhabitants still contrive to give bull-fighting exhibitions on the Contra Costa side of the bay, circulating the handbills announcing them in the public places of the city. These handbills are printed in Spanish and English. They are usually marvels of composition, being well worthy of their place among the literature of shows. A brave and gallant bull-fighter is Don Gabriel Rivers, as his name is printed on the placard I have before me. I do not doubt that he is a plucky Andalusian, but "Rivers" is very suggestive, and I beg his pardon for suspecting him of having learned the elements of his graceful art in one of the *abattoirs* of New York. He announces that he is "King

of the Sword," and that he will have the honor of introducing "six savage, wild, full-blooded and desperate bulls. These six bulls were lassoed
on the loneliest mountains of the coast, where they are not accustomed
to see human society. They have a fiery hatred to the civilized world.
Their disposition is on that account fierce and frightful; so that the
fighting of them can only be done by him who is a grand master of the
sword, and by *matadors* of acknowledged reputation and honor. There
will be a magnificent display of first-class fire-works when the bulls
have the pleasure of appearing before the public."

But the Spanish inhabitants of San Francisco occasionally desire to
have amusements of a more intellectual kind, and the Spanish drama
is performed for them in the grand language of old Spain at the American Theatre, Sansome Street. The French part of the population are
frequently treated to a drama played in French; the German inhabitants to a comedy or tragedy in German. While in San Francisco, I
attended the performance of a German play wherein one of the actors
played admirably. His name, if I remember rightly, was Maubert.
When will so many nationalities be theatrically represented in London?

Asia as well as Europe asserts the right of having its amusements
represented in the metropolis of California. The Chinese population
being very large, and there being whole streets in which the houses are
occupied by immigrants from the Celestial Empire, a Chinese theatre is
a matter of necessity. Artemus Ward, in his Lecture on the Mormons,
used to refer to his experiences of the Chinese drama in San Francisco.
I accompanied him on the occasion, and in a subsequent chapter will
attempt to describe what we both saw.

Fond as the inhabitants are of more exciting amusements, the English drama is, after all, the form of entertainment most fashionable in
California. Opera invariably draws good audiences, but the difficulty
is to get good artistes. A troupe chiefly composed of ladies and gentlemen who came from London made a very large sum of money in San
Francisco during one of my visits to that city. The *prima donna* of the
troupe was Miss Lucy Escott, and the tenor Mr. Henry Squires. Then,
for Italian opera there were the Bianchi family, together with a dozen
or two of other artistes who have a celebrity in the "Far West." The
usual rule is for opera artistes to play in California till they cease to be
attractive, then take ship and go off to Australia, Hong Kong, or South
America, and, after having made a tour of the Pacific, return to Cali-

fornia. Fancy *Amina* and *Elvino*, *Norma*, *Adalgisa* and *Pollio*, *Azucena* and *Manrico*, taking a professional tour over waters which Grijalva and Sebastian Viscanio, Drake, Anson, and Captain Cook explored with wondering eyes, in days which have hardly yet become those of antiquity!

Maguire's Opera-house, Washington Street, is the theatre which has enjoyed the longest run of good fortune. It is not a large house, but very compact. Some of its arrangements used to be peculiar. For instance, all around the back of the pit was a series of private boxes for the exclusive use of the *demi-monde* of San Francisco; while on the first floor, over the entrance, were extensive gambling rooms, where he who might be desirous of "bucking the tiger," or, in other words, playing the game of faro, might have a chance of breaking the bank if skill and fortune were with him, or a still greater chance of becoming "broke" himself, to use the Californian synonym for impecuniosity.

Most of the "stars" from New York, from London, or from Australia who have chanced to visit San Francisco in past years, have displayed their talents at Maguire's Opera-house. New plays, as soon as produced in the English or American metropolis, are sent on to San Francisco; for Mr. Maguire has agents in both capitals. Sometimes it is surprising how the plays find their way to San Francisco without their authors knowing that they have set out on the journey; and sometimes the authors receive remuneration. But San Francisco is a long way off, and, though gradually becoming inclosed in the garden wherein the playwright culls the flowers of pecuniary reward, it has not yet been the most prompt and punctilious of places in rendering to the auctorial Caesar that which Caesar rightly claims to be his own.

"Come and let me show you what a place I have made since you were out here last," said Mr. Maguire, taking me by the arm, leading me through mysterious passages, and ushering me into a large hall in which were many desks. "I have built them a Stock Exchange. Here's where they sell their 'feet' and shake about their dollars."

As far as I could make out, the dollars were shaken about on the very spot where, a few years before, I witnessed the ladies of the ballet disporting themselves on what was once the stage of the Lyceum Theatre, in the days when Mr. Lewis Baker was the proprietor thereof. The Lyceum has ceased to be. Adjacent to its former site, but round the corner in Montgomery Street—or "on Montgomery," to write as a

Californian would speak—stands the Metropolitan Theatre, a very commodious house, built on the spot where another theatre of the same name once stood. It is now owned by a wealthy brewer of San Francisco.

Farther up Montgomery Street—the Regent Street of that part of the world—was a small house known as the Eureka Theatre, used at the time of Artemus Ward's visit as a minstrel hall, the minstrel company belonging to Mr. Maguire. Near to it Mr. Maguire was commencing the building of another house. From the plans of it, which I carefully looked over, it must have been, when completed, one of the most charming theatres in America. The name given to it was The Academy of Music. Round goes the whirligig of change, and hey, presto! the Academy of Music has become a furniture warehouse, while at the time that I am writing I can not find in the San Francisco papers the name of Mr. Maguire among the list of Californian managers, though his theatre still bears his name, and but a year or two ago his dramatic friends used to style him "The Napoleon of the Pacific." In addition to his theatres in San Francisco, he had one at Sacramento, another over the Sierra Nevada, at Virginia City, and a third beyond the Reese River desert, at the Silver Mines of Austin. I should not be the least surprised were I to learn that he had gone up to Alaska, the territory purchased recently from Russia, and that he is building a series of Opera-houses along the borders of Behring's Straits.

Dramatic artists are an adventurous class. In illustration of which I may mention that among the letters of introduction I took with me to San Francisco were two to gentlemen of some professional eminence. On asking for one of these gentlemen, I was told that he had gone off to start a theatre at Yokohama, in Japan; and on inquiring for the other, I was informed that he was managing a play-house up in Puget Sound. The latter had been manager of the American Theatre in San Francisco; and on going there to seek for him, a hole in the middle of the road reminded me of what I had witnessed in the same street a few years before. The incident is illustrative of the mode in which San Francisco is built. As I have before stated, a very large portion of it stands on piles driven into what was once the bay. In many parts the water still flows under shops, warehouses, and hotels. The old American Theatre in Sansome Street has a similar foundation. I was standing in front of it early in an evening of the year 1860. A friend was conversing with me. A carriage with a pair of horses was coming up the street. Suddenly, while we were still talking, the carriage and its horses disappeared. Not round any corner, nor behind any building, but vanished in the middle of the street, while coming along at a brisk rate. "Where is that carriage?" we asked each other at the same moment. "That carriage," horses, driver, and ladies inside, had all gone through the plank-road bodily. Rotten and ready to fall in, the planks had given way, and in an instant the equipage, with those belonging to it, had been precipitated into the foul water and the black mud over which Sansome Street extends.

The American Theatre has served its purpose, and may possibly by this time be demolished. Its fame in the past will not preserve it from destruction in a land where age hallows nothing. Since I left America another new theatre, more magnificent, I am told, than any one of its predecessors, has arisen in San Francisco, and is under the management of two very talented American actors—Messrs. Maccullogh and Lawrence Barrett.

As a matter of course, San Francisco has its Museum or miscellaneous collection of shows. It has also an Anatomical Exhibition, and a sort of Cremorne Gardens, known by the name of "Hayes Park," where there are various amusements provided for the pleasure-loving citizens, especially for those who seek their recreation on Sunday.

To the traveller recently arrived from one of the Eastern States the fact of the theatres and other places of entertainment being open to the San Franciscans on Sunday evening is a matter of surprise. Many of the actors and actresses strongly object to the custom, and I believe that a new order of things is in progress. Meanwhile actors and actresses have to congratulate themselves on the fact that they are better paid in California, according to their scale of merit, than they are anywhere else in the world.

Let no one suppose that because there is nothing but a little water between San Francisco and the island on which Captain Cook was slain by the savages of the Pacific, that any of the inconveniences of savage life are to be met with in the city to which you voyage through a Golden Gate. There are many pleasures, many comforts, and luxuries without number, to be enjoyed in Chrysopolis, as some of the more pedantic of its inhabitants like to designate the treasure-laden town. You get good hotels there. They are something to get. In the hotels you may find Parisian furniture, and tables well spread with the best of food pur-

chased in the market; which for its fruit and vegetables is not to be sur-
passed by any in the cities of other lands. These also are good things to get.

I have already noticed the Occidental Hotel. Besides that, there was
at the time of my visit the Lick House, a hotel of very imposing
appearance, and the Russ House, which occupied an extended front on
Montgomery Street. At the Russ House Miss Adah Isaacs Menken was
living in stately style, together with the gentleman who was understood
to be her husband, and whose literary name is Orpheus C. Kerr.

Still another hotel of larger proportions than those already completed
was in process of building. It was opened towards the close of the year
1864, and is known as The Cosmopolitan. The announcements stated
that it was to cost two hundred and fifty thousand dollars for building.
Another two hundred thousand dollars was to be expended on the furniture, which was to be wholly composed of "solid black walnut with
brocatelle trimmings."

Next to the grandeur of the hotels, the beauty of the churches is very
noticeable in San Francisco. The religious edifices are numerous, many
of them having marked architectural excellence. The good Californians
are fond of sensational preachers. They like their clergymen to have
great oratorical and rhetorical power. A prosy parson would stand no
chance among them. The people themselves are full of "go," so also
have to be their preachers. I have already noticed the eloquence of the
late Rev. Starr King, who was not only the great preacher of his sect
but also the most popular man of any sect among the churches represented on the Pacific. But the Presbyterians have their "stars" of the
pulpit. Chief among them is the Rev. Dr. Wadsworth, from Philadelphia. So successful is he in attracting congregations that I was assured his church was the wealthiest in the city. "He draws elegant
houses," remarked my informant to me. "He's got the real grit in him,
and makes an awful pile of rocks." By which I understand that the
reverend doctor's congregation is largely disposed to liberality in the
way of remunerating him for his services.

From the churches of San Francisco to its bar-rooms is rather a
strange transition, but not more so than the way in which things are
jumbled up in the Californian metropolis. To attempt any sketch of the
place, however hastily filled in, and to omit its bar-rooms, would be a
great mistake. They are at one and the same time places of refreshment, of business, and of information. In no way except that drink is

dispensed in them, do they resemble the public houses of England. They are divided into two classes; those at which the drinks are charged at "two bits" each, and those where the price is only one "bit." A "bit" is a ten-cent piece or "dime," but "two bits" are supposed to mean a quarter of a dollar, or twenty-five cents. Where two bits are charged for a drink the vender will accept two dimes, but expects the quarter dollar, and he who offers two dimes on every occasion is soon regarded contemptuously as a shabby fellow who belongs to the rank and file of the ignoble army of "bummers."

No better illustration of a Californian first-class bar-room can be adduced than that of the one which stands on the corner of Washington and Montgomery Streets. It is designated by the name of the Bank Exchange. Carrying out that odd fancy which the good people of the West have of calling things and naming places by any but their right names, it is no uncommon practice to designate a bar-room an "exchange." In any Californian mining town The Exchange is sure to be a liquor-store, and a Magnolia is equally as certain to be an establishment of a similar description. The Bank Exchange in San Francisco is a gorgeous temple of Bacchus, conducted in the best manner. Its appointments are all sumptuous without being meretriciously gaudy; its liquors are of the very best, and its arrangements peculiar to California. For instance, during two or three hours of the morning there is a free lunch spread, at which the visitor can partake of fish, flesh, and fowl. For his drink he is charged twenty-five cents, and in that charge his luncheon is included. When there is no luncheon the table the cost of a drink is just the same, but for the twenty-five cents you may select what drink you please, even to sparkling Champagne supplied to you in a silver goblet with a gilt lining to it. Lunch, Champagne, cleanliness, and civility—all for an English shilling! A good land is California.

In addition to the drinking and eating, the intellectual wants of the visitors are attended to in the San Franciscan bar-rooms. For instance, at the Bank Exchange, Mr. Parker, the proprietor, takes care that the latest telegrams shall be posted up, and the news of the world be at the command of his patrons. "Punch," the "Times," and the "Illustrated London News," are there side by side with the "New York Herald," "Times," "Tribune," and "World." Over the bar is a billiard-room fitted up with great luxury, having ten of Phelan's famous tables; its floor covered with Brussels carpet, and its chairs fit for a Parisian palace.

The "Bank Exchange" is a great focus for the gentlemen of San Francisco. It is the rendezvous at which you meet your friend on any matter of business. Ladies of course do not visit it, for no American female, however humble her position, would enter a bar-room. The only feminine adornment the Bank Exchange possesses is Potiphar's wife, or Delilah, I forget which, the size of life, in oil-color at the back of the bar.

Peculiar is the custom in San Francisco of anticipating the morning and evening papers in the news posted on what are termed the "Bulletin-Boards" of the bar-rooms. The latest telegram from the East, the arrival of the last steamer, the names of the passengers who have left at noon by the boat for Panama, the most recent accident, any valuable lost, or any celebrity coming, are all items which find their way to the bulletin-boards with extraordinary rapidity. At the time of my visit, there was a man employed to do this sort of work who had been on the press of New York. He was paid for his bar-room penny-a-lining by a subscription among the various liquor-sellers. Being as fond of his whisky as he was indefatigable in hunting up news, and being free to drink at almost any bar, his occupation was as congenial to his tastes as it was serviceable to the public.

When Artemus Ward did arrive in San Francisco, every bulletin-board in the city had an announcement of the fact within six hours after his landing.

❖ 20 ❖

The Echoes Wake and Reply • Comedy and Tragedy at the El Dorado

PRECISELY what I expected would happen occurred in due course. On the morning of the second day after my friend had promised to "wake the echoes," I found the echoes to be wide awake. Half a dozen people called at the hotel to make proposals for engaging Artemus Ward. There was one enterprising gentleman whose proposal had the merit of novelty.

"I'll jine in with you on shares," said he. "I'll take him up the country with a tent. I'll have the best brass band there is on the Western
slope, and I'll hire a dozen boys to dress up for his wax-figgers and go on
horseback through the mines. He'll make dollars. So shall I. I'm posted
up about him. There's stuff in him, and he'll pan out good."

Thanking the gentleman for his proposal, I declined his offer. The
tent, the brass band, and the boys dressed for wax-figures, were not in
accordance with the way in which a lecture tour should be conducted
even in California. But it was most satisfactory to listen to the prog-
nostication that Artemus would "pan out" well. I was familiar with the
phrase, having heard it in the mines years previously. The diggers use
it in referring to the yield of golddust in the washing of a pan of earth.

Another gentleman prefaced his tender by asking, "What sort of a
show does he give? It isn't a steamboat, is it?"

I assured him that it was not a "steamboat," for I knew that in the
singular phraseology of California the word meant an imposture or
fraud; and that "to steamboat" a man signified to chase an impostor
out of the town.

There came offers from managers, from secretaries of institutions,
and speculators ready to speculate in any thing. Then came Mr. Maguire, who drove up to the door with a pair of spirited horses, and asked
me to go for a drive with him as far as the Cliff House to see the seals.

The day was fine; the offer was not to be refused. Besides, I felt that
it meant business. We drove out behind two of the best horses in the
State, along a newly-made but excellent road. On each side of us villa
residences were built, or in process of building, and a good opportunity
was afforded of glancing at the Belgravia of San Francisco. Driving
past Lone Mountain Cemetery, we pursued our way between ranges of
sand-hills, till at length, the Pacific Ocean opening to view, we saw on
our right the Golden Gate, through which a steamer was passing outward bound to Victoria, in Vancouver's Island.

We halted at the Cliff House, a hotel built on the edge of the rocky
coast; its windows looking out upon the most romantic ocean of the
world, and upon a high rocky island close by us in the midst of the surf
and spray which were washing the huge brown masses of stone of which
the island was formed.

In front of the hotel was a wooden balcony, with chairs for the use of
visitors. Sitting down, we had a good view of the great sight to which

San Francisco treats its citizens and its visitors—the seals belonging to the State.

Waddling up from the water on the stones around, and perched up on projections of the rock which forms the island, were some hundreds of large seals, some of them with their glossy heads only just above the surface of the waves, but the greater-part of them basking, sliding, or crawling over the rock, many asleep, some at play, and a few of them apparently enjoying a little family quarrel among themselves. The proprietor of the Cliff House keeps opera-glasses and telescopes for the use of his guests. We borrowed a glass, and through it watched the seals at their gambols as they bit at each other, seemingly more in fun than in anger, barked like playful dogs, flopped from rock to rock, climbed the stony heights, or plunged into the sparkling sea. More pleasant was it to scan those which lay extended on their spray-washed couches, their large, soft, gleaming, womanly eyes turned toward us, and the folds of shiny skin on their sleek necks having the tone and texture of velvet. Some of the seals were so large as to warrant the belief that they weighed at least two hundred and fifty pounds. They are the pets of the San Franciscan public, and are preserved from being shot, caught, or disturbed in the enjoyment of their rocky island adjacent to the Golden Gate by a special enactment, wherein they are made the property of either the city or the State itself.

We had watched the seals for some time, and had also discussed the quality of a bottle of Champagne, when Mr. Maguire asked me in a pleasant manner:

"Well, what are you going to do with your man?"

That was the question I had been waiting for. I knew that it was coming. "My man" was Artemus. I replied that I was going to settle where he was to lecture very shortly, that I had received many proposals to engage him, and that if Mr. Maguire had one to make in addition I was very ready to hear it.

"You don't want to trade with him, I see," he continued. "Well, I have made up my mind what I mean to do. He's a nice fellow, I believe, and you and I are old friends, so there's my Opera-house. I mean to let you have it for a night for nothing."

Thanking the manager for his liberality, I replied that I was not quite certain whether it was the right place for Artemus Ward to deliver his lecture for the first time in California. There were many people willing to go and hear him who would have objections to enter a theatre, and my own impression was that Platt's Hall in Montgomery Street was the right place.

"Your head's clear," replied Mr. Maguire. "It is the right place. I should like him to come to my house, because it's where all stars do come; but you're right. Don't sell him to any body. Take Platt's Hall."

We took another peep at the seals, remounted our buggy, and drove off along the shore towards the Ocean House. Exciting and full of interest was that glorious drive, the broad sands glittering in the afternoon sun, the white surf washing our horses' hoofs, the ocean without a vessel of any description to relieve its grand and limitless expanse. The breeze which blew around us came across the waves from islands where palm-trees grow—from shores where luscious fruits ripen and fragrant flowers bloom. Straight across those waves were China and Japan, the Sandwich Islands, and the spice-laden isles of the Philippines and of Molucca. It was worth being a showman to drive along that sandy beach on the world's western fringe of earth, far from the bustle, smoke, and noise of London and New York.

On the way home Mr. Maguire again became generous. "I have been thinking over it," said he. "You take Platt's Hall. My Opera-house wants cleaning up. I wouldn't like to oppose you. So I'll shut it up for cleaning, the night you open, and let you have the field to yourself."

Very good, indeed, of Mr. Maguire; but, as I subsequently learned, his business just then was at a low ebb. He knew that Artemus Ward would be attractive, and it was better for him to enact the magnanimous than for the good citizens to crowd Platt's Hall and he to have an empty house.

Without further hesitation I saw Mr. Platt, arranged terms with him, and engaged his hall. Then came all the work of gradually stimulating the public with newspaper paragraphs, and notifying them by means of circulars, bills, and posters.

In the evening I was again waited on by the gentleman who proposed to take Artemus up the country "with a tent."

"Do you mean to let me jine in?" said he. "My brass band will be worth all the money to you. A show isn't worth a red cent up the country without a brass band, and mine will play louder than any two in the State. It's elegant to listen to. There's one of my boys at the Bella Union. Just you go and hear him tonight. I'll get him to give you 'Hail

Columbia' on the trombone. When he pulls up the slide it makes all the benches move, and when he lets it out you can see the roof go up."

I had seen so many queer performances at the Bella Union in days gone by that I promised to go and hear the vigorous trombone-player. I had to give my promise to that effect as being the shortest mode of getting rid of my visitor. Walking down Montgomery Street some hours after, I found him waiting at the corner of Washington Street. He seized me by the arm and impelled me towards the Bella Union. When we were inside the concert-room he pointed out one of the gentlemen of the orchestra who was seated in a comfortable chair, his head drooping, his hands in his pockets, his legs extended straight before him, and a trombone between his knees.

"There you have him! He's elegant—he's just elegant. He gets steam out of that trombone. The instrument's got a soul to it—you'll hear it. The judge will tune it up presently."

"Is he a judge?" I asked.

"Well, I guess he's a kinder sort of one. He used to be in a law office. That's when he learned his instrument. He used to take it up for exercise after writing out a lawyer's letter. You'll hear. When the judge does take it up, he'll let her rip."

My impression was that "the judge" was not in a fit condition to take any thing up. Unless I was much deceived by appearances, he had already taken up enough whisky to render his ability to play a trombone very problematical. Presently the time arrived for him to display his talent, but when his fellow-artists began to finger their instruments the judge still remained motionless. My companion first gazed with a look of wonder, which presently changed to one of vexation, and then to an expression of rage.

"I guess the judge has been on it to-night," said he. "But he ain't a-going to peter out in that way. Just you hold on while I go and straighten him."

Rushing down the hall and through a little door beside the stage, the patron of the judge made his way towards the trombone-player, seized him by the shoulder, and hauled him through an opening, trombone and all. There were sounds of a scuffle behind, and of an altercation in the distance. After the lapse of about ten minutes the angry man made his reappearance through the little door, his face flushed, his manner excited, and a battered fragment of the trombone in his hand.

"The mean coot!" he exclaimed, "I've straightened him. He can't leave his rum alone—can't he? To think he'd serve me a trick like that! I've taken all the tune out of his instrument over his thick head. He's done it before, but I've straightened him now—I've straightened him!"

That little door beside the stage through which the man had gone to "straighten" the judge, reminded me of another scene which had transpired at the same place when I chanced to be in San Francisco in 1860.

There came from New York a young man with a rather pretty and youthful lady, who was at first supposed to be his wife. He professed to act, and she to sing. They lodged at the El Dorado, opposite the Bella Union. The talents of the young man were not appreciated, while those of the young lady, combined with her good looks, gained her many friends. By-and-by it became rumored about that the lady was treated harshly by her companion, made to work for his support, and chastised if she did not. Any such conduct was repugnant to the ideas of gallantry which every American possesses, but which Californian gentlemen have to even a Quixotic extent. For some few weeks the lady displayed her abilities at the Bella Union. Meanwhile the presumed husband busied himself in fitting up a small concert-hall in Montgomery Street, to which he attached the maiden name of the lady as an attraction, and called the place—well, I will not mention the right name, but suppose it to have been entitled "Miss Melinda Smith's Olympic," and, not to annoy the gentleman, who I believe, is still alive, I will write of him as Mr. Richard Jones. The Olympic had been duly advertised; the evening came about for its being opened. Mr. Richard Jones was there; so also was a large audience. When the time arrived for Miss Melinda Smith to appear, according to the programme, she was not forthcoming.

Now, audiences, as a rule, are not very patient, and those of California are peculiarly fond of the excitement of a programme being continuous. A clamor arose for Miss Melinda Smith. The curtain remained down. The lady did not present herself. In her place appeared Mr. Richard Jones, who apologized to the people for the absence of the prima donna, and promised to go and fetch her. Meanwhile a report spread in the room that the fair one had received a beating that morning from him whom she called her husband; that the beating had taken place at their apartments in the El Dorado, and that the lady had fled for refuge and protection to the Bella Union. A portion of the audience followed Mr. Richard Jones into the street, along which he rushed wildly in quest of the truant Melinda. He darted into the Bella Union, and after an interval reappeared on the thoroughfare, a handkerchief to his face, and only one of his eyes visible. It had so happened that he had attempted to pass through the little door to the stage that he might seize Melinda, take her off in triumph, and flog her well afterwards when at home, but that his passage had been barred by a strong arm, while a blow from a stout fist had dissipated his courage and overthrown his plans. Mr. Richard Jones returned to the Olympic, showed his bruised features to the audience, and, apologizing for their disappointment, solicited their sympathy. He received it in the shape of some stools and billets of wood projected at his head.

Mr. Richard Jones sought solace in whisky, and returned home late to find the door fastened and admission denied him. When the next morning came about, a happy thought struck him. The lady had evidently rebelled against further chastisement, and had obtained friends who were willing and able to fight for her. Without her, Mr. Richard Jones saw no prospect of making a living in San Francisco. She was no longer to be retained by force; but might she not be won back by love and by an appeal to sympathy? The manner in which he made that appeal was unique. He procured a plate, contrived to put some dried blood on it, wrote an affectionate note, expressed his sorrow, and requested the lady to notice the blood which he had lost in his endeavor to see her on the previous evening. He placed the note on the plate, took both across to the El Dorado himself, besought an interview, and, on being denied it, left the plate outside the door. The relentless Melinda retaliated in her own fashion. She caused the plate, with its unseemly contents, to be exhibited in a shop window, and beside the plate she deposited the note of appeal, open for all who pleased to read. By next steamer Mr. Richard Jones departed as a steerage passenger for Panama.

Female vengeance in this instance assumed a comic aspect; but a story was told to me by a young Englishman belonging to the press of San Francisco, wherein the revenge of woman assumed a more tragic form, and wherein the El Dorado also partially figured as the scene of the transaction.

The El Dorado building fronts the Plaza, on the corner of Washington and Kearney Streets. In olden days its fame was great, for it was the principal gambling-house of San Francisco at the time when every-body gambled. Within its walls the miners who worked hard for wealth on the gold-fields staked their gold at faro or roulette, and lost their hard-gained earnings to sharpers from New York and cunning Jews from New Orleans. Pounds upon pounds of gold, in dust and in nuggets, used to be staked upon the tables of the El Dorado. The place was fur-nished in magnificent style. There was a free supper for all who chose to gamble. There was wine to excite to play, and there was ruin to await the player. On the turn of a card frequently depended whether the pistol of the suicide should do its work without further delay, and add one more to the victims of the El Dorado.

In the early days of San Francisco there was a handsome young man who gambled much, and who had brought with him from the East a lady who appeared to be partly Louisianian and partly Spanish in her extraction. She manifested great attachment to him, and on many oc-casions was noticed urging him not to enter the great gambling-house. At a subsequent date the lady was found in a dying state in the room of a small hotel in the Southern mines, where before her death she told the story of her wrongs and of her vengeance. Briefly related, abridging the rather dramatic version of it which my informant favored me with, it may be thus told:

The lady and the gentleman were not married. She had left home and friends in Louisiana to accompany to California the man who had pos-sessed himself of her affections. In California the man had rapidly made money. The gambling fever had then seized him, and day after day, night after night, he spent his time at the El Dorado. At one time he won a little, at another lost much, and returned home in savage mood, frequently bringing with him a fellow-gambler who displayed more than pleasant courtesy towards the lady. The poor woman tried hard to dissuade the handsome man with whom she had recklessly come to the land of gold from pursuing the path which was leading him to mad-ness and to destruction. Luck went against him. The more he played the more he lost. At length one evening he staid later than usual at the gambling-table, and the woman, anxious for his return, went to seek him. Through a hole in the door she witnessed him at play. She had arrived just as he had staked his last dollar to the man whom he had so often brought home with him. The two were playing with dice, not cards. The woman was an unobserved listener, and for some reason she did not allow her presence to be known. When the ill-starred gambler had lost all, the winner coolly proposed to him that he should throw again, but that this time the stakes should be heavy. There was the beautiful dark-eyed girl from Louisiana. Let him stake her, and against her his opponent would stake five thousand dollars. One throw each of the little blocks of ivory in the dice-box was to decide the issue. The throw was made. The beautiful Louisianian was lost. A cry of terror betrayed her presence. She fainted, and was carried off by the victor.

A year or two afterwards the gambler who lost his last stake, and the woman whom he thus made light of at the gambling-table, met at a hotel in Calaveras County. According to the dying statement of the woman herself, she had dissembled to him, at the time of meeting, until they were both in one room together, at a time when she knew him to be unarmed. Then it was that, after fastening the door, she first drew from her pocket a dice-box and dice, and then a loaded revolver. With desperate coolness she told the man that, as he had once staked her happiness on the gambling-table, so now she intended to stake his life. Both were to throw the dice. If he won, he was to leave the room alive. If he lost, he was to die. The dice were thrown. The man lost, and the woman shot him through the heart. She attempted to kill herself afterwards, but the shot not being immediately fatal, she lived long enough to tell the story of her singular revenge.

The El Dorado has been the scene of a thousand strange stories. Its walls inclose chapters from nearly every romance in the early days of San Francisco.

◦ 21 ◦

Trotting Out the "Babes"
beside the Pacific

IT is an axiom in show-craft, and he knows nothing of his profession who has not mastered the secret, that no performance nor any exhibition or entertainment will be a success unless it appeal to the tastes and sympathies of the fair sex. That play will have a long run for the representations of which ladies urge their husbands, fathers, or brothers to take seats, and that performance is a decided success at which every female in the audience is seen occasionally to hide her face behind a white pocket-handkerchief. Never mind whether the gentleman visitors weep or smile, if the ladies are interested; then, in the language of the brotherhood, "the show is safe."

Anxious that Artemus Ward should be very successful in California, I endeavored to discover what amount of popularity he had already acquired among the ladies of San Francisco. My anxiety was dissipated when, after the announcement of his appearance had been made, a gentleman waited on me at the hotel to inquire if he could have the choice of the first seat sold. I replied that it was not intended to reserve seats. "But my wife must have the first ticket," said he. "She insists on my buying it for her. If you can not sell me a seat, can not you let me have the whole row? All my lady friends are coming, and I will get to the hall early to see no one jumps their claim."

I was satisfied. An arrangement was made with the gentleman that he should have the "claim" and that he should be allowed to attend early to prevent any body "jumping" it. The front row of the hall filled with ladies was precisely the very thing to have. In England that front row of a place of entertainment has too often to be filled with free admissions, the party to whom the task of filling them is assigned playfully designating the process as "dressing the stalls."

Resident at the Occidental Hotel at the time was a young lady who was most pleasantly prophetic of the success of Artemus. As she was peculiarly typical of California, I may be pardoned for referring to her and her history. Let me call her Miss "No. 5," and so call her because she always wore upon her dress a large "5," either in the shape of a solid gold ornament or embroidered upon a scarlet jacket.

Miss No. 5 was the accomplished daughter of a gentleman who had officiated as a surgeon in the army during the war of the United States with Mexico. Her father was rich, and the young lady herself was the owner of some scores of thousands of dollars in her own right. Being good-looking, having a merry disposition, and being thoroughly a Californian "girl of the period," she was the observed of all observers in the San Franciscan ball-rooms, and a specially attractive personage whenever riding or driving in the city or its suburbs. It had happened that when she was very young she had been rescued from a house on fire by the members of an engine company known as "The Knickerbocker No. 5." It suited her whim in after-life to don the red jacket of the firemen, and wear the number of the company on her dress. The firemen had duly elected her one of their members, and she was always ready, when in San Francisco, to run with them and the engine to a fire, assist in extinguishing it, encourage the firemen, deliver speeches to them, treat them with drink, and make them costly presents of elegantly manufactured insignia of a fire-company. Miss No. 5 resided at the Occidental Hotel simply because, like many American ladies, she preferred hotel life to any other form of living. But she was thoroughly Californian. She despised all conventionality, dressed as she pleased, went where she pleased, talked with whom she pleased, entered into the sports of her gentlemen friends with the keenest of relish, would challenge any of them to take a horse where she would take one, or fire a pistol with as steady a hand and as true an eye. One of her mad escapades was to seat herself on the iron bars in front of a railway engine—the "cow-catcher," as it is called in the States—and ride at express speed along the Napa Valley Railroad. Her parents seemed to have little or no control over her. She spent her money freely, and gave away largely for charitable purposes. She could be the most fascinating of young ladies one moment, and the next be acting the part of a great boy rather than that of an educated and accomplished girl. When tired of San Francisco, she would rush off to New York, and thence to Paris. She would be heading a fire-company in the streets of California to-day, and two months afterwards she might be seen gracing with becoming demeanor an Imperial ball at the Tuileries or figuring at Ascot races. She married some short time since, but left her husband in the most abrupt manner, though I believe that she has again rejoined him. Miss No. 5 was an exceedingly good-hearted young lady, but she was Californian female eccentricity developed in its most intensified form. She took much interest in the entertainment which Artemus Ward was about to offer to the San Franciscan public, and was a most obliging and energetic advertising agent. Californian wild oats grow profusely. By this time I hope that Miss No. 5 has sown her stock of that description of grain, and that, having been a good friend to showmen, she has duly met with her reward.

Another and valuable class of advertising agents in San Francisco were the negro minstrel companies. They were next in importance to the newspapers, the clergymen, and the ladies. At the Eureka Theatre, the Melodeon, and at other places, the negro minstrels drew large audiences. At the suggestion of a shrewd friend I supplied the "end-man" of each company with one of Artemus Ward's books, and left him to cull from it as many jokes as he pleased wherewith to entertain his audiences, exacting from him in return that he should mention the name of their author, and let the Californian public have notice of his early arrival. In the hope that Artemus would recompense the minstrels by supplying their exhausted *répertoires* with a few new jokes, they very readily consented to lend their aid in stirring up the excitement requisite to insure success.

San Francisco not being a good city for bill-posting stations, and some novelty in the way of announcement being desirable, the curb-boarding of the wooden side-walks was brought into service. Bound round the curb at all the principal corners of the streets of San Francisco appeared the following notification:

"ARTEMUS WARD WILL TROT OUT HIS 'BABES IN THE WOOD.'—PLATT'S HALL, NOV. 13."

The announcement was just in that form which best suited the tastes of the Californian public. "Are you going to see Artemus trot out his 'babes?'" became a question on the streets.

The press of San Francisco behaved in the most generous manner. The gentlemen connected with it were not only willing but anxious to aid one who had been himself a pressman, and who always felt pleased in referring to his connection with newspaper literature. From the published volume which I presented to the editors extracts were freely made; short biographies of the writer of the book appeared in the daily journals, and very lengthy notices of his previous career helped to fill the columns of the weekly papers. Magnanimous was the behavior of Colonel Lawrence of the "Golden Era," who begged to be supplied with any amount of copy, and with enthusiastic liberality declared that he would make the forthcoming number of his paper an Artemus Ward number. He was duly furnished with biographical notes, critical essays, and samples of the humor of the new humorist. But not satisfied with the quantity of matter with which he was already stocked, he "took a drink," and then blandly said, "Can't you let me have an article about him in connection with Shakspeare and spiritualism?"

To confess inability to a Californian would have been absurd. Colonel Lawrence was therefore informed that he could have such an article if he particularly wished for it, though how Artemus Ward was to be connected with the spirits or with Shakspeare, or why he should be connected with either, did not strike the mind as questions being easy of solution. Spiritualism was a prominent topic in San Francisco just then. Hence it admitted of being used to advantage, but why Shakspeare? The Colonel pointed out a ready mode of making up an article. "Get Mrs. Mary C. Clarke's Dictionary," said he, "and see what you can find about 'Ward' in it."

Thanking the Colonel for the idea, I suggested that I might find some difficulty in obtaining Mrs. Cowden Clarke's "Concordance to Shakspeare" in a San Franciscan library.

"Guess we've got her upstairs," was the reply. "Mary C. Clarke, Webster, and Lippincott are kinder useful tools in an office."

It happened that, on seeking for her, we found that "Mary C. Clarke" had gone out for a visit; but I easily obtained a copy at the office of the "Daily Call." Subsequent experience taught me that there were few newspaper offices in the Western States at which a copy of Mrs. Clarke's valuable "Concordance" is not procurable.

Colonel Lawrence required a sensation article, and here is the one with which he was supplied. That its literary merit amounts to nothing I am well aware, but as it pleased the Californian public, served the purpose of a preliminary puff, and was a source of much amusement to Artemus on his arrival, I may be excused for giving it insertion:

"Shakspeare, an agent for Artemus Ward.

"—A Strangely New Phase of Spiritualism.—Spiritualism has originated many new and startling ideas. The mental vagaries of some of its professors outstrip the wildest conceptions of the most imaginative poets. The latest theory propounded is, however, by far the most surprising; while the proofs adduced are of the most extraordinary description.

"We will give the theory in a few words. Incorporate mortals now existent can not only hold communication with decorporated spirits, but the spirits of all who are to wear fleshly garb can also hold present intercourse with other spirits which have yet to be incarnated.

"This theory is based on the doctrine propounded by the Rev. Charles Beecher, for which he was recently denounced by the convention of ministers at Georgetown, D. C. It is the doctrine of pre-existence— that our spirits have lived from all time, as they are to live to all time. That the soul of John Smith lived long ages ago, as it will live in the immeasurable ages to come. Herein arose the opportunity for Belshazzar of Babylon to know all about the soul of John Smith, whom we meet on Montgomery Street to-day. This is the strange new theory.

"It is proven by the fact that Shakspeare knew Artemus Ward three hundred years ago, and acted then as 'agent in advance' of Artemus, by advertising him to the full extent of his ability. Now Shakspeare must have known that the spirit of Artemus, when fleshified as Ward, would produce a good fellow, or he would not have done it. For Shakspeare himself was a good fellow, and ought to have owned as many feet in the 'Gould and Curry' as the best of us.

"Here are the facts, startling we admit, but as undeniable as any fact ever yet adduced in support of a theory:

"Shakspeare's acquaintance with Artemus was of long-standing. 'Thou knowest my old *Ward*,' says he. (1 *Henry IV.*, act iv.) That he esteemed him highly is manifest, for he calls him 'The best *Ward* of mine honor.' (*Love's Labor's Lost*, act iii., scene i.) That he advises every one to hear him and to know him is plain, for says he not, 'Come to my *Ward?*' (*Measure for Measure*, act iv., scene iii.) That he himself had diligently to attend to the business of Artemus is certain; for his own words are, 'They will have me go to *Ward*.' (2 *Henry VI.*, act v., scene i.)

"Sometimes Shakspeare appears to have been persuaded a little too strongly by Artemus, for his words are, 'I can not *Ward*, what I would not' (*Troilus and Cressida*, act i., scene ii.); and again—wary fellow —'There are many confines, *Ward*' (*Hamlet*, act ii., scene i.). Strangely prescient of the future fact that Mr. Browne would achieve fame about twenty-four months after adopting his *nom-de-plume*, he says of Artemus's father, 'His son was but a *Ward* two years.' (*Romeo and Juliet*, act i., scene v.) That he thought him to be smart, and to know as much as half a dozen men, is evidenced by his assertion that there are 'men in your *Ward*.' (*Measure for Measure*, act ii., scene ii.) And that he believed him to be guileless is demonstrable, or he would never have called him 'The *Ward* of purity.' (*Merry Wives*, act iv., scene iii.) Just as he knew him to be shrewd when he entitles him 'The *Ward* of covert.'

(*Measure for Measure*, act v., scene i.) How plainly evident, too, it is, that the spirit of Artemus used to call upon Shakspeare (whether by raps on the table or at the door we know not), for does not the poet answer him and say, 'I am now in *Ward?*' (*All's Well that Ends Well*, act i., scene ii.) And that he felt certain Artemus will one day get married, though at present a bachelor, is patent, for does he not speak of the 'Wife of the *Ward?* (1 *Henry IV.*, act iii., scene ii.) Ward's spirit, however, was not always truthful to Shakspeare; the principal did not treat the agent candidly, for Shakspeare says, '*Ward*, you lie.' (*Troilus and Cressida*, act i., scene ii.) And shortly afterwards, 'All these *Wards* lie.' (Same play, act, and scene.) Possibly, however, Shakspeare was irritated at the time, and Artemus may have sent him a message by telegraph, which was slightly spoiled by the operator.

"The above facts prove, however, that Shakspeare knew the great humorist of America in spirit; that where he had a chance of saying any thing for him he did it; that he never lost a chance of mentioning his name, and was always an industrious agent. It now remains for Artemus to do his part; and, having become incorporate, to look about him in San Francisco, and do the handsome in return for his spirit friend.—E. P. H."

San Francisco was well advertised. Artemus was the talk of dinner-tables, the subject of jokes at the ministrel halls, the topic of humorous conversation on the streets. That he would attract a crowded audience to his first lecture became matter of certainty. His arrival was eagerly expected, and the steamer which was to bring him was over-due. The show was ready. It was the showman only who was wanted.

On a bleak, windy afternoon—and the wind can blow bleakly in San Francisco at times—the telegraph announced that the steamer was in sight of the Golden Gate. The day was Sunday; precisely the day on which crowds of idlers could stroll down to the wharf and greet the new arrivals. Artemus landed amidst acclamations, and he and I drove off together to the Occidental Hotel. In the hurry of disembarkation one of his boxes was left on board the steamer. It contained his best clothes. After a convivial welcome at the hotel, a hospitable gentleman seized him by the arm and insisted on taking him away to dinner. Artemus declined the invitation, explaining that he was not sufficiently well attired to sit down at a dinner-table with ladies, and that the box containing his apparel had not yet come on shore.

"Never mind," urged the gentleman. "It doesn't matter what you wear in California."

"That's fortunate. I never *was* much," replied Artemus.

The joke told. It travelled over San Francisco that evening.

◦ 22 ◦

A Dance on a Floor of Gold, and Experiences of Chinese Theatricals

THE appointed evening (November 13, 1863) arrived. Platt's Music Hall, San Francisco, was crowded. The price of admission was one dollar, and the receipts exceeded one thousand six hundred dollars, not in paper currency but in gold. Had the hall been larger we might have taken three thousand dollars, so great was the excitement and so numerous the people who presented themselves for admission. We never knew to a dollar the exact sum taken, for the money-box was carried away by the pressure of the crowd, the money-taker escaping with difficulty. Aided by the police, a man was stationed with a hat in his hand for the people to throw in the silver dollars as they passed into the hall. Just as the hall became full the crown of the hat gave way.

Artemus delivered his old lecture, entitled "The Babes in the Wood," interspersing it with a few new jokes applicable to California. The lecture was well received, the lecturer loudly applauded, and the Rev. Starr King graced the platform precisely as Artemus had requested me in New York to arrange, if possible. Mr. Maguire closed his Opera-house that evening, as he had promised to do, and when we returned to the hotel Artemus was serenaded by a brass band under the direction of the gentleman who, on a previous evening, had "straightened" the trombone-player.

So successful was the first delivery of the lecture, and so many were they who had not been able to obtain admission, that a repetition of the "Babes in the Wood" was at once announced for the evening of the 17th of the same month, but to take place at the Metropolitan Theatre instead of Platt's Music Hall. In the intervening days Artemus amused himself by seeing a few of the sights of San Francisco.

"Would you like to walk on a gold floor three inches thick with gold?" inquired Mr. Maguire.

"I should like to dance on it," replied Artemus.

His wish was gratified. Mr. Maguire asked Artemus and myself to accompany him to the banking-house of Messrs. Donahoe, Rallston & Co., on the corner of Sansome Street. He introduced us to the manager—one of the partners in the firm—and by him we were conducted into a small back parlor. On the floor, closely laid together, not long brought from the mines and awaiting shipment, were a series of large ingots of gold having the form of bricks. To Artemus the sight was a novel one, and after participating in a bottle of Champagne with the manager of the bank, he requested permission to dance on the ingots, stating that he knew he should never have a similar opportunity, and that it would be something for him to tell about when he returned home. We whistled the air of "Hop Light Loo," while Artemus executed a "break-down" with admirable skill.

The Chinese quarter of San Francisco possesses irresistible attractions to an European, especially if he has not visited Asiatic countries. So intimately is it associated with the American portion of the city that the visitor can be among a community of "Down-Eastern" Yankees one minute and in a "Down-Eastern" Mongolian settlement the next. China and Boston jostle against one another. They are adjacent, but not intermixed. They are together, yet distinctly separate. Boston can climb the stairs to its roof-top and look down into China; while China can smoke its little brass pipe filled with opium, and gaze with moony, almond-shaped eyes into the dwellings of Boston and New York. The street which is American is that called Montgomery, and leading from it towards the hills is the street called Sacramento, which is most decidedly Chinese; crossed by the street called Kearney, which is half French and one-eighth Spanish, and crossed again by the street called Dupont, that possesses attractions for all nationalities. Then there are lanes and alleys in the very heart of the city in which the houses are inhabited by Chinese women, imported by Chinese merchants; women who follow a life of sin while acting as wealth-producing slaves to their importers. There is also a joss-house or Chinese temple in San Fran-

cisco, to visit which on the Chinese New-year's day is a treat of which
many strangers avail themselves.

Take a stroll up Sacramento Street, and there is scarcely a product of
the Celestial Empire which is not on sale. The names of the Chinese
merchants are displayed over their stores, most of them in large gilt
letters. Chi-lung, Hop-Quy, Whang-Fung, and Ahloo are among the
names which tell of the places of business where tea and dried oysters,
fire-crackers and desiccated snails can be purchased by Mongolian,
Caucasian, or Ethiopian, if he please to buy, and have the dollars
wherewith to make the purchase. To the street boys of San Francisco it
matters not whether the name of a Chinese gentleman be Whang-Ho,
Chung-Moy, Hop-Loo, or Chow-Bent. He is sure to be addressed as
"John." Enough that he has the features of a Mongol and the dress of a
Chinese, and his name to the digger and the *gamin* will be "John
Chinaman."

A thrifty race are these Californian Chinese. In the mines a Chinaman will find gold enough to buy his necessaries and to save for future
use, where an American miner would not consider it worth his while to
waste an hour of his labor. "John" will dig and delve, wash the soil or
wash linen for the hotels, sell birds'-nest soup, scorpions' eggs, and
fish-sinews to his own people, or turn cook and scullery-man to an
American, as long as he can make money thereby. What he makes he
saves, or expends among his countrymen on products of his native land.
That which Western "barbarians" will give him he will take, but none
of his own earnings is he willing to give them in exchange. Whatever he
requires for domestic consumption he prefers should come from China.
The dried meats from his own country are thought by him to be better
than the fresh meats of an alien race. Prime beef and well-fed mutton
are not prized by him. He will eat American poultry, but he likes to
feed it himself. He will feast on cabbage grown on foreign soil, but it
must be Chinese cabbage planted and reared by Chinese hands. Even
his mining implements—his picks and spades and sieves, he imports
from the Celestial Empire. Though living in California, his heart is in
China. Should he die in America, his bones may repose in American
earth for a brief period; but after a time they are taken up, scraped
clean, tied into bundles, and consigned, duly labelled and assorted, to
be deposited among the bones of his forefathers in the land where his
pigtail first began to grow.

Ah! that pigtail! the scrapes it has brought poor John into in California! Rude miners have seized it in ruthless manner, and lopped it off with savage glee. Before now, John has been hauled about by his pigtail, tortured by having it severely pulled, and flogged with it after it has been severed from his head. The pigtail question became a grave one at last in the halls of the Legislature at Sacramento. Californian Legislators met in solemn conclave and declared that John Chinaman had a perfect right to his own pigtail. By a law of the State, he who cuts off John's pigtail, without having John's consent to do so, is now liable to be sent to the State's prison. The pigtail of a Celestial is no longer a trophy which a valiant miner can hang up in triumph in his tent, just as the red Indian suspends the dried scalp of his victim to his girdle.

Chinese thriftiness and the adventurous spirit of many of the Chinese traders, have resulted in the Chinese merchants of San Francisco having become a very wealthy community. They form themselves into companies or "hongs." There are five or six of these "hongs" in the city—the Yung-wo and the Yan-wo, the Sze-yap and the Sam-yap, or San-yup. The president of this last-named "hong" or company is a very whole-souled Chinaman. His name is Chi Sing-Tong. He is a gentleman every inch of him, the inches of his pigtail included. He is liberal, munificent, enterprising, and intelligent, besides being a thorough good fellow in courtesy, suavity, and fair-dealing. Chi Sing-Tong, with his long, carefully-preserved finger-nails, is a model Chinese gentleman, one who is literally "*ad unguem factus homo.*"

Being numerous, wealthy, and fond of amusement, the Chinese of San Francisco have their own theatrical entertainments on a grand scale. The Chinese drama is peculiar. A good healthy Chinese play has an abundance of acts, and will last for three or four nights at the least. It is played in nightly installments, and the spectator is supposed to be able to remember on Thursday night all the incidents which he chanced to see on Monday and Tuesday. John goes to the theatre as he goes to the mines, with a full determination to work hard and get all that can be got. He likes his amusement to be steady, continuous, not too exciting, but of that mild character that a large quantity of it must be taken to produce any effect.

Artemus Ward was a capital "audience" to the Chinese on the night he went to their theatre. The performance was to him so intensely ludicrous, that when he left the house he wandered around the streets of San Francisco for two or three hours, stopping every now and then to laugh heartily as he recalled something which he had seen in the course of the performance.

Let me briefly describe what I saw at a Chinese theatrical performance in San Francisco. To a showman the manner of doing things on the Chinese stage was peculiarly interesting. A Mongolian drama is not to be witnessed easily without visiting Asiatic shores. To see one on the Western shore of the Pacific was a treat to be enjoyed.

The theatre was the Opera-house. It had been hired by the Chinese for a brief term. On entering, I found boxes, parquet, and gallery filled with an audience of Celestials. Here and there a few Americans and Europeans were discernible, but nearly all the visitors were male members of the Chinese community. The green curtain was down. Below its lower edge the thick-soled shoes of the Mongols were visible. No musicians occupied the orchestra, but from behind the curtain came the sound of a tomtom and the squeak of some villainously-attuned catgut.

Up went the curtain, disclosing what is technically named a chamber set. There were two large door-ways in the "flat" or back of the scene, each filled up with superbly embroidered curtains, the ground-work of each curtain being blue, and the pattern in crimson and gold. Behind the door-ways, and at the very back of the stage, were the musicians. They had no music-stands, nor any of the usual arrangements of an orchestra. The leader had a sort of violin resembling a mandolin in form. He supported it on his knee, using the bow after the mode of playing a violoncello. The notes were squeaky and harsh. Next to the leader sat a man who played on a clarionet-looking instrument, which gave out sweetly musical sounds resembling those of the bagpipe. Next to him was a Chinese Orpheus who played on a cocoa-nut, and another who thumped away vigorously on a tom-tom. One of the performers attempted to get music out of a piece of solid wood by smiting it with artistic precision, while another tinkled away at a triangle. The music throughout the evening seemed an endless accompaniment like that played to a pantomime, with the difference that one monotonous air ran through it, and that the players sometimes allowed their voices to assist their instruments. Let the n's in the following lines be pronounced in the same manner as the Spanish ñ is in the word cañon, and some idea may be formed of the sound:

Nang—nang—nang—nang
Nya—nya—nya—nang
Nang—nang—nya—nya
Nya—nya—nang—nang.

A polite Chinaman, who could speak broken English, kindly informed me that the play was to be an historical one, and that the heroine in it was supposed to be very valorous. So far as I could learn, she was a sort of Chinese Joan of Arc.

On the prompt side of the stage, and at the "second entrance," was a cloth stretched upon a number of upright sticks. The cloth was painted black, and had white lines upon it, to give it the appearance of a wall of brick or stone. This, I was informed, was intended to represent the fortress which the Chinese Joan of Arc had to take. Behind it a man was stationed, ready, when the right time arrived, to open a slit in the cloth and allow the conquering army to pass through the breach made in the wall of the fortress. A Chinese property-man, in the ordinary attire of a Chinese shop-keeper, was busy on the stage when the curtain rose. In the theatres of the Western World the property-man is a functionary who furnishes the stage, and supplies the actors with weapons, letters, purses, and snuff-boxes, but who is not visible to the audience. At this Chinese play the property-man was continually obtruding himself to public view. He brought swords and spears into the chamber scene when a battle was about to be fought; hoisted a chair upon a table, to serve as a throne when a king had to be crowned; and brought on a banner with "victory" emblazoned on it in Chinese characters, to be displayed when the fight should be terminated.

Presently, the property-man having placed a table and chair in order, the curtain of one of the door-ways drew aside, and a magnificently attired Chinaman made his entrance on the stage. Behind him followed a man bearing aloft a crimson umbrella of a tub-like shape; while behind him, again, were some gorgeously-arrayed gentlemen who had golden tigers embroidered on their backs, and flying dragons over their stomachs. They came to the front of the stage, put their hands to their heads, bent their arms at right angles, and bowed profoundly. The gentleman over whose head the umbrella waved its crimson fringe then came down to the foot-lights, raised his left hand, extended two of his fingers, and, after winking at the audience, proceeded to sing through his nose, the music keeping time to his nasal recitative. So far as I could learn from my Chinese informant, the singing performer informed his audience, in the course of his song, that he was a great emperor, who could fight, would fight, and was not to be beaten. Having thoroughly explained that much, he spun himself round four times on his left heel and marched out at the door to the right, winking again as he went.

More loudly squeaked the stringed instrument and the clarionet with the bagpipe tone, as through the door to the left came sixteen valiant soldiers with their sleeves tucked up, each holding a sword in his right hand. Marching forward to the foot-lights, the leader of the valiant band duly declared his intention to fight for the illustrious emperor who had just made his exit. Having made this declaration, he and his followers turned themselves round four times on one foot and marched out in the direction which the emperor had taken, flourishing their swords as they went.

Twang and squeak went the music, and the emperor reappeared, came to the front and sung for ten minutes, the purport of his song being, so far as I could learn, to inform the audience that he was really king of the castle, and intended to remain so. When he had sung this three times over, he recommenced, and sung it three times over again. Then the man behind the cloth wall opened the slit in it and spread out the sticks. Marching very grandly, the monarch strode through and passed from sight. Now came the turn for his valiant army of sixteen to reappear. On they came, again tucked up their sleeves, and sung that they would fight for ever and ever in defense of the king and his castle. Then the cloth wall opened, and they also marched through with the step of heroes.

The castle being no longer required, the property-man came on and helped to roll up the sticks and canvas into a bundle, which he deposited against one of the wings for future use. Now came the appearance of the insurgent chieftain who had resolved to depose the king of the castle. The emperor *de facto* had presented himself in a bright blue dress. The rebel chief appeared in one of a bright scarlet color. His face was painted, while that of the Emperor was partially concealed by a mask. Refreshingly absurd was the manner in which the rebel leader had "made up" for the occasion. One of his cheeks was colored red, the other white. The eye over the red cheek was closed up and painted white, as also was that portion of the forehead above it. The eye over the white cheek was open, but around it was painted a circle of black, and around that again a circle of crimson. The nose was colored half crimson and half white. The painted face was evidently intended to awe those around by the fearful sublimity of its expression. On the Chinamen it seemed to have some such effect. On the Europeans and Americans present I am afraid that it produced a contrary impression, and brought to mind recollections of pantomimes and burlesques.

Down to the front came the rebel chieftain, to tell the audience in a dreary song who he was and what he meant to do. Then snorting like a horse, shrieking like a peacock, and braying like a donkey, he spun himself round on his heel as all the others had done, and passed out of view.

Enter again the sixteen soldiers, but with their sleeves this time tucked up inside instead of rolled up outside, to indicate that they now represented the rebel army instead of the imperial one. More singing, more turning on the heel, and out they went by the way in which they came.

Re-enter the rebel chief. Again the cloth castle was erected; and, after singing that he meant to go through its gates with all his army, the brave fellow spun round like a teetotum, and passed through the aperture in the cloth. Then returned the sixteen soldiers, sung what they meant to do, twirled themselves round, and followed their leader through the castle wall. Now for the first time during the evening a young lady made her appearance, but whether she represented the empress, or the wife of the rebel chief, or the sweetheart of one of the soldiers, I could not decide. She hobbled down to the front, wearing very small shoes, did her share of singing in a high shrill voice, turned up the white of her eyes as if she were going to die, and otherwise distressed herself in an extraordinary and most unnecessary manner. While she was singing, the property-man was busy fetching and placing upon the table a formidable array of warlike instruments. There were triangular pitchforks, cutlasses made like a ploughshare, two-handed swords, spears with huge prongs to them, and with tufts of colored silk at the junction of the prong with the shaft. Then there were heavy clubs for felling a man at a single blow, and spikes for impaling him after he was slain. The melancholy singing-lady made her exit. The emperor, attended by his servitors, reappeared, with the rebel chief following him. His imperial majesty armed himself with one of the two-handed swords, while the arch-rebel possessed himself of the most formidable of the spears. Now commenced a fight between the two principal personages. Not a fight to music, after the fashion of the terrific and sanguinary combats common to the English melodramatic stage, but a proper Chinese fight, arranged according to the ideas of fighting prevalent in the Flowery Land.

The general plan of the combat appeared to be that each belligerent should spin himself round on his heel three times, and then make his cut or thrust. If either failed to complete the third gyration at the right time, so as to ward off the attack of his enemy, he received a stroke from the two-handed sword across the nape of his neck, or a thrust of the three-pronged pitchfork in the lower portion of his back. The Orientals appeared to enjoy "any amount" of this sort of fighting, but to a Western the protracted character of the fight became very tiresome. At length each combatant grew equally tired, and marched off to allow the sixteen soldiers, half with their sleeves tucked up inside and the other half with their sleeves tucked up outwardly, to continue the combat between them. There was no general *mêlée*. Pairs of the respective combatants engaged separately. One had a sword and shield; the other a spear. Much ingenuity was displayed in each turning three times round, and the swordsman falling on his knee to receive the thrust of the spear upon his shield. At length, throwing away both shield and sword, each pair of fighters commenced wrestling for the possession of the spear. In the course of the wrestling each dispossessed the other of the weapon by lifting up the right foot, planting it suddenly against the chest of his opponent, and forcing him down upon the floor. Then each made a bound in the air, threw a somersault, and placed his foot on the neck of his fallen foe. The rebel party became the conquerors. One after another of the imperial army fell down dead, and apparently had the three-pronged pitchfork thrust through the small of his back by the victor. The moment a noble warrior was slain the property-man made haste to place a small pillow beneath his head to give him ease in his deathly attitude.

After resting a short time with the back of his head on the pillow, the dead man arose and walked away, to reappear again in a few minutes and swell the ranks of the conquering army. To die right out one minute and arise resuscitated the next, appeared to be no infringement of the rules of dramatic propriety. When alive again, the revivified soldier seemed to have perfect liberty to belong to which of the two armies he pleased.

Victory resting with the rebel party, the gentleman with one white cheek and one red one came to the front and sang a song of triumph, with an air of the utmost self-complacency and the most remarkable leer of his single eye. While he was singing, the property-man hoisted a chair upon the table behind to constitute a throne. Portly as Falstaff was the rebel chief, and to hoist him up on the throne was a work of difficulty. When seated on it, he stroked his chin three or four times, assumed an air of dignity, and proceeded to chant in a wearisome mono-tone the might of his majesty, the bravery of his arms, the awfulness of his power, and the terror of his one eye. His courtiers entered, twirled their right arms round their left ones, bowed low, spun round, and sang a song of flattery. Then the victor, being helped down from his throne, came to the front, twirled himself round three times, and marched off followed by his friends.

Enter now the Chinese Joan of Arc. She made her appearance in a flowing robe, strode down to the foot-lights, and sang in a doleful strain who she was, and what she meant to do if she knew her own mind. On a sudden she gave a shriek, rent off her outer robe, displayed the attire of a soldier, drew a pair of swords from her girdle, flourished them aloft, and spun herself round like a top. Then she bounded up, threw three somersaults, flung herself flat on her back, leaped up again, executed a back somersault, and then rushed madly out at the door, intent on pursuing the one-eyed monster, and on reconquering for her monarch the territories of which he had become dispossessed. Joan was worked up to it, and evidently intended business.

Once more appeared the emperor and his army, and once more en-tered the one-eyed terror and his adherents. This time the spears were all of extra length, the three-pronged pitchforks were much more for-midable, the men had arrayed themselves in fighting uniforms far more awe-inspiring than those they wore previously. Shriek, scream, twist, twirl, spin, leap, bound, thrust, strike, wrench, struggle, and the fight went on furiously. But always before a blow was struck the striker jumped round three times, while he whom he was about to strike jumped three times round to meet him. The fight was grand; but the Chinese audience looked stolidly on, and seemed to be far too much engrossed with the serious state of affairs to move a muscle. The American spectators laughed boisterously and applauded with ecstasy.

Now came a great scene. In the very heat of the fight one of the curtains at the back was drawn aside, and in bounded Joan of Arc, turning head over heels twice to bring herself down to the front of the stage, and into the very midst of the combatants. She was armed with a pair of globes, fastened to the end of a stick by means of a cord. Whirling these round her head, she brought them down with a thwack on the shoulders of the one-eyed usurper. He endeavored to spear her; but, seizing his spear with her left hand, she belabored him with the globes held in her right. Fairly conquered, he fell at her feet and died. The property-man first placed a pillow under the usurper's head, to assist him in letting his last breath pass away quietly, then rolled him over to the back of the stage, and gave him a kick to admonish him that he was dead and no longer required. Whereupon he rose and walked off decently.

While the property-man was getting rid of the rebel chief, Joan of Arc knocked down the rest of the insurgents, belaboring them first with the globes and then thrusting her foot against the chest of each to topple them over. Her followers assisted her. Then entered some very terrible men, who, springing upward, alighted upon the soldiers and knocked them over one after another. The fight became a matter of leaping, vaulting, and tumbling. The dead men rose and joined in it. Joan of Arc was infuriated, and, going to work vigorously, turned somersault after somersault, throwing over all her foes. The property-man brought the table down to the front, to represent the walls of the fortress. Soldier number one threw himself over in the air, alighted on the table, and bounded over the painted cloth into the fortifications. Soldier number two followed him, Joan of Arc sprang up, cleared the table at a bound, and was at once mistress of the fortress. The emperor re-entered, Joan sang to him her victory, and he sang to her his thanks. Charles VII. was not more grateful to the French heroine than his majesty of China appeared to be to the Chinese one. The actors were tired out, and so, I think, were the spectators.

When the green curtain fell a Chinese came in front of it and addressed the English-speaking part of the audience, anxious for their patronage on another occasion. This was his speech:

"'Melliky man no sabe China play. All welly well this night now. Plenty more welly good to-morrow night. All same other sort of play. Tanky you. Welly good-night."

By which was implied that an American man does not understand a Chinese play, and that the Americans among the audience had better come again the following evening and witness some more of the same kind of performance. My own opinion differed from that of the courteous Chinaman.

On another occasion Artemus Ward and I went to a Chinese theatre in California, where we witnessed the first act of a drama, the entire representation of which was to extend over a week. In order that the drama should be thoroughly complete, the birth of the hero was represented in the course of the first act, the baby was exhibited to the audience, and the medical attendant sang a long song eulogistic of his own skill as an accoucheur. Still later in the evening, the same Chinaman who played the doctor joined Artemus and myself in a game of American bowls. We asked him how he liked acting.

"Welly good," was his reply. "Me killy pigs sometimes. Me welly good cook for 'Mellikans. Welly good actor too."

Pig-killer, cook, and actor! John was one of those useful artists who are well fitted to make their way in a new land.

◦ 23 ◦

The Genial Showman in Strange Places

THE "Babes in the Wood" were "trotted out" for the second time in San Francisco at the Metropolitan Theatre. Pecuniarily the second lecture was as successful as the first; for although not so many dollars were taken at the doors, the expenses were considerably less.

Before delivering the lecture a third time in the same city, it was thought advisable to pay a visit to some of the towns down the bay, especially as invitations had been received from many of their influential inhabitants. The railway then extended as far as San José.

Pretty, picturesque, sleepy San José! Spanish in name, half Spanish in appearance, and about one-eighth part Spanish in population. San José has its mission church, its convent, its alameda, its huts built of adobe, and its quaint old Spanish inns. Side by side with them are American hotels, American drinking-saloons, Yankee-notion stores, and railway booking-offices. The Spaniard has lingered long in the pleasant valley. The New Yorker and the Bostonian are fast thrusting him aside.

Charming, sunny San José! nursed in the lap of Nature where she is enthroned with luxury, sheltered by mountains, and fanned by the breezes of the Pacific. With eyelids closed, and more than six thousand miles away from your sunshine and your flowers, you are as visible as though I looked down upon you from the hills steeped in sunlight, which shelter your gardens, your orchards, your drowsy old priests, your peaceful religious retreats, and your card-playing, cocktail-drinking Californians!

San José is not an American town; that is, if one of the busy towns of New York or Massachusetts be taken as the standard whereby to judge. The inhabitants seem to have strength enough of mind to resist excitement, and philosophy enough to appreciate the excellence of inaction. The good people of San José take life calmly. They accept the fact of their being alive, and don't make a fuss about it. Had the San Franciscans been kind enough to leave them alone and not trouble them with a railroad, I believe their own exertions would never have brought one to their doors in the next two hundred years. And why a railway should have been introduced among them, I know not. Far more pleasant was it, a few years ago, to go down the bay in the steamboat, and, after navigating through a net-work of marshes and channels, arrive at Alviso in the steamer "Sophie McLane," land on a little wharf whereon were a few wooden huts, a flag-staff, and a coal-yard, away out in the fields; with a coach to take you past groves and gardens, in sight of mountains and meadows, to the sleepiest of sleepy little towns, a seven-miles' drive of rural loveliness and atmospheric enjoyment. The old college of Santa Clara, partially discernible among the trees to the right, and the nestling places of cosy, antiquated mission churches visible in the valleys far away to the left, amidst the drowsy hills—hills whose sides are ever glowing with golden light, and their glens hazy with purple shadows.

"It all depends where you make your pitch. There are not many good pitches in California now," said Mr. Alexander to us, in reply to a question as to how many towns in the State we could visit with a good

chance of making money in each. Mr. Alexander had pioneered circuses
and travelled with minstrel bands. To him, as to most old showmen,
the excellence of a town consisted not in its architectural beauty, its
historical interest, or its picturesque position, but in its capabilities as
a place wherein to make money. The "agent in advance" surveys a
town, and judges of it, first, to calculate the number of people in it who
are likely to come to a show; and, secondly, with regard to how many
good walls it has for billing and posting.

Mr. Alexander continued: "Of course your best stands will be at
Sacramento, Marysville, and Stockton. Folsom isn't much, and I guess
you won't get much out of Oroville. North San Juan is a very good one-
night town; so's Forest City, so's Downieville. Nevada City and Grass
Valley are good one-night places for any show. Placerville's caved in
considerably. Jackson will do for a pitch. So will Mokelumne Hill.
Murphy's ain't worth shucks. You may make out at Sonora. Columbia's gone up. I can't say how Coulterville would turn out for you. If you
go to Copperopolis, tell old Cardinell at the Hall to let you have some
music. Ione City don't count. Campo Seco's nowhere. San Andreas never
was much, and it's wilted considerably lately. But there's Vallejo, and
Napa, and Sonoma, and Santa Rosa, and Petaluma. They are all good
pitches. Dollars are lying around loose for you in all of 'em—you bet."

"And how about San José?"

"Shy. I don't go much on her—not for your show. She's a sweet
little town for a circus. Then's when her greasers turn out."

By the term "greasers" we knew Mr. Alexander to mean the Spanish-
Mexican part of the population. As a matter of course, they were not
the right kind of people to attend a comic lecture by Artemus Ward.
For all that Mr. Alexander had to say to the contrary, to San José we
determined to go. Not only had offers been made and invitations tendered, but there were friends resident there on whose influence the
lecturer thought that he could build prospects of doing a fair business.

The hotel at San José had a polite landlord. He was a good host, with
but one salient failing—he cared more about horses than he did about
lectures. Very prophetic was he that Artemus Ward would be a great
success in San José, and that he was just the very man whom every
body wished to see and hear. On the night of the lecture I looked
around the theatre for him, but caught no glimpse of his radiant face.
I saw him the next morning at the hotel when the bill was asked for.

The theatre at San José, was of wood. It had been built a few years previously by Mr. James Stark, an actor of some celebrity on the Pacific coast. Its interior was in a dilapidated condition. The boy who found the keys for me, in taking me round the building, pointed out a hole in the dress-circle through which another little boy, while witnessing a performance, had suddenly dropped down and fallen into a barrel of whitewash. At one time the stalls and dress-circle had been nicely carpeted, but the taste for the drama had decayed in San José; so had the carpets.

The agent at the Express-office had the letting of the theatre. His charge for it for a night was twenty dollars. He prognosticated great success.

"You must have a band outside," said he.

Why a band for a lecture? I objected to it, and I knew that Artemus would.

"We always have a band," said he. "There's a small balcony in front for them to play in. When they've done outside let them tune up in. You'll have a big rush as soon as the band strikes up."

I concluded to have one. The Express-agent promised to arrange it for me on economical terms.

"And get up a bonfire," he added. "It's the greatest thing out. The boys will light you up one in the road. It's a sure thing. You can't have a better advertisement. When they see the smoke, they'll come in from all parts."

There were two newspaper offices to visit; that of the "San José Patriot" and that of the "San José Mercury." At the latter I found one of the proprietors. He was working at case. Putting down his composing-stick in a decided manner, he replied to my announcement of my business:

"You'll want a lot of dodgers. We do them very cheaply at our office. Send your dodgers about and you'll have a good house. Well, I *am* glad to hear that we are going to have Artemus Ward. He's a man I have long wished to see. I think much of him and would do any thing to serve him—Dodgers of this size would suit you best. You'll want about a thousand."

By "dodgers" the disinterested gentleman meant small handbills. I ordered the number required, and wrote out the prefatory notice I wished to appear in the paper. The worthy proprietor suggested that, as he had been working hard, he would put on his coat and take a stroll with me round the town for a little enjoyment. I found him to be an agreeable, well-informed, communicative companion. He proposed to point out to me a few of the noteworthy things of San José. I accepted his proposal with gratitude.

"That white building with the trees round it used to be our court-house," said he. "Look at the bullet-holes in this door-post. They were trying a man inside for murder. The people outside were afraid he would not be convicted, and had him brought forth. A shower of bullets was sent into him at once. Some were sent through him, and are stick-ing in that post now. Here's our mission church. The old one was falling to ruin, and we have built up a new one around it, with the old one still inside. That queer-looking old adobe-house over there, all of one story, with the white shingle roof to it, used to be the State-house of California, and was so up to 1850. San José was the capital of Cali-fornia then, just as Sacramento is now. The Legislature used to meet in that old house built of dried mud, just as you see it. A high old Legislature it was, too. They were the hardest-drinking lot of cusses California ever had. It used to be called 'The Legislature of a thousand drinks,' and the name wasn't a bad one. They'd drink whisky, aguar-dente, cassis, or cold poison, it was all the same to them. They made very good laws, for all that, though they were the cussedest lot."

Thus discoursing, my acquaintance of the "San José Mercury" wan-dered on. I remembered that on a former visit to the little town I had chanced to make the acquaintance of a nurseryman by the name of Lowe, who had in his garden some hawthorn bushes grown from berries plucked by Colonel Younger of San José, at Newstead Abbey, and brought over loose in his pocket. Mr. Lowe referred to his bushes as "Byron's hawthorns." I inquired if the nurseryman were still alive, and if the hawthorns still flourished. My companion replied to my inquiry, and then, after being silent a minute or two, spoke out abruptly, just as though he had hit upon some new and happy thought:

"Byron was deep—wasn't he? He got off some good things."

I evaded any comment on the criticism, and continued the ramble.

Mr. Lowe, the San José nurseryman, was originally from Chester-field in Derbyshire. I had a conversation with him in 1860, when he told me that he was once an assistant of Sir Joseph Paxton's; that he went to California shortly after the Great Exhibition of 1851, and landed with little or no money; that he was engaged to lay out a garden, and soon obtained other employment of the same kind. In his first year he cleared nearly four thousand dollars, and now possessed land all over the country.

"I have a league of it at San Luis Obispo," said he. "There's three hundred head of cattle on it. My second son is down there. He can throw the riata with any Mexican."

The proficiency of his son in the use of the lasso seemed to afford Mr. Lowe great satisfaction. Very pleased, also, was he with the diplomas of the State Agricultural Society, awarded to him at Stockton and at Sacramento for being "the best cultivator of the smallest quantity of land." There was also another diploma awarded to Mrs. Lowe for having exhibited "the best specimens of tomato sauce."

"And it wasn't tomato sauce, after all," said Mr. Lowe, rubbing his hands with glee. "It was mushroom catsup, and they didn't know the difference!"

Every thing in San José reminds the visitor of the Spanish origin of the place. At the telegraph office was written up, *Telegrafo de la Compañia del Estado. Se communica con todas las ciudades de California, la linea Pacífica y Atlántica por Los Angeles.* Opposite the mission church was an announcement, *Officina de Diligencias de las Minas de Guadalupe y Enriqueta.* Near to the stage-office was a dealer in wines and strong liquors, whose sign was, *A Quevedo. A la Iberia. Vinos, Licores, y Viveres.* The bakers' shops have the word *Panaderia* painted up beside the word "Bakery," and the restaurants, after notifying you that you can be refreshed with breakfast or dinner for fifty cents, inform you that you may have *almuerzos y comidas* at the same price. There was also a Chinaman who had painted over his door, and who probably has the same announcement there still—"*Com Son. Washing and Ironing, Lavados y Planchados. Blanchisserie, Soap-place. Hooray!*" The last word was evidently a joke of the sign-painter. Possibly Com Son supposed it to mean clear-starching or mangling.

Great artists in their way are the Chinese laundry-men of California. They are to be found not in San Francisco and the large towns only, but in all the mining camps throughout the country. As a rule, John Chinaman, when developed as a washerwoman, is to be seen in a small shop, ironing shirts or petticoats at a table close by the window. On the table is a pan of burning charcoal, and near to it a large wash-basin filled with rice-water. John does not sprinkle the linen with his fingers, but dips his face into the wash-basin, fills his mouth with the rice-water until his cheeks are well distended, and then blows the glutinous fluid in the form of spray over the linen he is in the act of ironing. The large heavy irons are heated on the pan of charcoal, and John puffs out his rice-water spray without stopping the motion of the iron. As a getter-up of fine linen, he is highly to be recommended. He manipulates a shirt-front to perfection, washing it spotlessly white, and polishing it to glossy smoothness.

The devotion of the Chinese to the laundry art has been a great boon to Californians. A few years ago it was difficult to get any thing washed in San Francisco. The female inhabitants had minds superior to soap-suds, while even the poorest of the male population preferred to wash the golden soil rather than rub and rinse soiled garments. The hotels had to charter small vessels to send their bed-linen to Honolulu, in the Sandwich Islands, to find a laundry. A pair of sheets or a table-cloth then had to make a voyage of more than a month out and home, to be cleansed by natives of the islands where Captain Cook was slain, and of which Kamehameha is king. They were sent to the blacks to be whitened.

Apathetic San José had been duly dosed with "dodgers." The editors of both the newspapers had befittingly heralded the lecture, and the evening for its delivery had arrived. From the paucity of applications for tickets at the various places where they were deposited on sale, there was reason to expect that Mr. Alexander would be right in his prophecy of San José being "shy," and that, however much it might be a "sweet little town for a circus," its sweetness was not likely to prove very saccharine to a comic lecturer. But, for other reasons than simply to get dollars, Artemus had desired to visit San José, so that if expenses should chance to be taken, together with the slightest margin of profit, there would be no disappointment.

Carpenters had repaired the dilapidations of the theatre, and a black man had swept the floor, brushed the seats, and made ready the stage. Into the little balcony in front of the house went a noble band of musicians, consisting of one clarionette-player, three gentlemen with horns, and one with a drum; the latter slightly the worse for whisky, and consequently more vigorously disposed for music. A goodly group of enthusiastic little boys volunteered to light up a bonfire, and the loafing part of the community soon began to appear upon the scene

A troupe of Mexican youths smoking cigarettes arranged themselves in line against the side of an adjacent hotel, the name of which was the Mansion House, and a bevy of giggling girls, very dark in complexion, and each with a bunch of flowers in her hand, collected around the coach office opposite. Looking up the road to the right, some wagons were seen coming in from the country bringing a portion of the destined audience, and looking down the road to the left toward the town, the good people of San José were noticeable, sauntering slowly along towards the theatre with provoking tranquility of manner.

Loudly played the band, brilliantly burned the bonfire, gently came the crowd.

"A gentleman round the corner at the Express-office wants to see you," said a little boy, running up breathlessly—the first energetic individual except the excited drummer who had appeared upon the scene.

I obeyed the summons. It was Artemus who had sent for me. "Shall we have any house?" he asked.

I replied that it was early yet, and that I knew from previous experience the people of San José were not the same as other people of the American continent, nor disposed to do any thing too hastily.

"Confound that band! The whole thing is ridiculous. What do you want with a band to a comic lecture?" observed Artemus, in an irritated manner.

"Well, it's our ordinary way," replied the man in office. "Our people go great on music. They don't know when they've to go in till they hear the band strike up. Take care and liquor up that drummer. He'll beat 'em in like thunder."

There was no need for the advice. As I returned round the corner, the drummer was hauling up some whisky into the balcony by means of a string to which a bottle was attached.

The bonfire blazed, the band blew bravely, the public of San José had assembled, but the theatre was still empty.

"Massa muss get de musicianers in soon when de ladies and gen'elmen are all ready," suggested the African gentleman, who acted as bill-poster, cleaner of the theatre, whitewasher, and custodian of the Congregational church close by.

I found upon inquiry that the negro was correct in his information. The evening was fine, the bonfire brilliant, and the music attractive.

Not until I allowed the fire to go out and the instrumentalists to go in was there a likelihood of our having a good house. I acted accordingly, and proceeded in quest of Artemus to inform him that his audience were inside, and that he might safely make his way to the theatre.

"What have you done with the artist on the drum?" he inquired.

I replied that the drummer was in the orchestra fronting the stage, playing his instrument courageously.

"But I am not the Colleen Bawn nor Richard the Third. What do I want with an orchestra? What will the people expect? Do stop them before I go in, or those musical idiots will start up 'See the Conquering Hero' or some other nonsense. And turn out that drummer—he's abominable."

Hastening to execute my errand, I met half a dozen people assisting a wounded man from the theatre. At a glance I recognized the drummer. He had left his whisky-bottle in the balcony, and during my absence had quitted the orchestra to fetch it. The stairs were narrow, the drummer unsteady. To use Mr. Alexander's phrase, he had found a bad "pitch" at San José.

Artemus lectured. I am afraid that the good people of the town were slightly disappointed. They laughed heartily at what they heard, but there were some among them who, as they went out, expressed regret at not having seen "Mr. Ward's wax-works." They wanted a show to look at, not to listen to. Had they been treated to some "ground and lofty tumbling," a little conjuring, a cock-fight, or any thing equally intellectual, I believe their minds would have discovered more matter for meditation and have been better satisfied. Dollars enough were taken to pay expenses and leave a slight surplus. So far things had gone well with all but the drummer. As we left the theatre a gentleman from the neighboring town of Santa Clara introduced himself to Artemus, and urged the advisability of lecturing there.

"You are sure of an immense house," said he. "I will do all I can for you. You can charge just what you please. We are warmhearted people in Santa Clara, and we want you bad. Sakes alive, man! they'll come to see you with a rush, like a shower of little apples."

I suggested that perhaps the enthusiastic gentleman would be willing to speculate, and to pay down a certain sum with a chance of making a profit for himself. He evaded the proposal, remarking:

"It don't run in my line. Besides, I want Mr. Ward to have all the money he makes. There's a pile waiting for him over there in Santa

Clara. He might give his lecture in the college first, and then in the little chapel behind. We are all warm-hearted, and he'll have a good time of it. It's the best little place in all the valleys, and full of big-souled people."

Artemus promised to lecture in Santa Clara. The town was only three miles distant. We had a day or two to spare, and if no money should chance to be made, none was likely to be lost.

On the evening after the lecture in San José we were wandering through the city together, when, passing a small Spanish-built house in the outskirts, we noticed a pair of handsome Mexican saddles. The door of the house was half-open, the saddles were hung up inside. Seated near them, smoking a cigarette, was a young and pretty Spanish woman, far more handsome than the saddles.

"We could make a sensation riding down Broadway, New York, on those saddles," observed Artemus. "Let us go in and look at them."

An English saddle of common pig-skin and a well-made Mexican saddle with all its adornments are about as like to one another as a school-boy's "fizgig" of wet gunpowder rolled into a cone is to Mount Vesuvius in eruption.

The Mexican saddle is large, heavy, showy, and often of many colors. It has *macheos*, or large flaps of leather, very grandly embossed, and leathern casings for the stirrups of marvelous construction and solidity. A Mexican saddle would not be a saddle if it were not a thing for show as well as for use. So the *macheos* are embossed, and also the *tapaaeros* or stirrup-casings. So are the long leather *chicaros* which are interposed between the horse and the rider; and so is the *ancara*, on the back of the animal. The *fraena*, or bridle, is made as ornamental as possible, while the *foosta*, or high pommel in front for holding the *riata*, or lasso, is a curiously-constructed and characteristic portion of the extraordinary mass of leather, iron, wood, brass, and twisted hair which a Mexican horse has to carry for the comfort and ideas of grandeur that have possession of the mind of its rider.

We were examining the saddles, and asking a few questions of the Spanish lady relative to the value of the highly-decorated pieces of leather-work, when an olive-complexioned, dark-browed, tall fellow, wearing a very wide sombrero, and having in his grasp a heavy riding-whip, rushed into the house, glanced first at the pretty Spaniard, then at Artemus, and closed the door with violence.

"Como esta usted, señor?" said Artemus, airing his recently-acquired Spanish to assist him in the emergency.

The man made no reply, but strode up to the woman and brandished the stock of his heavy whip. At the same moment we noticed that his other hand was fumbling with the hilt of a pistol in his girdle.

Drink and jealousy had evidently got the upper hand of the infuriated Mexican. Artemus and I comprehended our position, and the poor woman glanced pityingly towards us as she cowered back into a corner of the apartment.

In the middle of the room was a stout heavy table. On it a lamp was burning. The one chance of escape was perceived by both of us simultaneously.

Artemus blew out the lamp as I pulled back the latch of the door. In a few seconds we were in the open street. Before we could turn the corner, we heard the report of a pistol. I fancied that I felt the bullet whizz by my ear. Almost at the same moment we heard the drunken fellow who had fired at us fall on the ground, uttering a loud oath as he stumbled.

When we had gained the open road Artemus laughed, and observed jocosely:

"Comic lecturing has nothing to do with saddlery. Old fellow, just keep your comic lecturer to his business, or you'll lose him. That Mexican wanted to saddle the wrong horse."

In half an hour afterwards we met the gentleman who had printed the "dodgers" for us. To him we told the particulars of the adventure. His sympathy manifested itself in an invitation to take a drink.

"Them Greasers are a caution," said he. "I guess the man was tenacious—a kind of tenacious, you see."

The Mexican's tenacity reminded me of the Yankee's criticism on a boa-constrictor. Being asked what he thought of one, he replied, "Wall, he ain't what yeou may call a playful kind of a critter, but I guess he's got a considerable heap of affection in him when he twists."

⚬ 24 ⚬

The Warm-hearted People of Santa Clara

W E are all warm-hearted people in Santa Clara," was the alluring commendation of the gentleman who invited us to visit the little town. As we rode along towards the place, I asked Artemus in what way he thought the warmth would be manifested.

"Warm hearts always want free tickets," he replied. "I once lectured at a place in Connecticut where a whole-souled manufacturer of sewing-machines asked me if I didn't feel a great wish to be introduced to his family. I told him that my inclinations were that way. People said he was the warmest-hearted man in the whole place. In the evening he brought himself, his wife, and sixteen nephews and nieces. He introduced them all, and said they would just take seats and listen. They filled all my front-seats. Next day I sent for the admission-money. Answer came back that a mistake was made. They were all Mr. Ward's friends, and couldn't think of paying; but their hearts were as warm to me as ever—bless them!"

The road from San José to Santa Clara is about three miles in length, and exceedingly beautiful. Grand old pollard willows overshadow it on each side. In days past it was the Alameda along which the priests of the San José mission walked in procession to visit the Jesuit fathers of Santa Clara. Though profane intruders have now populated the district, the old Catholic faith still retains its hold among the people. The priest is still a power in the pleasant valleys of Southern California, and the mission churches are some of the most picturesque objects in the land. While travelling in this part of the world a doubt is apt to cross the mind of the traveller whether he is really in California. Can this be the new country, the name of which was scarcely seen in print a quarter of a century ago? Can this be the land of gold to which fortune-seekers from all parts of the earth have recently found their way? Here, where the convent bell tolls and the wooden crosses by the roadside invite wayfarers to pray? Are we on the far side of the American continent, or are we in Southern Europe?

We had left the Colegio de Niñas behind us, and were hastening along the willow-shaded road when we were recognized by a gentleman who had met Artemus in New York.

"Rip, slap, here we are again!" exclaimed the traveller mirthfully. "Glad to see you, Mr. Ward! Heard you lecture in 'Frisco the other evening. You'll do business out in this country."

A few compliments passed. Artemus then inquired what errand had brought the gentleman to California.

"Just started an Anatomical Museum—branch of the one in New York," replied our new acquaintance, who was a young Jew, with very pronounced features and much suavity of manner. "Have large collection of models—good show—give anatomical lectures every evening —got a smart man to do that—make a fortune with museum here— bad luck, though, last week with a new Venus from Italy."

We sympathized with the museum proprietor, and requested further particulars relative to his unlucky Venus.

"She was a beautiful figure," he continued; "splendidly modelled made in Florence—best wax—quite as good as Sarti's one used to be— was packed in a case along with a pair of Napoleon's hands, modelled in harder wax. Steamer people were cautioned to be careful how they stowed the case on board. Would you believe it? The fools put it near the engine-room. What with the hot weather in the tropics and those plaguy boilers, my Venus was a gone goose. When I came to unpack her, I found her lower parts all melted away. Napoleon's hands had welded themselves clean on to her knees. D—n me! if she hadn't four hands, and no feet at all! My brother took some models out to Australia, and they melted up just in the same way."

"I should exhibit her all the same," remarked Artemus.

"I think I shall," was the reply. "Good notion to call her a freak of nature—eh? Born in the middle of Asia. D—n me if I don't! The Circassian phenomenon modelled after life. I'll do it, and have her history written up tomorrow."

We laughed and parted. Our Jewish friend—who, by-the-by, styled himself a doctor—took the direction of San José, and we that of Santa Clara. After an interval of silence, Artemus observed:

"There are two social puzzles I can not solve. Perhaps you can, old fellow. One is why bakers' stores have a monopoly of the church notices and go-to-meeting bills in their windows, and the other is why advertising anatomical museums are always kept by Jews, who in reality are money-lenders?"

We arrived at Santa Clara before we had solved satisfactorily either of these problems.

Near the gates of the Jesuit College we met the gentleman who had guaranteed the warm-heartedness of the little town, and whose advice had prevailed over Artemus to consent to lecture in the place. He approached us in a jaunty manner, and was profuse in his expressions of welcome. We inquired if he had made any arrangements for the lecture to be delivered. His reply was that he was then about to call on the Principal of the college, and hoped to be able to secure the college lecture-room, which would also include the attendance of the students, who were numerous and for the most part wealthy. He added that the Principal was a very warm-hearted man, and that he had left a copy of "Artemus Ward—His Book" with him to read. An immediate introduction to the Principal was proposed. Artemus, after much hesitation, consented.

We were ushered into a little room on the left of the entrance. Religious pictures adorned the walls. A crucifix was over the mantel.

"They won't stand comic lecturing here," suggested Artemus to our guide.

"Oh yes, they will. Very good boys all. Like a little fun. Are always having lectures on one thing or the other."

Artemus smiled incredulously. Presently the Principal made his appearance—a portly father of the Church, very gentlemanly in demeanor. In his hand was the small volume of which Artemus was the author.

Introductory preliminaries being over and the nature of our visit explained, his reverence gravely inquired:

"Do you propose to lecture on a philosophical subject?"

"No—history," replied Artemus.

The Principal informed us that he had looked over the little book, the character of which he confessed that he could not clearly comprehend, though it did not appear to him to be historical. After apologizing for not being better acquainted with the literary reputation of Mr. Artemus Ward, he concluded by asking what department of history was intended for the subject of the proposed lecture.

"Early history," replied Artemus—'The Babes in the Wood.' "

"Do you mean Romulus and Remus?"

"No, little Billy Smith and his sister. It's a fairy tale of the ancient Greeks in New England. Your college would like it, I am sure," continued Artemus, gravely. "All colleges do. Students howl over it."

After a few minutes' deliberation the Principal shook his head and politely declined the proposal, intimating that he was afraid the subject was not suited for the institution.

"Never mind," said our introducer, as we passed out at the door. "I guess we'll go round and take St. Mary's Hall. The students will all come round and hear you there. They are all warm-hearted boys."

St. Mary's Hall we found to be too dilapidated, but there was a small Methodist chapel close by, the use of which was offered to us. We accepted the offer, and issued our bills with as little delay as possible.

The evening arrived. We opened the chapel doors in good time. From the road, people on the outside could see the lecture-table, with two large tallow candles burning on it. We awaited the warm-hearted public of Santa Clara.

Two or three boys looked in at the chapel door, and in course of the first quarter of an hour after opening one man paid. Artemus walked up and down on the opposite side of the road, smoked a cigar, and watched results. Our enthusiastic friend who had induced us to visit the place presently made his appearance on the scene: He brought with him three of the town officials and asked that they might be passed to seats. He also informed us that the Principal of the college had given orders that all the students should be locked in, and none of them allowed to attend the lecture; a proceeding on the part of the Principal by no means complimentary to Artemus, but testifying to a commendable zeal in superintending the historical studies of his collegians.

Eight o'clock, and only eight persons for an audience; three had paid, and the other five were "dead-heads."

"Is this about the usual heat of their generous hearts?" asked Artemus.

"They're mean to-night—very mean," replied the eulogist of Santa Clara. "I attended myself to your bills going out properly. I guess they all know you are here. Perhaps the tickets are a little too high in price."

"For a warm-hearted people?" asked Artemus.

"You see they are a little cantankerous at times. Besides, Mr. Ward, we are all farmers here in the valley, and there's been a good deal of blight about this season, and all the Judge's children have got the scarlet fever. Smallpox is considerable too in most families, and—"

"For goodness sake go and send those people home and blow out the candles," interrupted Artemus, imploring me to dismiss the audience.

I urged him to undertake the task of dismissal himself, but he declined the honor, preferring to stand in the road and laugh at my perplexity in having to tell eight good people of Santa Clara that they must return to their homes without hearing the lecture. I explained to them in a few words that it would be impossible to deliver a humorous lecture to so scant an audience, and handed back to the three who had paid the dollars they had disbursed. One of the three gentlemen asked me if Mr. Ward was near by. I accompanied him to the door, and introduced him to Artemus.

"Sorry for you, Mr. Ward," said he. "It's a hard place this, but just bring your candles across to my store at the corner over there. We'll soon have a fire built in the office. Our friends here will come with us. If we can't have a lecture we'll have some whisky."

We accepted the proposal. The gentleman by whom it was tendered kept a large grocery and hardware store, behind which he had a comfortable room used as a counting-house or office. We locked the chapel door, carried the lighted candles across the road, and adjourned in a body to partake of the grocer's hospitality.

With good whisky and funny stories an hour passed pleasantly away. Two sisters of the grocer and three of their young lady friends came in and desired to be introduced to Mr. Ward. They had intended to be in time for the lecture, but had promised to call for their doctor, and had been delayed.

"Our doctor is provokingly punctual," said one of the young ladies. "He always has his watch in his hand. We were to have been at his office at a quarter to eight. It was just twelve minutes to it when we got there, and he said it was too late. The cross old fidget wouldn't come."

"Punctual men are nuisances," remarked Artemus. "Where their heart should beat they have only a clock ticking. Your doctor is like the New England doctor I tell about sometimes. He was very punctual. When his wife died he went to her funeral. As the earth fell on her coffin every body around cried. All he did was to take out his watch, look at the time, and say: 'Well, we've got her under, and it's just twenty minutes past two!'"

Conversation was brisk. The grocer and his friends were very merry. Presently we ascertained that the young ladies came from New York, and that, late in the evening, they were going to make up a "surprise-party," to pay a visit to a newly-married pair not long settled in Santa Clara, and who also came from New York. Invitations were tendered to us, and accepted, to join the party. Other young ladies soon came in, and with them came three or four young men bearing a hamper, together with a gentleman who brought with him a violin. It was not long before we learned the cause of our having failed to attract an audience to the lecture. In Santa Clara it was a night of party-giving. People were too busy visiting to go out listening.

"But, really, it is a shame! We should so much have liked to hear you lecture. Oh, do let us hear some of it!" petitioned the ladies to Artemus.

Petitioners so pretty and so pressing were irresistible. Artemus told them that if they would go out in the front store and there make an audience, he would do his best in the way of comic oratory.

Lamps and candles soon illuminated the store. A flour-barrel was hoisted on the counter to serve as a lecturing-desk, and the ladies disposed themselves on chairs, tea-chests, bags of rice, coils of rope, or whatever came handiest for a seat. Some coffee had been hastily made. It was passed round to the ladies before the lecture commenced.

Artemus perched up on the counter, a candle burning on the flour-barrel before him, and a small parcel of mouse-traps dangling from the ceiling over his head; gentlemen seated smoking cigars on the counter, and ladies sipping coffee while they enjoyed the impromptu style of entertainment: such were the surroundings of the lecture in Santa Clara.

After the lecture came the adjournment to the surprise-party. The peculiar form of social fun known as a "surprise-party" in New York and elsewhere in the Union is characteristic of America. Considered as a compliment paid to those to whom it is given, some people would regard it as an unwarrantable intrusion of privacy.

It consists in making up a number of jovial acquaintances to go in a body to the house of one whom they know, surprise him at bed-time or thereabouts, compel him then and there to give a party, and accept the visitors as self-invited guests. Usually the host and hostess have some slight notification of that which is about to happen, but frequently no previous notice is given; and if the good people to be complimented have retired to rest, they have to rise again immediately, turn on the gas, and join in the night's festivity. They are put to no further trouble, for the surprisers bring with them their own servants. Expense there is none, for in hampers and baskets the guests carry with them to the house of the party surprised all the eatables and drinkables required for supper and refreshment during the night. Nor is it unusual to take with them plates, knives and forks, salt-cellars, and pepper-boxes. The guests really take full possession of the house, give the entertainment, provide every thing required, arrange the programme of amusements, constitute themselves their own masters of the ceremonies, and do just as they please. The master of the house and his family are for the time nothing more than privileged persons in their own domicile.

Thoughtfully and judiciously the ladies had packed the hampers at Santa Clara. Cold meats and cake and wine were in abundance. Artemus and I felt that we could not go empty-handed. I noticed that among other articles in the store was some French brandy of a good brand, and purchased a couple of bottles to stow away in the pockets of my outer coat. Artemus looked round, and discovered on a shelf half a dozen jars of olives.

"Hand me down those olives," said he. "We are going to visit newly-married people. I shall present them with those jars of olives and a pot of honey. The honey they can eat, and keep the olives to grow and have branches."

Thus laden we went to the surprise-party. Music, dancing, and flirtation constituted the entertainment. The surprised host was exceedingly forgiving to his intruders, while the lady of the house was amiability itself. Morning arrived before the merriment terminated.

Artemus, tired and sleepy, was silent and grave in the carriage as we travelled to San Francisco. I remarked to him that he did not look like a humorist. He replied:

"No, I am a headachist."

❧ 25 ❧

Spiritualism and Conjuring

Gentlemen, I have got a big thing—very big—and money in it," said Mr. Samuel Wilder, calling in the evening at the Occidental Hotel, and finding Artemus and myself busily engaged arranging the lecturing tour through the gold mines.

Mr. Wilder spoke in a low voice, as though he was afraid that some outsider would hear of his good fortune and do him injury. He drew his chair up close, and, having made his announcement, proposed in true Californian style to stand drinks at his own expense before proceeding to business.

To Artemus Mr. Wilder was an old friend, while to me he was but a recent acquaintance; but I knew enough of him to be aware that he was an enterprising man, ready to enter into any speculation that might offer a chance of being remunerative. Among many other avocations he had been proprieter of a circus or two, a dealer in real estate, an entrepreneur of acrobats, a wholesale jeweller, a trader in mining stock, a proprietor of coaches, and I believe at one time a banker. He was a capital illustration of the adaptability of the American to any pursuit, a peculiarity which forms a national characteristic. Apprenticeship to any art or calling is not thought to be required in the United States. A Yankee learns a trade in six months to which an English youth is apprenticed for seven years. In professions, instead of a man waiting till he is middle-aged before he commences to practise, he gallops through all the sciences he has to learn, or makes a *coup-de-main* on all the art he has to acquire, and begins his profession and his manhood together. Should he commence as a doctor and not like his calling, he will probably turn to be a lawyer. If still dissatisfied, he will possibly try hotel-keeping, horse-dealing, or architecture. None of these suiting, he will attempt something else. Before he is forty he may have been a soldier, captain of a vessel, proprietor of a theatre, contractor, stone-merchant and piano-forte manufacturer. By the time he attains his climacteric he may have exhausted all the professions and tried every trade.

"How big the thing is depends on what we make out of it," continued Mr. Wilder. "There has not been a conjuror in this city for some time, and I've got one. But he'll want a lot of working-up."

Artemus suggested that Mr. Wilder was the very man to "work up" a show.

"Not as it should be done. I have not had enough to do with hanky-panky artists. This man has just landed from Hong Kong. He has plenty of traps with him. Says he is very clever. Has no money. Wants some one to bring him out. I am game to try him; but he'll have to be engineered. If I take him, I shall want you to make me out some bills and lend a hand to start him. We must give him a big name, and keep him dark till we are all ready."

We inquired whether the conjuror had any celebrity, and by what name he was already known to the world.

"Calls himself Perkins, or Simpkins, or something like that," replied Mr. Wilder. "Some name that don't amount to shucks. We must make a 'professor' of him. I don't go on any conjuror if he's not a professor. Give him some long Greek name that no one can understand. He don't know too much himself, so you call him what you like and say about him what you please. But people like long names—regular jaw-breakers. So give him a twister."

We agreed to assist Mr. Wilder in his speculation with the conjuror, but suggested that it would be advisable to see the man of mystery first, and have some conversation with him before interfering with his destinies in California.

Mr. Wilder informed us confidentially that he already had his magician under lock and key over the way at the Russ House, and asked us to go over and be introduced to him.

The weird necromancer of the past and the prestidigitator of the present are very different sort of beings. All the atmosphere of supernatural solemnity which enveloped the sorcerer and the cabalist of ancient times has dissolved away. The conjuror of modern days is as commonplace and unromantic as the rest of his fellow-men; sometimes he is a little more so.

We found the newly-arrived conjuror to be a pleasant, ruddy-faced, merry-eyed, thick-lipped, talkative, and dapper little fellow, who had the bearing of a man recently from behind a counter in Whitechapel or a desk in Liverpool, rather than a magician who had astonished, as he assured us that he had, the Emperor of China at Pekin, Prince Satsuma at Hakodadi, and Indian rajahs innumerable. A few questions I addressed to him elicited answers that convinced me of his having been to Australia, some of the Pacific islands, and in Batavia.

"The Emperor of China gave me this," said he, exhibiting a ring. "This gold-headed cane is a present to me from the brother of the tycoon. This snuff-box was given me by the Queen of Madasgascar, and I've sent no end of presents home."

We pitied the poor little man's simplicity. All his travel had not taught him to distinguish between the old birds that are not to be caught with chaff and the half-fledged young ones who will peck at any thing. In my mind's eye I could see him driving a hard bargain for the Emperor of China's ring, going back three times to the same shop to offer for the brother of the tycoon's walking-stick, and standing meditative in front of a pawnbroker's window, enchanted by the glamour of the Queen of Madagascar's snuff-box.

"I am but a child of nature," said Artemus to the conjuror, very gravely. "Pardon me for asking the question. Did the Queen of Madagascar snuff with you when she gave you that box—is she a snuffist?"

"That box!—why that box is an event," replied the conjuror emphatically, with a Cockney accent. "That there box pretty well got up a revolution in Madagascar. The queen had to get it made for me, and I had no time to stop. The native goldsmiths were ordered to make it in a day and a night. I was a great favorite with her majesty, and she wouldn't let me go without it. I was dining with her at the palace when her goldsmith came to tell her it couldn't be done in time. She's a fine woman with no end of a temper, and—well, I don't mind saying it to you—she was nuts on me. So she called her guards, and told them to keep the chief goldsmith in charge and see that he got the snuff-box ready by eight o'clock in the morning; and if it wasn't they were to cut his head off. It wasn't ready till nine, and they did cut his head off—fact!"

"Honest Injun?" inquired Mr. Wilder, using a Western phrase equivalent to demanding of the narrator of a story whether he is strictly adhering to the truth.

"'Pon my solemn word of honor!" replied the conjuror. "The people were all very fond of the goldsmith. When they knew he had been executed they raised an awful bobbery, and I nearly lost my life too.

Her majesty slipped the snuff-box in my hand, and I had to run for it—fact."

"That man will do," whispered Artemus to me aside. "He has that sweet respect for truth which most noble conjurors have. If he can force a card as well as he can a lie, he's a lovely artist."

It was decided that the Madagascan magician should be brought out. Artemus and I were to concoct the bill for him. It appeared that he had never possessed a good startling poster, nor had any well-arranged programme. Mr. Wilder believed largely in a grand posting-bill. The conjuror had no special titles for his tricks, and sanctioned our entitling them as we pleased. Mr. Wilder's idea was that the programme should have some drollery in it, be preposterous enough to set the people talking, and sufficiently wanting in intelligibility to confuse the readers, and to cause them to imagine very much more than they were likely to see.

"There's all my bag of tricks," said the conjuror. "I'm in your hands, gentlemen. There's a mint of money in me. I am an artist. It's different with me and them there fellows who have never been brought up to the profession. Say what you like about my experiments, but go it strong on my blood-red writing on the arm."

"The trick of the Spiritualists?" inquired Artemus.

In reply the conjuror assured us that it was the same "experiment" of which the Spiritualists made so much mystery, and that he could perform it as well as any medium in existence. He asserted that not only could he cause names to appear in blood-red letters on his arm, but that he could also produce raps, and pick out the name of a deceased friend written on a slip of paper, rolled up in a pellet and placed among a dozen other similar pellets on a table. This last feat of the Spiritualists I had seen a "medium" named Forster perform in Boston some few months previous. The *modus operandi* had puzzled me exceedingly. Being anxious to know how the trick was performed, I promised to lend my aid in concocting a poster if the conjuror would enlighten me as to the way the Spiritualists effected the mystery.

"I'll do that and I'll show the blood-red writing too," promised the conjuror. "It's all hanky-panky, every bit of it. I'm as good a Spiritualist as any of them. I'll give you a *séance* to-morrow night —fact."

"Do you know the trick of rubbing two rabbits into one, like Hermann does it?" inquired Artemus. "I want to learn that trick. Teach me, and I'll help you."

"Know it? In course I do. I'll *learn* it you in no time. We'll have it at the *séance*. You shall do it yourself—fact."

Spiritualism was in the ascendant at San Francisco. The lady with the large teeth, who had accompanied me on the steamer, had given many lectures and become popular. Her trick of lecturing seemed to be to talk glibly an unintelligible jargon of mysticism, mixed up with daring assertions and occasional dashes of the sentimental artfully interfused. Plain language she ignored. Her Spiritualistic theories were expounded in carefully selected words of not less than five syllables each. Evidently she composed a lecture in the same way that Mr. Wilder wished a poster to be written, and regarded the public from the *omne ignotum pro magnifico* point of view.

The interest the California public took in the matter of Spiritualism revived in my mind a latent desire to understand the trickery of the so-called "mediums." I have already alluded to a Mr. Forster of Boston, to whom I once or twice paid a visit. One of his most astonishing feats was performed in this way: Previously to calling at his house, I had written on two slips of paper the names of relatives some years dead, one name on each slip of paper. On ten other slips I had written ten other names selected at random, and not those of any party with whom I wished to communicate. Each slip of paper was the same size, and each I rolled up into a little pea-shaped pellet, and I placed the pellets on a table before Mr. Forster. Had I tried to pick out the two on which were written the names of my dead friends, I could not have succeeded, for one pellet in appearance was precisely like the other. Yet Mr. Forster first passed his hands over the pellets, then, using a common lead-pencil as a small wand, knocked away pellet after pellet, until, on his touching one of them, three loud raps were heard under the table. He paused, directed my attention to a card with the alphabet printed on it which he had placed on the table before me, and desired me to take a pencil and touch with it the several letters. When I came to the letter "J" three raps sounded under the table. Then I was told to go back to the first letter. The "spirits" rapped at that. They rapped again when I came to "M," and succeeded in rapping out the name of "James," as well as the surname following it, which I had written on the slip of paper. How came Mr. Forster to know that the name written within that pellet was that of the dead friend with whom I wished to communicate? That was the question I put to the conjuror when we met him on the evening appointed.

"We will do the experiment. Then I will show you the trick," replied the obliging little fellow.

Artemus and I produced our pellets. We had prepared them at the hotel before starting. The name that I wished to be rapped out was rapped in due order with as much celerity, and with equal attendant mystery, as if a spiritualist instead of a conjuror had been the operator. But when Artemus experimented with his pellets, no raps resulted and the conjuror was unsuccessful.

"Ah!" he exclaimed, "you have not written the name of a dead friend whose spirit you really wished to hear from."

Artemus replied that he had written the name of Captain Kydd, the famous pirate of days gone by, adding that he particularly wanted to hear from Kydd's spirit, that he might learn where the pirate had hidden his booty.

"There is just where you have made the mistake," said the conjuror. "You have written Captain Kydd's name on one slip, the King of the Cannibal Islands on another, and Rip Van Winkle on this one."

Artemus laughed, but was fairly puzzled. "How do you know what I have written?" he asked. "You have not opened any of them to see, though you have got the right names."

"There's the trick of it. You see I know already what's inside the little balls. Now go into the next room. Make up six more little balls, and write on one of them the name of somebody who is dead, and whom you would really like to hear from. We'll try the experiment again."

A fresh set of pellets was placed on the table. The conjuror, after a few manœuvres, commenced knocking aside with his wand one pellet after another. On his touching the fourth one, there were three vigorous raps. Artemus was told to take a pencil and go over the letters of the alphabet. He did so, and a name was rapped out to him in due "spiritual" form. His surprise was great.

"That's the name of an uncle of mine who died down in Maine," said he. "It is the very name I wrote. I thought it was a likely one, because he was given to talking when alive. But what is the old man rapping away under the table for?"

"Wait, and you shall know all about it. You see, when you did write the name of one you really desired to hear from, the raps came all right. Now here's the trick of it. You make up twelve little balls. You write a name inside of each. You place all the twelve upon the table. There they are. I pass my hand over them. There they are still."

"I see them," said Artemus.

"No, you don't," asserted the conjuror, with a laugh, "for here they are."

He opened his left hand. There were twelve other pellets in the palm of it.

"Observe my table," said he. "It has a pattern on it—all inlaid wood in squares and stars. Now look closely at that little square in the centre. You don't see it's a little trap-door, but it is. The pattern of the table hides where it opens. Now there are twelve little balls on the table. I palm these other twelve little balls, which I have already prepared, in my right hand. As I pass my hand over the table, I touch this spring. The trap opens. Down go the twelve little balls on which you have written into the table. The trap closes, and I put the other twelve little balls in their place. You think they are the same. There, you see, the hand is quicker than the eye. First lesson in conjuring—fact! Then I divert your attention while I unroll and examine the twelve little balls which have fallen through, to find out the name of the spirit you want to hear from."

"But how do you find that out?"

"That's science, not hanky-panky," answered the man of mystery. "You see you write on twelve slips, and you write twelve names. One name is that of somebody you do wish to hear from, and the other eleven are nobodies. You think you write all alike, but you don't. You are sure to write the name of the spirit you want to rap more carefully than all the other names. You can't help doing it. Ninety-nine people out of a hundred would. I open all the little balls, and I run my eyes over them. I see which is most carefully written, and I say that's the one. I've got a rapping-machine in the leg of that table and I make it rap. When you wrote the name of a real uncle I could tell you. When you wrote a lot of nonsense, I couldn't. While you are going over the alphabet, I palm the little ball back on the table. If I have made any mistake, I soon find it out when you go over the alphabet, because if the name is Harry, you are sure to hesitate when the pencil comes over the letter 'H.' You are sure to do it—fact: though you don't know it. And I've got my eye on you."

The conjuror's explanation was a great lesson in "Spiritualism." I next asked him to elucidate the trick of writing on the arm. On the occasion of my visit to Mr. Forster, when the raps indicated the second pellet, he required the "spirit" present to write its initials on his bare arm. Mr. Forster placed his arm under the table for a moment, then raised it in front of a lamp burning on the table and quickly rolled up the sleeve of his coat. The skin was without stain or mark. He passed his hand over it once or twice, and the initials of the name I had written on the second pellet seemed to glow on the arm in letters of crimson.

"It's a trick I do every night. It goes with the audience like steam," said the conjuror. "Very simple. We'll suppose a name. What name would you like?"

"Henry Clay," I replied.

Down went the conjuror's arm under the table. In a few seconds he raised it and exposed the bare fore-arm without mark upon it. He doubled up his fist tightly, so as to bring the muscles of the arm to the surface, and rubbed the skin smartly with his open hand. The letters "H. C." soon appeared upon it in well-defined writing of a deep red color.

"There you have it, gentlemen—that's the blood-red writing. Very simple. All you have to do is to take a lucifer-match and write on your arm with the wrong end of it. If you moisten the skin with a little salt-water first, all the better. Then wet the palm of the other hand, rub your arm with it. Send up the muscles, and the blood-red writing will come out. It will fade away again in no time. If you look under the table you will see that I have a little piece of pointed wood. I can move my arm under that and write the letters without using the other hand. But that's a fakement which wants practice. Lor', how I had the Queen of Madagascar with this experiment!"

We thanked the conjuror for his elucidations of the tricks of the spirit-rappers, and reminded him of his promise to enlighten Artemus relative to the feat performed by Mr. Hermann, who, bringing before the audience two white rabbits, contrived, apparently by simply rubbing them together, to blend the two into one.

"Simple as possible," said the conjuror. "My great trick when I played before the tycoon in Japan. First of all, we want two rabbits.

Bless my heart! Mr. Ward, you have one in your waistcoat, and your friend has another!"

Cleverly enough the little conjuror succeeded in producing a small white rabbit, alive and active, apparently from within our waistcoats, just as I have seen other magicians pretend to extract large potatoes from a man's nose. He held the rabbits by the ears as he proceeded to illustrate the feat.

"We will use this same table again," said he. "See, I place the rabbits on it. I rub them. I touch the spring with my foot. The trap opens, down goes one of the rabbits into a little box. Here is the other, and I seemed to have rubbed the two into one. Lor' bless you! you can do any thing with a well-made table. They sell them in Paris with springs and traps in them to do any trick. But when a magician always uses one, he's only an old bungler. See, I can do the rabbits again without any table at all. But then the hand deceives the eye, and I slip one into this little pocket made for the purpose. I have a coat fitted up with pockets and spring-hooks. Cost me twenty pounds—fact! That's how I do the gold fish and the bowls of water. I don't use any Zoroaster's robe —not I. I can do seven bowls—fact. Each glass bowl, you know, has a thick rim to it, and an India-rubber covering, which stretches over and keeps in the water. I hook on three bowls inside the back of my coat, and do two inside each breast. Beautiful! gentlemen. Only write me some good bills, and I'll get the people, you'll see. I'll warm them! I'm an artist, I am!"

He was a kindly-hearted little conjuror; we therefore determined to do our best to aid him. Mr. Wilder again reminded us of the necessity of inventing some high-sounding name.

"I've got one," said the conjuror; "a gentleman made it for me in Australia. He called me a 'Basiliconthaumaturgist.' Isn't that grand?"

I raised a question relative to the Greek being correctly compounded.

"Don't be hefty on your Greek," interrupted Artemus. "It's splendid. It's the very thing. We must have it on a long streamer. Now make out the posting-bill and the advertisement."

Here is a copy of the advertisement we issued, with the single exception that I have substituted another name for that of the conjuror, who, if he be still alive, might possibly object to seeing this narrative in print. His name was not "Juleps."

Grand Performance of

PROFESSOR JULEPS,

The Renowned

BASILICONTHAUMATURGIST,

In his Marvellous, Magical, and Mystical Feats of

NECROMANCY,

And terrific and absolutely confounding

Paradoxes.

———

PROFESSOR JULEPS

Has recently performed in all the chief cities of

CHINA,
 JAPAN,
  THIBET,
   COCHIN CHINA,
    SIAM, and
     AUSTRALIA,

BEFORE
The Emperor of China at Pekin,
The Tycoon at Jeddo,
The Fontai and Toutai of Shanghai,
Prince Satsuma and suite at Nagasaki,
The Governors and Princes of Japan at
 Yokahama,
The two Kings of Siam at Ofuslo,
The Grand Llama of Thibet,
The Khan of Crim Tartary,
The Mogussulite of Cochin China,
The Dyacks of Borneo,
The King of the Gorillas in Central Africa,
All the Governors of Australia,
The Sentries at Alcatraz, San Francisco,
Maximilian, Emperor of Mexico, at Acapulco,

Buffalo Jim, the chief of the Pi-Utah Indians,
Artemus Ward, and the Twelve Bannack
   Robbers who were executed at Bannack City,
The Select Men of Waterford, Maine; and the
Presidents of the various Banqueting Halls
   on the Stations East of Bridger.

The following will be the Great Weird, Wondrous, Basiliconthaumaturgical and Invincibly Incomprehensible

PROGRAMME:

Previous to the rise of the curtain, there will be an Enharmonic Prolegomena by the Orchestra.

MYSTERY No. 1.—The Magic Wove Handkerchiefs of Othello's Mother. "That handkerchief did an Egyptian to my Mother give; there's Magic in the Web of it;" or, the transposing textile Problem.

MYSTERY No. 2.—The Columbian Paradox; or, the ornithological labyrinth of perplexity.

MYSTERY No. 3.—Pecunious Conversation; or, very dollar-ous intimations from articulate silver sybils.

MYSTERY No. 4.—The perplexity of a Pomaceous Puzzle; or, how one Apple can be grown to be of the value of twenty dollars, and made to ripen on a frosty night better than in the laughing sunlight of a sunny clime.

MYSTERY No. 5.—Christopher Columbus; our hat and the completeness of repletion, as illustrated by how any thing can be placed where nothing can go, and nothing can be compressed until it becomes something considerable.

MYSTERY No. 6.—Plum-pudding Problematicalities: or a very familiar illustration of the applicability of woven textures to the construction of coquunterial stoves for the providing of Basiliconthaumaturgical banquets.

MYSTERY No. 7.—The great Japanese Papilionaceous Puzzle taught the Professor by the principal juggler to the court of Prince Satsuma, Japan.

MYSTERY No. 8.—The great Abracadabra Secret of Confucius, which, after having lain dormant for two thousand years, was resuscitated in China specially for imparting to Professor JULEPS.

MYSTERY No. 9.—The Chronological and Panisti-
cal Inexplicability; or, the intimate association of
watches and hot rolls.

MYSTERY No. 10.—Thomas Zpiwldildethzy, the
Learned Traveller, who can travel much faster than
the lightning stages from Salt Lake to Denver City.

MYSTERY No. 11.—How to make Artemus Wards by
the wholesale, without immaterially co-mingling the
co-ordinate tangential forces with the primum mo-
bile, except so far as regards the sumptuous banquets
of the overland mail.

MYSTERY No. 12.—The great Forster Feat of Writing on the Arm in Letters of Blood; or, the incarna-
dined chirography.

MYSTERY No. 13.—The Calculator which admits of
no more adding, dividing, or multiplying; being the
great mathematical puzzle which occasioned the building of the pyramids and the short route over the
Sierra Nevadas.

N.B.—The Professor will perform his feats *velocius
quam asparagi coquuntur.*

Prices as usual.

BABIES IN ARMS TEN DOLLARS EXTRA.

The intention was to make an unintelligible programme. I believe
that we succeeded. As the Professor found it difficult to explain to us
what particular tricks he would be able to perform, we studied to make
the enumeration of them as foggy as possible, and to use words not
readily to be understood by every body. Our *Basiliconthaumaturgist*
appeared at the Metropolitan Theatre in San Francisco, and drew a
large house. His tricks being few, and his style not according with the
tastes of the Californians, his career was brief, though brilliant. He
turned out to be an annoying illustration of the story of Frankenstein.
We had called into being a something which haunted us throughout
our subsequent journey to Salt Lake. Wherever we went the Professor
preceded or followed, and posted his bills in contiguity with, and in
some instances covering, those of Artemus. Worried by his keeping on
our track, Artemus met him in one of the mining towns and drew him
aside.

"Professor," said he, "two Basiliconthaumaturgists can not get on together in one town. If you don't keep off my track I shall turn blood-red writist myself, and do it in my lecture."

The threat told; the Professor kept far in the rear; but he followed us to the city of the Mormons, and became conjuror to the prophet —Brigham Young.

◦ 26 ◦

In the Capital of California

SAN FRANCISCO was far behind us. We were steaming up the Rio Sacramento towards the political capital of California. A thin-faced, large-nosed, long-haired fellow-passenger joined us, uninvited, as we paced the deck together.

"I reckon you air Mr. Ward?" said he.

Artemus replied that the interrogator had reckoned correctly.

"I attended your lecture in San Francisco, and I must say that some of the things you got off were elegant. What's the matter with you is, you've got some ideas—mighty good ideas, Mr. Ward."

Artemus bowed acknowledgments. "Have you got any?" he inquired.

"I reckon I have, Mr. Ward. I'm bursting all over with ideas. I am in the same line as you, and travel on my lecturing. Now, if you and I were to jine together, I should just feel about as happy as a clam at high-water."

"What are the subjects of your unparalleled discourses?" demanded Artemus.

"I am advocating the good cause, Mr. Ward. I am a Dashaway, and I lecture on philosophy generally, with its bearings on the Dashaway system."

The "Dashaways" in California are synonymous with the teetotallers of England. They have a hall in San Francisco, and number among their adherents a percentage of the population remarkably large, considering the class of persons who peopled the Golden Land. Artemus and I noticed the seedy appearance of the lecturer. He had the scar of a severe cut over his left eye, and walked as though he were lame.

"Have you been a Dashaway long?" I inquired.

"Well, I have—in my sentiments. My mind was organized that way. But, stranger, my second conversion was only about nine months ago. I was converted practically by getting this broken leg."

"Is breaking your leg good for conversion?" asked Artemus.

"It was for me," replied our teetotal acquaintance. "I had been having a high old time of it up in Sac city, where we are going. Coming home at night with the cussed whisky in me, I fell into a big hole in the road. My leg went snap like a bit of old wood. I had to stick in that hole two hours before any one came to get me out. My early education came back on me, and I knew it was the whisky had done the mischief. So I lectured myself mighty hard in that hole. Says I to the whisky in a friendly way, 'You and I have been fightin' together pretty considerable. We've fit it out together for a long time. Whisky, you are stronger than I am. I acknowledge it honorably, and cave in. We'll shake hands and part;' and I reckon we did."

The steamer "Chrysopolis," bound for Sacramento City, left San Francisco at five in the evening. We expected to arrive at our destination shortly after midnight, a voyage of 127 miles. Suisun Bay had been crossed, and in the bright moonlight the peak of Monte Diabolo was disappearing from view in the distance behind us, when we entered a reach of the Sacramento River, where the banks were low and the land on each side apparently swampy.

"I guess the settlers about here grow a fine crop of chills and fevers," remarked a chatty passenger. "It's to be hoped they manage to get good whisky hereabout to keep the life in them."

Overhearing the remark, the Dashaway lecturer interposed energetically. "There you are in the wrong," said he. "Whisky is like greased poison. It slips away down easily, and kills while you are looking after it. The manufacture of it must be stopped by Act of Congress. I reckon, sir, you air a Britisher?" he observed, turning to me. "Well, I wish I were your queen."

I inquired why he had that wish.

"These here United States make the greatest country on airth," he replied. "There's no getting over that fact, as you and I know. But our Government wants arranging. We can't get Congressmen at Washington to vote down whisky when they make their pile by distilling it. That's against human nature. But your queen can do what she likes. It's the one good thing about a monarchy when the monarch is as good as she is. Now she can say, 'Stop the whisky-trade,' and I reckon her soldiers could stop it right smart."

"Why don't you go to Europe and see her on the subject?" suggested Artemus. "Call upon her at the Tower of London."

"If I could get to see her, I reckon I'd straighten out her ideas on the whisky-trade," replied the Dashaway. "I am going on a trip to Europe soon. If I am in London on one of your queen's reception-days, I shall make a call."

"You would find it a little difficult to get to see her," I remarked.

The gentleman smiled knowingly, and replied, "I reckon there's a way to do it. Her soldiers want their hands greased with a few dollars, like our Congressmen do."

"There's a better way than that," said Artemus. "You get a letter of introduction from the Mayor of Sacramento City to the Mayor of London. Call upon the Mayor of London with it. He'll put you in his carriage and drive you to the Tower, just as the queen comes in from her walk with the royal family."

Not a doubt seemed to cross the mind of the poor man that Artemus was in jest. Well-informed as Americans usually are, there are still thousands in the "Far West" who believe that an English monarch nowadays has the same power that a King of England had three hundred years ago. Of court etiquette they know nothing, and some, I presume, imagine that her majesty takes her breakfast and writes her letters wearing her crown upon her head. In hazarding this opinion, I am, as a matter of course, not referring to Americans in general, but only to the less-informed of those who inhabit the distant valleys and least travelled portions of the country. As a rule, Americans know more about Europe than Europeans do about America.

The "Chrysopolis" steamed up to Sacramento at two in the morning. During the early part of the evening moonlight had rendered our trip up the river comparatively pleasant, but now the sky was overcast and rain was beginning to fall. Sacramento presented any thing but a cheerful aspect as seen from the river. Built on a low flat plain, having few lofty edifices, the streets being very wide, and the river front consisting of a series of stores with no architectural pretensions whatever, the heart of the Golden Land by no means appeared to beat warmly towards us in the darkness and drizzle of a November morning.

A high bank or levee along the river-side shut out the lights of the town from view. The lanterns on board the steamer were not as numerous or powerful as desired. There were other steamboats in the way. Every one was anxious to get on shore. Confusion was at its height, when a splash in the water, followed by a cry from some one in the darkness, warned us that an accident had happened. Lanterns were quickly held out over the side of the vessel, and some men came running down the levee to assist. We soon learned what had happened. In his eagerness to get on shore, the Dashaway lecturer had fallen overboard.

Well soaked, cold, and almost senseless, the poor fellow was hauled out of the water and mud, and brought up the bank. A minute or two elapsed before he spoke. Then, as we stood surveying his condition and debating what should be done with him, his lips opened, his teeth chattered, and he muttered faintly:

"Whisky—get me some whisky."

A bottle was soon forthcoming. The half-drowned man took a deep draught.

Artemus looked at me, and remarked, with a quaint smile:

"There'll be a third conversion—sure!"

We proceeded to the Orleans Hotel, where the Californian Senators most do congregate. Though two hours after midnight, the bar had many gentlemen in front of it, and billiard-playing was going on briskly.

What the city of Sacramento lacks in beauty of architecture it makes up for in simplicity of plan. Its streets are in straight lines and its houses in square blocks; the ground-plan being, in fact, an exaggerated chess-board. The streets running parallel with the river are numbered, not named—those which run at right angles take an alphabetical arrangement. "J" and "K" streets are the principal ones. I failed to discover an "A" street or a "Z." Prudently considering that Sacramento would in time expand laterally, the founders of the city began with the middle of the alphabet, trusting to prosperity for C to follow D and Y to follow X; whence it results that one side of the city augments with alphabetical propriety, while the other side goes alphabetically backward as it proceeds architecturally forward. The correct side will have the better of the arrangement by-and-by, because after it has attained to Z it will be able to add on an &, but with A there will be finality. Thus are those who do rightly always rewarded.

Sacramento dates back to the year 1839, when Captain Sutter claimed the land and built a fort, the ruins of which are still to be seen. Unfortunately, California selected it as the city in which should be held the councils of her Legislature. In it stands the Californian capitol. Around the city is a huge dike, levee, or wall of earth, to prevent the Capitol from being washed away. Sacramento is situated where the American River and the Rio Sacramento meet. When the snow dissolves on the Sierra Nevada mountains the rivers overflow, and the city becomes liable to inundations that greatly interfere with its prosperity. Even the great and learned legislators have had, on some occasions, to hire boats and be rowed up "J" Street to the Capitol.

Bad as its position is with regard to immunity from undue cold bathing, Sacramento possesses advantages of site which readily suggest themselves to the traveller. It is at the head of a navigable river, in the midst of a fertile country, and an excellent centre of travel for either the Northern or Southern mines, as well as a convenient *entrepôt* for their productions. In summer the city is not the most agreeable place to dwell in. The sun's rays swoop down on the wide streets and roads, unshaded by lofty buildings; while clouds of dust, set in agitation by any passing vehicle, induce a passenger to wish the river would be kind enough to overflow in summer as well as in the early spring. There is this compensation—that while a visitor has his nostrils filled with dust, his face scorched with the extreme heat, and his lips disagreeably dry, he can turn his eyes to where the white snow still lingers on the summits of the Sierra Navada, and at the next whisky-shop moisten his lips with spirits and iced water, while he cools himself, in imagination, by gazing at the distant mountains, their peaks glistening with snowy diadems—their sides shady with forests of pines.

Apropos of whisky-shops, as public bar-rooms are familiarly termed in these parts, it occurs to me that in Sacramento they constitute about one-fourth of the places of business. The streets of the city have planked foot-paths with awnings projected over them. Walk in what direction you will, you can not go many yards in the business part without coming to an open door-way with a screen of white or green laths just inside it, giving free access to the shop, but concealing from the view of passers-by the gentlemen within. From behind these screens the ear will catch the chink of glasses and the clang of the metal cup in which the bar-keeper is commingling the ingredients of the cocktail, the julep, or the swash. At the bar of the Orleans House I believe that the preparation and dispensing of drinks go on without intermission, especially when the Legislature is in session—the first cocktail of the daily series being made precisely at daybreak, and the last one two minutes before daybreak on the following morning.

Its whisky-shops notwithstanding, the city of Sacramento is a place of considerable business, and can boast the possession of much for which it has just reason to be proud. There have been agricultural exhibitions held in it worthy of a town ten times its size and thrice its age; and it possesses a newspaper—the "Sacramento Union," which for careful editing and selection of news ranks among the best papers in the United States.

Sacramento in its palmier days—for *fuit Ilium* may be written of it, as well as of a dozen other towns in California—possessed three or four theatres. At the time of my last visit the Metropolitan was open, but the Forrest Theatre, with its marble front, was half in ruin; while the old Sacramento Theatre looked like a place haunted, shunned, and suggestive of rats, spiders, and festoons of dust-laden cobwebs. I had arranged with Mr. Maguire in San Francisco, to whom the lease of the Metropolitan belonged, that Artemus Ward should deliver his lecture in that theatre. On our arrival, the night before its delivery, we found the house in the possession of a celebrated tragedian, who had made his living for some time past on the Pacific coast by playing Lear and Macbeth when audiences were to be obtained, and poker and faro whenever simpletons overladen with wealth challenged him to a trial of skill or a test of luck.

The ponderous tragedian seemed to think very lightly of the ability of Artemus Ward to draw a good house. In this opinion he was seconded by a gentleman with him who was about to appear the week following as a dramatic star, and who took particular pains to assure us that he was "an artist."

As a rule, the actor who endeavors to exalt himself above his associates by offensively declaring himself to be an artist, instead of allowing the public to discover that he is one and pronounce accordingly, is an impudent fellow, whose art consists in thrusting every one else aside and taking the middle of the stage, quite regardless of whether that is his place in the picture, and caring nothing for art itself, but all for personal vanity.

"As an artist, I must say that I can see no humor in Mr. Ward," said the dramatic star, addressing me. "People are such fools nowadays that they may come to hear him, but from an artistic point of view I should say that he would be a fizzle."

"He is a great favorite among actors and actresses," I replied.

"But what *are* actresses and actors?" rejoined the star, contemptuously. "Poor people, I pity them! A lot of sticks. None of them have any love of art."

"You have, I perceive, for that is a very fine lithograph," said I, noticing a large portrait of the gentleman, in which he was represented in a defiant attitude, his hair brushed back and hanging in slight curls behind, his eyebrows knit in a magnificent scowl, his head thrown up, and his chin pointing in a direct line towards the north star.

"It is merely for advertising in bar-rooms," replied the actor-artist. "It might be better, but those draughtsmen never do an artist justice. Do I look like that? Where are my eyes? Where is my soul—my intellect?"

The question was difficult to answer. Turning away, I left the gentleman in the act of reprimanding the tradesman in whose place we had met for not putting the portrait in a more conspicuous position, so as to attract more attention to the great and marvellous genius that Sacramento had in its midst.

The "Sacramento Union" and the "Sacramento Bee" duly informed all the good citizens that Artemus Ward was among them, and that he was going to lecture. Reporters called upon me to ask for facts in his biography, while he himself was "interviewed" at the Orleans House by newspaper men, politicians, gentlemen anxious to obtain his signature for their collection of autographs, and strangers generally, who simply called to proffer the courtesy of taking him a drive round the town, or of tendering any other little act of politeness. Society is not so sociable in many places as it is in Sacramento.

Then came the night of the lecture, when the Metropolitan Theatre held an audience whose admission-money amounted to about six hundred dollars. On the following day Artemus and I were in front of the theatre during the passing round of a subscription-list to assist the widow of a play-actor whose dwelling had recently been burnt. The subscription went on briskly; for no class of people are more practically benevolent or kindly-hearted than those who follow the profession of the stage. Petty animosities, envy, and jealousy may disturb the serenity of their minds in the green-room; the use of too small type in the printing of their name on the playbill, or the omission of the initial letters of their prenomens in the programme, may render them furious in the street; but though within them there may be a pent-up fountain of gall, there is always an ever-flowing river of the milk of human kindness when charity invokes their aid, or distress appeals to their feelings.

The company attached to the theatre had subscribed liberally according to their means, when at length the great "artist" to whom I have alluded, and who also chanced to be present, was asked for his subscription.

"Is this a public affair?" he inquired.

"No. Only a private subscription among ourselves."

"Very good, no doubt, "said the great man. "But I object—I object on principle."

Artemus drew me aside and whispered, "There were six hundred dollars in the house last night. How much will the expenses be?"

"About a hundred," I replied.

"And there will be five hundred left?"

"Yes."

"Then pay over the odd hundred to this charity fund. But don't let them put my name down on the list. Let them say, 'Subscribed by a religious Indian.'"

৹ 27 ৹

The Show in Sight of the Sierra

TAKE your 'Babes' into the Northern mines and you'll do well; but I guess you'll find it all poppycock if you try the Southern ones. They've all gone up. No spons there—you bet," was the advice of an astute showman in Sacramento.

As we did not wish to find any "poppycock," which we knew to mean worthlessness, and as we did wish to find "spons," which we knew to mean money, and to be a contraction of the word "spondulics," we determined to try the Northern mines.

Less than four years previous to the present visit I had rendered myself familiar with all the mining towns of California, and had seen them in the days of their prosperity. Returning to them now after the lapse of so short a time, I found many of them to be "gone up," "caved in," and "fizzled out," as the Californians, in their own phraseology, expressed the defunct condition of their once gay and festive Timbuctoo—the formerly frolicsome Butte City, and cheerful, unruly San Andreas. In England a place goes down when the grass begins to grow in its streets. Away in the Far West it is said to "go up," and, having "gone up," to be "caved in." The latter phrase is very expressive. It takes its origin from the system of mining adopted in the country. When the mine is too much hollowed out, and rendered too cavernous, it "caves in," and sometimes buries a dozen or two of the miners in a grave of golden earth.

Twenty-two miles from Sacramento is the little town of Folsom. Thither, for sundry reasons, we determined to go first. Partly because it was a queer little place to go to, partly because Artemus had an evening to fill up somewhere, and partly because there was a railway on which the trip could be made with comparative ease.

That railway was a marvel then; that same railway is a marvel now. People used to smile at it for its eccentricities and its unpretending character. People may now wonder at it for its grandeur and its immensity. A few years ago it had its commencement in the middle of a road, and its termination in the midst of a field. Now its first rail is laid in California and its last in New York; for it is a part of the great iron band which links the shores of the Atlantic to the sands of the Pacific.*

A quaint little railway was that Sacramento Valley line half a dozen years ago. Its terminus in Sacramento itself was simply a shed in the middle of the street beside the river—no grand building of brick or stone, but a few boards, with the iron rails coming to an end in the roadway, right in front of the windows of the stores. Very handy for the passengers by the steamboats, the wharf being alongside, but very dreary on a wet day for passengers waiting to get into the train, and finding no waiting-rooms on the platform, no cloak-room, and no refreshment buffet. The tickets were taken at a whisky-shop called the

*The *Union Pacific* Railway is now connected with the *Western Pacific* line. Travellers leaving San Francisco for New York cross the bay of San Francisco in a steamer, and take the train at Oakland, Vallejo, or Alameda.

"What Cheer," on the corner of K Street, where it was possible for the traveler to wait and to shelter himself amidst the luggage and the tubs of axle-grease.

After three hours and a half of successful struggling along the twenty-two miles of railway, including a break-down of the engine at a miserable little station called Salsbury, I arrived at Folsom and made my way to the principal hotel, a wooden building of shaky appearance, called the Patterson House. Opposite to it was a roughly-constructed edifice, also of wood, which I discovered to be the theatre. I engaged it for Artemus—the terms to be ten dollars for the evening, to include the oil-lamps. On entering the place, I found the seats to be of rough, un-planed material, built up one above the other, like those of a circus at a country fair.

"Will your man give us a dance?" asked the individual who showed me the interior of the theatre.

I replied that dancing formed no part of the lecture.

"I guess, then, he's some as a roarer?"

The question puzzled me. I intimated that Artemus was not partic-ularly loud-voiced, but that his lecture was very humorous.

"I mean, can he sing a bully song?" continued the custodian of the theatre.

My answer was that singing was not included in the programme.

"Our people have considerable music in their souls," observed my companion. "You tell your man to get inside a good song before he comes up here—one with a chorus. Our boys will jine in handsomely."

After engaging the theatre, it was requisite to call at the newspaper office and see the editor. The paper was the "Folsom Telegraph," and the gentleman to whom I introduced myself was Mr. Avelin.

"You had better sketch out all you want to say," was Mr. Avelin's obliging remark as he tendered me paper and pencil. He was in want of copy, and an essay on the life and lectures of Artemus Ward was charity to him.

Some one to take the money on the night of the lecture, and another person to receive checks, being required, I engaged the sub-editor of the "Telegraph" for one, and a clerk from Wells and Fargo's bank for the other. The price of admission to the lecture was to be a dollar, and the officials in front were to be paid two dollars each for their services. My plan of operation was to make contracts, sign them, and leave copies of them with those with whom they were made, for Artemus to pay the amount after the contract had been fulfilled.

Three or four days passed before I met Artemus. I asked him how he was received at Folsom, and whether the audience were pleased with the lecture.

"The maniacs stopped me when I was orating sublimely, and called upon me to sing," said he. "They howled for a song."

"And did you sing?"

"I had to, or they would have thrown cartwheels at me."

Knowing that he had no vocal abilities, I expressed my surprise, and wished to know what song he selected for the occasion? He replied, laughingly:

"The cheerful lunatics wanted 'Maggie by my Side;' they pitched the tune, and I joined in with them. It was a farce altogether. Down at the bottom of the bills, No singing allowed—that's a good fellow, or I shall have to be a walking Opera-house before I get through many more mining camps."

From Folsom I returned to Sacramento, and started by the stage-coach at five o'clock next morning for Marysville. The weather was unpleasantly cold for California, and as the coach bowled over the open plain, and I peered out through the window, the snow-capped peaks of the Sierra Nevada, glistening in the early sunlight, formed any thing but a cheering prospect. Twelve miles out the coach halted at a wooden shanty in the middle of the plains, where, while the horses were being changed, I endeavored to get some warm coffee. The owner of the shanty surveyed me with disdain, as though he thought me to be some luxurious Sybarite fresh from a couch of rose-leaves and a banquet of sweets. Instead of coffee he offered me a drink of whisky—the inevitable, ever-recurring whisky! I had no inclination to taste it, for the odor was of that vile strength that, if the horses had not been able to pull the coach, the scent of the whisky might have assisted.

We were a mixed party inside the vehicle. Opposite me sat a sickly looking woman with an infant in her arms. Next to me was a Chinese woman wearing the dress of her country, and having with her a gigantic umbrella. There were two more occupants, one of whom was a miner in a state of semi-intoxication, although the time was early morning; the other traveller had rolled up his head in a blanket, gone to sleep and coiled himself up in a corner.

Before we had proceeded many miles on our journey, the sickly-look-ing woman with the baby was seized with an ague-fit, and I had to hold the infant while the poor creature shivered and struggled with her malady. The Chinese woman looked on stolidly, simply remarking that it was "welly cold." The miner produced a bottle of spirits, and pressed the woman with the ague to take "a long drink," assuring her that it was the best remedy in the world for chills and fevers. The coach rolled on at a good pace, through oak-groves and across shallow water-courses, till we arrived at the village of Nicolaus, where we procured some warm milk for the ague patient, again changed horses, and were enabled to take a little exercise. In remounting, the male passengers selected the outside of the coach and left the Chinese female and the sick woman, who had recovered from her fit, to full possession of the interior.

No sooner did the fresh air begin to blow upon the face of the traveller who had slept during the early part of the journey, than he woke up and became noisy. He vehemently cursed all lawyers in general, and one special lawyer in particular. We learned that he had been to Sacramento on legal business, and had lost a lawsuit.

"Lawyers are mean cusses," he exclaimed, with bitterness. "I'd drown the whole biling of them in the Yuba, if I had my way."

"They are not always smart," remarked the driver. "I come from the State of Georgia. Now do you know what happened to them down there?"

"Did the State pass an act to smother them?" asked the angry traveller.

"No, we were not as rough on them as that; but some one introduced a bill to tax all jackasses ten dollars a year. One of our Legislators moved an amendment. He wished lawyers and doctors to be put into the same act. Our Legislature was in high spirits that day, and wanted a little mischief. So, when the amendment was put, they carried it, and passed the bill. They've tried to rub it out since, but they can't do it. We've got it on our statute-books. Just as sure as I'm driving you down to the Yuba, the act stands good in old Georgia—all jackasses, lawyers, and doctors have to pay up ten dollars a year. It's hefty on the lawyers, but it's *so*."

Early in the afternoon we arrived at Marysville, driving up to the St. Nicholas Hotel. Few towns in California have a better appearance than Marysville. The streets are wide, the stores good, and the houses for the most part built of brick instead of wood, as in other cities of the Golden State. I intended to put up at the Merchants' Hotel, where I had stopped a few years before. When I went to seek it I found nothing but its ruins. The Yuba River had overflowed in the middle of the night, and washed away the hotel and its contents. I asked for one of the former proprietors, and received for reply, "Well, he went hard at brandy, and it fetched him dead."

To arrange for the theatre was my first duty. I found the house to be neat and clean, fresh painted, and the seats covered with red cloth. I ascertained that it would hold four hundred dollars, and I obtained the use of it for one evening for thirty dollars. I had with me an introduction to Judge Lucas. Inquiring for his residence, I was directed to an office adjacent to a small shop, where, painted on a tin plate attached to the door, I read "Lucas, Justice of the Peace." The Judge's office was furnished in very primitive style—a table, a stove, a few law-books, and an inkstand. Cordial and thoroughly American was the manner in which the judge received me. His first act of kindness was to take me round and introduce me to Judge Fowler, Mayor of Marysville, and agent for the California Stage Company. We found the mayor seated on a box at the corner of the street, cleaning his nails. I saluted him in orthodox fashion, and was soon asked to "take a drink." Judge Lucas then proposed escorting me to visit the proprietors of all the principal bar-rooms, and be introduced to them. According to his way of thinking, that would be a great point gained; but I preferred being first taken to see the editors of the "Marysville Appeal" and of the "California Express." The Marysville public was a reading one, and knew all about Artemus Ward. Even the bar-tender at the Magnolia exclaimed enthusiastically, "I'm bound to go my bottom dollar but I'll hear that man."

From Marysville I determined to proceed to Oroville, and see what the prospects were for Artemus to visit the Rabbit Creek diggings. In making this trip I could avail myself of the facilities offered by another queer little railway—the California Northern. Like the Sacramento Valley line, it was but a fragment of a grand scheme—the commencement of an iron road destined to connect California with Oregon, and wend its way through the solitudes in the shadow of Mount Shasta—the Mont Blanc of America of the North Pacific, whose snowy peak rises fourteen thousand four hundred feet above the level of the sea.

The California Northern line had its Marysville terminus in an open field. The distance to Oroville is twenty-seven miles; but the railway at the period of my visit was completed for twenty-two of those miles only, and broke off abruptly in the middle of another field, at what was termed Rose's Station. The remaining five miles of the journey had to be performed by means of a stage-coach. I went to the railway at half-past six in the morning. Adjacent to the rails was a small newly-erected house, one room of which was used for an office. In it sat the money-taker, ready to receive my three dollars for fare. There was no other attendant. One man served for superintendent, money-taker, conductor, policeman, and porter. The share-holders had no cause to blame the directors for want of economy. There were but five passengers, but a fair amount of freight in the way of parcels of fish intended for sale to the Chinese at Oroville. The fish had been caught in the Rio de las Plumas, or Feather River. The passengers had to wait for the locomotive to get up steam, and the morning being chilly, they endeavored to warm themselves by jumping over the fish parcels and assisting in firing up the engine. That engine had been made in Philadelphia, taken to pieces, brought to Marysville in separate portions, and there put together again.

The money-taker saw the passengers safely in the train, then locked the door of his office, and took a seat inside the "car." The engine-driver and he seemed to be the sole officials of the railway.

Smoothly enough the little engine dashed across Marysville Park, as the partially wooded country adjacent to the city is called. Marysville is known as the "City of the Buttes," and rising in the middle of the plain, to our right, were the "Buttes," after which it is so named. They consist of a range of mountains eight miles in length, towering up in isolated grandeur, and lofty enough to be visible for many miles around. Beyond them the snowy Sierra extended in gloomy grandeur, far as the eye could see, trending northward to join the Blue Mountains of Oregon.

Cold and hungry I arrived at Rose's Station, where the stage was in waiting to convey the passengers to Oroville and to breakfast. Fortunately a wood fire was blazing in the little shed at the station. For refreshments there were whisky, brandy, and apples. With pockets apple-laden, I took a seat on the coach beside the driver for an exciting drive, consisting of five miles of bumping over rough ground and heaps of gravel, winding in and out among dugout and deserted gold-holes, across muddy water-courses and over stumps of trees, with shattered windlasses, broken water-sluices, and mounds of well-washed earth to make up the scenery of the fore-ground; while in the distance was a long, low, flat mountain, apparently perfectly level on the summit, which the driver pointed out as being Table Rock.

Oroville—or Gold Town, as its name implies—was one of the first of the surface diggings of California; a "surface digging" being one where the miner has but to remove the upper stratum of earth, wash it, and pick out his share of gold. In the language of the West, the Oroville diggings are now "played out." All the gold worth the getting has been extracted, and the well-dug soil is now in the possession of the Chinese, who contrive to earn a living where an American would not gain money enough with which to buy his "chewing tobacco."

The hotel at which I stopped was called the St. Nicholas. A great saint in these parts is St. Nicholas. His name is painted in black letters on a white cloth stretched across the roof of the hotel. I asked for the theatre, and found that it had been turned into an armory. Though the American war was yet young, there were old bills on the theatre wall of "Pearson and Wilder's Panorama of the Rebellion." Among my letters of introduction was one to Judge C——. All lawyers are "Judges" in these parts. I went to the Judge, and found him in his office. He apologized for yawning while he read the letters, saying, "I was out on a drunk last night." After reading the letter, he promised all the assistance in his power, and invited me to take a cocktail and smoke a cigar.

With the judge for my companion, I called upon Mr. Crosette, the editor of the "Weekly Butte Record," to whom I had also a letter. We held a consultation on the best means of procedure. "There's the court-house," said the editor; "we'll go over and look at it. Perhaps that will do for Mr. Ward."

At the court-house we find the sheriff of Oroville sitting in his office, with his feet on the top of the stove. The sheriff has been "out on a drunk" too, and is unwashed and unshaven. He suggests that the Brick Church would be better suited for my purpose than the courthouse. "If you want to see it," says he, "just catch hold of that rope and ring the big bell on top of the court-house till the night comes." I do so, and am shown across to the church.

Oroville, I was told, had no parson of its own, but borrowed one every alternate Sunday from Marysville or some other town. The church was neat, clean, and held about three hundred people. I bargained for it with the school commissioners, and arranged to take it for five dollars, which amount it was understood was to pay for the lighting and for the attendance of the nigger to open the pews.

Before leaving Oroville, I took a stroll down the long street inhabited by the Chinese. Situated in the outskirts of the little town, this street consists of two rows of wooden, unpainted, dirty houses, most of them having red papers, with Chinese characters written on them, attached to the door-posts. There are stores for supplying all the wants of the Chinese population; barbers' shops, with the tub of water on a four-legged stool as a sign outside, while inside are Chinamen sitting on high chairs having the top of the head shaved and the pigtail dressed. Then there are Chinese gambling-shops, with large tables covered with matting for shaking the coins about while gambling; butcher-shops, with pieces of pork cut as none but Chinese butchers would cut them; and poulterers'-shops, with fowls split open and pounded out flat ready for frying, hanging outside the front. At the end of the street is the temple or joss-house, gayly decorated with little scarlet flags and glaring inscriptions in gold and scarlet. The joss-house is built in a small garden. On one side of it is a brick altar, with three huge oval stones set up on it to represent deities, and a little place in front for burning offerings. The priest came to the door as I stood gazing at the little structure. He was very dirty, and was picking a chicken-bone.

Returning to Marysville, I met Artemus at the railway station. Seating ourselves on a log, we compared notes and studied our prospects.

"They tell me," said he, "that if we make a journey to Salt Lake at this time of the year, we shall be a pair of icicles by the time we arrive among the Mormons."

I pointed to where the fields of snow on the top of the Sierra Nevada mountains gave us a glimpse of the sort of scenery through which we would have to pass, and suggested a more pleasant and possibly more profitable way of spending the winter. Artemus found it difficult to make up his mind. He took a twenty-dollar gold piece out of his pocket.

"We'll toss for it," said he. "If it comes down eagle we'll go to the Mormons."

The coin came down eagle-side up. Our destiny was fixed. We determined to cross the continent and call in among the Mormons on our way.

∘28∘

Among the Gold Mines with our "Babes"

REAL miners wearing red shirts, and real stones sparkling with specks of gold. Why not come and see them?

Question No. 1—Will the real miners appreciate the lecture?

Question No. 2—Will the real mines yield to us a portion of their golden ore?

My belief was that the miners would be kindly, and the mines remunerate us for our visit. Poor Artemus was afraid of being "steamboated."

To "steamboat" a show means, in the phraseology of California, to refuse to accept the showman, deride his show, and chase him out of the place.

The towns we had already visited were places where there was a settled population subsisting chiefly by commerce. We now determined to try the real diggings, where the processes of mining were still in operation.

Five o'clock in the morning, and I take my seat on top of a stage bound for North San Juan (pronounced San Hwan). We are four on the top of the coach, but Artemus is not with us. After much jolting over rough roads, we halt, at ten o'clock, at the Empire ranch, where we change horses. Though the term "ranch" means a farm, it is very commonly applied to road-side inns in this part of the world. Presently we come to where the road becomes divided into two branches. That to the right leads to Nevada—that to the left is our road to San Juan. A few more miles and we arrive at Live-Oak Ranch, beside which is a beautiful garden full of vines and flowers, many of the latter being in full bloom, though we are travelling in the last days of November.

At Live-Oak Ranch a lady is waiting for the coach. She has with her a large parcel. She takes her seat inside. The parcel is handed up to the roof. There is a cloth wrapped round the parcel, but it is very loosely wrapped; and, as the parcel is of peculiar shape, our curiosity is excited.

One of the passengers unrolls a portion of the cloth, and reveals a wooden image, representing the upper portion of the figure of Liberty. The discovery excites our merriment, for the image seems to have been carved for the figure-head of some small sailing-vessel, and the lady is recognized by the driver as the proprietress of a not very respectable establishment in a neighboring township.

The incident reminds me of a report in the "Albany Argus."

To foster the cultivation of the fine arts, the United States Government admitted statuary to pass through the custom-houses free of duty. According to the returns, during the late war the rush of statuary was overwhelming, and all the statues took the shape of Goddesses of Liberty. At the same time, there was a great falling off in the importations of pig-lead. Could there be any connection between the two? How was it that, when Goddesses were in, pigs were out? Congress discovered the secret. Mr. Morrill reported a section to the bill prohibiting the importation of lead as statuary. Mr. Kernan, of New York, asked why there should be such a prohibition, and was answered because lead was imported as statues of Liberty, and of Washington and Jefferson. Mr. Morrill stated that the statues were imported into New York, and Mr. Stevens gave information that the importers were a well-known mercantile firm in that city, whose names he quoted. What became of the statues? On the authority of the "Argus," the Goddesses were melted down into bullets, and sold to the Government at double cost, for use on the battle-field.

Our coach has hilly ground to traverse, for we are slowly ascending the base of the Sierra Nevada mountains. Around us are all the characteristics of a mining district. We are in the region where free men work harder than slaves to find gold.

We are at the "Diggings," a most inappropriate name for these mines of California. The "washings" would be a much more truthful term, for the miners use the hose more than they do the spade, and a ditch full of water at a high elevation is more useful to them than a hundred pickaxes. All around us are exemplifications of the paramount importance of water as a mining agent. Deep water-courses artificially made run around the sides of high hills, conveying water from lakes far away up in mountain recesses. Great aqueducts, made of wood and supported on trestles, cross the valleys at altitudes of thirty, forty, or fifty feet. The miners call the water-courses "ditches," and the aqueducts "flumes." At the post-office is the notification: "*Water 12½ cents an inch.*" How do they measure out an inch of water?—simply by opening a little sluice at the end of the aqueduct and fastening on a hose. According to the number of square inches in the calibre of that hose the miner has to pay; at the other end of it he will have a metal jet, holding which he will advance upon a hill whose sides are rich in gold dust, and wash away not those sides only, but the entire hill. From out of the slime thus formed the particles of gold will subside, and be caught in the sluices along which the liquid earth has to run.

Gayly goes our coach over stones and through the beds of half-dry creeks, under high flumes and across ditches full of rushing, muddy water. We have passed through Sweetlands and Sebastopol, arrived at North San Juan, and come to a dead stop in front of the National Hotel. It is Sunday, but the stores are all open, and groups of idlers are smoking cigars on the "stoop" in front of the hotel. It scarcely wants a month to Christmas, but the sky is blue and cloudless, and the day warm and pleasant.

California mining towns very much resemble each other. Let me take North San Juan as a specimen.

A wide street, with stores on each side mostly built of wood, and never more than two stories high; a few brick stores having huge iron doors to them. The brick buildings very red, the iron doors very green, and the wooden houses very white. A planked road-way to the street, with raised planked foot-paths. Signs hanging out from the various stores; large livery-stables; many drinking saloons. Numerous cigar-stores open to the street, with no window between that and the counter. A few white cottages away beyond the stores, and a very tall "liberty-pole" beyond the cottages. Telegraph-posts on one side of the road; and high up aloft, crossing the main thoroughfare far above the houses and the hotel, a large aqueduct supported on trestles, conveying water from the distant mountains to the gold mines in the rear of the town.

The signs of the saloons are pretty much the same in most of these mining towns. The "Magnolia" is sure to be one of them. Then there are the "Sazerac," so called from a celebrated brand of brandy; and the "Fashion," so named after the once famous trotting mare.

Peep in at any one of the saloons, and you will see the characteristics to be a gaudy bar, three or four round tables for card-playing, one or two billiard-tables, a large stove for burning wood, and a group of roughly-attired men clustering round it, if the weather happens to be chilly. The road-way in front of the saloon is certain to be strewn with playing-cards that, having been once used, are first cast upon the floor and then swept into the street.

On the bright afternoon of the Sunday on which I arrive in North San Juan, the landlord of the hotel where I stop is playing cards with his guests in the office of the hotel. He is a burly man, wears a rough white felt hat, a loose jacket, and large boots, with his trowsers tucked into the top of them. He sees that I am a showman, makes me welcome, asks me to take a drink with him, and, as he tosses off his own, remarks; "Here's old Blases's toast—Thus we cross the Yuba!"

I drink "old Blases's toast," and proceed to business. San Juan has a new theatre built of wood, with a circus-like arrangement of the seats. I secure it for Artemus at the small cost of sixteen dollars. The rent I pay at once to the proprietors, Messrs. Block and Furth, whom I find in a store where they buy gold-dust, and sell coats, boots, shirts, gun-powder, and cigars. Then I have to seek the editor of the "San Juan Press," to whom I have my usual introductory letter. His name is Judge Stidger. He's another judge. The judge undertakes to devote his newspaper to my interests, attend to my business, get out my bills, post them, and sell my tickets. Yet the judge is a great lawyer. He broke his leg a short time since while travelling by the stage, sued the Company, and has just recovered $18,000 as damages. Neither the accident nor the damages have impaired his agility; for, when he learns my errand, he jumps over the table in his office, and exclaims:

"I am on it, you bet, for Ward's wax-works! Will he hev his snakes with him?"

I explained that he does not travel with a wax-work exhibition, as described in some of his writings, but that he is about to lecture on *"The Babes in the Wood."*

"I am on for the 'Babes' too," says the judge. "But tell him to fetch along his wax-show. We'll give him a high old good time of it in this city—you bet."

Of that "high old good time" more anon.

The mining towns of California have each their Chinese quarter or suburb. At North San Juan the Celestials have a little town of their own, shut in with wooden walls. It would be more correct to say that

they have two little towns, one for the tradesmen and one for the females. That devoted to the trading community forcibly reminded one
of an Eastern bazar, or one of the special quarters of a Levantine city.
It is a town within a town—a square patch of China removed to the
side of the Sierra Nevada mountains, and stuck down in the midst of
a Californian settlement not twenty years old.

Adjoining the Chinese shops the Chinese women have their nest of
houses. A mere glance is sufficient to inform the traveller of the social
position of these women. Sweeping as the assertion may be, I believe
that I am right in stating that there are no respectable Chinese ladies
in California. Large as the Chinese population is, and numerous as are
the Chinese women, there are few if any females among them whose
moral status is above reproach. Though in a land of freedom, though
the liberty-pole stands in the public square of every township in which
they live, and though they are sheltered by the wings of the American
eagle, they are slaves of the basest description—held in slavery by the
most brutal tryanny, and devoted to the vilest life of degradation.
Whole cargoes of Chinese girls are imported by the Chinese merchants
for purposes of prostitution. They are sent over from China consigned
to merchants in San Francisco and Sacramento, these merchants being
in many instances Chinese gentlemen of good position and great
wealth. An average consignment is said to be worth from five to six
thousand dollars. The merchants by whom the women are purchased
find habitations and dresses for them, appoint clerks to receive and
check their earnings, and treat them precisely as though they were a
consignment of animals or a stock of goods. True it is that the Legislature of California has interposed, but not so as to produce any real
check on the sad traffic. The chief importer is a Chinese named Ah
Fook, who lives in Jackson Street, and who in his time must have
imported some thousands of wretched girls into San Francisco from
various ports of China.

Passing one of the houses of the Chinese in North San Juan, I noticed two men at work preparing the dead bones of a disinterred coun-
tryman for transmission to his native land. As I have stated in a former
chapter, when a Chinese dies in California he is buried for a time only.
In taking him to the grave, small pieces of perforated white paper are
strewn along the road and over the place where he is buried. The per-
forations are usually of a diamond shape; the paper is of a peculiar thin

texture, and where it falls it is allowed to remain. The poorest Celestial strives that his skeleton shall at some day be duly returned, polished and parcelled, to the home of his fathers in the Flowery Land. Among the Chinese are artists who have attained to celebrity for their skill in preparing these parcels, and in polishing the bones of their dead brethren to perfection. "Unusquisque valeat in arte sua."

In the rear of San Juan are the gold mines. My arrangements for Artemus to lecture being concluded, I strolled out with Judge Stidger through the chapparal, or shrubby undergrowth which surrounds the town, to look down upon the source whence the place had drawn its wealth.

Here is the picture: A vast hollow, fully two square miles in extent, and three or four hundred feet deep, the sides for the most part perpendicular, the earth red and gravelly. At the bottom of the immense excavation are tramways, on which trucks convey the golden soil to where it is to be robbed by water-power of its hidden treasure; tunnels driven into the sides of the great hollow, and trucks emerging from them, laden with auriferous earth; huge black flexible hoses trailing about in all directions like gigantic serpents; great aqueducts supported on trestles; men working, horses pulling, and the depth of the excavations so deep that scarcely a sound reaches the ears of those who stand upon the brink looking down upon a scene where the grandeur of the work accomplished is magnified by the sublimity of the natural objects around; for across the great hollowed-out city, in the bottom of which are huts and houses, rise the pine-covered hills and forests of firs, untrodden, black, and gloomy; while again, beyond them, tower up the snowy peaks of the Sierra, glistening majestically in the last rays of the autumn sun.

From San Juan my course lay towards Nevada City and Grass Valley. The distance to Nevada is eight miles. My fare on the coach-top amounted to three dollars. The road wound through a forest. We crossed a few creeks and then ascended Montezuma Hill. Here from the summit was a good view of hills beyond hills, and valleys beyond valleys, black with pines and firs—a world of trees, glorious in its vast expanse and stately silence, the dark foliage rendering the view inexpressibly impressive in the limitless grandeur of its gloom. On the top of Montezuma Hill was a small inn, round the doors of which half a dozen suspicious-looking fellows were lounging, each having a revolver conspicuous in his belt.

Down the mountain side, over the muddy Yuba, across Shelby Flat, and the coach stops in front of the drinking saloon kept by the far-famed Mr. Blases, whose celebrity has arisen partly from the quality of his whisky and partly from his being always ready to drink the famous toast of his own invention—"Thus we cross the Yuba!" Every stranger calling upon him has to drink that toast. Not a miner in the Northern mines but has "crossed the Yuba"—with a glass to his lips.

On my arrival in Nevada City I found that it had just been burnt up for the fourth time. The coach drove along through streets where there were no houses, but heaps of black and charred ruins. In some places there were new walls already going up where the piles of burnt timber were still smoldering and smoking. The good people had become used to large fires, and, instead of repining at their loss, were going to work bravely to build up another and a better city immediately. I know of some countries where, in the event of a town being burnt, the ruins would be suffered to remain till two or three years of deliberation had rendered rebuilding practicable, but in California he who procrastinates is lost, and the city which does not rise again from its ashes immediately had better never attempt to be a city any more.

Theatre and hotel were both consumed, but the citizens were not going to be denied hearing Artemus Ward on that account. "We will give him a show in the Baptist church," says Mr. Waite, the editor of the "Nevada Transcript," and within an hour from his so saying the Baptist church was duly engaged, and the sum of fifteen dollars paid for its use. The church was full of apples when I went to see it, but the apples were to be cleared out and the lecturer accommodated. The hotel being a smoking ruin, a private family undertook to take Artemus as their guest. I was in doubt whether it would be worth while for him to come to a city of smoldering embers and streets of ashes.

"Keep yourself animated on that point," said my guide. "The fire has done us good and put life into us. My head's clear. The people are not burnt up. They are still on the track. They haven't been out since the fire. Mr. Ward will fetch 'em, and all will be elegant."

Mr. Ward did "fetch em," as the sequel will show.

From Nevada City to Grass Valley was the next stage in the journey. The distance being about four miles and the road a good one, I sent my baggage on by the coach, and decided on a pleasant walk through a part of the country where gold-mining takes another form than that which it assumes in North San Juan, and where the precious metal is found imbedded in quartz reefs, whence it is extracted in subterranean quarries.

Outside Nevada City were a dozen or two of Indians belonging to the Digger tribe. The noble Red man differs materially according to the tribe to which he belongs. As a Sioux, he is tall and graceful; as a Digger, he is the squattiest, dirtiest, and most offensive form of humanity. He derives his name from his habit of delving in the earth after roots and tubers, as well as to form a place wherein to take shelter. In intelligence he is a booby—in his instincts a mole.

The party of Diggers I passed on the road were in mourning. Some of their tribe had fallen victims to an epidemic, and the decencies of Indian society had to be observed. To mourn with propriety it was necessary to pierce the pine-trees, obtain a good supply of tar, mix that with wood-ashes, and smear the whole thickly over the head and face, leaving apertures merely for the ears, eyes, nose, and mouth. The head of each Indian, female as well as male, was enveloped in a hard crust of black pitchy composition, nearly an inch in thickness. How the mourners were to go out of mourning without having recourse to a hammer and chisel, I am not able to say.

Grass Valley is a town, and one of considerable size and importance. It takes first-class rank among the quartz-mining towns of California. In it are more than twenty quartz-crushing mills, constantly employed crushing ore, which yields a return of from five to twenty-five pounds a ton, and sometimes as high as seventy or eighty pounds sterling.

The queer little town is intimately associated with the career of a most eccentric woman. In 1854 the celebrated Lola Montez paid it a visit. A rich quartz miner fell in love with her. Lola, countess of Landsfeldt, from having been the favorite of a Bavarian monarch, became the mistress of a Californian gold miner. He was rich but not strong-minded. In a few years she succeeded in reducing him to poverty and lunacy. I visited the little cottage where they had resided, and asked the landlord if he knew any thing about the fate of the miner who had loved not wisely but too well.

"He was a muggins," was the reply; "he did what all muggins do. When he'd lost all his gold, he took a lead pill out of a steel pillbox."

Many were the strange stories I listened to in Grass Valley that evening relative to the doings of Lola Montez. Poor wayward Lola!

In the city of New York I called upon her a few days before she died. She who had lived in a palace at Munich, had become the occupant of an up-stairs back room in a small house; consumption had reft her face of its beauty, while it had added to the brilliancy of her wondrous eyes. Her couch was a humble one, and round her room were Scriptural texts written in large legible characters. It is to be hoped that as her feverish, burning eyes gazed upon them, the heart of the contrite woman derived consolation.

In Grass Valley I obtained a hall for the use of Artemus. Similar good fortune did not attend me in every town; for in the next one I visited, a billiard-room was the only place I could obtain in which the lecture could be given.

At Placerville I was fortunate enough to obtain the theatre, and made certain that the lecturer would find every thing to be comfortable, but on the night he lectured one of those offensive animals known as the skunk (*Mephitis mephitica*) found its way under the boards of the pit, emitted its unbearable odor, and caused half the audience to leave the building.

I arranged for Artemus at Auburn, Drytown, Jackson, Sonora, and other places. At Jackson there was a new hall. Some difficulties were at first placed in the way of my obtaining it. I had an introduction to the sheriff. He took me to see the prison in course of erection, and, pointing to a rectangular space around which were a series of cells with iron doors, said:

"Sakes alive, man! I see how to do it. Let your comic man make his speech here. You can have the place for nothing. He can stand up on a table in the middle. We'll place forms for the people, and there's the place for your boxes."

"Where?" I asked.

"Those cells. They are made to put murderers in, but they've not been let yet. We can put chairs in them, and charge double price."

Artemus Ward and I had arranged to meet at Auburn. When we met I asked him how he had succeeded at Oroville, and found, to my satisfaction, that the brick church there had been crowded.

"And North San Juan—how did you do there?"

He laughed, and hesitated before giving his reply. "They had no lecture out of me there," said he, shaking his head.

"But why not? I paid fifteen dollars in advance for the hall; and Judge Stidger was to write you up well in his paper."

"Write me up! I should think he did. He told the noble inhabitants that I was coming with a whole menagerie of snakes and animals, and half a dozen wagon-loads of wax figures. When I got into the town and found what the people had been led to expect, I left by the next stage. Do you think I would have stopped? Why I should have been steamboated first and lynched afterwards."

"And the burnt-out city—Nevada; did that pay?"

"Here's the money-taker's return. It is just half of what I received. The people opened the windows and sat on the sills, while others stood in rows round the church. When I came out they all waited to see me, and paid up their dollars for standing-room. I like churches to lecture in, but if you take another one for me, get some foot-lights to the pulpit."

❧ 29 ❧

With Our Faces Towards the Mormons

EITHER Placerville or Hang-town—which you please. They call it Hang-town because men were hanged there pretty freely in days gone by, and Placerville because the name is more euphonious, and the place was once famed for its rich *placers* or surface mines.

At Placerville we were at the foot of the Sierra Nevada, and at the starting-point for leaving California and ascending to the great plateau whereon is the American desert, and where, far away, beyond mountain ranges and barren tracts, is the home of the Mormons, in the fertile valley of Salt Lake.

Very few were the showmen who had been to Salt Lake, at the time of our journey. Next to the missionary, I count the showman to be the greatest pioneer of civilization. I once met a man who had been down in Patagonia with a magic lantern, and I know a professor of legerdemain who has been in Tartary and among the Russian Esquimaux of Alaska Territory. Minstrel bands with blackened faces have explored Australia, and concert-parties have sealed the Andes and the Himalayas. The mystery of Central Asia will one day be solved by a showman, and a playbill be found clinging to the shrubs on the other side of the Caucasus.

The few slop-sellers who abound at Placerville had called my attention to the blankets of uncommon thickness, and the overshoes of marvellous make they had on sale for travellers about to ascend the mountains. I bought a black felt Vecuna shirt, half an inch in thickness, and a pair of moccasins to wear over my boots, with straps of buffalo-hide and a lining of wool. After partaking of a hearty dinner at the Cary House, I consigned myself to the mercies of the Pioneer Stage Company to be hauled up the mountains.

Night came on by the time that the heavy lumbering coach reached Sportman's Hall, a miserable little hostelry by the road-side, thirteen miles on the journey.

And here let me again change the key of this narative, and again make use of the historical present as the rhetorical form of my description.

Artemus Ward is left behind to fulfill the engagements I have made for him in California. He is to follow in the course of two or three days. In the coach with me are three fellow-passengers; two are men of coarse exterior; the third is a lady with many diamonds on her fingers, and much mischief in her eyes.

Strongly-built, and intended for rough usage, is the Pioneer Company's coach. It is constructed to suit the worst of roads and the most daring of drivers. In the course of the journey it will have to be pulled through mire, bumped over ridges of rock, made to roll over blocks of stone, trunks of trees, and slabs of ice—to go through the mud like a plough, over the snow like a sleigh, and down the mountain-side like an India-rubber ball. Its form is that of an old-fashioned stage, and its workmanship is the best of its kind that a New England workshop can furnish.

To our coach there are leathern blinds instead of glass windows. Glass would be inconvenient when the time arrives for the vehicle to topple over in ascending a mountain-pass, or descending to the bottom of a ravine. Better to have your bruises without any cuts; better to travel in darkness than receive light through windows which may suddenly be transformed into knives.

A newly-ploughed field would be a level mead in comparison with the road along which we travel at night. Our coach rolls like a ship becalmed where there is a heavy under-swell in the ocean. It pitches and

tosses like a cockleboat in a rough sea. It leans to one side, and, thinking that we are going over in the darkness, we hold our hands to shield
the side of the face on which we believe that we are going to fall. Suddenly the coach rights itself, lurches over on the other side, and bang go
our heads against the wooden bars. We grasp the edge of the seat tightly,
the coach leaps over a rib of rock, and we are bumped upon the hard
cushion, as though that were a stone of a carriage-way in course of
construction, and we the rammer in the hands of the paver. Five minutes after we plunge into a deep hole, are knocked upward with a jerk,
and butt the roof of the vehicle with the crown of the head; our teeth
are jolted in their sockets—the tongue is bitten at its tip. Sleep is
out of the question when we are in full expectation of being, in the
course of the next ten minutes, whirled down a precipice, thrown over
on a ridge of jagged rock, capsized in a muddy slough, or transformed
into a heap of ruin in the middle of the road. Imagine that you have
attached a chain to a water-butt and hooked it to a locomotive—that
you have placed the water-butt on its side, laid it on a railway, got
within it, fastened down the lid, and started the steam-engine at a
speed of sixty miles an hour. You will form a mild idea of our midnight
journey up the Sierra.

Twenty-five miles from Placerville we plunge into deep snow, and
our path becomes more impeded. Just before daybreak we arrive at
Strawberry Valley, where we take breakfast. I remark to one of our
fellow-passengers that we have had rough travelling during the night.

"Not a touch upon what we shall have going down the second summit," he replies. "Last time I went over I held on with my teeth to the
roof for ten miles. Swing by your teeth if you can, and keep your feet
off the floor of the coach. It saves a sight of jolting."

We change our coach and driver, and start for the first summit. There
are six horses to pull our Concord coach. The driver appears to be a
man of nerve; his eyes are keen, his hands large, his shoulders broad,
his voice deep, his manners rough but cheery. He wears a fur coat. His
cap has large flaps of fur which come down over his neck and ears.

Upward at a brisk pace; past great blocks of granite and of porphyry,
past fields of snow and half-formed glaciers, past immense pine-trees
and boulder stones of prodigious dimensions—upward still upward,
till we have gained the top of the Sierra Nevada, and are at the head of
Johnson's Pass, 6750 feet above the sea-level. Behind us is California;
before us the whole breadth of the American continent, across Nevada

to Utah, from the Great Salt Lake to the Rocky Mountains, thence to the plains of Colorado, across them to the valleys of the Missouri and the Mississippi, again beyond them the prairies, hills, and rivers of the West—the hamlets, villages, and cities of the populous East. We are in a straight line with the Capitol at Washington; but the line happens to be more than three thousand miles long.

There are some sights which, once seen, are never forgotten. The one now before us will hold firmly to the memory. It is grander than sunrise on Monte Rosa, and more magnificent than the sunset I once beheld off Hauhine, in the mid-Pacific. It is morning in its earliest beauty, as seen from the summit of the Sierra.

Far away below is Lake Bigler, as they called it at one time—Lake Tahoe as they call it now; still and beautiful, sleeping amidst a forest of pines. Beyond it are the snow peaks of the Second Summit; and over them, in rays of rose-color, amber, and gold, stream the glories of the morning sun. Snow-white pyramids change into ruby monuments, frosty pinnacles become silver spires, icy domes are transformed into gigantic opals, iridescent with every tint of crimson, green, violet, and gold. Sunrise on the Alps is magnificent, but sunrise on the Sierra is sublime; for here are the wilder solitudes, and here the grandeur and impressiveness of the remote New World far away, beyond the centres of civilization.

We drive at headlong pace down into the happy valley in which Lake Tahoe is situated. The lake is about forty miles in length and twenty-one in breadth. We are told that it contains three varieties of trout, and that at the Glenbrook House, where we stop for refreshment, fine fish breakfasts are obtainable.

"When we get the Pacific Railroad through," observes the landlord, "we shall have picnic parties here from New York and Boston."

I look round at the scenery, glance at the long range of snow-covered mountains, then at the calm, bright, sparkling lake, and then at the pleasant sites for pretty villages far away among the pine-trees. A few small churches with tall spires, and a sprinkling of white and green châlets are all that are wanted to complete the picture. One day they will be there. No Californian will then have occasion to travel to Switzerland, for Switzerland will be in the Sierra Nevada.

We start for the Second Summit, and see it far off, snowy, and golden gleaming in the morning sun. Our coach drives through a pine forest where every pine is a giant. I learn that pines have been felled in this neighborhood the trunks of which measured from eight to nine feet across, at a height of seventy-five feet from the ground. There is timber enough in this grandly-timbered region to keep all the carpenters in California at work sawing and planing for the next fifty years—not pines only, but balsam-firs, red-wood, cedars, and white oak; every tree huge in size and noble in conformation. Here in the Sierra is the very home of the pinetree. It was from these mountains, but farther south, in Calavéras County, that the bark of the great pine was brought which, within the Crystal Palace at Sydenham, was exhibited as being that of the mammoth Californian tree.

One of our passengers has become much excited since leaving the Glenbrook House. He seems to have received unpleasant news, and drunk too pleasant whisky. The lady with the diamond rings appears to share in his excitement. He draws his revolver, looks at it eagerly, examines its trigger, with the muzzle of the barrel uncomfortably pointed towards me, and clutching the weapon with a convulsive grasp, exclaims:

"By ———! there will be a man for breakfast to-night!"

I do not comprehend the exact meaning of the phrase, but shrink back with fear into the corner of the coach. My excited *vis-à-vis* rolls his head, and mutters to himself for fully twenty minutes. His female companion urges him to put away the pistol. Instead of doing so, he plays with it nervously, and yells out:

"Boys, look out! By ———! I'm on it. There'll be a man for breakfast over in Carson City. I tell you so—*sure!*"

The revolver has an ugly appearance. I study the probability of there soon being a man dead in the coach, should the pistol go off by accident. We come to a halt to rest the horses. I get out and beg for a seat alongside the driver.

As we toil upward towards the snow I tell the driver of the eccentricities of the inside passenger.

"Did he say there would be a man for breakfast in Carson?"

"Yes, and said it savagely. Who is he?"

"Not a bad fellow; but he has an ugly kink in his brain. He's not to be played with."

"And the lady in the coach with him. They seem to be acquainted. Do you know who she is?"

"She! Wh-e-e-ew! I reckon I do. She's a blazing ruin."

While the driver thus enlightens me, the air blows chilly from off the slopes of snow. I prefer being chilled as an outside traveller to reentering the coach, there to share the society of "blazing ruins" and men with a "kink in the brain."

Our road-way is narrow. The ravines beside us are a quarter of a mile deep. At the bottom of one of them I see the fragments of a coach. No wonder that they are fragments only; for, in rolling over down the precipitous side of the mountain, that coach must have fallen five hundred feet. I ask the driver if there were any passengers in it at the time of the accident. He replies that there were; that two of them were killed and three severely injured.

"A bad job for the Company, that," says he. "Cost them a pile of dollars. The injured people brought actions and made small fortunes out of it. But that will never happen again if the coachman isn't killed too."

"What preventive have you?" I ask. "As far as I see, if it were not for careful driving this coach might turn over and roll down."

"I reckon it might."

"And I might get my arm broken and sue the Company?"

"Never in this world—not if *I didn't get smashed too*," says the driver, with emphasis.

I am puzzled, and desire more explicit information.

"It would be out of order," is the reply. "If you brought law against the Company, I should suffer, and the Company also. You wouldn't be allowed to do it. If you were only badly hurt, I should have to knock you on the head. Dead men don't bring actions."

Arrived at the Second Summit, we again halt. The scene is the grandest I have beheld for many a day.

There may be bathos in making the comparison, but the idea is one which suggests itself on the spot. I am standing at one end of the uppermost row of the highest gallery of a theatre. The theatre is of horseshoe shape, the walls are granite, the roof is the open sky; and, from where I stand, down to where I see the top of a tree in the middle of the pit, must be at least two thousand feet. Where the tiers of boxes should be, slopes down in winding curves the road by which we have to descend. Instead of arabesque work, the front of the boxes is ornamented with pine-trees, some of them a hundred feet in height. Around the uppermost tier is a cornice of glittering snow. Looking across the

Titanic theatre, whose walls upreared themselves in primeval time—
across the stupendous pit, the floor of which has scarcely been trodden
by the foot of man—Nevada appears upon the stage in scenery more
impressive, more dreary, and yet more wondrous than ever painter's
hand painted or scenic artist devised. Far as the eye can see is one
broad expanse of brown, arid, treeless, cheerless, solemn desolation—
a series of volcanic-looking hills, of a burnt, dusky hue, apparently
devoid of all vegetation, and looking as though never watered by the
rain of heaven, the bright blue sky above them only enhancing their
dreariness, and the white snow in the foreground lending force and
color to their gloom.

We have to descend from the gallery to the stage. We shall accomplish the descent driving at a rapid pace. Should our coach turn over
we should be hurled down to destruction. Should we roll to the depths
below no one would take the trouble to find our grave. To our left as
we descend is a wall of rock crowned with an inaccessible coping of
snow; to our right is an almost perpendicular precipice, the base of
which is an untrodden ravine. At the angles of the road, where it curves
upon itself, are wide hollowed-out recesses for a vehicle ascending the
mountain to wait the passing of a descending one.

The hind wheels of the coach are locked. We glide down at a rapid
rate. There is peril enough to cause silence, and danger sufficient to
make the traveller cling to the coach with nervous grip.

Half-way down we are startled by the report of a pistol. Our passenger with a "kink in his brain" is flourishing his revolver out of the
coach-window and pointing it towards where, behind the mountains,
Carson City awaits the "man for breakfast."

The "grade" down which we are descending is a toll road, and is the
property of the Pioneer Stage Company. Over the same mountains
that road traverses, but farther to the south the Pacific Railway con-
veys its passengers at the time when these pages go to press.

We are at the bottom of the descent—have driven round the mountain—have passed some corn-fields and some cabbage-gardens, to find
which fringing the dreary wilderness excites our surprise, and we stop
at the St. Charles Hotel, in Carson City.

California, with its golden soil, is on the other side of the Sierra. We
are now in Silver Land.

The Show in Silver-land

NEVADA is the first child of California," to use the phrase of Mr. Bowles, of Massachusetts. The child was born with a silver spoon in its mouth, for nearly the whole State is one vast silver mine. When first explored by miners in 1859, it was called Washoe. Then it was known as the Territory of Nevada, and now it has become a State of the Union.

The soil of Nevada is literally manured with uncoined dollars. In the first six years of her being known to the world she yielded sixty millions of those dollars for coinage. At the time I write these lines she forms a prominent topic of the London Stock Exchange, and twenty-two of her silver mines are advertised as let on leases at rentals amounting to £52,000, which, with royalties, are calculated to yield to a company a yearly income of nearly £70,000. The gloomy-looking land we saw from the summit of the Sierra is probably the richest silver region in the world. Once it belonged to Utah of the Mormons. Now it has an existence of its own, and Carson City is its capital.

A wild place is Carson. As uncouth and semi-civilized as in old time was the famous hunter and trapper Kit Carson, from whom it takes its name.

We look at the straggling, half-built city from out the windows of our hotel after a good night's rest. We see that it is at the base of the Sierra, that the mountains rise behind it, that dreary plains extend around it, but it is laid out in squares, that its houses are nearly all built of wood, and that its streets are lively with coaches, wagons, and drays.

For breakfast there are eggs and bacon, hot cakes and molasses, good coffee and some apples. Though we are on the outskirts of the American wilderness, there is a morning paper. It is brought in damp from the press.

I unfold the "Carson Daily Independent," wondering what matter the editor can find for news. The first paragraph that attracts my attention informs me that the Genoa coach, which I had seen on the

First Summit, turned over yesterday descending the Kingsbury Grade, and, to use the expression of the writer, "killed the turn-overs."

Paragraph No. 2 in the Carson paper is headed "A man for breakfast." I read that late last night a man was shot dead in one of the drinking saloons of the city. On inquiry I find that the murderer is my coach companion with the "kink in his brain;" that the affair is thought to be nothing more than an ordinary occurrence, and that paragraphs recording such little events are usually headed "A man for breakfast." Possibly the good citizens value such a stimulant with their morning meal.

Carson City, as I see it, contains about four thousand inhabitants. It has a theatre, but no church; though there is a small brick one nearly finished.

I intend that Artemus Ward shall lecture in Carson City, and I go to the theatre to make arrangements. I find it to be an ill-built, dirty wooden structure; the auditorium consisting of a pit with raised seats, and the chief entrance being through a very forbidding-looking drinking-bar, in which, early in the morning as it is, many men are lounging, some drinking, some smoking, and some playing cards. They are roughly clad, and wear large slouching wide-awake hats. Beside the door leading from the bar into the theatre proper is a painted notice:

"NO WASHYBUMS ADMITTED HERE"

On inquiry I find that the notice is intended to warn those who have spent all their money in the drinking saloon that they can not go into the theatre without additional payment.

I ask for the proprietor. I am told that he is "a genius," that his name is "Dr. Schemmerhorn," and that he originally came from the City of Baltimore.

The doctor presents himself. He is a tall, gaunt, large-limbed man. He wears a red shirt and a broad slouch hat, but is without coat or waistcoat. I easily arrange for the use of the theatre, and after a preliminary chat I ask Dr. Schemmerhorn how he came to leave Baltimore to live in Carson. His answer is:

"I have lived in these d—d mountains, and the Rocky Mountains, and all other d—d mountains for the last eighteen years."

He himself is a curiosity. So is his theatre. I ask him where he gets his actors from.

"Make them here, and write my own pieces," is his reply.

"What sort of pieces?" I ask, wondering whether high comedy or heavy tragedy is most appreciated in Carson.

"My last was 'The Tempest at Sea,' replies the doctor. "It was a bully piece, and went well with the boys. One of my actors—a new one—had to be in a storm. There was to be thunder and lightning they like plenty of that here—and he had to say, 'Let it come.' When he did say it, I had all ready. Out went the lights, and down came a tub with forty gallons of water right on top of him. He was sitting in a chair with a bunch of fire-crackers tied underneath it. We let them off as soon as the water was down. Never had such an effect in any piece before; but my actor swears he'll never go on the stage again. What are you going to do this afternoon? We've got a rooster-pulling match on. Come and see it."

I promise to accept the invitation. But business has to be attended to first. The editor of the newspaper must be called upon. They tell me he is a major. I discover him in his office, and arrange to advertise "four squares four times" for the sum of twenty dollars. A "square" being as many lines of type as will be equal to the breadth of the advertisement. Then I engage two printers to take checks at two dollars each, and the keeper of the postoffice to take money, for which he is to receive five dollars. I find him to be a very intelligent man, and I remark, in a complimentary manner, that I presume he will one day hold a much higher position in the commonwealth. He replies:

"My brains are in a muss. If I had education to contract my brains, and had a delivery, I'd make a speaker."

In the afternoon I saunter outside the town to see the "rooster-pulling," not knowing what kind of an entertainment I am destined to witness. That the inhabitants of Carson City are not given to elegant frivolities I am quite prepared to expect; but that they should indulge in any such villainous sport as that to which I am treated, is matter for sincere regret.

A "rooster" is the American term for the male bird among poultry. Many roosters have been provided for the match—fine strong fowls. Each competitor seats himself on a log of wood with his feet against a board. He first deposits a dollar, and then takes one of the roosters, places it between his legs with its head downward, and, seizing the feet of the poor fowl, pulls with full force. If he succeed in pulling the legs of the rooster clean off, he will win the bird; if not, he will lose the dollar. Few succeed in the attempt. I notice that the fowls, though subjected to such severe torture, do not make any noise, and I ask Dr. Schemmerhorn the reason.

"They can't," answers the doctor. "They are too much absorbed."

I conclude that eighteen years of life in the mountains is not favorable to fine feeling; and am not sorry when the time arrives for me to remount another coach and start for Virginia City.

Seventeen miles across the Silver Land. As we leave Carson the coach rolls through deep, sandy soil, and on each side is a sandy plain devoid of verdure, but spotted as far as the eye can see with the gray and hideous sage-brush.

Oh that sage-brush! How many tens of thousands of acres of it were Artemus and I destined to see in crossing the American continent! How we got to detest its gnarled, stunted, tiresome ubiquity! How we came to hate its all-pervading aromatic odor! In the American desert it is the very emblem of sterility—of cheerless tracts, want of water, and intensified dreariness. Its dull gray color becomes wearisome to the eye, and its camphorlike fragrance detestable to the nostrils. Botanists call it *Artemisia tridentata*. I remember a miner calling it "demon's garden-stuff."

As we bowl over the sandy plain we see smoke ascending in the distance, and are informed that it proceeds from camps of Washoe Indians. Before us is a ridge of reddish-brown hills. We drive towards them over what seems to be blocks of broken lava. Everywhere around are indications of igneous origin in the rocks.

We pass the hills, and in passing see the openings of tunnels in them, with piles of bluish earth heaped up at the mouth of every tunnel. Into those tunnels men have gone in search of silver. Here miners do the work of rabbits, and these are their huge warrens.

Down we plunge into a valley, through which runs a small stream. The few wooden houses away to our right constitute Empire City; the long street of wooden houses and large sheds through which we pass is called Silver City. We enter a magnificent ravine, the sides of which are formed of gray mountains, almost perpendicular, and we come to a toll-bar, the name of which is "The Devil's Gate." We drive through it up a steep hill, past barren mountains with rounded sides and jagged summits—past wooden huts—past great mills keeping up a continuous roar as the steam-driven stampers within them crush with the noise of thunder the silver ore—past mounds of blue earth, full of the material out of which dollars and half-crowns are made—past heavy masses of machinery and piles of timber, till Mount Davidson rises in full view, and we toil up Gold Hill to find ourselves in Virginia City, 7827 feet above the level of the sea.

You know how high up you are in the world after you have spent a day in Virginia City, for the elevation is so great that the rarefied air tells immediately upon the lungs of a traveller not accustomed to the region. The city is built on the side of the mountain, and, from a distance, seems clinging on to it. Above it, as well as on a level with it, are the mouths of the tunnels leading to the great silver mines. A thousand five hundred feet above the city is the summit of Mount Davidson.

The coach drives along C Street, and stops at the International Hotel, the proprietor of which is a Mr. Winn. The booking-clerk is entitled Dr. May. I arrange for a bedroom, and then purchase ten "meal tickets" for five dollars, for such is the mode of doing business at a hotel in Silver Land.

From the windows of the hotel, high up in the bedroom allotted to me, I can see across the twenty-six miles of desert I shall have to traverse in the next stage of my journey towards the Mormons. Away in the distance I can almost discern the "sink" of the Carson, where that peculiar river becomes lost in the desert. I can see, from my position in civilization, the land where the Indian roams, and where barrenness extends in plains covered with bitter alkali.

Rambling through the city I find the main streets to be built one tier above the other, and the cross streets to be steep hills. Any one familiar with the town of Dartmouth, in Devonshire, can readily form an idea of the ground-plan of Virginia City. In the course of my ramble I pass the entrance to the famous Gould and Curry Mine, on the celebrated Comstock Ledge. This grand ledge of silver ore runs along the side of the mountain above the town for nearly three miles. In width it varies from fifty to one hundred feet. How far deep it extends into the bowels of the earth no human being knows.

Here I am, where every man who is at all rich is a centipede. He possesses a hundred "feet" in one or many mining claims. On the streets, in the hotel, go where you may, the talk everywhere is concerning "feet." The whole business part of the city is one great mining Stock Exchange. Every store-keeper can tell you the value of a foot in every mine in this part of Silver Land.

Many and rich are the "feet" of the Gould and Curry. The mine is twelve hundred feet in length on the surface of the ledge. It has been delved to a depth of eight hundred feet. Then there are any number of cross excavations. More than five millions of cubic feet have been excavated at the time of my visit. The mine has two miles of tunnels and subterranean passages, and there is more timber within it than there is in all the structures of the busy city outside. I am told that it has produced over eleven millions of dollars' worth of silver ore, and paid nearly four millions of dollars in dividends. I ask in return who is Gould and who is Curry?

"As to Mr. Gould," says my informant, "he never got more silver out of it than a barrel for a pistol. Curry is pretty well off. He speculated in building the Territorial prison, and is the owner of it now."

It is the old, old story of him who originates an enterprise. I next inquire after Mr. Comstock, whose name the great ledge of silver bears, and who must assuredly be a man of immense wealth.

"Hasn't got a dollar," is the response. "Comstock is only a poor bummer. You may find him loafing in the saloons of Carson City."

In Melbourne, Australia, I have seen Mr. Fawkner, the founder of the colony of Victoria, sitting in his fitting place in the Parliament House. Things are otherwise with the pioneers of Nevada. I ask who first bought up the land from the Mormon settlers in 1859, and am answered: "Proctor, the Sayers, Phillips, Green, Goodrich, Abraham Curry, and Comstock." Curry, landlord as he is of the stone prison, appears to be the best off of the whole party. From having been an explorer of silver he has become the custodian of crime.

Two days of rambling among the mines of Virginia City yield me notes enough for a volume. Here I see one of the two precious metals in the place of its nativity. I see it reft from the arms of Mother Earth, cradled by machinery, and brought up to brightness by the fall of the stamper, the revolution of the iron washing-pan, and the fire of the furnace.

For miles out of the city, on the road by which we entered it, are a succession of mills, each fitted up with huge, ponderous iron-shod stampers. Thump! thump!—thud! thud! they go unceasingly day and night, Sunday as well as week-day, so long as there is ore to be pulverized and silver to be beaten out. Marvellous is the magnitude of the operations, wonderful the enterprise, and astounding the industry.

Every piece of timber in those great mills has been brought miles over hills and valleys; every massive iron casting and cumbrous engine has been hauled over the summit of the Sierra Nevada. Nothing is too difficult to daunt the energy of the lusty miners around us, who have speckled the mountains with heaps of blue earth, and rendered cavernous the hills with subterranean streets paved with silver, and in some localities glittering with gold.

"What are they throwing into those wagons?" I ask.

"Bricks," is the reply.

They are very white and shining bricks, and I go nearer to look at them. I find them to be great ingots of silver, tossed into the wagon just as laborers would toss bricks of clay, or as a carter would throw Dutch cheeses to a cheesemonger.

Artemus Ward rejoins me in Virginia City. He has given his lecture at Carson, and found Dr. Schemmerhorn's friends to be as rough as I have intimated to him by letter it would be his fate to find them.

Here, nearly at the top of a mountain in Silver Land, the lecture is delivered at the Opera-House, another of the buildings owned by spirited Mr. Maguire, of San Francisco, who has kindly given us the use of the building merely for the cost of lighting and warming it. It holds nine hundred dollars, even at the low price of admission we have to charge—one dollar to the dress circle and orchestra seats, and fifty cents (2s.) to the parquette or pit. In front of the outside of the building is a gallery for the brass band requisite to play in the people. Next door is a stable with a hay-yard attached.

I ask about the people who perform at the Opera-house, and find that they consist of occasional performers sent over from California by Mr. Maguire. I inquire after them as the "artistes" of the theatre. My informant, who is a wag attached to one of the newspapers, calls them the "Opera-ators." And why not, if "opera" is derived from *opus?*

A strange Opera-house is this one in Virginia City. I peep out at its back windows and see the desert. The Indian in his furs and feathers can look from his hiding-place in the distance, wonder why the lights are bright in these windows, and then why they become dim. He knows not that Amina is crossing the plank; and the music of "Somnambula" is a mystery to him.

Here, in Virginia City, we meet the Governor of the Territory, Mr. Nye, and listen to him address the people. He is followed in his speech by a red-headed, light-bearded, foaming-hot politician, who bears the name of Bill Stewart, and of whom we hear the remark made: "If Heaven gives up the poor miner he'll be turned over to Bill Stewart."

Our city of silver has a population of twelve thousand. It also has three daily papers, two of which are published in the morning and one in the evening. Yet five years antecedent to our visit there was only a pony path over this mountain side, where now are streets filled with noisy throngs.

At the office of one of the morning papers, "The Territorial Enterprise," Artemus meets with Mr. Samuel L. Clemens, one of its editors, who is destined to distinguish himself in American literature as Mark Twain, the author of the "Jumping Frog." At the time of our being in Virginia City, Mr. Mark Twain's brother, Mr. Orion Clemens, is Secretary of the Territory.

The sides of Mount Davidson must ache with laughter, for Virginia City is continuously gay and festive. As we ramble through it in the evening we find innumerable dance-houses wherein miners in their red shirts are dancing to the music of hurdy-gurdys played by itinerant maidens. At Sutcliffe's Melodeon a ball is taking place; and at the Niagara Concert Hall there are crowds assembled round the door, while from within come forth the sounds of negro minstrelsy, with the clack of bones and the twang of banjos.

Artemus spends his spare time with Mark Twain, descending silver mines and visiting the strange places of the city. I drive around the neighborhood and make arrangements for lectures at Gold Hill, Silver City, and Dayton. Christmas-day arrives. There is turkey for dinner, but no plum-pudding. After dinner, thinking of Christmas spent elsewhere, and feeling moody, I put a bottle of Champagne in my pocket, take a stout stick in my hand, and climb to the summit of Mount Davidson. With Nevada at my feet, Utah in the distance, and behind me the snows of the Sierra Nevada extending south to where in the unseen distance is Mexico, and north to where, beyond vision, are the wilds of Oregon, I drink "Merry Christmas!" to friends who are far away.

◦ 31 ◦

Straight to the "Saints" of Utah

ANY chance of being scalped?"

"Not if you wear your hair long behind."

"But that would give the brave Indian better hold."

"Take my advice. Keep your hair long, and no Indian will hurt you. All the Indians around Utah have an understanding with Brigham Young. Not one of them will touch a Mormon. They'll take you for Mormons if you have long hair. It's a good passport—you bet!"

Such is the conversation we have in Virginia City with a gentleman who knows Salt Lake and its people. Artemus and I take the advice, and do not visit a barber, as we were about to do. That Indians are on the path we are going is almost a certainty, and that they are not gentle-spirited and sympathetic ones is evidenced by the fact that a station has recently been attacked by them, and that two white men have been scalped and tomahawked.

At the booking-office in Virginia City of the Overland Mail Company, owned by Messrs. Wells, Fargo & Co., we purchase our tickets entitling us to be conveyed *via* Salt Lake City to Atchison, in Kansas, on the Missouri River. Our route is to be through Austin to the capital of the Mormons, a distance of about four hundred miles; and thence over the Rocky Mountains by Bridger's Pass, across the Laramie Plains, by the Cache la Poudre River, along the Cherokee trail into the Valley of the Platte, then through Colorado and Nebraska over the great plains to the Missouri, a farther journey of about twelve hundred and fifty miles.

We are travelling in the year 1863. By the time the world is half a dozen years older there will certainly be one direct line of railway across the wilderness we are about to traverse, and there will be at least two other lines in process of construction. The line destined to be first opened will be the Union Pacific, and will proceed along the Valley of the Platte. The next will be the Kansas Pacific Line, which will run from Kansas City by the Valley of the Kansas River to the City of Denver, in Colorado; the third railway will be an extension of the Mississippi and Lake Superior Line to Fort Abercrombie, on the Red River, whence it will take its course to the Upper Missouri, and pass through Dacotah.* Another twenty years, and the trail of the Indian will be the street of a city, the scent of the sage-brush will have given place to the odor of new-mown hay, and the wilderness will literally "blossom like the rose."

What seems to be so odd in our enterprise is, that we are going into the desert with a show. We are not missionaries starting forth to convert heathen Indians, not geographical explorers intent on investigating the physical features of the country. Artemus Ward is travelling with a comic lecture, which he is about to take into the land of the coyote wolf, elk, antelope, and buffalo; and I am Sancho Panza to my American Don Quixote. It seems to me like Punch and Judy being taken into the African Sahara; only that Punch would there be uncomfortably warm, and we have the clearest prospect of being most miserably cold.

As for the Indians we are about to see and to meet, we are quite well aware that we are not to shake hands with any of the chivalrous, amiable, and romantic gentlemen who figure in the pages of Mr. Fenimore Cooper. We have already seen the wretched Digger Indians of California, and we have looked on some very unsavory specimens of the Washoe tribe in Carson City. We have now to pass through the country of the Snakes or Shoshonees, then through that of the Utes. We are likely to meet with the Pey Utes, who confine themselves to fish diet, and the Gosh Utes, who are not anglers, and who prefer a few lizards and grasshoppers roasted with roots for their morning and evening meals. Then, when we have crossed the Rocky Mountains, and seen the waters of the Platte, we shall make the acquaintance of the warriors and the huntsmen of the Sioux.

We are notified that our drivers along the road will be armed, and are advised that we had better have revolvers in readiness. Artemus buys one in Virginia City. He buys a case for it also. Throughout our ride to Salt Lake, except on one occasion, he provokingly keeps the weapon in its case unloaded, and, locking the case, never remembers

*This third railway to the Pacific is already in progress. Messrs. J. Cook and Clark, the American bankers, have undertaken to furnish five million dollars for its construction.—*December, 1869.*

into which of his pockets he has put the key. That pistol is useful for sudden emergencies.

For extra clothing we each purchase a pair of thick coarse blankets, with straps to bind them round the body. Our hats are of fur, and drawn down over the ears; our gloves and the lining to our moccasins are of fur also. In addition, Artemus purchases a buffalo-robe of ample size to wrap round us when sleeping in the coach at night, and to throw over us in the open sleigh when gliding down snowy mountains by moonlight, with the thermometer a dozen degrees below freezing-point.

Friends who know the road warn us that we shall probably be in want of wholesome refreshment. To obviate any difficulty in that way, we purchase a large ham and have it boiled. To this we add half a dozen roast chickens, a bag of biscuits, another bag filled with coffee, a pot to boil the coffee in, and a lantern to light us when riding at night.

Our coach looks any thing but a comfortable vehicle. It is lightly built, though doubtless very strong. Its form is that of a van. We enter it from behind. There is a seat along each side, and a framed roof, covered with leather. It has no windows, but in place of them leather curtains, which admit of being rolled up whenever we want more air and light, and which, though intended to button close to the framework, have an unpleasant trick of flying open at the corners and letting in cold blasts of air upon us just as we are falling off to sleep. There are one hundred and seventy-five miles of desert, hill, and plain to be traversed in this uncomfortable vehicle before we arrive at any town or village; for there is no mining settlement between Virginia City and Austin, on the other side of Reese River, in the Toyabe Mountains.

Lyrical chronicles tell of a celebrated cobbler who "lived in a stall," and who found it to serve the purpose of kitchen, parlor, and every other description of apartment. Would that we were of the cobbler's contented disposition! for in the coach now waiting for us we have to ride, and live, and sit, and sleep, for the next two days. In it we are to be taken across the desert, jolted over the rocks, pulled through the sand, and dragged up the mountains. There are four strong little Mexican horses to pull us; and the passengers for Austin consist of a ruddy-faced jocose farmer from Sacramento, a Jew gold-dealer from San Francisco, Artemus Ward, and myself.

A dozen good friends assemble to see us start. One kindly fellow makes us a present of a demijohn of whisky; another gives us some scrip entitling each of us to twenty feet in a silver mine somewhere in

the rear of Mount Davidson; another brings an offering of a pouch full
of tobacco; and a fourth insists on Artemus accepting an old bowie-
knife, warranted to have killed two men, and to be as useful for carving
our ham as for a weapon of self-defense. Mr. Mark Twain gives us the
latest copy of the "Territorial Enterprise," and Mr. Dan De Quille of
the same paper contributes some hardboiled eggs.

Our road is down the side of the mountain. "Good-bye!"—"Hurrah!"—"Whoo-roo-roo-roo-rooh!" and away we spin, holding on to
the coach with one hand and waving our traveling-caps with the other.
We start at eight o'clock in the morning. The air is cold and clear, the
road dusty and rough.

Through sand and sage-brush, across desert plains, and over a
seemingly endless expanse of white alkaline dust, till at six in the evening we stop to dine at Cottonwood Station, forty-five miles from
Virginia City, and not far from the sink of the Carson, where that odd
river, like its equally odd neighbor, the Humboldt, loses itself in the
earth, disappearing in what in this part of the world is called a "sink."

At ten in the evening we cross the Carson River by a wooden bridge,
and at midnight arrive at Stillwater Station. The night is cold, and
the keepers of the station sulky. We want hot coffee for supper, and
find that the best way to get it without loss of time is to go out, cut
some cotton-wood and grease-wood, and light up a fire ourselves, while
the horses are being changed, and a new driver is getting himself
thoroughly awake for his journey.

Brightly shines the moon and frosty is the air as we again resume our
seats in the coach. Artemus tries to sleep, and with that intent uses the
bag of coffee for a pillow. The coach plunges down into the bed of a
creek, Artemus rolls into the straw provided for keeping our feet warm,
and the coffee-bag falls on top of him.

After that adventure no more attempts at sleep. Our nerves are not
yet used to this kind of travelling. By-and-by we shall be more inured
to it, and able to slumber soundly whether jolting over ruts or bumping over stones.

Hark! is that the cry of hostile Indians? We listen, and learn from
our fellow-travellers that the noise is one made by coyotes or prairie-
wolves, who are howling at us as we drive along, and who if they dared
would attack our horses. An unpleasant animal is the coyote. He is
described to us as having the form of a dog, the voracity of a wolf, the
cunning of the fox, and manners of a jackal.

While we are listening to the coyotes, and are being told by our friend from Sacramento that it is always as well to have your name and address engraved upon the handle of your jack-knife, so that if your bones are picked clean by the coyotes, a stranger finding your skeleton with your jack-knife beside it may know who you are and where you lived, we are startled by a wild yell:

"Cush! cush! cush! cush-oo-oo-oo!"

The cry seems human, but it is like the screech of a madman. A minute passes before we recognize it as proceeding from our own driver, and intended to warn the men at Mountain Wells Station that the coach is coming, and that the horses will have to be changed.

At daybreak we stop at Fairview. By eleven o'clock on the morning of the second day of our ride we make Westgate Station, 115 miles from Virginia City. It consists of a rudely-constructed dwelling of one story, built of rubble masonry. Around it are great dreary mountains. In the distance is a hilly range covered with snow. At Westgate we take a hurried breakfast of fried bacon and coffee. Our appetite is fierce. Artemus thinks that if he had a coyote cooked he could eat even that.

Thence on to Cold Springs; then to Brewster's Ranch for supper; and on to New Pass, where we halt at midnight.

The station is composed of four walls, inside which is a hut for the keepers, and stables for the horses. A pair of huge wooden gates are thrown open to admit the coach, and are closed quickly when we get inside. Looking round, we notice that some old muskets are placed in a position where they could be readily made available. Other signs of precaution attract our attention, and we ask the reason.

"An Indian got killed here a few days ago for stealing. His tribe have threatened us with an attack."

"When do you expect it?"

"Perhaps to-night. If you like, gentlemen, you can stay and jine us in the fight. We've got guns enough. The more hands we have, the better stand we shall make against the sons of—[lady-dogs]."

Artemus looks at me, and draws a circle with his forefinger round the top of his head. I ask him if he knows any thing of the nature of the road on which we have to travel for the next thirty miles of our journey, and explain to him that, having studied the map, I know that we have to pass through a canyon, where, if attacked, we shall have no chance of escape. I suggest that we had better stay where we are till morning, and that if Indians come we can fire at them better behind walls than if we have to fight them from the coach. The driver settles the matter by preferring to have four fleet horses in front of him to any walls of brick or stone.

We leave the station, the gates are closed rapidly behind us, and we dash into the gloomy canyon. Each of us holds his revolver with a tight grip. Even Artemus has found the key of his, and the Jewish gentleman travelling with us has loaded it for him, but forbidden him to touch the trigger unless called upon to do so, lest in his nervousness he should shoot one of us in the coach. We sit listening in the darkness. Presently the driver cries out:

"Quick! Hand me a pistol!"

We do so. He fires it. The echoes of the report roll up the canyon.

"Keep cool, Mr. Ward. Don't fire till you see a savage right before you," advises our brave Hebrew friend.

The driver pulls up the horses, returns the borrowed pistol, and remarks:

"I saw his eyes, and I shot him in the forehead clean between them."

"An Indian?"

"No; a wolf. The thieving beast was following us. He scented your cold ham, Mr. Ward."

Freezingly chilly is the wind that blows around Mount Airy, and welcome is the bright wood fire we find at Jacobsville. We cross Reese River by a wooden bridge, and, driving past some huts and stores, wind up a steep hill into Austin. Again we are among silver mines, and hear the heavy thump of the ore-crushing machines, and see tunnels in the mountains, and heaps of silver-laden soil at the tunnel's mouth.

Austin, at the time we visit it, is only one year old. Built along a ravine between steep mountains, it is a place of many marvels. Its mines are rich in silver; its stores are stocked with goods; it has a French restaurant, any number of bar-rooms, and—a daily paper! —the "Reese River Réveille." Yet Austin is nearly two hundred miles from anywhere westward; has no acquaintance with any town to the south; has nothing to the north nearer than the mining camps of Idaho, and no connection with anywhere to the east except Salt Lake City, four hundred miles away.

There never has been a show given in Austin, and Artemus determines that he will be the first on its list of showmen. A court-house has been erected, built on piles by the side of a hill. A flight of wooden steps leads up to the justice-room, and a group of Shoshonee Indians are lolling against the piles beneath it. We make the acquaintance of Judge Brownson. The judge is willing that we shall have the use of the court-house, but suggests that, as it is not strongly built, if too large an audience be gathered together in it, it might break down and roll to the bottom of the hill. He advises us to take "Holbrook's new granite store." The proprietor grants the use of it; and we announce in the "Reese River Réveille" that the "Babes in the Wood" will be given as "The Pioneer Lecture in the Shoshonee Nation." That we are among the Shoshonees is without doubt; for there, in front of the International Hotel, a real Shoshonee is cutting fire-wood. He wears an uncurried sheep-skin for a covering, but is using a bright saw which not long since came out of a store in Boston.

The International Hotel is where we live. It is a peculiar institution, and makes no pretensions to rival the hotels of London, Paris, or New York. In front of it is an apartment which serves as bar-room, coach-office, parlor, drawing-room, and general rendezvous. Behind that is the dining-room, with rough planks for a table and hardened mud for a floor. Beside and behind the dining-room are the sleeping apartments, where the guests are stowed away for the night—not in beds, but in wooden bunks, built one above another in wine-rack fashion. The floor of each dormitory is earth, the walls wood and canvas.

We determine to stop a week in Austin, that Artemus may lecture there, investigate its wonders, and prepare for the long ride to Salt Lake City. We fall in with two miners who were the first to come here a twelvemonth ago. By name they are Mr. J. B. Marshall and Mr. George Peoples. Both have once been showmen. They enter into the spirit of our enterprise with enthusiastic alacrity, and undertake the distribution of our handbills among the miners at the adjacent camps. I engage a Shoshonee Indian to accompany them and distribute bills also. Conciliated with a glass of whisky, he allows one of the bills to be pinned to his sheep-skin. Thereupon Artemus becomes struck with a bright idea.

"When we do our show in New York," says he, "we'll have a dozen Indians to deliver bills. We'll arm them with tomahawks, and give them umbrellas to carry."

New-year's-eve arrives while we loiter in Austin. Judge Brownson invites us to spend it with him at his chambers. We find the "chambers"

in a field in the rear of the main street. They are built of logs, have a
mud floor, are furnished with a couch, a table, half a dozen stools, two
law books, and a dozen empty bottles. The judge provides some lager-
bier for refreshment, and we are joined by another judge, whose name
is Crane, and a colonel whose name is Williams. Pleasantly the evening
passes; many are the jokes and quaint the stories. Late at night we
sing "Auld Lang Syne" in chorus, the judge playing an accompaniment
on the flute.

"There was a deal of music in that flute once," observes the judge.
"But it's a drunken old engine now. A kind of faithful in its ways,
though. The more lager-bier I drink, the drunker the old flute gets."

On New-year's-day, 1864, we wish to follow out the American custom of paying complimentary visits to the ladies. Unfortunately Austin
has few of the fair sex for inhabitants, and they are mostly engaged
in business. So, after two or three calls, we accompany Mr. Marshall
to see the Pioneer Mill, and here in the course of half an hour we learn
many facts about a silver-mill. We ascertain that it cost $75,000; that
the freight bill for bringing the materials of it to the spot amounted to
$25,000; that the roof, made in Carson City, cost $363; and that the
haulage of it to Austin involved an expense of $1980. We are told that
one stamp crushes a ton of silver ore in twenty-four hours; that the
charge for crushing a ton is $75, including amalgamating and retorting;
that the furnace is made of fire-stone procured in the neighborhood;
that the price of wood is $12 "a cord;" and that a pound of mercury from
the Almaden mines of California can be had for $1. Then we ask the
cost of provisions, and find the bread we eat at Austin is made from
flour supplied by the Mormons at Salt Lake City, and that its cost
is $20 per hundred-weight, or $40 a barrel; that potatoes are 20 cents a
pound, beef or mutton 25 cents, and pork 50 cents, or in English money
about two shillings. So much for statistics of Silver Land.

Wandering about Austin we make the acquaintance of a man who
has two dogs, and who propounds a queer theory regarding them. The
dogs have been his constant companions for some years of a roving life,
and he himself has at one time been a telegraph clerk. We notice him
waving his arm systematically to one of the dogs, and the animal seems
to understand the movements. We are told that the man "has a craze"
about understanding the language of dogs, and we get him to converse
on the subject.

"My dogs talk as plainly as you do," says he. "All dogs have a language. It only wants studying out. Here I take my knife and tap twice on this table; then I tap twice, pause half a second, and tap again. Now I tap two sharp taps, pause and give two more quick taps. If you were a telegraph clerk you would be able to read off those taps just as plainly as I am speaking. A sound, and time between the sounds, is all that's wanted to make the alphabet. It's just the same with a dog. When he says 'Bow!' that's his tap. When he says 'Bow-wow!' that's his two taps; and when he says 'Bow-wow—wow!' that's his two taps, pause, and tap again. That's dog language, and it only wants to be studied out. When you hear the instrument going in a telegraph office you don't know what it's saying, because you haven't given your mind to the subject; and when you hear a dog barking you are just as much in the dark. But I've studied them, and I'm getting at their code—I'm getting their code fast."

"But what has the waving of your arm to do with it?" we asked.

"That answers to the movement of the dog's tail. His tail's a needle. Do you know how the letters are made in a needle telegraph? It's just the same with the wag of a dog's tail as it is with the needle."

"Then a dog can talk at both ends?" observes Artemus.

"Of course he can," replies the dog man. "One wag to the left and one to the right may mean 'A' with the telegraph. It means something else with the wag of a dog's tail. But there's a code for it just the same. Dogs are sensible beings; so are all animals. We shall know the language of all of them some day."

"Dog-Latin is known already," remarks one of our party as we compliment the owner of the dogs on his discovery, and watch some of his experiments in holding telegraphic conversation with the animals.

When the time arrives for Artemus to lecture, we find that the plasterers have scarcely finished the walls of the store in which the lecture is to be delivered. There is no time to have the floor washed, and there are no seats nor lamps. The latter we soon procure, but the seats are more difficult to improvise. We borrow chairs from the hotel and restaurants, and the friendly miners assist us in procuring some timber and empty barrels, out of which we make temporary forms. Artemus walks across the road from the hotel to the lecture-room bearing a lighted lamp before him, and many of the audience are thoughtful enough to bring chairs with them from their homes. The lecture is received with shouts of laughter. When it is over a dance is proposed, and Austin determines to have a night of jubilation.

Twelve miles from Austin is a small mining camp, called Big Creek. Artemus is solicited to lecture there. Though the inhabitants are not more than three hundred, a good house is promised, for all are guaranteed to attend. We drive over to Big Creek, and Artemus lectures in a large bar-room, with a huge wood fire blazing at one end of it, a floor of bare earth, a roof of dried sage-brush, and walls of rough pine. Some candles are stuck to the posts which support the roof. Artemus stands on a chair behind one end of the bar to lecture, while at the other end of the bar the keeper of it, with his shirt-sleeves rolled up, is busy selling beer and slicing loaves. Whenever Artemus pauses, and the audience applaud, the bar-keeper yells out, "Bully, boys—bully!" and, once becoming over-excited, he exclaims: "That's Artemus Ward from New England. Listen to him! Ain't he sweet? Ain't he h—l!"

On the 5th of January we leave Austin for Salt Lake. Before quitting the most genial community we have found in the course of our trip, we hold a merry meeting, and bid many farewells. Artemus perversely insists on having his boots blacked, though we are going to travel in the wilderness, and the ground is covered with snow. It is not easy to find a boot-black, and the freak costs fifty cents.

Next to the hotel is a cigar-shop, kept by an enthusiastic and educated young German. Whenever I have dropped in during my stay in Austin, I have found the cigar-seller studying Virgil or reading German poetry. We become on friendly terms. As Artemus and I take our seats in the coach, the German brings cigars to each of us, and begs me to accept his card. I have it before me as I write—"S. M. Ehrlich, Austin, R. R. N. T." On it the "classical cuss," as Artemus called him, has written "Nostra amicitia sempiterna sit." We shall not be troubled with Latin again for some time, for the Indians are not learned, and the Mormons are not scholastic.

Our start is at midnight; at seven in the morning we arrive at Dry Creek Station and take breakfast. Thence we go on to Grubb's Well; then to Robert's Creek; and then to Sulphur Springs. Here we change our driver. Mr. Hodge, who has driven us the last fourteen miles, has driven us to distraction as well as to Sulphur Springs, by blowing a bugle during the whole journey, knowing only one tune, and that very imperfectly. Our new coachman, who announces himself as being

"Frank Jordan from Maine," is a most acceptable driver. We know that the road before us at night is a rough one; a whisky-loving driver would increase its danger, but when some spirit is offered to Mr. Frank Jordan, he declines it indignantly, saying, "I don't drink; I won't drink; and I don't like to see any body else drink. I'm of the opinion of these mountains—keep your top cool. They've got snow, and I've got brains; that's all the difference."

We arrive at Diamond Springs, and change our Concord coach for an open sleigh. Diamond Mountain is before us, coated with glistening snow. The ascent to it is gradual; but when we have gained the summit we have to sleigh down on the steepest side. To assist us in the operation our driver takes two men up the mountain with him. When we have made the ascent, we are cautioned about how we are to behave in descending.

The sleigh is nothing more than a wide, shallow, open box, mounted on runners all round it; and fastened to the frame-work of the runners projects an outrigger, consisting of a small plank platform, on which our conductors stand, and shift themselves quickly from side to side to balance the sleigh. The mules are harnessed "wide;" that is, they are attached to the ends of a long bar, which keeps them at least six feet apart. The mail-bags have been placed at the bottom of the sleigh; on top of them have been laid our travelling-bags and small store of provisions. There are four of us in the sleigh; we are directed to lie down at full length, wedge ourselves close together, and not to roll out if we can help it, because the snow is frozen and the icy spiculæ would be likely to pierce the skin if we and the snow were to come in contact. We cover ourselves up with our blankets and buffalo rugs, leaving just enough space in the covering through which to see the moon shining coldly splendid in a sky of intense blackness. A guide runs down the mountain with some lanterns and a long pole. He feels for where the snow makes the best roadway, and places the lanterns down in the depth below us to indicate the route. The driver stands in front of the sleigh, yells to his horses, the men on the outriggers balance the sleigh, and away we glide down, down, down over fields of snow. Though we are extended full length face uppermost, we are every now and then almost vertical with the zenith.

From Jacob's Well to Fort Ruby, and thence to Mountain Springs. Sixteen miles more driving brings us to Butte Station, and another sixteen to Egan. Our pace is about seven miles an hour. At Egan, on a dung-heap beside the station, are squatted five or six Gosh-Ute Indians, cleaning some freshly-procured skins. More dirty, offensive, repulsive specimens of humanity it has not been our lot to see during the journey.

Egan is left behind, and we are spinning along with fresh horses towards Schell Creek. The road is slightly hilly, the ground hard with frost; for two nights we have had no sleep; the excitement has been too great even to admit of our dozing in the coach. Artemus is overcome with fatigue, and expresses his delight when he perceives that Schell Creek Station is large and commodious.

"Let us stop here to-night, and go on by the next coach to-morrow," says he. "But when shall we get into Mormon territory?"

"We've been in Utah for the last seven miles," replies the driver. "The people who keep this station are saints. Very good sort of saints too—bully ones!"

❧ 32 ❧

Safe in Salt Lake City

IT will be done by the Urim and the Thummim."

"And not by a knowledge of Hebrew and Greek?"

"No; that would be an uninspired translation, and no better than the one you have," answers Mr. Walter Davis, telegraph operator and Mormon "saint" of Schell Creek. "The Bible will be translated by the Urim and Thummim some day. Then all America will be of our faith."

"No doubt it will be," remarks Artemus. "But is your head clear about how the translator will go to work? Will the Urim read off the Hebrew, and the Thummim write it down in English?"

"It will be like looking through a divining-stone," explains Mr. Walter Davis, rather foggily.

I observe to Mr. Davis that the Urim and Thummim were oracles having to do with the breastplate of the Jewish high-priest, and that the breastplate is probably irretrievably lost.

"It will be found," says Mr. Davis, solemnly. "President Young knows where it is. Our President has had many revelations which he has never disclosed."

"Plenty of wives to every body was one of them—was it not?" suggests Artemus.

"Not to every body," replies Mr. Davis. "I have but one wife. I have never been commanded to take another. When my faith is stronger I may take one more if the Church desire it."

Mrs. Davis listens to her husband in silence, seemingly quite willing that his faith should remain at its present strength, or become strong enough for the Church to require an additional wife to share it with her. She has a pale, wan look, and an air of thorough resignation.

Hospitable as the Arab of the Old World's deserts are these Mormon settlers in the desert of the New World. The keeper of the station, Mr. Newton Dunyon, has gone to Salt Lake City to select a wife. In his absence Mr. Davis acts as deputy. There are seven other people at the station. Schell Creek is a place of workshops belonging to the Overland Mail Company—a place where broken-down coaches are repaired, mules doctored, and harness mended. Its buildings are arranged as a street, inside of a corral, or four-cornered wall of stone. The stone wall is pierced for firing through. The former station was burned down by Indians, and Indians may come again. Hence it is necessary to be fortified. Not all the Indian tribes are kindly to Mormon scalps. The Gosh-Utes are said to respect the long locks of a Mormon no more than the short crop of an unbeliever. Mr. Davis has long hair. So has the blue-eyed, lame old Dane, who can hardly speak English, and who officiates as cook. He spreads for us a supper of fried beef, boiled onions, excellent boiled potatoes, and very palatable coffee. After supper Artemus and I retire to a sort of loft over the telegraph operating-room, where for one of us is a small truckle-bed, and for the other a shake-down of blankets on the floor. The loft is cold, for there are port-holes all round it for firing through at the Indians. We notice that every man in the employment of the Overland Mail Company is furnished with a carbine and revolver. Before going to bed we stop up the port-holes with old rags to keep out the cold, and place our revolvers beside us to keep out the Indians if called upon to do so. Artemus has his revolver in its case, as usual. I ask him if the case is unlocked. He replies that it is not. I then inquire if he knows where the key is.

"Oh! don't bother," says he. "I never know where the key is. When the Indians come, blow open my case with your pistol."

As we fold the blankets around us we hear the click—click—click of the telegraph instrument in the room beneath, and we know that Mr. Walter Davis is sending information to Mr. Brigham Young that new visitors have entered Mormon territory. Mr. Davis has listened very attentively to our conversation. He may be retailing some of it to the Mormon chief two hundred miles away.

Then we go to sleep, but we have scarcely slept half an hour before we are startled by a wild cry in the distance. We each ask the other what it means. Then we rest on our elbows and listen.

"Whir—roo—roo—roo—roo—roo!"

Again it is repeated, louder and nearer.

"Are the Indians upon us?"

Artemus asks me the question in a voice of trepidation. As I am about to answer there is the sound of a horn, followed by the rumble of wheels. We listen, learn that the coach is coming in from Salt Lake City, and that the driver uses the Indian yell to warn the station-keepers of his approach.

"If I were a cheerful Indian I'd scalp that noisy fellow myself," says Artemus, turning over to go to sleep again.

Schell Creek has an open plain in front of it and snow-clad mountains behind it. The creek furnishes water, the sage-brush fuel, while the piñon pine, here growing profusely, supplies the Indian with nearly all the diet he requires. He plucks its nuts in the autumn, and buries them in deep pits for use in winter. Any one anxious to know what their flavor is like, has only to take the kernel of a Brazil-nut, soak it for twenty-four hours in strong turpentine, and then eat it with a little tar for sauce.

While at Austin the idea struck Artemus that it would be funny to have some bills printed to take with us on our journey across the plains, and tack up in the huts of the various station-keepers. To be advertised in such a way across the American continent would be at least a novelty, and the probability was that the men in charge of the stations would preserve them to show to every passing traveller. Artemus dictated the wording of the little bill thus: "A Lecture will be delivered here, in sweet voice, by Artemus Ward, the Wild Humorist of the Plains." The idea of any lecture being delivered in the stations of the

American desert was in itself a farce. No doubt the announcement has caused many a laugh, and possibly some of the bills still remain.

We spend the hour or two after breakfast before the coach starts in posting up these little bills and warming ourselves for the journey by taking a smart walk across the snow-covered plain. Then, with Mr. William Corbit for driver, we start for Spring Valley Station. On arriving there we find the keepers attending to their duties, with their fire-arms, primed and cocked, on the table of their hut. An Indian attack is anticipated. We change our mustangs quickly, and drive away. We shall learn by-and-by that the Indians came two days after we left; that the men who harnessed our mustangs were slain and scalped, and the station was burned to the ground.

At the next station—Antelope Springs—we find the chief of the murderous Gosh-Utes sitting before the hut-keeper's fire. Artemus has picked up a few words of the Shoshonee language in Austin, and attempts to flatter the Indian by telling him that he is "*Tibbets-hansch*" (good-hearted). The chief nods his head, and makes signs that he wants tobacco. We give him some. In lighting his pipe some of the burning tobacco falls among the hair of a dried scalp attached to the chief's girdle. As he brushes it away we notice that the hair is long and beautiful, and we wonder if it is that of a woman.

From Antelope to Deep Creek, through a canyon guarded by lofty rocks, and marked with Indian trails. Thence to Willow Springs, Boyd's Station, Fish Springs, Black Rock, and Dugway. But where is Dugway?

That is our puzzle. "We shall soon be at Dugway," says our driver. His whoops and yells confirm us in that belief. We fancy, too, that we can scent the strong odor of the fried rusty bacon which we know will be our meal. But where is the station? Stretching out before us as far as our sight can range is a vast barren plain. To our left are hills. We see the road on which we have to travel for the next ten miles. Then where is the station?

"Wor—r—r—r—roo!" shrieks the driver; and out of the earth in front of us emerges a man, bringing up with him two horses.

Dugway is dug in the earth. The stables and the sleeping-place of the poor fellow whose doom it is to live here are under the surface of the ground. We might drive over the roof of the stable with ease, though the roof being of boughs and pieces of cedar wood, the wheels might go through. Here, in this subterranean abode, the station-master sleeps on a straw bed, and serves up hot meals for travellers on a black, unplaned table. He is a forlorn-looking man, whose eyes have a continuous stare, whose cheeks are hollow, whose matted hair hangs in elf-locks on his shoulders, whose arms are lank and angular, whose woollen clothing seems not to have been taken off nor known any cleansing process for years, and whose appearance altogether suggests the idea of a man expiating in solitude some fearful crime, and self-banished from society which he feels he has no right to share. We pity him, and express curiosity as to what incidents of earlier life can have brought him to a position so unenviable.

"Murdered his mother, perhaps, on his birthday," whispers one of our fellow-travellers. "I have been told that every murderer who has escaped from Texas and Arizona is to be found along this line of road. And I guess Texas is pretty liberal in keeping up a supply."

Dugway is a sorry specimen of a "station;" but most of the stations are miserable stopping-places, where the only accommodation to be obtained is a wood-fire, some hot coffee without milk or sugar, some coarse bread baked in the hut, and some fried bacon of the strongest flavor. We have fried bacon and coffee for breakfast, coffee and fried bacon for dinner, bacon fried and more coffee for supper. At some places the complaint is that the Company has forgotten to send on any bacon, and we must be satisfied with the coffee and hot bread. If we have brought on any whisky, and give a glass to the station-keeper, he is a happy being. As a rule, the drivers along the road abstain from drinking whisky while driving in winter. They tell us that with hot coffee just before starting on the journey they are much better able to withstand the cold.

For our meals at each station we pay a dollar per head. After a few days of overland travel we feel that we would gladly give twenty dollars for a meal in an American restaurant car, while a refreshment station on the London, Chatham, and Dover Railway, with a Spiers and Pond's buffet on one side, and Smith & Son's newspaper-stall on the other, would be a dream of paradise. But the Pacific Railway will soon extend across the desert, and something better than strong bacon will be obtainable in the neighborhood of Dugway.

From station to station, each from fifteen to eighteen miles apart, day and night, cramped up in our narrow coach, jerked forward, tossed backward, jolted from side to side, tumbled over, thrown out, bruised, battered, and sore all over, irritable through want of sleep, nervous with continuity of excitement, and weary of the cheerless monotony of the scenery, we are too jaded to talk and too drowsy to be convivial. Our driver for one stage of the journey is a Connecticut man, and knows the famous showman Barnum. As we dismount and toil up a mountain with him, the horses going at a slow pace, he tells us two or three anecdotes of Barnum, and presently says, "I guess you should hear him tell the story of the smart minister."

We ask what the story is, and the driver thus narrates it, but with more idiomatic expression:

"I guess it's the darndest story about a minister I ever heard. He was a parson in our old State of Connecticut. His name was Day. He used to pitch it mighty strong in his sermons, till his church got a kinder skeered, and fancied he was going all the wrong way. So they called a grand church meetin' at Middletown, and commanded the minister to appear before them. On his way to the grand meetin' the minister happened on another clergyman, who was the very man who had called the church together to punish Mr. Day. One didn't know the other, for they preached miles apart. I'm dubersome about the name of the old parson, but as the other one's name was Day we will call him Night. He was a hard-hearted man, stiff in the back, and down upon all his brother ministers if he heard any thing against them. He asked Mr. Day for his name. 'My name is Mr. Richard, from Fairfield,' said the minister, for his right name was the Rev. Richard Day, and he was keepin' to the truth. 'Then you know the Rev. Day who lives there?' says the Rev. Night. Mr. Day said he did, and he oughter pretty much, I guess. 'What sort of a minister is he?' asks Mr. Night. Whereupon Mr. Richard, as he calls himself, tells the other minister that Mr. Day is not a man he should like to say any thing against, but he's an all-fired hypocrite, and bad at heart, and don't believe in any thing, and has been caught out in many bad acts. 'Can you tell me one? I want to know one or two,' says the Reverend Night. 'Caught him out more than once kissing my own wife,' says Mr. Richard. 'Horrible! and I believe it of him—I believe any thing of him,' says Mr. Night. 'That's not the worst part of it, but I've caught him at it in my wife's own bedroom.' 'And where was your wife, Mr. Richard?' says the other. 'In bed,' says the minister who was having the fun. 'Quite enough,' says Mr. Night. 'That will do. It's all I wanted. We will soon dispose of Mr. Day at our Church Assembly.' Next day the Assembly of all the ministers met.

They charged Mr. Day with heresy. Up jumps Mr. Night. 'Never mind the heresy,' says he. 'I am in possession of facts against the Rev. Richard Day which will be enough to expel him from our Church. Providence has put the facts in my way. I can prove he has been caught kissing the wife of another minister of our Church in her own bedroom.' "

"Gentlemen," said the driver of the stage, "you can imagine the shindy there was among the ministers. All of them looked straight at Mr. Day, for all of them knew him except Mr. Night. 'Bring your witness into court,' cries the parson. Mr. Night stood up and said, 'I call upon the Rev. Mr. Richard, of Fairfield, to affirm to you the facts upon oath.' Mr. Day never moved, and the Chairman of the Church wanted to know where Mr. Richard was. 'Here he is,' says Mr. Night, stepping straight out and laying his hand slap on Mr. Day's shoulder. 'Here he is. And it was his wife that our erring brother, Mr. Day, kissed.' Gentlemen, you can imagine. The hull [whole] Church burst its sides with laughter. 'That is the Rev. Richard Day,' says the Chairman. The Rev. Night couldn't see the bearings of the case at first, but when he got it all into his wool he wilted [when he understood it, he broke down]. He looked round for the way out, and went off like a streak of lightning. There wasn't any more heresy in the Church after that."*

Our drivers across the desert are all eccentric characters, and each has his stock of quaint stories. Unfortunately we get but few opportunities for conversing with them, shut up as we are within the coach. Nor do we care to roll up the leathern blinds and look out, for the wind is keen, and the land through which we are going is dreary in the extreme. It is a land in which no living thing seems to find a home. For miles after miles the desert is covered with a carpet of alkali, and even the sage-brush and the grease-wood give up their right to the desert and cease to grow.

From Look-out Mountain to Rush Valley, and on to Camp Crittenden, where we arrive an hour before midnight. Here to our surprise we are among ruins, and ruins of any sort are to us curiosities. The camp was once called Camp Floyd, and was then a lively military outpost, consisting of a number of huts built of adobe or sun-dried bricks. Mr.

---

*While these pages are going through the press I learn that Mr. Barnum has recently told this story himself in another form.

Floyd went over to the Southern cause, and loyalty has changed the name of the Camp to that of "Crittenden." The adobe huts are roofless, and the mud-built walls are full of gaps and fissures.

"Thar's no crossing the Jordan till daylight," says our driver. "The river is frozen over. You can take a sleep on the floor in the back office if you like."

At seven in the morning we leave Camp Crittenden and drive on to Jordan Station. Eight miles beyond the station we come to the river, plunging down to it through high banks of snow. The telegraph-posts indicate the route, jutting up as they do above the snowy wilderness. The frozen surface breaks beneath the wheels of our coach, and we ford the stream amidst the splash of water and the crash of breaking ice. By the time we have crossed we are wet and chilly, well-sprinkled as we are with the waters of the Jordan of the Western World.

Across more plains of snow and over snow-covered hills, and we arrive at Rockwell, where we find a well-built adobe-house, with a capital farm-yard adjoining. We are informed that this is the residence of Mr. Porter Rockwell, of whom we have often heard as being one of the chief officers in Brigham Young's *Danite Band*, or secret corps of "Destroying Angels." Artemus, pricked in conscience by the burlesque on the Mormons he wrote a year or two ago, is not desirous to make the acquaintance of a Destroying Angel. He becomes calmer on learning that Mr. Rockwell is not at home, and accepts an invitation from one of Mr. Rockwell's wives to go into the farm-yard and look at two large pigs, the larger of which weighs nine hundredweight. Among other of Mr. Rockwell's characteristics is his fondness for fat swine. Notwithstanding all that we have heard concerning him, we presently come to the conclusion that he must be better than rumor has represented. We find on a chair a copy of the "Times," published in London about seven weeks previously; and we doubt if a man who takes in the "Times," and has the enterprise to bring it into the midst of the American desert, can be altogether unsociable, even though he be a Destroying Angel; and even though, at the command of his Church, he has shot a few sinners who have stood in the way of the "saints."

At Rockwell we dry ourselves after our drenching in the Jordan, and drive on nine miles more through the snow, to a stopping-place called Trader's Rest. Here we find a lone house, in one room of which a sickly-looking woman is cooking dinner for herself and six ill-clad children.

She tells us that her name is Mrs. White; that she came here from Doncaster, in England; that her husband has been dead fifteen months; that she has had thirteen children altogether, and that seven of them are buried here. Her husband, she says, was a Mormon; but she is not. "And I don't want my children to be," says she. "I am going back to Yorkshire as soon as I can get away."

We are thirteen miles from Salt Lake City. As we hasten towards it from Trader's Rest, we pass from the wilderness into a garden. Indications of fertility of soil become apparent on each side, though the time is midwinter, and the ground covered with snow. We drive by neat little farm-houses, cross many small bridges, notice how well fenced in are the several lots of land, and how good the road is, notwithstanding its wintry drawbacks. In front of us and to our right are high mountains. To our left is another range partially shutting in the valley. But the mountains on the left do not join those in the front. There is a great gap between; and, as though the rock-wall of the valley had suddenly opened and the mountains glided back, we see through the open space snowy peaks in the far-off distance. In that gap, and steeping in its waveless brine the bases of those distant mountains, is the Dead Sea of America—the Great Salt Lake of the Mormons.

"Gentlemen, that is Brother Townsend's," says our driver, as he drives past the Salt Lake House where we are going to stop, and proceeds to the office of the Overland Mail Company. "Brother Townsend will take care of you well; but you can't get him to give you any whisky. If you want that, you'll get it at the dry goods store just beyond."

○ **33** ○

Inside the Mormon Hotel

S EE all as if you were not looking, and keep your thoughts to yourself." That was the advice of Captain U——, of the Third Californian Cavalry, an old acquaintance whom I had warned by telegraph of my coming, and who was waiting for me at the Salt Lake House.

"The people in this place," continued the Captain, "will try to be very friendly with you. They will let you see the best side of every thing. If you believe all they tell you, you will go away without knowing any thing about them. They are hospitable because they want to be well reported to the world. They are courteous because they think it to be the right policy to insure your being so courteous in return as to say nothing about them. But they would rather you had staid away; and, if Uncle Sam didn't keep us up there in Camp Douglas to protect you, you might find their hospitality to be a *grave* matter."

Here let me again change the key of my story, resume the past tense, and write of Salt Lake City as Artemus and I became acquainted with it in the early part of 1864.

There are travellers who pack theories in their carpet-bags, and who never travel without a pair of tinted spectacles. They know what they mean to see before they start, and they see it, where nothing is visible to any one else. Being neither politician nor philosopher, I determined to look around me in Salt Lake City simply as a showman, to note what I saw, and not allow myself to be hoodwinked by my brother show-man—Brigham Young and his Mormon elders.

In less than an hour after our arrival we were waited on by a gentle-man who wore a large, rough poncho cloak and a Scotch cap, and whose throat was well wrapped up with a worsted comforter. His manner was bland in the extreme. His step was of a gliding character, suggestive of one who was accustomed to go on delicate missions. He snuffled as he spoke, and announced himself as being the postmaster of the city, and brought some letters from his office for Artemus Ward.

"That is one of the great saints," said Captain U——, drawing me aside. "He is Elder Stenhouse, Brigham Young's confidential friend. He comes to reconnoitre. On guard!—Be wary!"

Elder Stenhouse soon became very chatty, but mingled questions with his information. A Scotchman by birth, the proverbial caution of his race was evident even when he was most communicative. Nothing could exceed his urbanity. To be the means of making us supremely happy during our stay in Utah seemed to be the business to which he had generously devoted himself. He had once been a reporter attached to the staff of the "New York Herald," and did not omit the opportunity of ingratiating himself with Artemus on the ground of being a fellow-professional. Gradually, Elder Stenhouse succeeded in extracting from Artemus a statement of why we had come to Salt Lake, what we proposed to do, what time we intended to stay, and the fears Artemus had of not being well received in consequence of what he had written.

"The President has your book in his library," said Mr. Stenhouse, who always spoke of Brigham Young by his title in the Mormon Church. "He has all the books that have been written about him. You ought not to have made ridicule of our Church."

Artemus explained that he wrote the article under pressure, that he knew little about the Mormons at the time of writing it, that he was sincerely sorry if he had given them pain by what he had written, that he hoped they would allow him to lecture among them, and that if Brigham Young would condone the offense and allow us to see real Mormon life in the Mormon capital, more justice would be done to the "Saints" in future writings.

To all this Elder Stenhouse replied that he would see the Head of the Church on the subject, put the matter in a proper light before him, procure an introduction for Artemus, and, if possible, win him pardon for his offense. When Mr. Stenhouse left, we rejoined the military gentlemen who had welcomed us on our arrival. Artemus remarked to one of them that the postmaster appeared to be a very well-informed man.

"He is about the only educated man among these people," replied one of the officers, confidentially. "He has been a missionary for Brigham Young in England, France, Switzerland, and Italy. He edited the newspaper here, and can write poetry. His wife speaks good French, and is the fashionable milliner."

I remarked that Mr. Stenhouse appeared to be the very soul of courtesy and affability.

"Were he not, he wouldn't do for a spy of Brigham's," replied my informant. "He is the look-out crow for him, who tells him when danger is approaching; and he's Brigham's pump to pump up all his master wants to know. He's smart as a steel trap in his way, and would have your eye-teeth out before you knew he was drawing them."

Artemus observed that the poncho cloak and the general attire of the postmaster gave him the look of an amiable brigand.

"There's a pistol under that cloak; and as for his amiability, it's all very well so long as you don't touch him on Mormonism. He's sold himself body and soul to Brigham, like old Faustus sold himself to the devil.

There isn't a word Brigham would say but what that post-office apostle would swear to."

Our hotel in Salt Lake City was, at the time of our visit, the only one of any importance. I believe that it still retains its superiority, though rival establishments have recently arisen. It stands on Main Street, and is called the Salt Lake House. The present landlord is Colonel Little, a military Mormon. When Artemus and I took up our quarters within it the host was Mr. James Townsend—hotel-keeper, farmer, and missionary.

In 1864 the Salt Lake House was a two-story wooden building, with a covered balcony or gallery in front of the upper story. There was a planked foot-path in front, with wooden posts for idlers to lean against and whittle away. Opposite was a little smithy, and next door was a razor-artist who styled himself, on the showboard in front of his shop. a "Physiological Barber."

Inside the Salt Lake House there were no luxuries, and few conveniences. On the left of the chief entrance was a room with a large stove in the middle of it, a few chairs, and some forms. In this room were always to be found three or four travellers and many loiterers. On the right of the main door-way was another room with a private door opening on the street. It was furnished with two beds, two or three chairs, one small table, and a miniature stove. The walls were of rough wood. There was no carpet, and no attempt at decoration. Bad as it was, it was the best room of the house, and Artemus and I were allowed to be its occupants.

At the back of the hotel was a long room, bare and cheerless in its appearance, with a table down the middle of it, and windows through which you could look out on a yard incumbered with rubbish. This was used as a dining-room, and the kitchen was at the end of it. Overhead were sleeping apartments for travellers, and in contiguity with the dining-room were a number of ill-built outhouses.

Of our landlord, Mr. Townsend, or "Brother Townsend," as Mr. Stenhouse always called him, we saw but little. He was constantly busy attending to his farm or to duties required of him by the Church, and appeared a very quiet, inoffensive, rural-minded kind of man.

Domestic affairs in the hotel were controlled by Mrs. Townsend, a lady much younger than her husband. She was a lively, kindly, gentle, and attentive hostess, who nursed poor Artemus during a season of severe illness with all the care and solicitude of a mother, and whose cheery disposition made sunshine in the shadiest places of that very shady hotel.

We had not long been guests at the Salt Lake House when I learned that our amiable landlady was Mrs. Townsend No. 2. Where was Mrs. Townsend No. 1? I asked for her; was informed that she was living and on the premises, but was never seen in the hotel. Anxious to become acquainted with the social phases of Mormonism, I desired to know more of the hidden wife who never appeared upon the scene. I discovered her in an outhouse behind the hotel, where she lived apart in comfortless seclusion. No. 1 was much older than No. 2, and by no means so presentable. It was hinted to me that her wits were a little wavering, and that she had never thoroughly reconciled herself to the will of the Church that her husband should take unto himself another bride. Here, in the position of this neglected woman, I obtained one glimpse at the working of the Mormon system worth more than a volume of theories.

Let me frankly state, however, that I have no reason for believing that No. 1 was badly treated by No. 2; for so kindly-disposed was the Mrs. Townsend we met daily, that I doubt if she could have behaved harshly to any living creature. It struck me also that the thought at times presented itself to her that, as her predecessor was, she might come to be; and that when No. 3 should be deputed to receive the guests, No. 2 might have to betake herself to an outhouse like to that occupied by No. 1.

There were no female servants attached to the hotel. At Salt Lake, instead of a man engaging many female domestics, he marries many wives. In one of them he finds all the qualifications for a parlor-maid; in another he detects the attributes of an excellent nurse; in a third he perceives the virtues of a laundress; and in a fourth the requirements of a governess competent to attend to the education of the children of all her "sisters"—to use the word by which a Mormon wife refers to those who share with her in the affections of her polygamous husband.

Artemus became accustomed to call Mrs. Townsend our landlord's "best-third." The exile in the outhouse precluded there being any "better-half."

There was a profane merchant resident in the city who used to speak of the wives in the Mormon households as "the numerals," and who puzzled Artemus, shortly after our arrival at Salt Lake, by saying that he had "just met Apostle Benson walking out with his numerals." I believe that Apostle Benson rejoiced in only 1, 2, 3, and 4.

What we lacked in female domestics at the Salt Lake House was made up for in the person of a mysterious old man known as "Thomas." Thomas was the clerk, porter, messenger, acting-manager, chamber-cleaner, and fire-lighter to the establishment. To him we applied for any thing wanted, and from him we obtained our daily information. He was a white-haired old man, born in Devonshire, if I remember rightly, and converted to Mormonism before he left England. Thomas had a shuffling gait, great activity, a habit of always turning up, no matter in what part of the hotel one might happen to be. He had keen old eyes that seemed to be always on the watch, and a peculiarity of carrying his head slightly twisted to one side as if he were continually listening. Thomas waited upon us at table, and glided noiselessly into our room in the early morning to attend to the fire. Though bald-headed and slightly bent with age, he appeared never to tire nor ever to go to sleep. Stay up as late as you pleased, Thomas was inclined to stay up with you. Rise as early as you liked, you found Thomas bustling about the premises. Under the stairs leading to the upper story was a cupboard, and of that cupboard Thomas had the key. In it he kept the candles which he gave out nightly to the guests, and in it he kept also—poked far away out of sight in a corner—the cynosure of the establishment—a bottle of good whisky.

Brigham Young prohibits drinking-bars and billiard-rooms in the territory over which he rules. He considers that neither are good for the much-married community of the "Saints" at Utah. In the Salt Lake House there was no bar, nor any barrels, bottles, or bacchanal belongings exposed to view. Any person selling ardent spirit in the city was liable to a heavy penalty. The maker of this law was the only one permitted to break it; for a few score yards up the street above the Salt Lake House was a place at which *Valley-Tan* could be bought, and Valley-Tan is the Mormon name for home-made whisky, manufactured by Brigham Young at his own distillery, sold by him at a properly appointed office, where it is only to be bought wholesale by those who are permitted to purchase, and who must take it to their own homes for private consumption.

Valley-Tan is not likely to find a large export market. It is the vilest whisky I remember tasting. Worse even than some I once moistened my lips with at Cairo, in Illinois, when, arriving very late at night after a cold and dreary journey on the Illinois Central Railway, I asked a "bar-tender" for a drink to warm me. "Which will you have?" was his question—"Sudden Death," or "Live a Week?" I was bold enough to ask for some Sudden Death. Half a tea-spoonful was enough. Only a sufficient quantity was required to make good the right to the name.

Strong drink was to be had in Salt Lake at the stores of the Gentile merchants, but they gave it away—not sold it. There were various large stores kept by traders who were not Mormons, and in the rear of each was a little "office" where a stimulant was always obtainable after making a purchase in the front shop. You could buy a pick-axe and be treated with a glass of Bourbon, or purchase a pocket-handkerchief and asked to taste "a little old rye." But the black bottle in the back corner of old Thomas's cupboard was a treasure to the thirsty spirits who chanced to travel in Utah. When you had gained the confidence of Thomas he would unlock the cupboard noiselessly, even if the hour was as late as midnight, take out the bottle in a furtive manner, and dole out a drain with cautious charity. What puzzled me for a time was the fact that Thomas would treat a new-comer as liberally as he would a guest of the hotel. But Thomas drank little himself at the time of treating. Whisky made travellers communicative. Thomas listened to what they had to say. No one was afraid of saying any thing to an old man so kind and harmless. They told him why they had come to Salt Lake City, and what their ideas were relative to Mormonism. What did Thomas care? He gave them another dose, and let them talk. When they had done he put away the bottle. Next morning Brigham Young knew all about the latest arrivals at the Salt Lake House: why they came and what they thought. A splendid fellow was old Thomas!

And strange men were many of the guests in that Mormon hotel! Grouped around the stove in the evening would be types of nearly all the conditions of humanity to be met with on the borders of civilization—exemplars of most of the aberrations of social human nature developed in the American wilderness—miners, travelling traders, trappers, hunters, drovers, teamsters, fugitives, and *mauvais sujets* of the roughest kind. To get a place in the circle with them round the fire was not easy without running against the projecting barrel of a revolver or the protruding end of a bowie-knife sheath. A few days before our arrival a man named Jason Luce—a Mormon, by-the-way—had killed a miner of the name of Dunning, by stabbing him in the back with a bowie-knife in front of the door-way of Mr. Townsend's hotel. A Mormon jury tried the murderer, and Mormon soldiers shot him.

Artemus and I would take seats among these strange men round the stove, and listen to their stories of adventure. One evening the group was added to by a tall, gaunt, hollow-cheeked man with long black hair and shaggy eyebrows, whose dress was that of a miner, with a dash of the garb of a brigand thrown in. He wore a dirty sheep-skin over his red shirt, and a fur cap which came down over his eyes. In his belt was a pistol, and slung at his back a gun. He had come down from the Bannock mines, and had brought with him a full verbal report of the hanging of the notorious Jack Gallagher and eleven other men at Bannock City, in Montana, by the Vigilance Committee. Our new arrival was known to many of the men round the stove. They saluted him as "Judge."

"The committee had eighty-three on their black-list," said the judge; "they have hanged twelve. I had notice to leave Bannock within half an hour; I was to be hanged if I was caught within twelve miles of it in two hours after leaving. I got a horse and came away without bringing any thing with me. I rode fifteen hours, then my horse and I cached in the snow [sheltered in a hole]. Next day my horse died, and I was so hungry I had to eat some of him. I've travelled over the mountains, and slept five nights in the snow; both my feet are frost-bitten, and this left ear seems to be turned into leather. What am I to do now? I have got a bad name, and I know they won't let me stay here; I shall have twenty-four hours' notice to clear, and then I must start for Nevada. When I get there I shall have to clear again, and make tracks for California; when I get there they won't have me—I know they won't. I have been hunted out of New Zealand, hunted out of Australia, hunted out of Oregon. I've got the curse of Cain on me. This d—d world won't let me have a corner to myself!"

The "Judge" was right. Orders came that he was to leave Salt Lake City within twenty hours, in the best way he could.

Smoking a black pipe beside the stove in the evening was another eccentric character, whose cheeks were puffy, whose eyes were bleared, and who, though dejected in his manner, was disposed to be chatty and communicative. He was a miner, but not a fortunate one.

"All my ill-luck comes about through my having married a mystery," said he.

He had referred more than once to the cause of his misfortune, when one night he became more informative than usual, and told his story:

"My friend Harry Rickards here knows to the truth of what I say. If I had never married a mystery there would have been no Utah, Idaho, or Montana for me. I never knew which I married."

"But you said just now that she was a mystery," observed one of his companions.

"Yes, *she*—but which she?" he continued. "It was just this way: There were two sisters in our village; one of them loved me considerably, and I loved her pretty much for a time. Her name was Grace; the other one's name was Hester. At last I got to love Hester best, and all of a sudden I made up my mind to marry her. Both were nice girls, very like each other, and they had a rich uncle who had made his pile in the East India trade years ago, and lived out at Salem. It was a dark winter's day when we got married; we joined hands before the minister; my wife spoke so low I could hardly hear what she said, and she would hold down her head and wear a white veil. We were married at my wife's house; when the minister said, 'I pronounce you to be husband and wife,' I supposed I'd married Hester. She bobbed away from me right smart, and I guess I waited for her quite a while. Presently in runs Grace, throws her arms round my neck, kisses me, and says, 'You are my husband now, dear Josh, and I am your wife!' I got scared, and told her she was not right in her calculation, for I had married Hester. Up comes Hester, and tells me I had been a kinder taken in in the matter. Grace wanted me, and she had let Grace have me. I had married Grace, and did not know what I was doing. I asked the minister about it; he told me I ought to know which was my wife. With that I got riled; so I put on my hat and went off like all fury, and as mad as all wrath, to Lawyer Briggs; and I said some very rough things to poor Grace before I went. I told Lawyer Briggs all about it. He went on opening some letters while I talked to him. Presently he threw down his spectacles, stared me in the face, and asked me if I had married Grace? Says I: 'Grace says I have; but I guess my intentions were towards Hester.' Lawyer Briggs whistled, and told me not to be a fool; says he: 'You've done the slickest thing you've ever done in your life. The uncle of the girls has just died over at Salem, and left all his dollars to Grace; if you are her husband, you've married an heiress!' With that I rushed back to the cottage to find Grace. She wouldn't come to me when I called her; when she came she was crumpling up a letter and putting it in her pocket. I told her I had forgiven the trick, and meant to have her for my wife. With that she laughed right in my face, and said they had only been trying to rile me, for it was Hester, after all, I had got myself married to. Says I: 'I guess you can't come that on me: you are my wife, and I don't mean to have any other.' While I was trying to quiet her spirits, Lawyer Briggs rides up to the door like a man all possessed, and draws me aside. Says he: 'I've got another letter from Salem; the first was a mistake; the property is left to Hester, not to Grace.' I felt quite beat; so, 'cute like, I went up to Hester and said I'd take her. She burst out a laughing, and told me not to be a fool; but, as I'd married Grace, to keep to her. Then they all fell to laughing at me. I got into an all-fired rage, ran out of the cottage, went to Boston, drank whisky for a week, then shipped myself down to New Orleans, and here I am out in Utah."

"But you are married to one of those girls, Josh?" suggested the listener to the narrative.

"I guess I am—I guess I am; but it's a mystery. I married a mystery, and it's been my ruin!"

"You should go back to New England and solve the mystery," I ventured to remark.

"I guess I'd better stay where I am," he replied; "I shall make out pretty well up at the Alder Gulch mines, and I'd better not get my brains crazy with any more mysteries."

◦ 34 ◦

The Church in the Theatre and the Theatre in the Church

THE theatre will be open to-night. The play will be 'The Stranger.' Brigham Young will be there with most of his family. You must go." So said one of the cavalry officers to Artemus Ward a few hours after our arrival in Salt Lake City.

Unfortunately poor Artemus was too jaded, travel-worn, and exhausted to avail himself of the opportunity. To me the attraction was powerful enough to overcome my fatigue, and draw me away from a bright fire and an easy-chair.

A theatre in the midst of the wilderness! A theatre in a valley shut in by mountains and surrounded by a thousand square miles of desert! A theatre with Indian savages almost within hail! A theatre near the shores of the great Dead Sea of America! A theatre belonging to a Church—erected, managed, and frequented by "Saints!" Could a showman abstain from going?

"The City of the Saints" is the favorite name for the metropolis of Utah among the Mormons. Its inhabitants manifest no diffidence in arrogating to themselves peculiar holiness. They consider the saintly character to be exclusively their own, and all who are not Mormons are "Gentiles."

Brigham Young, arch-priest and saintliest of the "Saints," built the theatre; to maintain it the Church lends its authority, and to go to the play is a duty in the code of Mormon ethics.

I left Artemus slumbering before the fire; and in the midst of a heavy snow-storm sought my way to the theatre. I found it on the corner of an adjacent street. People were wending their way to it along the middle of the road, for the snow-drift was too deep for them to use the foot-path. There were a few small houses with wooden pales in front of them, and beyond them a large rectangular building, so large as to dwarf every other structure in the neighborhood. The long black side-wall visible through the snow-storm recalled to my recollection the Waterloo Road side of the Victoria Theatre in London as seen from the New Cut. On a nearer inspection I found the building to present few claims to architectural merit externally, though it is but fair to acknowledge that its exterior was then incomplete. The style of architecture was the Doric, with Mormon modifications.

In a small office to the left of the entrance was the money-taker, handing out tickets at a window. I found that admission to the dress-circle was only a dollar. As I paid the amount in a gold coin bright and fresh from the Californian mint, I noticed that the money-taker took stock of me. I returned the compliment, and listened to him whistling the air of "The Groves of Blarney." I was not aware at the time that I was gazing at a bishop!

Internally the theatre presented as incomplete an appearance as the exterior. There was very little attempt at decoration other than that obtainable by the use of white paint and gilding. There was a large pit, or "parquet," as the Americans call it, having a high rake from the orchestra towards the back, thus allowing occupants of seats in the rear to have as good view of the stage as those in front. I counted the pit, and found that there were about eight hundred people in it. The price of admission was seventy-five cents. Over the dress-circle was an upper box tier, the admission to which was fifty cents; and over that again a gallery, to which the charge was twenty-five cents, or about one English shilling.

Some of my cavalry friends undertook to point out the arrangements of the house. They told me that the dress-circle was the part which Gentiles frequented, and that the pit was specially reserved for Mormons, with their families. I noticed that nearly every man in it was accompanied by two, three, or more ladies, and that in some instances an entire family occupied a row, there being only one adult male among the number.

On each side of the proscenium was a private box, on the same plane as the dress-circle. These boxes were fitted up with green curtains. No other drapery was used for decoration elsewhere in the house.

Under the dress-circle to my right, and a little more elevated than the floor of the pit, were a series of seats like pews, running parallel with the side wall of the theatre. Occupying them were fifty-nine women and children, all very plainly dressed, and none of them remarkable for good looks.

"That is the Prophet's Pen," said my Gentile informant, "and those are his wives and daughters. There are more of them in those seats of the parquet where you see the large rocking-chair."

"Whose is that, and why is it there?" I asked.

"That's where the Prophet sits when he is in the bosom of his family. It's a pretty large bosom," remarked the officer, dryly.

"But where is the Prophet himself?"

"That's he. Over in yon proscenium box with the green curtains to it. The lady beside him is his favorite wife—Sister Amelia. Brigham likes to sit up there because he can keep an eye upon his family down below, and see the Gentiles in the dress-circle. He's having a look through his opera-glass at the General just now."

The General referred to was General Connor, the commander of the troops in Camp Douglas. As I was subsequently informed, the General had been stationed in Utah for nearly two years, and during the whole of that time had resolutely refused to have any intercourse with Brigham Young, regarding him in the light of an enemy to the United States, with whom one day he might have to come in conflict. General Connor was a frequent visitor to the theatre, where he was in full view of the Mormon President, but no sign of recognition passed between them.

The *Mrs. Haller* of the evening was Mrs. Irwin, a lady who, under her maiden name of Miss Rainforth, I had seen a few years before on the stage of the Museum in Boston. Mr. Irwin, her husband, enacted the part of *The Stranger*. Both were Gentile "stars," who had come on a professional trip to Utah. Some days after my visit to the theatre, I had an opportunity of spending an evening with them at their private residence, and found them to be loud in their praises of the kindly treatment they had received among the saints. Their eulogies were many, not only of the hospitality they had experienced, but also of the general management of the theatre, and of the courtesy shown to them by all behind the curtain. They were almost the first "stars" who had found their way across the wilderness to play in Brigham Young's Theatre. Since then many actors and actresses of note have appeared on those boards. With the Pacific Railway in full operation there will be few histrionic artistes in the United States who will not take a trip to the Mormons, don the sock and buskin, and use the hare's foot, on the shores of the Great Salt Lake.

I asked who were the other ladies and gentlemen of the company, and received my reply in nearly the following words:

"They are all Mormons—every one of them. The part of *The Baron* is being played by Mr. Caine, the stage-manager. *Countess Wintersen* is Mrs. Clawson, wife of Hiram Clawson, the manager. He has three wives. This lady is No. 2. The part of *Peter* is being played by Mr. Margetts; he is one of their low comedians, a very good fellow. He has three wives also. All their wives learn to play; so that if one gets ill they can easily send on another for the part."

After the play of "The Stranger" came the farcical piece known as "Paddy Miles's Boy." The part of *Henry*, according to the bills, was played by Mr. Sloan. So soon as that gentleman came on the stage I recognized him as being the money-taker to whom I had paid my dollar on entering.

The Mormon President left his box, came down to the pit, and took his seat in the rocking-chair. During the performance of the farce he laughed heartily, and entered into conversation with two or three of his wives. I had been led to expect that in Brigham Young I should find a man of severe aspect, stately presence, and solemn demeanor. My misconceptions were dissipated when, looking at him through an opera-glass, I saw a robust, jolly, pleasant-faced gentleman, with a ruddy complexion, hair of the color of sand, light eyes, the lines of the face curving upward instead of downward, his chest broad, his hands large, his age apparently about sixty; his appearance that of a well-to-do farmer, and his manner cheerful and agreeable as became a man who had forty of his children around him, and I know not how many of his wives. In the early morning I had crossed the Jordan; the waters of the Dead Sea of the West were not far from me. Could time have gone backward with me to patriarchal days, and was it Solomon in modern clothes who sat before me?

So cold was the evening and so chilly the interior of the theatre, that the Prophet, like every body else, was well wrapped up. Nothing in his attire denoted his rank, nor was there any attempt at dress among the members of his household. There was no display of silks and satins. Every one was plainly clad. Most of the ladies wore on the head what in the States is called a "Nubia"—a sort of knitted woollen scarf, with long ends to it. The men were mostly clad in homespun. As I afterwards learned, the policy of the Mormon leader is to discourage the wearing of any articles of attire not manufactured in the Territory. His aim is to make his people independent of the outer world, and with that end in view he has established and owns cotton mills and woollen factories. The Gentile rulers at Salt Lake take care to import novelties and fineries from New York; but Brigham Young has a keen eye and a denunciatory voice for those who indulge in the pomps and vanities of fashion. He once preached a sermon against the use of crinoline. The language he used on that occasion, and the plain, strong, coarse phrases and allusions in which he indulged, have become historical. He characterized the wearing of hoops as a nasty practice, and in denouncing it he used the nastiest language.

No audience could have behaved better than did the one I saw at Salt Lake. There was no whistling in the gallery; no cries of "Now then, catgut!" no stamping of feet, nor vacating seats before the downfall of the curtain. The performers on the stage met with much applause and very deservedly so, for the amateurs were not far behind the professional stars in their knowledge of stage business. Every performer was well dressed for his part. The scenery was good, and there were no mishaps on the part of the stage carpenters. Evidently the rehearsals had been well attended to; there was no laxity of management behind the curtain, and the voice of the prompter was not heard in the land.

"*Panem et circenses!*" cried the old Romans. "Corn and comedies!" cries Brigham Young. He desires that his people shall have food alike for their hunger and their laughter. Hence he disapproves of tragedies, and prefers that comedy and farce should constitute the chief performances at his play-house. Mr. Irwin told me that there were two or three tragic parts he wished to play, but that Brigham Young opposed the pieces being put in rehearsal. Said Mr. Irwin: "Brigham is of opinion that there is grief enough in this world without having it in imitation on the stage." I subsequently learned that the "Lady of Lyons" and the "Marble Heart" were two very favorite dramas among the Mormons, and that the Prophet had no objection to plays in which the crime of adultery is represented as being severely punished, but that he preferred dramas wherein the passion of love is depicted, and the comic and sentimental elements well blended. Considering that Brigham Young "loves not wisely but two hundred well"—to use a joke belonging to poor Artemus—it is not incomprehensible that he should uphold the claims of love to public appreciation. Perish the man who in Utah would decry the tender passion! "*Chi dice mal d'amore, dice la falsità!*"

Digressing from my narrative of what I saw at the theatre on the evening of my first visit, it may not be out of place to refer to the position of the play-house among the institutions of Salt Lake. The theatre is essentially a national concern. It enters into the general system of government—social, moral, and religious. Socially, because all classes visit it; morally, because Brigham Young considers it the best substitute for amusements of a less harmless character; and religiously, because its profits go to the support of what is called "The Church." The performances are advertised from the pulpit, and attendance at the play-house is preached to the people as a portion of their duty. The actresses are for the most part the wives and daughters of church dignitaries. Even the daughters of the Prophet himself occasionally assist in the representations; and Mr. Hiram Clawson, on whom the management devolves, is a son-in-law of Brigham Young.

Mr. Clawson was kind enough to take me over to the theatre a few days after my arrival in the city. Well acquainted with some hundreds of theatres, I do not remember one in which the comfort of the actors is more studied than in the theatre at Salt Lake, nor one where the arrangements for the business of the stage have been more thoughtfully attended to. The wardrobes are extensive, clean, and commodious. There is a capital workshop for the tailors, and equally as good apartments for the dress-makers. The library is nicely arranged, free from dust, and well stocked with plays. The propertyman has excellent accommodations and a large stock of well-made properties. No dressing-rooms could be more convenient, nor any green-room better fitted for its purpose.

Brigham Young is as careful of the comfort of his audiences as he is of that of his actors. The theatre was built under his inspection, and he has taken care that visitors shall not be incommoded. In all his arrangements the fact is apparent that he understands what so many managers in London and elsewhere do not comprehend—that the auditorium of a theatre should be attractive simply for its qualifications as a place in which to sit at ease without being cramped, crushed, or annoyed—that it should be the drawing-room to retire to after dinner. He understands also—and herein he is ahead of many other managers, and anticipates the theatre of the future—that the play-house should be a place for paterfamilias, to which without apology he could fearlessly take all his kith and kin, not an institution depending for its success upon ministering to the tastes of fast young men, nor for its patronage on its advantages as an exhibition-room for marketable beauty. But a place to which human beings with head and brains can go, and feel that they are not degrading themselves by witnessing senseless trash, nor having their patience tested by listening to uneducated and unqualified performers.

The Salt Lake City Theatre is open in winter and closed in summer. If the season of the year admits of agricultural labors being attended to, Brigham Young requires his flock to work. If the weather be ungenial, the shepherd allows his lambs to play. Better, he thinks, that they should laugh than moan; better be histrionic than hypochondriac. If they have no money with which to pay at the doors, they can take their flour or their dried peaches to the "tithing-office" during the day and barter them for tickets of admission to the theatre. At the tithing-office any thing of any value will be accepted—eggs, apples, wool, cabbages, or feathers. During my stay in Salt Lake, I remember a man obtaining entrance to the theatre for half a dozen glass bottles. Let it be borne in mind how many mountain-tops those glass bottles had to be brought over before they arrived in the city, and it will be understood how they grew in value with every mile traversed. Should it be that a newly-arrived immigrant wishes to visit the play-house, that he be poor and have no resources, he may go to the tithing-office and obtain a dozen *coupons* of admission by pledging a portion of his labor during the ensuing summer to assist in building the Great Temple, or by otherwise devoting himself to the service of the Church.

Just as the people can visit the theatre when they have no labor to occupy their time, so the actors can learn new parts and study for the stage when they can not carry on their ordinary occupations. I met an amateur tragedian who owned a saw-mill, and the best low comedian in the city was a blacksmith. The saw-mill tragedian—Mr. Bernard Snow—played *Matthew Elmore*, in the drama of "Love's Sacrifice," one evening during my stay. I have seen the part played much worse on the boards of a large theatre in London. In Great Salt Lake City it is not thought to be derogatory to the highest and holiest lady in the land to play even a subsidiary part on the stage. Three of Brigham Young's daughters posed for the statues of the three Graces in the "Marble Heart;" and I looked in at the theatre one morning when the daughter of an "apostle" was practising for the *rôle* of Columbine.

My first experiences of the Mormon theatre were on a Saturday night. On the morning of Sunday Artemus and I determined on paying a visit to the Great Tabernacle in the hope of hearing Brigham Young preach. As we strolled towards it, we met many Mormon families on their way to the same place. Every one was clad in garments of warm but coarse texture, and there was no display of finery. Half a dozen wives of the same husband walked along lovingly together; their children following after them, hand-in-hand.

On the Mississippi River, far away up, just where the stream leaves the fields of Iowa to fertilize those of Missouri, stands a ruin on a bluff, the only ruin worthy of being so called I saw anywhere in the United States. It is that of the first Temple of the Mormons, destroyed by fire in 1848. Driven from Nauvoo, on the Mississippi, and their lands taken possession of by a party of French Socialists, led by M. Cabet, the Mormons planned the erection of a larger and far more magnificent Temple in their new home at Salt Lake. Whether it will ever be completed is doubtful. In the state in which I saw it, it appeared as much of a ruin as its prototype at Nauvoo. Pending its erection, the services of the church are carried on in what is termed the Tabernacle—a long building with a semi-cylindrical roof, situated within a walled inclosure. Beside it is a singular structure called the Bowery, consisting of a number of poles stuck in the ground, supporting a roof formed of branches of trees, and sheltering a vast space covered with settles and forms. Under the green leaves of the Bowery, with the sunbeams swooping down through their interstices, and the cool breezes from the Sea of Salt blowing in at the sides, the Mormons worship in the summer; during winter they assemble in the Tabernacle.

Snow underfoot and a bright blue sky overhead, Artemus and I found our way to the doors of the sacred edifice. On entering, I noticed an organ to our left, and, looking down the long tunnel-like interior, perceived the pulpit backed by a rostrum, on which were raised seats for the elders. The congregation came in slowly; as they took their seats we had an opportunity of observing their faces and scanning their outward developments. There were very few who arrested attention by attractiveness of feature or intelligence of expression; a single glance was enough to ascertain that none of them could boast of "blue blood," noble birth, gentle nurture, or high intellectual culture. A similar assemblage might be seen at a Methodist meeting-house in a Lancashire manufacturing town, or attending an open-air discourse in the neighborhood of Whitechapel, with the exception that cleanliness reigned supreme, and that no one had ragged attire.

The service commenced by the choir singing a hymn, accompanied by the organ and a small instrumental band. The congregation preserved silence. After the hymn an elder came forward from among the group on the rostrum, advanced to the pulpit or tribune, and prayed an extempore prayer. Then came more singing, more organ, and more band; following on which the presiding elder rose and called on "Brother Sloan" to preach to the people.

Brother Sloan advanced to the pulpit.

"What are you excited about?" whispered Artemus. "Who is that preacher?"

"He?—he's the very man who took my dollar at the door of the theatre last night, and who played in 'Paddy Miles's Boy!'"

° 35 °

Looking Down Upon the Mormons

GREAT Salt Lake City has been described by many recent travellers. Let me endeavor to picture it as seen by a travelling showman. The description shall be brief; the picture shall be sketchy.

Main Street is the great thoroughfare. A traveller looking up it sees that the street gradually ascends towards the base of a high range of mountains. Some few hundred yards up the mountain range is a wooden building—that is the Mormon Arsenal; a few more hundred yards, and there is a flat ridge, forming what geologists term a "bench." Still some hundred yards higher up, and not by any means easily accessible, is a conical hill known as Ensign Peak. On the summit of this peak —according to Mormon history—the ghost of the founder of Mormonism, Joseph Smith, appeared to Brigham Young, and pointed out to him where he was to build the new Temple; to this summit also Brigham Young is said to go up, like a modern Moses to an imitation Sinai, to receive revelations.

To the "bench" below Ensign Peak I wandered some half a dozen times during my stay at Salt Lake. Let me suppose that I am standing on it now, and playing the part of a descriptive guide to a panoramic exhibition; let me also suppose that the reader is beside me.

We are standing in latitude 40° 45′ 44″ N. and longitude 112° 6′ 8″ west of Greenwich. It is as well to know exactly where we do stand in the world. Would you like to know how high we are up in it—somewhere about 4500 feet above the sea-level. We are looking to the south; there is no reason to dread a cold blast from the north, for we are screened by a wall of mountains from three to four thousand feet in height. The mountains form a portion of the Wahsatch Range, and you will observe that they extend round to the east on our left, rising in higher peaks and mantled in robes of snow. There are mountains in the distance to the south—the Traverse Mountains; and there is another high range, the Oquirrh, on our right. Beneath us is the Valley of Salt

Lake; and immediately at our feet, on rising ground, and at the northern end of the valley, is the Jerusalem of the new faith—the City of
the Great Salt Lake.

But where is the Lake? Streets and gardens are below us, beyond
them are cultivated fields. Precisely so. It is a common mistake to suppose that the city is built along the water's edge, like our English
Brighton beside the sea; or, like Chicago, on the southern shore of Lake
Michigan. Look beyond the city, and winding across the valley you will
see a line of light. That is the River Jordan, flowing from Lake Utah—
the American Sea of Tiberias, to the Dead Sea of the West. You will
observe that the Oquirrh Range on our right terminates abruptly, and
that between it and the spur of the Wahsatch, which forms the wall
behind us, there is a wide opening. Look in that direction, and about
fifteen miles from where we stand you will see the Great Salt Lake. The
mountains you dimly see rising in the middle of it are on Antelope
Island. The lake is about fifty miles wide and one hundred miles long.

Now let us look down upon the city. If you have travelled in classic
lands, you will probably notice how much this city resembles some you
have seen in the East; a few mosques here and there would make the
resemblance perfect. The houses, as you perceive, are of a uniform drab tint
—shall we say mouse-color? They are built of sun-dried, unburnt brick.
Nearly every house is in a garden; the streets are laid out rectangu-
larly, and flowing through every street is a stream of bright fresh water.

The wide thoroughfare immediately before us is Main Street—or
"Whisky Street," as it is jokingly called, and as it was referred to in a
sermon by Brigham Young, when he elegantly said: "The stinking
lawyer lives down in Whisky Street, and for five dollars would attempt
to make a lie into a truth." Main Street, you perceive, is very wide, and
differs from the other streets in not having trees on each side; in the
houses being larger, and each house adjoining the next, instead of having a garden space between. On the left of the road are telegraph posts;
in the middle of it are many bullock-drays, and on the broad footpath
Mormons and Gentiles pass each other on their way to business or
pleasure.

Nearest to where we stand, and on the eastern side of Main Street, is
an inclosure within which is one large house and other smaller ones.
That is the residence of Brother Heber C. Kimball, one of the three
Presidents of the Mormon Church. He is the most polygamous of Mor-

mons, and keeps within that inclosure about ninety wives. In the pulpit
he has called them his "cows," and, regarding them from a zoological
point of view, he divides them into classes and genera in separate
houses, just as in a menagerie the feline races are separated from the
ruminatia, and the deer are kept apart from the dogs.

Beyond Brother Kimball's house is a much larger inclosure containing many buildings, one of which has an imitation bee-hive on the top
of it. The stone wall surrounding the inclosed space shuts in the residence, seraglio, and offices of President Brigham Young. On the next
corner, proceeding down Main Street, is the home of the third President
of the Church, and commander-in-chief of the saints militant, Brother
Wells. Still further down is the telegraph-office; beyond that some large
stores occupied by Gentile traders; and farther still the Salt Lake
House, where travellers are entertained.

Taking the other side of the thoroughfare, we see the vast space
within which are the foundations of the new Temple. At the corner of
the next street we notice a square dark building, containing the apartments of the Territorial Legislature, the Territorial Library, and other
offices. That squat building beyond, with the gable roof to it, is the
post-office; and farther down is a wooden store wherein the quarter-
master of the United States cavalry transacts his business. Then come
some large, well-built stores occupied by Gentile traders, and a row of
smaller shops stocked with provisions, articles of hardware, and all the
thousand-and-one things which a storekeeper "out West" provides for
the choice of his purchasers.

Look down upon the whole scene and take it in at a glance—no
towers, no spires, no minarets, and no domes, except the tin one on the
court-house. The city divided into squares, the houses what in England
we would term "villa residences," the garden round each house well
planted with fruit-trees, the streets wide, the general appearance that
of prosperity and comfort.

Now raise the head and look round. Mountains seem to encircle you,
except where the Salt Lake extends in dreary solitude. On another
"bench," or step of the mountains away to your left, you may discern a
flag-staff, attached to which waves the striped and starry banner of the
United States. Around the flag-staff are huts, tents, and wooden houses.
They constitute Camp Douglas, where the great guns of Uncle Sam are
ranged in order, with their muzzles pointing towards the palace of the

Mormon President, constantly informing Brigham Young with signifi-
cant dumb-show that, though he is chief of the Mormons, he must be a
law-abiding citizen of the American Union.

We are looking at the scene in winter. The ground is white with snow,
the trees leafless, and the mountain-peaks stern in their stately coldness
and icy splendor; but let the summer come and the flowers bloom; let
the sun shed a rose-tint on the mountains, a golden glow upon the
fields, and this glorious valley will seem to him who looks upon it, from
where we stand, to be a garden of enchantment—a glimpse of fairy land
—a realization of Paradise; so fertile are the plains, so luxuriant the
vegetation, so green the trees, so abundant the fruit, so bright the
streams, so blue the sky, and so magnificent the scenery.

And this is the Canaan which the Mormons found! No wonder they
think that inspiration discovered the place, and that Providence led
them across the wilderness to its happy valleys; no wonder that they,
in their simplicity, believe their spiritual rulers, who tell them that an
angel came to Brigham Young in the night and revealed to him the land
wherein to dwell, and the spot whereon to build a Temple. Whoever
will take the trouble to investigate, will find that as Joshua sent out the
spies from Shittim to the land where Rahab dwelt, so Brigham Young
was discreet enough to send explorers from Nauvoo to the home of the
Indian Utes, in the Valley of the Great Salt Lake of Utah.

The Mormons will tell you that an angel had to do with the discovery
of the Book of Mormon. Unfortunately for them, there are persons still
living who know the facts of its having been written by an eccentric
clergyman named Spalding, and left in a Pittsburg printing-office. The
"Saints" will also assure you that an angel revealed Utah, and that
another angel proclaimed the privilege of polygamy. If you think the
statements to be inconsistent with what you know of the natural history of angels, they will try to annihilate your objections at one blow
by asking you what but a miracle could have made them the community they are, and what but a miracle could have rendered the Valley
of Salt Lake the Eden that it is?

Both questions admit of easy replies. As Napoleon III. has been to
modern France, so has Brigham Young been to the Mormon community. In the shrewdness, cleverness, and strong will of one man is the
miracle of Mormon prosperity. In the natural fertility of the soil, the
advantages of climate and of situation, is the miracle of the flourishing

city. Not one whit more miraculous in its growth than Chicago, whose immense warehouses are built where fifty years ago the prairie-grass grew; not one jot more marvellous in its history than that of the beautiful metropolis of California; not one touch more prodigious are its antecedents than are those of the great city of Melbourne, at the other end of the world, whose palatial buildings stand on ground for which John Batman traded with the Australian blacks no longer ago than 1835.

A city at one end of a valley surrounded by mountains—a city four thousand feet above the level of the sea—the streets broad, and lined with acacia-trees—the houses of unburnt clay, each nestling in an orchard where the peach ripens and apples hang thick upon the boughs—fields away beyond the streets, luxuriant with crops of golden maize—innumerable streams of sparkling water, and over all a cloudless, sunlit sky. Shut your eyes, paint the picture with your imagination, and you see where the "Latter-day Saints" dwell in their sequestered American Zion.

Externally this city beside the Dead Sea of the West is fair and fascinating. Does it want a symbol? Pass to the Dead Sea of Asia, and find on its shores one of those apples so tempting in their outward beauty —so full of dust and unsavoriness within.

∾ 36 ∾

Prisoners in Salt Lake City

YOU can marry your grandmother here; that's one advantage." So spoke Mr. W——, Gentile storekeeper, and real good fellow of Salt Lake City.

"Surely you do not mean to say that any Mormon would contract such a marriage?"

"Well, I guess a Mormon would marry any thing that wore a petticoat," replied Mr. W. "At any rate, that holy saint who has just passed out along with Mr. Stenhouse has three wives. He has married his first wife's daughter and his first wife's mother. He wished to have all the family home with him, so he got 'sealed' to the grandmother, the mother, and the daughter, and is husband to them all."

Artemus listened with a grave face to this statement, doubting, as I did, its truth. We questioned our informant more closely, and were assured that he had told us facts. Then we sought Mrs. Townsend, and, on addressing inquiries to her, became satisfied that we had not been misinformed. With some coaxing we induced her to talk on the subject of polygamy. She found much to say in its favor, finishing up by putting the question:

"Why should not a man be able to love two wives?"

Artemus replied that he suspected the heart had something to do with loving, and among his acquaintance he did not know a man who had two hearts.

"God loves all," she naively remarked.

We venture to observe that man is not a god.

"But man is a part of God," she continued. "And when a man belongs to the Church the image of God is in him. He loses his selfishness, becomes like God, and can love many. Those to whom he is sealed on earth will be his family in heaven."

Our interesting conversation was brought to a close suddenly, by Mr. Hiram Clawson coming in to say that President Young was willing to forgive Artemus for having satirized the Mormons, and to consent to his being introduced; that he was waiting in his office, and that it would be advisable to lose no time in calling upon him.

A long wall of rubble masonry, strengthened here and there with circular buttresses or towers; inside the wall a large house, with a stone lion in front of it, next to that a small office, next to that a larger one, and beyond that, again, a large building with a bee-hive on top of it. Such is the outward appearance of the palace of Brigham Young. In the house with the bee-hive he boards, lodges, and finds employment for his many wives; in the house with the lion to it he lives with her he loves best for the time. In the smaller of the two offices he receives visitors, and transacts business with the outer world.

Ridicule is almost too long a lance for fanaticism to parry successfully. Brigham Young, conscious of this fact, smarting under the wounds Artemus had already inflicted, and desirous of getting him to lay the lance in rest for the future, was peculiarly affable, gracious, and conversational. Artemus told him his object in coming to Salt Lake was simply to deliver his lecture as he had done elsewhere, and to engage the theatre for the purpose by paying rent for it, just as he would do with any other theatre or public hall. Brigham took some time to consider, and finally decided that he preferred to share the receipts rather than let the house; or that perhaps he would give the use of it gratuitously.

Brigham can be gracious, bland, and softspoken; but the impression he produces is not that of his being a man of large heart and strong sympathy. Volition, not feeling; persistency of purpose, not conciliative suavity; intense self-respect, but little or no benignity, are the characteristics which declare themselves in those cold light-gray eyes, and those hard, firmly-set lips. Some American has written of him that he has no "magnetism." If by that is meant that he does not cause you to love him at first sight, I understand the phrase; but it surely can not mean that he does not impress a stranger, nor that he fails to leave on the mind of whoever has been in his company the feeling of having talked with a remarkable man.

It may be asked how it is, if Brigham does not cause love at first sight, that he has so many wives? The answer is simple: The ladies of Utah love him as being the supreme head of their Church. I believe that in the first instance—no matter what phase it may have afterwards assumed—that the love of each wife was one of veneration, if not of adoration. The Mormon faith teaches that the Church on earth is but a faint counterpart of what will be the social condition in heaven. According to the position of a man in the Church here, so will be his standing in the Church above; and that all who belong to him in this world, if they maintain their allegiance, will share with him in whatever he may enjoy hereafter. Being president in this life, Brigham will be a god in the life to come. Just as Jupiter, in addition to Juno, could pay attention to Semele, Maia, Dione, Mnemosyne, and Latona, so Mr. Young is to be surrounded with sisters Lucy, Clara, Amelia, Zina, Margaret, and Eliza.

But where are those wives now, and how do they spend their time?

These were the questions which both Artemus and I wished to put to the Mormon president, but politeness forbade. More than once we wandered round the outside of the palace, and endeavored to get some glimpse of the ladies of the household. Subsequently we became introduced to many of them; but all that we could learn during the first few days of our stay was that Brigham had more than forty wives living in the Bee House, that they each had apartments similarly fitted up and furnished alike; that they were all compelled to be industrious, and that whatever articles they made more than were required for use on the premises were sold for the benefit of the Church.

That word "Church" perplexed us; its precise signification took us some time to understand. We knew that the people paid a tenth of every thing for the support of the "Church;" we were told that the theatre was conducted for the benefit of the "Church," and we were led to believe that all the riches of Utah converged in ceaselessly-flowing streams towards the great ocean of the "Church." Yet the bishops were all working-men—carpenters, tinkers, and such like; the Tabernacle was any thing but a gorgeous edifice, and the building of the new Temple was progressing very slowly. After a time we became enlightened. By the term "Church" is meant Brigham Young. We found that he represents the "Church" financially as well as spiritually; and that, being the foundation of all goodness, he also reserved to himself the right of being the reservoir of all riches. We were told that his wealth is enormous; that he invests his money in England and in France; that he is a speculator in European stocks, and that he shrewdly perceives how little difference there is between the two words—Mormon and Mammon.

"When one of these people becomes rich and discontented with his life here, I suppose he can manage to get away?" said I, inquiringly, to an acquaintance in the city.

"He can get away," was the reply, "but he can't take his money. Brigham is the only banker, all have to bank with him; and if they want to draw out their money, he must know what they are going to do with it."

"Some of the Mormon traders must be very wealthy?" I remarked.

"Yes; but when they are getting too rich, Brigham interferes and sends them on a mission to go and convert the heathen ten thousand miles away."

"Do they take their money with them?"

"No more of it than he allows. Perhaps they will never come back; if so, the 'Church' falls into luck."

"But their wives—do they take them with them?"

"Certainly not. The Church assigns them over to some of the brethren to be cherished during the husband's absence. Sometimes the Church wants to take care of them, and finds a mission for the husband as far off as New Zealand, or in some of the islands where there are healthy cannibals."

Our intention on arriving in Salt Lake City was to stay for a few days only; unfortunately Artemus became seriously ill, his lecture had to be postponed, and our visit was prolonged to many weeks.

Never shall I forget those weeks of anxiety and suspense. When my friend became indisposed, I endeavored to procure medical advice. The only doctor I could hear of in the city was a botanical one, in whose quackery I had no confidence.

"The saints get cured by laying on of hands," said a gentleman to whom I applied for aid. I had no faith in such mode of treatment. My belief was in quinine and calomel, if I could get them. There was a drug-shop just below the Salt Lake House. I went there and asked for quinine. None was to be had, nor had the proprietor any calomel; some one had bought the calomel bottle and taken it to the Bannack mines. Artemus showed symptoms of typhoid fever, and the case was urgent. I remembered the cavalry camp up in the mountains, and knew that it had a military doctor. I rode to the camp without delay. Dr. Williamson understood the condition of the patient immediately, and took medicine with him in starting for the city. On our way I told him that I had a sore throat.

"Take quinine," said he; "the altitude of this city affects the atmosphere. The rarefied air and the cold weather bring about a fever; sore throat is one of the first symptoms. Quinine is the thing to stop it; take some, or you will be down beside Mr. Ward."

Quinine and I became very friendly.

Artemus grew worse. Dr. Williamson looked grave. Leaving the bedside of his patient one evening, he said to me, "When that delirium quits him you had better say a few words to him about how he wishes to dispose of his affairs."

The first wife of any Mormon husband who had just married his twenty-second bride was not more wretched than I was when the doctor had left. In the rear of the room which we inhabited was a sort of yard devoted to boxes and old lumber. In it was a long box which had been pointed out to me as being "Jake Gooding's coffin." I was told that Jake Gooding had been an important personage in connection with the stage company, that he had died on the road, and that his body had been brought on in this roughly-constructed shell. More than once before I had looked at it in dreary anticipation, and now I made up my mind that it would have to be used for poor Artemus.

What was I to do with the body? I could not commit it to the earth in Salt Lake City, and go home without it. Could I take it on with me, slung beneath the coach?

Leaving the patient tossing his arms about wildly and muttering incoherent nonsense, I sought Mr. Stein, the agent of the Overland Stage Company, found him at his office, told him my distress, and requested to know in what way, should occasion require it, I could transport the remains of the Genial Showman to the Missouri River.

"We could not send them on by the stage," replied Mr. Stein. "The last time we sent on the body of one of our people, the wolves smelt it and attacked the mules. Our orders are never to send on another."

Miserable before, I was doubly miserable now. As I walked out of the stage-office into the deep snow, saw the white spectre-like mountains glaring at me on all sides, and remembered that between me and civilization were the barriers of the Rocky Mountains and a thousand miles of dreary desert and desolate plain, I felt the completeness of my isolation. I was the most forlorn, sad-hearted man in all Utah. I looked in at Artemus; he was still muttering, and Mrs. Battershall, the old English nurse whom we had been fortunate enough to find to attend upon him, shook her head dolefully as I re-closed the door and mechanically strayed into the street to brood moodily amidst the snow.

About four o'clock in the morning I noticed a favorable change in the patient. About seven Dr. Williamson came on horseback.

The doctor's face brightened as he stood by the bedside. "He's better," said he; "we shall have to take care of him and nurse him. He must not cheat us out of that lecture."

Careful was the nursing and worthy of all praise the nurses. The old woman we had engaged attended to her duties in a motherly manner; Mrs. Townsend, our Mormon landlady, was the very soul of human kindness; and there was a strong; stout-limbed, burly farmer of Sacramento, by name Jerome Davis, who had been our companion for a short portion of our journey, and who, having taken a fancy to Artemus, became the gentlest and most devoted of nurses. No sister could have been more kindly in manner, nor the most affectionate of brothers more assiduous in his attention. Rough-looking and ponderous in his outward appearance, the Sacramento farmer had the heart of a woman, and a sympathetic manner indicative of the tenderest feeling.

Let me also add that the Mormons were Samaritans to Artemus. Brigham Young commissioned Mr. Stenhouse to call frequently, and sent presents of dried fruit and wine from his private stores. As the patient grew better and became able to receive company, we had visits from many of the celebrities of Utah. Late one evening came a strange-looking personage, wearing large jack-boots and leathern leggings, having a thick muffler round his neck, his face very red, and the hair at the back of his head plaited and tied up with a piece of black ribbon. He introduced himself as Mr. Porter Rockwell, sat down by the bedside, and conversed pleasantly for half an hour. While he was talking I noticed Artemus surveying him carefully. When he left the room Artemus said:

"I am glad you were here. Did you see if he had any pistols?"

I replied that I thought the gentleman was armed.

"He's the great Destroying Angel," continued Artemus; "the chief of the gang who used to put people out of the way when Brigham wished them to be got rid of. They say that he has shot eighteen men at least. He's a cheerful angel to call on a sick man! Did you see he wanted to hand me my physic? No, don't you give it me; throw it away! He may have put some poison in it."

Ugly as are the stories told about Mr. Rockwell, no man could have expressed himself more kindly, nor have exerted himself more to enliven an invalid by pleasant talk and ludicrous anecdotes. During our stay in Salt Lake, I had an opportunity of meeting Mr. Bill Hickman, another of the small party of gentlemen who, according to Gentile report, constituted the Danite Band, or secret corps of Destroying Angels, whose business it was to silence the enemies of the Church. Neither Mr. Hickman nor Mr. Rockwell looked like a bravo of Venice. Neither of them wore a long cloak, nor a broad-brim cap, nor spoke in a deep voice, nor was often seen before breakfast sharpening his stiletto on a door-step. Both have had some rough jobs to do in their time, or else they are the most maligned men in Utah; but, for all that, they are good Churchmen, and just the sort of gentlemen you would offer cigars to and sit down with—at a proper distance—while they told you a few good stories of how they had roughed it in the wilderness.

Gradually Artemus grew stronger. General Connor sent him Champagne, and Brigham Young contributed some home-made wine of very pleasant flavor. The Mormon ladies brought offerings of eggs, dried

peaches, jellies, jams, and sweetmeats innumerable; but the great restorative—the food which the weak stomach most thoroughly enjoyed
—was discovered by the kindly Californian farmer, who, in ransacking
a neighboring draper's store, had found among the calicoes and stuff
dresses a dozen cans of oysters brought from Baltimore—a two-
thousand mile journey over the Rocky Mountains.

"Get out the bills for the lecture," said Artemus, after the first meal
of stewed oysters; "see Mr. Clawson, and arrange for the date. The
show is safe enough, now we've got an oyster basis."

❧ 37 ❧

Among the Ladies of Salt Lake

Y OU should go to-night and hear the low-comedy bishop," said
Captain U——. We had heard much of Bishop Woolley, and had been
assured that the Mormon Church owned no ecclesiastic more amusing.
He was bishop of the Thirteenth Ward.

With wisdom characteristic of the sagacity of Brigham Young, Salt
Lake City is subdivided into wards. At the time of our visit these wards
were twenty-one in number. Each ward is about forty rods square, has
its own fence around it, its own hall for preaching, and its own bishop.

The duties of a Salt Lake bishop consist in attending to the temporal
as well as the spiritual necessities of the inhabitants of his ward. He
has to know every one individually; to see how each acts up to his
faith, and how far the poorer ones are able to sustain themselves. Some
of these are recent immigrants who have not acquired riches. In winter
they will want flour for bread and wood for firing. The bishop has to
see that their wants are supplied. If any are unwell, he must use the
influences of the Church in curing them; if any are in trouble, he must
relieve them if he can. The heaven that he pictures in his Sunday
sermon he must endeavor to anticipate in his week-day work.

Besides being careful of his flock, the bishop must attend to his own
temporal welfare. He must look after his corn-mill, keep his wagons in

good repair, see that his farm is in flourishing condition, that his carpentry-work is not neglected, nor his smithy without the sound of the hammer. As a matter of course, he finds a felt cap to be more convenient than a mitre, and a two-foot rule more handy than a crozier.

Travellers may think as they please about Brigham Young; but whatever faults he may possess, he must be allowed by all to be a great organizer. The poorest man in Salt Lake is a son of the Church, to whom the bishop must act as a father. Through the bishop there is a ready avenue to the president. Every unit in the Mormon integer feels that he is a part of the great whole—that his Church and he are one. Churches elsewhere would be better were they as utilitarian.

With some of our military friends leading the way, we went on Sunday evening to hear the "low-comedy bishop." His church, or rather great school-room was crowded. The congregation was chiefly composed of females. The bishop had a small desk to preach from. To the left of it were seats specially reserved for occasional visitors; and as Salt Lake City was just then very full of travellers and Gentiles, those seats were pretty well filled.

Bishop Woolley was dressed plain homespun, with nothing about him to denote episcopal rank. A hymn was being sung as we entered. When we took our seats the bishop turned his face towards us and winked. He had a broad face, thick lips, and mirthful eyes.

The discourse was an exhortation rather than a sermon. It was mainly addressed to the younger portion of the female congregation.

Said the bishop: "Our city is very full of Gentiles. They talk to you, and you will talk with them. I can not help your talking to them. I guess talking is pretty safe if you keep a yard of daylight between your lips and their ears. You ask me how you are to behave to them. Well, I have told you before. I tell you again. Treat them courteously, treat them kindly, but not lovingly—mind that! If you do, you know what will happen. It will be no use your coming to me with a baby in your arms, and asking me what you are to do *then!*"

Bishop Woolley looked threateningly stern at the young ladies as he spoke. Then, turning round, he closed his left eye at the group of Gentiles, among which Artemus and I sat, smiled knowingly, and told us, by gesture, as plainly as if he had spoken loudly, that he thought he had done something towards destroying the prospects of any gay Lothario among us.

In the proneness of the young ladies of Utah to listen to the seductive voice of a fascinating young Gentile is one of Brigham Young's great sources of tribulation. The youthful belles of Salt Lake are not disposed to regard the soldiers of Camp Douglas with that aversion and contempt the Mormon President would like to see them manifest; and the soldiers are not inclined merely to flirt with the daughters of the Saints. In many instances they take them off to the camp and marry them. In other instances a Mormon wife, discontented with being married to a man whose wives are numerous, will charitably resign her share of his attentions in favor of her "sisters," and betake herself to the care of the military, trusting to finding in some son of Mars a husband with an undivided heart. Nothing vexes poor Brigham more than this defection of the female members of his flock, and the predatory raids on the sisterhood of Utah made by the soldiers of the United States. He stated, during the time of our visit, that he had no objection to see the Stars and Stripes waving from an encampment overlooking the city, provided the military gentlemen would abstain from making love to the daughters of the Church. It troubles Mr. Young to lose property so valuable as pretty young women, and it annoys him still more that any Mormon girl should bring scandal on her faith by allying herself with an anathematized Gentile.

Are the Mormon ladies contented? Not once nor twice, but a thousand times over, were Artemus and I asked that question on our return from Utah. I know of none better able to answer the question than the officers of Camp Douglas. They will tell you how many are the applications to them from Mormon wives asking for protection and safe-conduct out of the territory; they will tell you how many daughters of Mormons, dreading the future if remaining in the faith, flee to the military settlement as their best means of escape. I applied to the wife of an officer for information. She had resided some time at the camp, had been much in the city, and her accomplishments and beauty had caused her to make many acquaintances. I asked her what her experiences of the Mormon women were, and whether they were thoroughly contented with their position.

"Indeed not," she replied. "The more fanatical train themselves to obedience and contentment, the timid ones are afraid to say that they are unhappy, and the last new favorites are very well disposed to be pleased; but I know many who are very miserable, and who would be glad to get away. They are afraid to disclose their unhappiness to strangers, and I believe that they are punished if they are known to do so."

Yet, as these pages go to press, a petition is presented to the National Legislature at Washington, signed by three thousand ladies of Utah, and praying that the institution of polygamy may be allowed to continue. This petition would have some weight were it not that in every large religious community there are a certain number of enthusiasts slightly tinged with monomania, and were it not that a Mormon lady is not a free agent, but must do as her lord desires. The Church can say, "Sign that paper!" and the wives of bishops and apostles, whom faith has assured of future bliss if they obey their husbands, will sign meekly in obedience to the mandate.

As a contrast to the memorial of the ladies of Utah to Congress, let me record the facts that in the autumn of 1864 two companies of soldiers who left the Mormon territory for California took with them twenty-five wives escaped from the households of the "saints;" but in 1856—according to the authority of Mr. Bowles, who accompanied the present Speaker of the House of Representatives to Utah Territory —there were more than fifty women in Camp Douglas who had fled from the town for protection, or who had been induced to leave "unhappy homes and fractional husbands." In his letters from Salt Lake to the "Springfield Republican," Mr. Bowles says: "Only to-day a man with three daughters living in the city applied to Colonel George for leave to move up to the camp for a residence, in order, as he said, to save his children from polygamy, into which the bishops and elders of the Church were urging them."

It has cost the Church much money to bring many of those young ladies across the plains. They are valuable goods and chattels. Besides, according to ecclesiastical decrees, the Church has the first right to make a selection from the number, and the harems of the priestly dignitaries are entitled to be replenished before the right to choose passes to the brethren. That any presumptuous Gentile should interfere is therefore sacrilege, and in the days when Destroying Angels were free to roam it would never have been permitted. If Brigham could annihilate those lady-stealing soldiers he would do so, and his army of volunteers is large. Every Mormon is trained to use a musket. Brother Wells is head of the War Department of the saints; and the Prophet's son, Joseph

Young, who is also in command, looks a lusty and a doughty warrior. They will have to fight some day. Said Major Gallagher to me at Camp Douglas: "We have some guns up here in camp that would knock old Brigham's house about his ears in no time. He knows it, and he knows the General would like to try their range. If he didn't know it, there would be an outbreak some fine morning."

Artemus had recovered from his illness, and was desirous of seeing life in Salt Lake. We were discussing the best means of seeing it when we received an invitation to "The Apostles' Ball."

Social Hall is the Willis's Rooms of Salt Lake City. The ball was to be given there; Brigham Young was to be present, and all the apostles were to dance. An invitation to so great a treat was not to be lightly regarded. To go was a duty. Down with the man who would not tread the steps of an apostle!

Dancing dervishes we know of—King David is recorded to have danced; but fancy Mohammed and the Holy Ones of Islam dancing! Fancy Confucius or Buddha sporting the fantastic toe! Yet in Salt Lake City the "saints" dance, the bishops *chassez* and turn partners, the apostles excell in the ladies' chain, and Brigham Young understands the business of the ball-room as if he were a Baron Nathan, or an "M. C." at Almack's in the days of its glory.

The Head of the Church introduced Artemus to the company generally, from an elevation at the end of the hall. Then came the introduction to a dozen of Brigham's wives, who were presented separately as "Sister Jane," "Sister Eliza," "Sister Zina," and so on; then there were the presentations to the wives of the Prophet's sons, and those of his son-in-law, Mr. Clawson. The wives of the apostles followed in due course. The ball opened with a quadrille, in which Brigham Young acquitted himself with stately splendor, as became his position. The ladies were all nicely dressed, not in expensive silks and satins, but most of them in muslins, very tastefully made up. There were no circular dances. Quadrilles and cotillons are believed by the Mormons to be conducive to holiness, but the waltz is supposed to cause a lapse from the true faith.

Two of the Prophet's wives were very pretty; and some of his daughters would have graced with their good looks a London ball-room. One part of the arrangement was very characteristic—there were many more ladies than gentlemen, and an apostle could conveniently form top, bottom, and side couples out of the circle of ladies belonging to his own establishment, to each of which ladies he had given his hand and a decimal portion of his heart.

We were invited to another ball at a private house, where there were thirty-nine ladies and seven gentlemen only. During the evening I had ample opportunity of studying female character among the Mormon community. I came to the conclusion that the young ladies were not very well educated; that they were like children in their docility; and that if a dozen young Gentile gentlemen had driven sleighs up to the door, joined the company for an hour, and then proposed that a dozen of the young ladies should select partners and elope from Utah that very night, there would have been no difficulty in effecting a satisfactory arrangement.

Artemus and I were anxious to see the homelife of a Mormon family. We received three or four very kindly invitations, were introduced to the wives of Mormons who were "much married," and on two or three occasions took tea with the mothers and children as though we were familiar acquaintances. I must candidly admit that the homes of those we visited appeared to be happy ones; that in every instance we found all the external indications of domestic comfort; and that two houses were especially noticeable for the elegance of their internal arrangements. One was that of a gentleman who formerly lived at Bayswater, in London, who had settled in business at Salt Lake; was married to three wives had a piano which he had brought all the way from London across the Rocky Mountains, and furniture imported from Paris. His three wives waited upon us during the evening, and exhibited amiable rivalry in trying to see who could be most courteously attentive. Few of the Mormons have more than three or four wives. We were told of one singularly-constructed household, wherein there was contentment all the year round except during one month—the head of the family was married to thirty helpmates, and there was a fight among the ladies every February.

Going to balls and private parties was very good advertising for the lecture Artemus was about to deliver. Brigham Young did his best to render the lecture a success, and the Mormon ladies were anxious to hear a man who was reported to have said naughty things about manners and customs at Salt Lake.

On Monday evening, February 8, 1864, Artemus told his story of "The Babes in the Wood" at the theatre. There was a large audience, but the price of admission was low, and many of the chief saints were admitted free. The receipts amounted to no more than four hundred and ninety dollars. The Prophet seemed to appreciate the lecture thoroughly, and the more intelligent of the audience took the jokes with hilarious satisfaction; but in the pit there were many faces—especially among the females—which by their stolid seriousness plainly indicated that the fun was foreign to the listener, and that Salt Lake City would not be paradise to a professional joker.

With the delivery of the lecture, and what we had seen of Mormon life, our mission was accomplished. We prolonged our stay a few days for Artemus to gain strength for the long journey before us, and then took the coach for our trip over the mountains to Denver, in Colorado, and thence across the plains to the Missouri. As the coach ascended to the mouth of the rocky pass by which we were to leave the beautiful valley, I struck a balance-sheet in my mind of the state of affairs in Mormondom.

On the credit side of my balance-sheet I placed seeming prosperity —no poverty, no gambling, no intemperance, no public resorts of infamy, no beggars to importune, no street-walkers to annoy.

On the debit side I placed woman a slave, and not an equal partner; a community subject to the will of one man; a religion known by its more intelligent followers to have been founded on a fraud, and by its less intelligent regarded with all-believing fanaticism; a creed based on sensual enjoyment; a people without culture; a city without booksellers, and a living body without a soul.

My Mormon acquaintances in Salt Lake may demur to the part of an accountant being played by a showman—demur to the *role* of a "saint" being enacted by men who believe holiness on earth to be best exemplified by keeping a harem, and whose ideal of heaven is one vast and eternal seraglio.

But the end is not far distant. The Mormons form a sect whose development has arisen from "the law of natural selection." They are children of the plains and of the wilderness; and as the wilderness becomes cultivated, and the song of civilization is written on the music-staff of iron rails ruled across the plains, the disciples of Joseph Smith and the followers of Brigham Young will cease to be—their *raison d'être* will have passed away, and they must perforce become comparatively as scarce as Quakers are at present in Philadelphia, and a community as restricted as the Shakers of Mount Lebanon. Even now the bills before the National Legislature at Washington are comprehensive enough to sweep away polygamy in Utah if they once pass into law. It is on the cards that Brigham Young may call out his militia and give arms to his Indian allies, but his shrewdness will probably lead him to calculate how large a military force the United States could pour into Salt Lake from both ends of the Pacific Railway.

Rumor points to the border-line of Arizona and Mexico as the site to which the Mormon chief may remove his head-quarters. Another report is, that he is in negotiation for the purchase of one of the Hawaiian Islands, where he could have water all round him, and be far from railways, telegraphs, soldiers, travellers, and all other nuisances.

❧ 38 ❧

The Show Opens in New York

I THINK I ought to go back to my B."

"Who is she?" I asked.

"I mean the B in my proper name," replied Artemus, in a meditative manner, as we rode across the plains of Colorado homeward. He had been silent for more than an hour, and, as I thought, asleep. What he meant by his "B," I failed to understand at the moment.

"Artemus Ward," he continued, "is a very good name for newspaper-work and books; but I must go back to my old 'Charles Browne' to be a showman. All good showmen begin with a 'B.' There's Barnum and Boucicault, Beecher and Bennett, Booth, Burton, and Bateman."

"What about Sothern?" I asked. "You said the other day that you thought him to be a good showman."

"Well, he can't get on till he's got his B. That's why he's gone over to join Buckstone."

I endeavored to overthrow his theory by mentioning the name of Albert Smith, of whom Artemus had read much, and whose manner of conducting a show he was very desirous to imitate. He laughed, and reminded me that Albert Smith got in his "B" by making "Mont Blanc" the subject of his entertainment. "Then make yours 'Brigham Young,' " said I. We discussed for a whole day the manner in which the show should be organized in New York, and the list of subjects to be selected for panoramic illustrations.

Our discussion was brought to a close in the evening by arriving at Beauvais Ranch, and coming to a halt amidst an encampment of Sioux Indians. The sight was a novel one to both of us, for the Indians numbered more than two thousand, were clad in full Indian costume, and were disposed in picturesque groups over the plain.

Through Nebraska to Kansas, with glimpses on the way of more Indians, of the indigo-color water of the Little Blue River, of thousands of acres of burnt prairie, of emigrant trains and wagons bound for Idaho, of boundless plain and innumerable creeks, till we arrived at Kickapoo; and the scenery changing in its character, we hailed with delight the sight of real trees and well-wooded land. From Kickapoo to Kinnekuk, thence to Lancaster, and on to Atchison. The Missouri River was before us, and our long stage-ride—in the course of which we had seven capsizes and two very narrow escapes from serious injury—was brought to a welcome termination.

We rested twenty-four hours at Atchison, thence went to Lawrence and Leavenworth, in both of which places Artemus lectured; and then, taking a boat up the Missouri, found ourselves comfortably seated in a railway carriage at St. Joseph—or "St. Jo," as it is more frequently called—en route for the Mississippi.

Before the train started a boy came into the car. On his arm was a basket, in which were a number of books.

"Tennyson's 'Enoch Arden,' only a quarter!" he bawled out some half-dozen times in passing through the long carriage or "car."

We felt that we had returned to civilization. Only three or four months had passed since "Enoch Arden" had been published in London, and here it was being sold for a shilling, and purchased by many travellers. Yet from the windows of the car we could look upon the waters of the Missouri, and not far across the river were Indian "reservations," with Indians farming the land.

Artemus was desirous of making as many dollars as possible before proceeding to New York. Accordingly after duly paragraphing his arrival and some of our adventures in the papers of St. Louis, and giving "*The Babes in the Wood*" to a six-hundred-dollar audience in the magnificent lecture-room of the St. Louis Mercantile Library, we prepared for a rapid lecture-tour through Illinois and Ohio. I started ahead and made arrangements at Alton, Springfield, Bloomington, Peoria, and Chicago, while Artemus, following, drew large audiences to listen to him in every town. People expected that he would recount some of his Mormon adventures. But Artemus reserved all he had to say on that subject until he had made his appearance in New York. There was no reason why the good people should not pay to see him after his journey and hear his old jokes once more. What he had new to tell them would keep very well till they were ready to pay again.

Arrived at New York, many difficulties awaited us. The American metropolis was not well supplied with halls and exhibition-rooms. We had decided that a panorama was to be painted, and we wished to obtain a good room on Broadway, in which Artemus might give the entertainment every evening for so long as it might prove successful. After much search we came to the decision that Dodworth Hall, 806 Broadway, was the only place to be had.

"Before we proceed any farther in the matter, go down and see Mr. Barnum," said Artemus. "Tell him what we purpose to do, and where we think of opening. Ask his opinion, and whether he thinks it will make a good show and I a good showman."

Artemus always had great respect for Barnum. He believed fully in his judgment, and regarded the great American showman as an example worthy of imitation by any one aspiring to please the public with an exhibition. I found Mr. Barnum at his Museum, in his little office at the top of the stairs, where he was sitting writing, with the door of the office partially open. No one better than Mr. Barnum himself knew the convenience of that office. Being at the head of the stairs he could see his visitors as they entered, and—more important still—by having his door partly open they could see him. He knew that half his patrons regarded him as the greatest curiosity of the show. And as the admission fee was supposed to admit to a sight of all the curiosities except the "Moral Lecture-Room," it was but fair that the great attraction should be always on view. Mr. Barnum listened courteously to all I had to say, and gave me his opinion, emphatically expressed, that the idea of the show was good, the proposed manner of carrying it out perfectly correct, and the hall, though not a good place, one which might be made to answer.

To secure the hall was not an easy matter. Used frequently during the winter for dancing-parties, concerts, and other purposes, the proprietor was indisposed to let it to any one who wished for continuous possession. When we had obtained it we commenced the preparation of the panorama. Mr. Wheatley, then the lessee of Niblo's Garden, granted the services of Mr. Hilliard, his principal scene-painter, and we obtained the further aid of Mr. G. Maeder and Mr. Thorne. A painting-room was hired in premises adjacent to Wallack's Theatre; and Artemus, having made his arrangements in New York, left for his mother's home, at Waterford, in Maine, there to write a book and put together the materials for his lecture, leaving me to superintend the preparation of the panorama and attend to the preliminary advertising.

Lecture and panorama were ready by the autumn. The book was subsequently published by Mr. Carleton, of New York; the lecture was revised by literary friends of the lecturer, and the panorama was completed and placed in the hall.

A moving picture requires certain points to be well attended to for it to be exhibited with effect. Unfortunately, Dodworth Hall was not of the right shape nor the proper dimensions. It was too broad one way, and not conveniently arranged the other. There was just one mode of adapting it for our purpose, and that was to place the seats diagonally and show the panorama in one corner. The effect was odd, but so also was the entertainment, and any thing eccentric took the fancy of Artemus immediately. It was arranged that an old friend of his boyhood, Mr. Maxfield, should be money-taker, and that a companion of his literary career in Cleveland, Mr. Rider, should be his attendant. The general supervision and the out-door business devolved upon myself.

Desirous that the advertisements should be quaint, Artemus superintended their construction. One of the earliest read thus:

ARTEMUS WARD,

Which his Number is 806.

ARTEMUS WARD AMONG THE MORMONS,

DODWORTH HALL, 806 BROADWAY,
Just beyond Stewart's Up-town Stores,
Opposite Eleventh Street,
Next to Grace Church,
And over the Spa.

HIS ENTERTAINMENT,
HIS PICTURES,
HIS JOURNEY, AND
HIS JOKES.

After the entertainment had been given some weeks the manner of announcing it was changed, and the following became the form of advertisement:

ARTEMUS WARD AMONG THE MORMONS.

YOUR ATTENTION IS CALLED

TO

☞ A MILE OF PICTURES.

☞ FIVE SQUARE YARDS OF JOKES.

☞ SIXTEEN CUBIC FEET OF FINE MORAL SENTIMENT.

☞ FOUR RODS OF SAD AND BEAUTIFUL PATHOS.

☞ A DOOR-YARD FULL OF BURNING ELOQUENCE.

☞ A SMALL BLACK TRAVELLING-BAG containing
    Phosphorescent Quips.

☞ PETROLEUM OIL PAINTINGS by the HIGH OLD
    MASTERS,   etc.,   etc.,   etc.

ALL MOVING TO BEAUTIFUL MUSIC,

AT

ARTEMUS WARD'S

PICTORIAL ENTERTAINMENT

OF

LIFE AMONG THE MORMONS.

AT DODWORTH HALL, 806 BROADWAY.

57TH TO 62D NIGHTS OF REPRESENTATION.

STUPENDOUS SCENERY,

STEAM-MOVED MECHANISM,

and GORGEOUS GAS EFFECTS.

Every Evening at 8.

"We are Here." We think so.

Ever of those!

A certain number of complimentary admissions had to be distributed. To make them characteristic and in harmony with the entertainment, Artemus suggested that they should be cards with the address and the simple words, "ARTEMUS WARD AMONG THE MORMONS. *Admit the Bearer and* ONE *Wife.*"

An old friend of the lecturer, Mr. Booth, the printer, of Duane Street, undertook the preparation of the bills and posters. Artemus wrote a quaint programme, now reprinted in the little book containing his lecture as delivered at the Egyptian Hall; and we concocted a large poster for the walls, the peculiarity of which was that all the letters appeared to be intoxicated and reeling over. Then came the question of what we should do to astonish Broadway. I reminded Artemus of the idea which had struck him at Austin, to have a procession of Indians.

"Can you hire a dozen Irishmen in the Bowery?" said he.

"Yes, without any difficulty. We can borrow Indian dresses for them from Mr. Lingard, at the New Bowery Theatre, where they have been playing *Metamora.*"

"But you must borrow tomahawks too, and see to have your Indians paint their faces every morning."

I assured Artemus that our Irish-Indians should be provided with muskets, and bows and arrows, as well as tomahawks; and I undertook to get a dozen very large white umbrellas made, with the works "Artemus Ward—His Indians—Dodworth Hall," painted thereon.

"Couldn't you mount your Indians on donkeys?"

This was asking me too much. Donkeys were scarce in the United States, and I knew of no place where I could obtain twelve at any price. We concluded to be satisfied with walking Indians, procured our men, drilled them, taught them how to put on the war-paint, how to give an Indian whoop, how to do an Indian dance, how to carry their umbrellas, and how to deliver our bills. Then, one bright sunny morning when all New York was out for exercise, having seen that our Indians were duly equipped and fully rigged, we launched them on Broadway. The effect was all that we desired. The Irishmen enacted their parts admirably; the people stopped to stare; and Artemus, with his hat down over his face, followed on the opposite side of the street, enjoying the sensation as much as any *gamin* among the crowd.

ARTEMUS WARD

AMONG THE MORMONS;

——AT THE——

MELODEON,················Washington Street,

FOR SIX NIGHTS ONLY,

Commencing MONDAY EVENING, December 26.

Begins at 8.

Programme for this Evening.

Music on the Grand Piano—Operatic Medley, including

(☞ for the first time in this city ☜) the Soldier's Chorus, from Faust. This is a good thing.

I.

A light and airy Preamble by the Lecturer, with some jokes. (N. B.—ARTEMUS WARD will call on citizens at their private residences and explain these jokes, if necessary.)

II.

At Sea.—The Steamer Ariel.—Disgraceful treatment of the passengers, who are obliged to go forward to smoke pipes, while the steamer herself is allowed two Smoke Pipes amid-ships.—The Storm.—Orgustus and his fair young bride.—"Doth you observe these wet waves, my dearest Ellen ! and lo ! yonder them winds and breezes ? Why did we ever leave Rahway ?"—The steamer gets high, and imitates Mr. Clarke as Toodles.

III.

The Land of Gold.—The Broadway of San Francisco.

IV.

The Land of Silver.—Virginia City, the metropolis of the Bright New State of Nevada.—Can't think of anything smart to say about Virginia ; besides, she's smart enough herself.

V.

The Plains in Winter.—A dismal place, indeed.—Here's where a man feels that there's no place like Home, whether it is mortgaged or not.

VI.

Great Salt Lake City.—A Bird's-eye view, with some entirely serious descriptive talk.

VI

The West Side of Main Street.—The Salt Lake Hotel, &c.—It is a Temperance Hotel.—The landlord sells nothing stronger than winter butter.

VIII.

The East Side of Main Street.—The State House and things.—Also the Post Office.—A few years ago, an enterprising Mormon started an opposition Post Office, and by selling three-cent stamps for two cents, tried to run the regular Office out of town. He failed, and is now a flourishing Outcast in Idaho, and owns Gold Mines.

IX.

The Mormon Theatre.—The Lady of Lyons was produced at this theatre a short time since, but didn't give satisfaction on account of there being only one Pauline in it. Mr. Tom. DeWalden, of New York, is now hard at work revising this play, and by introducing twenty or thirty good square Paulines, he hopes to " fetch " the Mormon public.— This theatre has a large free list—but never speak ill of the Dead head.

X.

Brigham Young's Houses.—Brigham's Wives live in these houses.—They live well at Brigham's, the following being the usual

Bill of Fare.

SOUPS, &c.	COLD.
Matrimonial Stews, (*with pretty Pickles.*)	Raw Dog, (*a la Injun.*)
FISH.—Salt Lake Gudgeon.	Tongue (*lots of it.*)
ROAST.	VEGETABLES.
Brigham's Lambs, (*Sauce piquants.*)	Cabbage-head, Some Pumpkins, &c.
Minced Hearts, (*Mormon style.*)	
BROILED.	DESSERT.
Domestic Broils, (*Family style.*)	Apples of discord, a great many Pairs.
ENTREES.—Little Deers.	Mormon Sweet-Hearts, Jumbles, &c.

XI.

Heber C. Kimball's Harem.—This old Mormon is almost as much married as Brigham. His principal amusement, in fact, is getting married. It has become a habit with him. He says he can't "outgrow" it.

Selections for the Grand Piano............**Mr Forrester**

Mr Forrester once boarded in the same street with Gottschalk. The man who kept the boarding house remembers it.

XII.

The Tabernacle.—The Mormon Meeting House.—One of the Elders who preaches here actually plays Irish Comedy at the Theatre. We should like to know what Mr. Dan. Bryant thinks of this?—Brigham's son isn't an Elder. He's a Younger.

XIII.

The Temple as it is.

XIV.

The Temple as it is to be.

XV.

The Great Salt Lake.—An inland Sea of Brine.—There are no boats in this lake, but a Mormon lives near by who says he has "a whole raft of wives."

XVI.

The Endowment House.—Here is where disciples of Mormonism are initiated.—The Mormon's religion is singular, and his wives are plural.

XVII.

Echo Canon.—Too grand to make fun of.

XVIII

The Plains Again.—A more cheerful view.—A tribute to the memory of a celebrated Indian Chief.—"Listen to these tears!"

XIX.

Brigham Young and his Wives.—The pretty girls in Utah, mostly marry Young.

ANSWERS TO CORRESPONDENTS.

SACCHARISSA.—"I have no Home; where shall I go?"—If you want a "Home, Sweet Home." you had better go on a Sugar Plantation.

***

SHARKEY.—"How can a fellow get a Free Pass on one of the North River Boats?"—Any Judge of a Criminal Court can give you one—as far as Sing-Sing.

CONSCRIPT, (Canada)—"Do they think of me at home,—do they ever think of me?" No; but they do at the Provost-Marshal's Office.

.

LAURA MATILDA.—"I have an unfortunate tendency, even on trivial occasions, to shed tears. How can I prevent it?"—Lock up the shed.

.

ALFRED.—"Where, O where can the weary soul find rest?"—We don't know. You can get board in Cambridge Street, however, for five dollars a week.

.

GEORGE.—"How old is Jefferson Davis?" We can not say, precisely, but he is old enough.

.

MARIA.—No; Mark Smith never played *Little Eva*, at the Old Park.

.

TRAVELER.—"How long was Artemus Ward in California?"—Five feet ten-and-a-half.

.

BOUNTY-JUMPER, (Canada)—"Had I better come back to the States?"—Certainly not by all means. You had better hang yourself with a piece of the Canada Line.

.

LOYAL.—"I wish to procure some trophies of the present Rebellion; battle flags, &c.— How can I do so?"—One very good way is to shoulder a gun and go and take them.

.

SPECULATOR.—"Is Petroleum frequent in caves?"—No: but caves are frequent in Petroleum.

.

GRAMMATICUS.—"Which is the more elegant expression, 'People ought to go,' or 'People should go'?"—If you refer to Artemus Ward's Entertainment, it is perfectly proper to say 'People should go.'

.

ADOLPHUS.—"Sir: I took a young lady to a ball the other night, and paid all expenses, except seventy-five cents; but while there, she danced with another fellow twice, and made fun of my new clothes. What is the proper course for me to pursue?" Tell your Ma.

.

INQUIRER.—"I am desirous of becoming a Mormon: what shall I do first?"—First get good common sense, and then you won't want to be a Mormon.

———

ADVERTISEMENT.—If the gentlemen who recently spilled Phosphorus on the beds of certain New York Hotels will call on Gen. Dix, they will hear something to their advantage.

. Children under one year of age not admitted, unless accompanied by their parents or guardians.

. Ladies or gentlemen will please report any negligence or disobedience on the part of the Lecturer.

. Artemus Ward will not be responsible for any money, jewelry or other valuables, unless left with him—to be returned in a week or so.

. The manager will not be responsible for any debts of his own contracting.

. If the audience do not leave the Hall when this entertainment is over, they will be put out by the police.

. The Piano used is from the celebrated factory of Messrs. *Chickering & Sons.*

. MR. CARLETON, Publisher, New York, has in press, for speedy publication, Mr. Ward's new book: "ARTEMUS WARD AMONG THE MORMONS," splendidly illustrated with humorous drawings. Uniform with "Artemus Ward, His Book."

F. A. Searle, Steam Job Printer, 118 *Washington Street, Boston.*

Yours truly,

A. Ward

The entertainment was first given in New York on the 17th of October, 1864. On the opening night most of the *literati* of the city were present. Artemus had expended some thousands of dollars in the enterprise, and was sanguine of success. His expectations were only partially realized, for the hall was most inconvenient and far too small. But it was a success that had its results and its reward in the future. New York yielded the fame; cities and towns elsewhere were to contribute the profit. After a run of a little more than three months the panorama was rolled up, and the show taken for a trip through the towns of New England. Artemus discovered that the picture was too large and ponderous to be transported easily and fitted up rapidly. He also came to the belief that it was too well painted for his purpose, and that some inartistic and roughly-executed caricature of a panorama much smaller in dimensions would be better suited. A new picture was painted by some panorama manufacturers in Boston. It was this small painting which Artemus subsequently brought to London. When the lesser picture was ready, the larger one was left behind at Providence, in Rhode Island. What became of it ultimately I do not know.

Circumstances called me to Europe. Artemus entered into a contract with Mr. Wilder, of New York—the same gentleman whom he had met in California—and with him undertook a tour of the Northern States of the Union. When that contract was fulfilled, he travelled southward on his own account, and seriously injured an already enfeebled constitution by subjecting himself to the hardships and annoyances of visiting a country so recently devastated by war, and by daring at an unseasonable time the hazardous climate of New Orleans. In the latter city he gave a benefit for the relief of some distressed people of the South, who had become reduced to poverty by joining the ranks of secession. On his return to Boston this benefit formed a subject of newspaper comment. The press criticised it to his detriment. It evinced too much kindliness for the people of the South to be pleasant to some of the good folks of Massachusetts. But Artemus had a kindly heart, and was always disposed to assist the deserving, whatever their crime or creed. Broken in health, and annoyed with the snarls of the unfriendly, he sought his home in Maine, and, resting there, came to a determination to attend to the advice of myself and others, and pay a visit to England. He sent me a letter concluding with the following paragraph:

"I shall float myself across the big ditch soon. Get ready for me. See the Prince of Wales, and ask him to let me have a room for my show in St. James's Palace. Any room will do. I can run round and board with the Royal Family. Their dinner-hour will suit me. I am not particular."

◦ 𝟛𝟡 ◦

In London · The Fall
of the Curtain

IN the early part of the summer of 1866 I received a telegram from Liverpool informing me that Artemus Ward had landed in England. Following it came a letter from him asking me to meet him at Euston Square Terminus. He had made the trip across the Atlantic in the company of his friend, Mr. E. H. House, of the New York press.

On my way to Euston Square, I took occasion to describe to Mr. Pond, who accompanied me, the genial, mirthful, hilarious character of the American humorist. When Artemus and I shook hands on the platform, I was grieved to see that I had been describing some one whom I had known a year previously, and that the description did not tally with the worn, wasted, and more grave than merry man who stepped out of the railway carriage.

After taking a few hours' rest, Artemus expressed a wish to see some of the London streets. Making up a party of four, we started for a drive, having formed a plot to take our guest to the East End, and exhibit that part of the metropolis to him as representing London, so that in the morning he might afterwards be taken westward and be puzzled to feel assured that he was in the same city. He chanced to mention St. Paul's. We drove up Ludgate Hill and showed him St. Paul's from there; then we took him round the Cathedral, passed into Cheapside, turned back into Cannon Street, and brought him in full view of St. Paul's again. Then we exhibited the Cathedral from Knightrider Street, and then again from Ludgate Hill, until in the dusk of evening Artemus became confused, and wished to know if St. Paul's pervaded all London.

There was no good exhibition-room in London vacant at the time of his arrival, nor was the health of Artemus adequate to his immediate appearance as a public entertainer. Besides, he very naturally wished to spend a few months in becoming acquainted with English society and in familiarizing himself with English customs. Acting on the advice of friends, he removed from London to Broadstairs, trusting to receive benefit from the invigorating air of the east coast of Kent. The sea-side soon proved monotonous to him; he returned to London, became introduced to a literary club, of which he was afterwards elected member, made the acquaintance of many of the celebrities of the metropolis, frequented the theatres, grew friendly with many of the principal members of the dramatic profession, and amused himself by studying life and manners in the city he had for so many years desired to visit.

His reputation as a humorist had long preceded his arrival. One of his books had been published in London and extensively quoted from. An early copy of "Artemus Ward among the Mormons" had been forwarded by himself to Mr. John Camden Hotten, of Piccadilly, and published by Mr. Hotten at the request of Artemus. The publication of it by unauthorized parties subsequently formed matter for a Chancery suit, and the popularity of the author became greater through the reports of the law proceedings. At length Artemus received a compliment, considered by him at the time to be the crowning triumph of his life—he was invited to a dinner-party at the house of Mr. Willart Beale, was there introduced to Mr. Mark Lemon, and asked to become a contributor to "Punch." As a showman he was keenly appreciative of the value of advertising, and knew how much it was worth to him to have the name of "Artemus Ward" attached to his articles in the great comic journal, which usually ignores all signatures to contributions. Still more elated was he when the publishers of "Punch" posted up his name in large letters over their shop in Fleet Street. He delighted in pointing it out to friends, and in exulting that he had obtained the best posting-station in London.

Preferring the Egyptian Hall to any other place, Artemus succeeded in renting of Mr. Arthur Sketchley the room in which that gentleman had entertained the public successfully for a long period. Feeling doubtful about his physical powers of endurance, and by no means certain how far his entertainment would be acceptable to an English audience, Artemus refrained from making many alterations in the exhibition-room. To quote his own joke on the humorous programme he distributed: "During the vacation the Hall has been carefully swept out, and a new door-knob has been added to the door!"

There were many rehearsals of the lecture. On a large sheet of paper the lecturer wrote out his cues, placed them on a music-stand before him, and used them for his guidance for a week or two after the opening night.

Tuesday, November 13, 1866, was the evening of Artemus Ward's first lecture in London. The audience was large, but principally constituted of the literary friends of the lecturer and the representatives of the London press. The cash receipts amounted to only eighteen pounds.

Few entertainments have proved more immediately successful, or have been more unhesitatingly accepted by the public. For six successive weeks the little lecture-room was densely crowded, and people vainly struggled for admission at the doors. On the evening of Friday, in the seventh week, Artemus became seriously unwell, and the money taken at the entrance had to be returned, an apology made, and the audience dismissed. On two subsequent occasions the entertainer was unable to entertain, and the public were similarly disappointed. In fact, on many evenings, while the audience were laughing at the jokes of the lecturer, the doctor was in attendance behind the panorama with stimulants and restoratives ready at hand. Poor Artemus was very unwilling to give up; but on the 23rd of January, 1867, he lectured for the last time; his strength completely failed, and the door of the exhibition-room was closed, never again to be occupied by him.

The lecture, as given by Artemus Ward at the Egyptian Hall, has been printed, with an attempt on the part of the publisher and the editors to convey some idea of the manner in which it was delivered. No description, however, can adequately shadow forth its indescribable charm. The matter without the man is a musical instrument with no musician to awake the strings. I have heard many attempts to imitate the style and manner of Artemus Ward, but none have succeeded in a faithful reproduction. Perhaps the imitations of Mr. George Grossmith are about as near as any that have been given in public; but they are simple reminiscences of the lecture, and convey no idea of the personality of the lecturer.

Acting on the advice of physicians, Artemus left London and went to the Island of Jersey. He remained there a short time, failed to regain any strength, and, returning to England, died at Southampton. The particulars of his last illness, and of his death, have been too recently published to render it requisite that I should recapitulate the melancholy details.

In these pages I have told the story of our adventures in connection with what Artemus took pleasure in calling his "Show." With recollections of many happy hours spent together, rendered the happier in the retrospect by contrast with some sorrowful moments, I close my record of "The Genial Showman."

APPENDIX

Artemus Ward among the Shoshones

W̲ARRIOR, what do you say? Shall we go to Big Creek?" said Artemus. "Why not? It must be a queer place to see, and to lecture there will be something droll to do. We will announce *The Pioneer Lecture in the Shoshone Nation*," was my reply.

"We'll do it, Warrior. Only take care to have at the bottom of the bill 'Admission, one scalp; front seats, two scalps.' Noble Warrior, it's agreed to. Let's take a drink."

It was a playful idea of poor Artemus to call me "Warrior." Before leaving Sacramento for Salt Lake City, both he and I had rendered ourselves fully acquainted with the questionable character of the Indian tribes through whose territories we had to pass. Friends who had recently made the journey advised us to provide ourselves with good pistols, and to be always ready in case of a fray. We both bought revolvers. Artemus, with characteristic eccentricity, persisted in carrying his unloaded in his portmanteau—the ammunition in one corner, the pistol in another: whilst I, with a due regard for the exigencies which might arise, displayed the latest edition of Colt conspicuously in my belt, just as other travellers were accustomed to do. Hence the pleasant banter of my being addressed as "Warrior."

Our journey was made in the winter of 1863–4. The conversation above recorded took place at Austin, Reese River, Nevada Territory, nearly two hundred miles from any town we had left behind us, and four hundred from the next to which we were advancing. We were in the heart of the Shoshone land. Behind and before us were Indian tribes of the very worst classes of Indians: beings rightly representing the savage in all the lawlessness, cruelty, dirt, and degradation belonging to the aborigine of the western wilderness. Neither Artemus Ward nor myself were saplings enough to imagine that we were about to meet the noble heroes of Fenimore Cooper. Uncas is about as mythical as Actaeon, and Chingachkook as legendary as Ulysses. Mr. Hepworth

Dixon, in his recent journey to Utah, fell in with representatives of many of the Indian nations; but he did not travel south enough to see the most objectionable, nor west enough to meet the most degraded. We had been amongst the *Digger* tribe of California, than whom lower types of humanity can hardly be imagined; the *Cricks* and *Snakes* of Nevada, than whom none are more wily and more treacherous; and we were now among the Shoshones, who, if not the most to be dreaded, are certainly the laziest and dirtiest. It has been asserted of them— how truthfully I know not—that they have no idea of a Deity, nor any belief in the existence of a *great Spirit*. Thoroughly nomadic in their habits, they roam from place to place; feed on fruits, roots, and game; dress themselves in filthy skins; cut their hair straight across the forehead, and tie pieces of old iron to it at the sides; make their women do all the work; are polygamous as Mormons in their marital notions; and when they die have their wives killed and buried with them. Amongst these gentle creatures we found ourselves at Austin.

A strange place was Austin in 1863. To get to it we had left California, scaled the Sierra Nevada, visited the wondrous silver mines of Virginia City and Washoe, traversed the sterile desert of Nevada, crossed the "sink" of the Carson, where a river becomes absorbed and disappears abruptly in an arid waste; stopped at stations to change mules, where the poor fellows who had charge of the station were expecting hourly an Indian attack; and we were now some four thousand feet above the level of the sea, five hundred miles from the Pacific coast, high up in the Toiyabe range of mountains, with nothing but wild country, wild beasts, and wild Indians away to the north, and little else but wilder Indians, wilder beasts, and wilder country away to the south; desert in any quantity to the west, and desert in greater quantity to the east. We had plenty of fresh air.

Arrangements had been made for Artemus Ward to lecture in Austin, the Court-house having been retained for that purpose—a rough wooden building, stuck upon piles, by the side of a hill. The miners had agreed to bring their own chairs and stools with them. But previous to our amusing the Austin folks there was just one evening to spare, and that Artemus desired to devote to Big Creek, a mining village about twelve miles distant, and of only a few months' growth. Why he wished to go to Big Creek was simply because it was the wildest place he could go to for lecturing purposes. Big Creek was on the very edge of the wilderness; Big Creek had never had an entertainment of any kind; and Big Creek owned a mingled population of three parts miners and one part Shoshone Indians. No one else would have thought of lecturing there; and that was the very reason why Artemus Ward wished to go.

We "liquored up" at the International Hotel, an establishment constructed partly of wood and partly of canvas. We had also taken apartments there for sleeping. They consisted of two shelves, one above the other, in a room where there were eight or ten other shelves separated by linen partitions. The floor was of hard mud, the roof of boards, through the holes in which the wind whistled and the rain fell.

"This is pretty rough," observed Artemus; "surely they cannot have anything rougher in Big Creek!"

"Well, I guess they have," remarked Mr. William Albaugh, a stout miner, who stood at the bar beside us. "They're mighty rough over thar. If you are going over thar to lecture, you'll have to do it in the 'Young America Saloon,' and thar you'll see something; and you'll have to get thar over some very queer country, and thar you'll see something; and you'll find no beds thar, and have to ride back at night, when maybe you may see something too."

"Any noble savages about?" inquired Artemus.

"Shoshones? Yes, plenty; and not an honest Injun among them."

"Not much worse, I suppose, than that majestic child of freedom chopping wood in the road?" suggested Artemus, pointing to an Indian who, clad in a filthy fur, was cutting up firewood in front of the hotel for the use of the inmates.

"Worse than he?—worse than Buffalo Bill? ay, a thousand times. And he'd as soon tomahawk you as cleave that wood, if he dared. Mr. Ward, can you fight? are you armed?" asked Mr. William Albaugh very seriously.

Artemus replied that he was; and as for fighting, he presumed that he could do his share. But the impressiveness of Mr. William Albaugh made the Indian question serious. Our conversation had attracted the attention of some half-dozen loiterers in the bar, including a miner by the name of Marshall, and a stout, merry, red-faced man, who held the position of Wells and Fargo's Express agent.

"If you make up your mind to go to Big Creek, Mr. Ward," said the agent, "I would advise you to hire a black horse they have in the stables behind, put him in a strong buggy, and drive across. If any rascally Indians come in your way, drive all the harder."

Artemus Ward meditated for a few minutes; then, taking me aside, he pointed to Buffalo Bill, who was still chopping the wood. "Hingston," said he, "there's not much to fear from such fellows as that. Besides, if we jib on going a journey of twelve miles because of Indians, what's the use of our attempting to travel a thousand miles to the Rocky Mountains? Have your revolver ready, old Warrior, and we'll do Big Creek, if only for the fun of it. 'The Pioneer Lecture in the Shoshone Nation, by the Wild Humorist of the Plains;' that's the title. Never mind the Indians. Come along."

Every mining town of two hundred inhabitants "out west" has a newspaper-office. The *Reese-River Reveille* was the name of the one in Austin. There we succeeded in getting a dozen small posters printed; and having sent them on ahead, we started for Big Creek. Our start was an event of sufficient importance to draw together a large assemblage, composed of miners, Indians, coach-drivers, and "loafers." Buffalo Bill, the wood-chopper, his axe on his shoulder, stood the centre of a group of the wildest-looking Shoshones, all of them intently regarding our preparations for departure. When we had taken our seats in the buggy and gathered our furs around us, Mr. William Albaugh handed up a bottle of Bourbon whisky and a glass.

"Take a good hoist," said he. "Keep to the track through the sagebrush. Have your pistols ready, and look out for Injuns."

"Shoshones are thieving critturs, everyone of them," remarked Marshall the miner.

"Gentlemen, a pleasant drive to you, and take care to bring your scalps back to Austin," was the prudent advice of the Express agent.

Artemus replied to them all by imitating the wild screech of the Indian. Then off we drove through the grand mountain-gorge in which Austin is situated. High up in the sides of the hills were the huts of the silver miners, and away down in the valley were the roughly-constructed mills for crushing the silver ore. There were a thousand people in Austin; six months before there were not ten. Silver had done it all. The rocks on each side of us we knew to be full of silver; the road over which we drove was seamed with silver ore; and as we descended through Marshall's Canon to Clifton, the plains of Silver Land opened out to us, covered with stunted sage-brush, dreary, treeless, and desolate,—the cheerless basin of some ancient sea, the very waters of which would seem to have been liquid silver in the earth's first morn of being.

Our course was to the south, almost parallel with Reese River, having the river to our right and a range of mountains to our left. The plain was partially covered with snow. No Indians nor anything living was to be seen, nor any vegetation except tufts of the scraggy, gray-coloured sage-brush, the most forlorn and unpicturesque of vegetable formations. Here and there deep gulches crossed our track; but otherwise the road was pretty good, and not difficult to be traced through the thin coating of snow.

Big Creek was arrived at in due time, and the lecture delivered that evening. Our lecture-hall was a large bar-room, the roof of which was formed of pine-branches, supported by pillars of roughly hewn pine-logs. The seats were formed of planks resting on old barrels and wheelbarrows. Every miner had heard of Artemus Ward. Big Creek turned out enthusiastically to listen to the story of the *Babes in the Wood*. The price of admission was three dollars each (twelve shillings). We had an audience of nearly a hundred-and-fifty miners, wearing gray shirts and large slouch hats. Artemus stood up on one end of the bar to talk, while the process of liquor-serving went on industriously at the other end.

The lecture was over before nine o'clock, and, after partaking of a hasty supper and some whisky, we prepared to leave. Our hospitable friends supplied us liberally with cigars, and insisted on our taking a demijohn of whisky with us in the buggy. They also furnished us with a lamp and a box of matches; for though the night was fine at present, there were signs of a storm coming on.

"Did you see William Albaugh in Austin?" asked the landlord of the Young America Saloon, "and did he give you any caution about the Indians?"

"He did," replied Artemus; "but there was not a sign of an Indian all along the road."

"You might meet with them to-night, though. Don't go unless you've made up your minds to. We can find you a bed. If you do meet with Indians, keep a stiff upper-lip, and your hand on your pistol. The Shoshones are an awful lot."

Artemus had no fear. Poor fellow, he never had. He was determined to go back to Austin that night; and though I timidly suggested it would be wiser to stop where we were, he was resolute on going.

There was sufficient moonlight at the starting to enable us to see our way nicely through the creek, and we were soon out upon the open plain. For the first three or four miles we bowled along rapidly over the crisp snow, amongst the crackling sage-brush. Then the moon became hidden by clouds; there was no light. We had to trust to the horse.

"Where the plague have we got to?" suddenly cried out Artemus, who was driving. "Get out, Hingston, and see. Light the lantern."

I did so, and it was well that I did. We were almost at the edge of a perpendicular bank, full twelve feet high, at the bottom of which was an inlet of Reese River. A few yards more, and we should have toppled over headlong. The precipitous character of the gulch showed that we had driven too far to the left, and ought to have crossed the small stream higher up.

Lantern in hand, I led the way over the snow to where we could find a fit place for crossing. It was too dark to drive fast; so I picked out the road with the lantern, and Artemus walked the horse after me, until, arriving at a fordable place, we passed over the stream, found ourselves once more on the snow-covered plain, and I resumed my place in the buggy.

"Hide that confounded lamp between your knees, and let me make out, if I can, where we are driving," said Artemus suddenly. "It seems to me that there is a light ahead. What is it, my Warrior?"

I looked, and sure enough in the distance there was the gleam of what appeared to be a fire. How a fire should happen to be there, unless some one was encamped for the night, was more than we could guess. We commenced discussing the question whether it was likely to be a party of miners or a party of Indians, when the horse stumbled, the buggy capsized, and we found ourselves in a ditch, one of our shafts broken, and the lantern lost.

"Confound the road!" was my friend's exclamation, at the same time laughing heartily at our disaster. "Let us make for that light in the distance, whatever it is. You lead the horse, and I'll feel the way. The light must be from a fire. We shall get a warming, if we get nothing else."

Artemus affected to be careless of results; but the silence he kept, as he paced on in advance, was evidence of his anxiety. We were approaching the light, which manifestly proceeded from a fire behind a piece of rising ground not far in front of us. As we neared it, we heard a slight rustle in the sage-brush beside us, and in a moment two dusky figures rose out of the darkness and stood before us on our path.

There was no mistaking them. Dark as the night was, their outlines were clearly discernible. They were Indians!

Before I could draw my pistol, my arm was pinioned in a tight grip. Artemus was seized upon in a similar manner. Our captors at once gave a loud yell, which was answered by another of a similar kind from more Indians on the other side of the rising ground.

Neither Artemus nor I attempted to resist. The suddenness of the seizure had paralysed us both. Trembling and shivering, we allowed the Indians to lead us to the fire, grouped around which were five other Indians, dimly distinguishable in the dusky light, but each with his face painted, his long black hair straggling over it, and each armed with a rifle, the muzzle of which was instantly turned upon us. In front of the fire were two large scalping-knives, placed there, as it seemed, to be warmed, their blades reflecting the firelight with a sickening gleam.

Our captors motioned us to kneel down upon the earth, keeping guard over us with their rifles, while their five comrades retreated a little into the shade.

After half an hour or more of silence, during which my blood seemed to trickle coldly through my veins, and we both remained almost motionless, an Indian on the other side of the fire gave a wild whoop, brandished his tomahawk, leapt over the smouldering ashes, and, alighting in front of Artemus, demanded, in scarcely understandable English, his name.

"Artemus Ward," very tremblingly spoken.

"Wh-r-r-r-r-r-ah-e! Uo, uo, uo.* Americano talkee-man," cried the Indian, running his forefinger round each of our scalps, and imitating the process of scalping.

"Talkee, talkee!" chimed in the others, as if addressing Artemus.

"What do they want?" asked my friend of me very anxiously.

"They want you to speak to them. Say something, for Heaven's sake!"

"My good Indian friends," commenced Artemus, "I am a peaceful man.   I—"

"Wh-r-r-r-r-r-ah-e!" cried another of the Indians, skipping forward with a bottle in his hand, and offering it to Artemus. "Whisky—*devite, devite*. Drinky—lecture—talkee'"

---

* "Yes, yes, yes," in the Shoshone language.

"What do they want me to do?" asked Artemus of me.

"They want you to drink some whisky. *Devite* is Shoshone for 'good.' They must know you, for they require you to get up on that bank and lecture to them. Pray do it; do anything to please them."

We both took a drink from the proffered bottle. It did not escape my notice that, as Artemus put the bottle to his lips, his eyes rested very searchingly upon the stoutest Indian of the party, the one whose face was painted the most, and who had the most genial expression, though the most uncouth attire.

Giving back the bottle, Artemus stepped up on the bank beside the fire, and, in the coolest manner, commenced to talk:

"Noble Shoshones! Brave and heroic warriors of a mighty race! The constitution of the United States was framed by the great and glorious George Washington. He wrote it out at tea-time over a bottle of Bourbon and a hot corn-meal cake. He wrote in that glorious document that the Shoshone nation should ever be respected. He wrote, did that great and good man, that—"

"Bosh!" cried one of the Indians, in very good and very distinct English.

At the same moment a whisky-bottle was thrown at Artemus, breaking into twenty pieces as it fell at his feet.

The lecturer gave one glance at the stout Indian, whom he had noticed so intently a few minutes previously, jumped quickly from the bank, dashed at the savage, seized his long black hair, and tearing it away, revealed, when reft of their disguise, the unmistakable features of Mr. William Albaugh.

Almost at the same moment I recognised in my captor the face of Buffalo Bill.

A loud whoop from Artemus, and a louder burst of laughter from the Indians, was followed by Marshall the miner, and Wells and Fargo's Express agent, also divesting themselves of their Indian head-dress, and shaking us very heartily by the hands.

"Gentlemen, we apologise for the scare we have given you," said Mr. William Albaugh. "Let it be a lesson to you to be careful how you travel in Indian territory. We have waited for you out on the plain till we have got well chilled. Buffalo Bill, stir up the fire, set some water boiling, and let's all have a whisky-toddy."

We had some, and in an hour afterwards were on our road to Austin.

AW

THE GENIAL SHOWMAN has been printed for Imprint Society in an edition of 1950 copies. Klaus Gemming of New Haven, Connecticut, designed the book, using Thorne Shaded, Thorowgood Italic and Monotype Scotch Roman types. Composition and printing from the metal were executed by The Lakeside Press, R. R. Donnelley & Sons Company, in Chicago and the work was bound by them in Crawfordsville, Indiana. The watermarked wove paper, Imprint Society Text, was specially manufactured for this book by Monadnock Paper Mills in Bennington, New Hampshire. The illustrations, wood and steel engravings dating from 1860 to 1870, are taken from originals in The Boston Athenæum, while the handbills on the covers and slipcase and in the text are reproduced from originals in the American Antiquarian Society, Worcester, Massachusetts.

THIS IS COPY NUMBER

Walter Muir Whitehill